# Debating European Identity

# Debating European Identity

## BRIGHT IDEAS, DIM PROSPECTS

EDITED BY

Branislav Radeljić

PETER LANG
Oxford · Bern · Berlin · Bruxelles · Frankfurt am Main · New York · Wien

Bibliographic information published by Die Deutsche Nationalbibliothek
Die Deutsche Nationalbibliothek lists this publication in the Deutsche Nationalbibliografie; detailed bibliographic data is available on the Internet at http://dnb.d-nb.de.

A catalogue record for this book is available from the British Library.

Library of Congress Control Number: 2013946002

ISBN 978-3-0343-0964-6

COVER IMAGE: 'European Fingerprint' by Katarina Šašović, reproduced with permission.

Peter Lang AG, International Academic Publishers, Bern 2014
Hochfeldstrasse 32, CH-3012 Bern, Switzerland
info@peterlang.com, www.peterlang.com, www.peterlang.net



This publication has been peer reviewed.

Printed in Germany

# Contents

# List of Abbreviations

| | |
|---|---|
| AKP | Justice and Development Party (Turkey) |
| CEE | Central and Eastern Europe(an) |
| CiU | Convergència i Unió |
| DTEU | Draft Treaty on the European Union |
| DTH | Kurdish Democratic Society Movement |
| EC | European Community |
| ECCs | European Citizens' Consultations |
| ECI | European Citizens' Initiative |
| ECJ | European Court of Justice |
| ECtHR | European Court of Human Rights |
| EEC | European Economic Community |
| ELDR | European Liberal Democrat and Reform Party |
| EP | European Parliament |
| EPP | European People's Party |
| ERA | European Radical Alliance |
| ETA | Euskadi Ta Askatasuna |
| EU | European Union |
| EUMC | European Monitoring Centre for Racism and Xenophobia |
| FIFA | Fédération Internationale de Football Association |
| FPÖ | Freedom Party of Austria |
| GB | Great Britain |

| | |
|---|---|
| GDP | Gross domestic product |
| GRECE | Groupement de recherche et d'études pour la civilisation européenne |
| HČSP | Croatian Pure Party of Rights |
| ICTY | International Criminal Tribunal for the former Yugoslavia |
| MEP | Member of the European Parliament |
| NATO | North Atlantic Treaty Organization |
| NGOs | Non-Governmental Organizations |
| OJ | Official Journal of the European Communities |
| OLI | Ordinary language interviewing |
| PKK | Kurdistan Workers' Party |
| PNV | Basque Nationalist Party |
| PSE | Party of European Socialists |
| PVI | Basque Immigration Plan |
| SEA | Single European Act |
| SIS | Schengen Information System |
| SNP | Scottish National Party |
| TEU | Treaty on the European Union |
| UEFA | Union of European Football Associations |
| UEN | Union for Europe of the Nations |
| UK | United Kingdom |
| US(A) | United States (of America) |
| USE | United States of Europe |
| VIS | Visa Information System |
| WWII | Second World War |

# Preface and Acknowledgements

Europeans and non-Europeans alike have dedicated a remarkable amount of attention to the very concept of European identity – which aspects it covers and which ones it actually excludes, the progress of its application over time and, more importantly for us today, its future relevance. The struggle for a European identity is often perceived as necessary in order to complement the European integrationist project, launched and continuously promoted after the end of the Second World War. However, the diverse challenges the European polity has already faced reveal that the concept of European identity can be a rather unsubstantiated one, conditioned by the general economic and political climate existing across the European Union. In times of crisis, states tend to be primarily concerned with their own performance, meaning that various forms of cooperation can be severely affected.

This edited volume provides a critical examination of different conundrums closely related to the concept of European identity. The contributors, interested in the development and survival of the European integrationist project, tackle some crucial questions which have the potential to affect European Union performance if not addressed properly and in a timely manner. Accordingly, they evaluate the basic understanding and power of European identity as a medium in the overall process, as well as the responses offered by the individual states' and supranational elites and their respective publics. Needless to say, economic, political and social aspects are serious enough individually that each can challenge and erode further the often problematic connection between the elites and the public – a connection confirming its full relevance in times of crisis when the future of European unity seems even less certain.

To begin with, Chapter 1 elaborates on the concept of European identity by looking both at the official documents of the European Union and at the existing academic literature. The analysis offered points out that the concept itself is highly questionable, not only because it does not manage to provide us with a clear definition or limitations of such an identity and thus problematizes further theorizing and applicability in practice, but also because it runs the risk of alienating the involved parties and the peoples of the present European polity even further. As noted, the fact that when talking about Europe we do not usually imagine it in terms of the United States of Europe, but rather in terms of individual or a group of dominant European Union member states, means that various European representatives and their respective audiences interpret European identity differently.

In Chapter 2, Nick Stevenson seeks to take a historical and sociological view of the current European debt crisis. In particular, he takes a critical view of the rise of neoliberalism across Europe and seeks to return to a consideration of the displaced tradition of European liberal socialism. He argues that liberal socialism contains many progressive ideas that can be linked back to the European Enlightenment and offers answers to the current wave of market-led globalization. Here, in the author's view, the idea of critical memory remains crucial to Europe's future and its ability to be able to sustain a sense of citizenship and above all freedom for its people. Furthermore, he seeks to link debates about consumerism and citizenship to the growing sense of resentment and anger that is currently spreading across Europe.

Chapter 3 focuses on minor transnational and semi-peripheral viewpoints of the discussion on European roots and identity. Adam Kola examines the concepts going beyond the simplified schemes of the Greek-Roman-Christian trinity. Hence, minor Europe(s) offer(s) a more innovative and creative opinion about Europe. The aim is to provide a survey of East and Central European literature (academic, political, belles-lettres). As will be demonstrated, 'minor Europe' can offer courageous solutions to the process of building of a European community as an inclusive rather than exclusive model. This is important in the case of enlargement of the European Union or in the face of the growing numbers of immigrants.

For Emma De Angelis, the European Parliament's quest to provide a legitimizing discourse for European Union enlargement led it to develop a compelling historical narrative to justify the entry of eight Central and Eastern European countries in 2004. As explained in Chapter 4, this narrative was, however, built through the lens of Western European elaborations of historical myths and memory. Central and Eastern European representatives did not in fact share this historical identity, and use of the historical narrative fell by the wayside in debates of Romania's and Bulgaria's process of accession to the European Union in the period from 2004 to 2007.

In Chapter 5, Fran Cetti is interested in the forced migrant, who, while being increasingly subject to a harmonized and securitized European system of immigration and asylum, is fashioned at the European Union's external border into the embodiment of an alien threat to the national and cultural cohesion of its member states. As such, this constructed figure is an essential resource in the creation of a *hyper*-national European identity. Constructed from nationalist tropes yet given a global character, this figure has become an ideological pivot for the normalization of a *global* neoliberal system as manifest in Europe in its *national* form, and it consequently gains in substance when economic and political crisis enhances the need for Europe's political elite to promote the idea of a cohesive Europeanness.

The central part of the book is dedicated to the concept of European identity in times of crisis. Bo Stråth explains that the idea of a European identity was launched as an attempt to hide the failure to link the social and the economic in the Werner Plan. It was an escape from political action and responsibility in a situation of economic and political crisis in the 1970s. In the 1990s, the identity concept was linked to economists' internal market language. As outlined in Chapter 6, European identity and the subsequent European demos would emerge through European citizens performing on and driven by the market; the emerging identity through the market would provide the preconditions of a European demos and a European democracy. In the author's view, the concept of a European identity has lost meaning due to the neglect of the social.

Going further, Dora Kostakopoulou questions whether it is possible to talk about European identity amidst the turbulence the Eurozone faces. Given the prominence of European identity during the last two decades, the absence of European identity claims in the present era raises questions about its relevance and political functionality. As the author suggests in Chapter 7, it may be worth going beyond concerns about what Europe's identity really is or how a European identity can be more than a thin overlay of deeply rooted national identities to examine why political arguments are framed in ways that prioritize European identity in time $t$, while disregarding it in $t+1$. In other words, the question is about what European identity does when it is invoked and validated by certain political actors or forces at certain historical and political conjunctures.

For Victor Olivieri, the intertwined futures of European identity and the European project seem uncertain in the midst of a Eurozone crisis, a resurgence of right-wing extremism, and the ongoing call by nationalistic movements for further fragmentation of the nation state. Accordingly, Chapter 8 focuses on European identity from the bottom up, using horizontal interactions at the individual level in an attempt to highlight aspects of European identity often overlooked and to shed some light on the possible future of the European Union. Findings from a cross-regional ethnographic study indicate that EU citizens are becoming more inclusive despite being involved in a dynamic process of identity formation within and beyond the traditional boundaries of the nation state. In addition, they suggest that European society is constructing a supranational identity as an emergent behaviour and that the move towards more inclusion might signal the beginning of a European demos.

Chapter 9 discusses the notion of Europe and European identity in the programmes of three far right parties in the region of Central Europe: Austria, Croatia and Hungary. By opting for critical discourse analysis, Martina Topić shows that, while the parties present somewhat different discourses on the notion of Europe, they present entirely the same discourse on the Nazi past of each of the three countries, and these views nonetheless correspond to views of the general public in each of them. The chapter concludes by noting that we can talk about the Central European concept, but not about the Eastern European concept, and by warning us that if the European Union stands aside as a passive observer and allows new labels such as East-Central European, while at the same time it keeps paying little attention to what is going on in this region, then no integration in Europe based on diversity will ever occur.

In Chapter 10, Miluna Andreea Balosin deals with the European public space, a buzzword in the academic world that generates numerous questions and never-ending debates concerning its very existence. The author argues that there is a European public space that is more than just words, in desperate need of a structure of resistance and means of promoting its accomplishments. This veritable European public space demands true integration of the civil society in political debates and decision-making processes. At the level of citizens, this public space must give access, allow individuals to group around projects, and play a role in the political debate in accordance with their merits, their pertinence.

For Monica Merutiu, the challenges confronted by European civilization seem more intense now, in an era influenced by the process of globalization when local problems tend to become global, including terrorism, violations of human rights, pathologies of reason and pathologies of faith. As stressed throughout Chapter 11, the discussions over Europe's religiousness and secularity seem today more heated than ever, with serious implications. As observed, a closer analysis of the European Constitutional Treaty points out the struggle between religion and secularization mirrored in the controversies over mentioning Christianity or God in its Preamble. Understandably, the question that arises is whether the European unity can be stable unless it is built on durable foundations that are based on a spiritual dimension.

Ayhan Kaya is interested in the concept of tolerance in Turkey. In Chapter 12, he shows that the term tolerance has become more viable in the aftermath of the Helsinki Summit of the European Union in 1999. The definition of tolerance is confined to the acceptance of Sunni Muslims and their secular counterparts under the banner of the Sunni-Muslim-Turkish nation; however, it does not mean to embrace all different kinds of ethnocultural and religious minorities. This chapter claims that both the Ottoman imperial experience and the Turkish national experience approved the tolerance of non-Muslims, non-Sunni-Muslims and non-Turks as long as they did not disturb or go against the Sunni-Islam-Turkish order. Furthermore, the author argues that the discourse of toleration has become even stronger in parallel with the deepening of the European integration process of Turkey.

Finally, the Conclusion will round off the volume by stressing the existing problems as well as outlining some additional concerns that scholars, the general audience and, most importantly, policy-makers, could find of interest. As each of the chapters confirms, the number of dilemmas with regard to European identity is mounting; still, it is important to note that the aim of the volume is not to spread pessimistic feelings about the very concept and its applicability, but to clearly elaborate on diverse and often ignored challenges that, in turn, provide ideas for strategies to be considered and possibly pursued, all with an ambition to avoid divisions within Europe that might erode the European integrationist project.

The contributing authors deserve a great portion of the editor's appreciation; indeed, without their fresh ideas and hard work, this volume could not have materialized. Some parts of their valuable research have already been presented and discussed at various international conferences and workshops. Apart from the authors, it is a pleasure to thank Lucy Melville, Publishing Director at Peter Lang in Oxford, for her support from the very beginning to the finishing line. Also, it is important to thank the anonymous reviewers for providing insightful feedback and suggestions on the outline of the book as well as earlier versions of the chapters. In addition, it is imperative to acknowledge that working on this volume was substantially supported by a grant received from the University of East London's School of Law and Social Sciences.

BRANISLAV RADELJIĆ

# 1 Debating European Identity

Questions such as 'What is Europe?', 'Who is European and who is not?', and 'Is a European identity possible?' are heard regularly. Nowadays, the term 'Europe' is often used as a synonym for the European Union, thus to describe the process of European integration, a project that initially characterized the post-Second World War progress in Western Europe. The six signatories of the 1957 Treaty of Rome agreed to work together towards a better future, primarily focusing on economic advancement and political stability. With regard to the founding fathers, they seemed to be convinced about their European project. Later, in his memoirs, Jean Monnet, a chief architect of European unity, noted that 'the essential thing [was] to hold fast to the few fixed principles that [had] guided us since the beginning: gradually to create amongst Europeans the broadest common interest, served by common democratic institutions' (Monnet 1978: 522). From an academic viewpoint, the European project is often, quite rightly, viewed as a big work in progress, yet some question the very sustainability of the project. One author described it as 'an animal in motion', without 'fixed' destination and 'not something quite separate from and independent of the states that set it up'; while seeing the evolution of the European Community (EC) as a puzzling business and 'a strange creature, a kind of hybrid', the author underlined that 'the world of the Community is full of paradox and irony' (McAllister 1997: 7–9).

However, it did not take long before the European project advanced to the extent that many peripheral countries wished to develop closer relations or, if eligible, apply for membership of the European Community. At the same time, the Community was continuously faced with growing numbers of immigrants, from both within and outside of Europe.[1] The *Gastarbeiters* (as the Germans called anyone coming to work in their country, including citizens of other EC member states but, of course, who were subjected to different regulations) or the *extracomunitari* (as the Italians called anyone coming from outside of the EC), were allowed to come and reside in various EC states on a temporary basis, and many decided to remain permanently in their host country. This aspect became startlingly apparent during the 1973 oil crisis when many European governments offered to sponsor immigrants to return to their homelands, as there was no actual need for

1 For example, France became a host country for many Muslim men from Algeria, Morocco and Tunisia looking for jobs. In his study, Esman (2009: 16) classifies them as members of labour diaspora, usually 'undereducated, unskilled individuals of peasant or urban proletarian backgrounds' who migrate 'in search of improved livelihoods and better opportunities for their children'. Although they had decided to migrate alone and support their families back home, soon after, the process of family reunification in the host country followed. This was an obvious indication that they wanted to remain in Europe. The French openly maintained that most immigrants were not part of their society and that they would probably never become so – an attitude that inspired immigrants' growing attachment to Islam. As argued by Esman (2009: 24), more discrimination and exclusion led to stronger emphasis of their Islamic identity: 'They were told by religious leaders, most of whom were trained and imported from their homelands, that religion and government, church and state, cannot, under Islamic law and practice, be separated. Islam, as they preached it, is incompatible with the infidel, amoral, secular cultures of contemporary Europe'. In West Germany, after the erection of the Berlin Wall, the government signed bilateral agreements with Turkey in 1961, Morocco in 1963 and Tunisia in 1965, all of them permitting the entry of cheap labour. One scholar underlined that while the foreign workers were needed to sustain high rates of growth and keep jobs in Germany, the newly introduced *Gastarbeiter* programme had no single intention to offer settlement to the guest-workers (Hollifield 1992: 218). Contrary to expectations, they brought their families and became permanent settlers. The immigrants gathered at their homes and practised their religious values. For the Germans, this publicly invisible realm in the 1960s meant that the nature of exile Islam was rather quiet. More importantly, as summarized by Ezli (2007), Germany 'had conceived of immigration exclusively as working migration in which an ever fluctuating and always renewed population of workers would be involved. The cultural, and thus religious, dimension of immigration was not deemed important enough to warrant any special attention'.

them. This policy was not successful and, as illustrated by Milton Esman (2009: 27), the post-1973 development in France faced 'very high rates of unemployment, approaching 50 percent, produced sentiments of resentment, isolation, and powerlessness' and resulted in 'a street culture with the familiar accompaniment of drugs, violence-prone street gangs, petty crime, and hatred of mainstream French society'.

Thus, in addition to addressing a new set of economic problems, the Europeans realized that the initial ambition to shape the Community based on ideas that were primarily congruent with Roman Catholicism (the founding fathers of the EC – Konrad Adenauer, Alcide de Gasperi and Robert Schuman – were all Christian Democrats and devoted Catholics) was likely to encounter serious obstacles.[2] Aware of the circumstances, the heads of state or government of the nine member states of the EC met at the Copenhagen European Summit in mid-December 1973 to discuss the ongoing challenges and to suggest solutions. In fact, it was at this meeting that the representatives decided to introduce the common concept of European identity into their foreign relations. Accordingly, this chapter elaborates on the ideas following the introduction of the concept and its accommodation within both official EU and academic discourses.

## Origins

At the Copenhagen European Summit of 1973, the representatives of the nine member states of the European Community justified their decision to introduce the concept of European identity as a necessary step in order 'to achieve a better definition of their relations with other countries and

2 As Checkel and Katzenstein (2009: 14) put it, 'the historical foundations of the European Union are undeniably Christian-Democratic, a capacious political tradition that accommodates temperate offshoots of conservative political Catholicism as well as a social Catholicism'.

of their responsibilities and the place which they occupy in world affairs' (European Communities 1973: 118). At that event, the Declaration on European Identity was released, consisting of three sections: The Unity of the Nine Member Countries of the Community, The European Identity in Relation to the World, and The Dynamic Nature of the Construction of a United Europe. The first section of the declaration briefly acknowledged the existence of selfish behaviour that had undermined relations between European countries but, more importantly, stressed the capacity of the nine member states of the Community to 'overcome their past enmities' and therefore adopt the idea of unity as 'a basic European necessity to ensure the survival of the civilization which they have in common'; accordingly, the Nine agreed to preserve their national cultures, the principles of representative democracy, the rule of law, social justice and human rights, all perceived as fundamental elements of European identity: 'The diversity of cultures within the framework of a common European civilization, the attachment to common values and principles, the increasing convergence of attitudes to life, the awareness of having specific interests in common and the determination to take part in the construction of a United Europe, all give the European identity its originality and its own dynamism' (European Communities 1973: 118–19).

The second section of the declaration served to assure the non-member states that 'European unification is not directed against anyone, nor it is inspired by a desire for power'; in fact, the representatives stressed the relevance of close relations with the others: while relations with the Mediterranean, the African countries and the Middle East deserved greater cooperation 'over the establishment of peace, stability and progress', the relations with the United States of America had to be preserved due to the 'values and aspirations based on a common heritage' (European Communities 1973: 120). Finally, the third section briefly explained how the Nine understood the future development of a European identity. According to them, it 'will evolve as a function of the dynamic construction of a United Europe' and by becoming such a powerful tool, the Europeans 'will strengthen their own cohesion and contribute to the framing of a genuinely European foreign policy' (European Communities 1973: 122). Thus, European identity was imagined as a strong construct that would complement and sustain the economic and political aspects of European integration. However, from a contemporary perspective and with the benefit of hindsight, it would seem that the Nine were overambitious in their plans.

Although the three sections of the declaration tried to bring some rather contrasting points together, they did not offer any clear idea regarding how to achieve a common, supranational or European identity. For example, the nine representatives viewed a common European civilization as an ideal powerful enough to dominate the existing diversity of national cultures within Europe, but still did not suggest any strategies. In addition, the Nine wrongly argued that European unification and consequent development of a European identity were not directed against the non-member states, even though it had already become clear that being a European state outside the European Common Market was highly frustrating.[3] Finally, what seems most surprising is that the Nine limited themselves and their ideas to the then participating members only, thereby excluding any thoughts about the future composition of the Community and how, if enlarged, European identity might develop differently.

Since 1973, although the European Union has continued to enlarge and promote the relevance of European identity, there have been various points at which its overall aims and future were brought into question. In the meantime, it also became clear that the aspiration to form the European Community on ideas that are mainly corresponding to Roman Catholicism was going to face various challenges. Aware of the puzzle, the Europeans insisted on further strengthening of European identity, seeing it often as a powerful tool to face the presence of Islam. The successive waves of immigration and the proliferation of Muslim associations in France and Germany in the 1980s (Union des Organisations Islamiques de France, Fédération Nationale des Musulmans de France, Islamrat für die Bundesrepublik Deutschland, Türkisch-Islamische Union der Anstalt für Religion), fostered the relevance of Islam to the extent that it became

3 For example, for a detailed analysis of the EC's discriminatory approach towards the Socialist Federal Republic of Yugoslavia, see Radeljić (2012).

'an agent in the discourse of action or reaction' (Kastoryano 2004: 1238). Such a performance made a clear division between the two identities, European and Islamic. In this respect, the 1989 headscarf affair in France, when three girls came to their public school wearing headscarves, served to demonstrate that Islamic identity in the EC was still in the process of construction. According to one analysis, the outcome of this event challenged the relationship between the state, religion and public opinion, as '[m]obilizations around the headscarf issue have strengthened the leadership of Islamic associations as representatives of a community taking shape around Islam' (Kastoryano 2004: 1240).

In the early 1990s, while writing about Europe and, more precisely, the situation characterizing the immediate post-Cold War period, Jacques Derrida (1992: 6) observed:

> Hope, fear and trembling are commensurate with the signs that are coming to us from everywhere in Europe, where, precisely in the name of identity, be it cultural or nor, the worst violences, those that we recognize all too well without yet having thought them through, the crimes of xenophobia, racism, anti-Semitism, religious or nationalist fanaticism, are being unleashed, mixed up, mixed up with each other, but also, and there is nothing fortuitous in this, mixed in with the breath, with the respiration, with the very 'spirit' of the promise.

Indeed, the European continent witnessed simultaneously processes of integration (Germany) and disintegration (Yugoslavia) of states, powerful enough to question the very essence of European unity, especially given that those who strongly advocated integration at home decided to support disintegration abroad. However, since then, the enlargements of the European Union have demonstrated that the frontiers of Europe can shift and that some states and regions that at one point in the past were excluded from debates of European enlargement may be granted EU membership status.

The discourse about the other(s) in Europe was very present during the break-up of the Yugoslav federation. Some authors noted that the wars in Yugoslavia 'shocked the civilized West' (Lucarelli 2000: 1) and encouraged an endless debate about the Balkans as a region: 'The very word "Balkans" conjures up images of intrigue, war, and human suffering on a scale abhorrent to Western society. To some people, the Balkan countries lack a clear Western orientation and carry far too much cultural baggage to belong in the European club. Western leaders refer to the region as the back door to Europe, the Balkan powder keg, or Europe's doorstep. What these euphemisms hide is, perhaps, the wish that the Balkans were located anywhere other than in Europe' (Gerolymatos 2004: 4). Even though European policy-makers tried to address the wider European public and to justify their involvement in the Yugoslav crisis and consequent decisions to terminate the existence of the singular Balkan state, the public paid more attention to their national representatives rather than their EU equivalents. In terms of the overall situation in Brussels in this period, one account offered a rather damning indictment, stating that '[a]ll the talk about creating in the minds of citizens, a sense of loyalty and attachment to the EC is not worth much now, given that the new total structure will be as obscure as the Holy Roman Empire ... One may be called upon to die for the EC in war, but will not be able to say quite what one is dying for' (Allott 1992). In fact, contrary to the enthusiasm of the Brussels elite, the 1992 Maastricht Treaty showed that the Europeans were not very convinced about the new Union and their position within it. Soledad García analysed *Eurobarometer* surveys and concluded that a large majority of respondents in member states prioritized their national identity over their EU identity: 'One of the reasons why European Union identity is relatively weak, appears to be dissatisfaction of citizens concerning information from the Commission and their national government ... Equally discouraging has been the decreasing proportion of respondents who recognized benefits from European integration or who thought that membership is a good thing' (García 1997: 204).

Since the early 1990s the EU's position towards the previously mentioned European otherness has significantly changed, as Slovenia, the ex-Yugoslav republic, and Romania and Bulgaria joined the Union in 2004 and 2007, respectively. These enlargements confirmed that Western Europe, once imagined as an unreachable region of the European landmass, was no longer at such a distance. The consequent Berlin Declaration marked the fiftieth anniversary of the signature of the Treaties of Rome and while proudly listing European successes of the previous decades, stressed the EU's ambition to preserve 'the identities and diverse traditions of its Member

States' (EU 2007). Nevertheless, the participants admitted that we, as Europeans, are facing 'major challenges which do not stop at national borders' and used the term 'European Union' as a response to these challenges, but referred to 'Europe' in order to mark a common future (EU 2007). However, is European identity capable of addressing the above-mentioned challenges? In her analysis, Montserrat Guibernau (2009: 287) correctly warns that nation states sometimes 'employ the EU as an excuse for action or inaction within the domestic arena and, sometimes they even refer to the EU as a scapegoat, thus fuelling nationalism and reinforcing national identity' – an approach that is even better explained if we take European identity as a 'non-emotional identity, in contrast with the powerful and emotionally charged national identities of our time'. In addition, as pointed out by some other writings, '[a] European identity ... cannot be based on any one language, as most national identities are. A European identity is also not based on any clear borders, a capital, or a pre-existing state with long-held symbols and institutions' (Robyn 2005: 8).

## Identification with Europe and European Identity

Many Europeans struggle to identify with Europe as a whole, but see themselves as French, German or Italian, or even prefer to limit themselves further, to a particular region of their own country. This tendency has become even more obvious after the 2004 enlargement of the European Union. In one of his studies, Jürgen Habermas questions whether a European identity in such circumstances is necessary and whether transnational civic solidarity is even possible. In his view, the 2004 enlargement represented an immediate challenge for the Union, as it was obvious that 'active political interventions will be necessary to bridge the gaps in socio-economic development between the old and new members' (Habermas 2006: 69). The discrepancies between the old, pre-2004 members, and new, post-2004 members 'will aggravate conflicts over the distribution of the scarce resources of a comparatively small EU budget, conflicts between net contributors and net beneficiaries, core and periphery, old recipients in Southern and new recipients in Eastern Europe, small and large member states, and so forth' (Habermas 2006: 70). In order to minimize the existing concerns, Habermas perceived the European Union Constitution as an instrument which, while deepening integration, strengthening decision-making processes and reducing democratic deficit, could be 'a vehicle for forming a European identity, if [the governments] accepted an admittedly risky and unavoidably time-consuming change in their accustomed way of doing business, and if they involved the citizens themselves in the process of shaping the constitution through referenda' (Habermas 2006: 71). As we witnessed, the involvement of the citizens resulted in the rejection of the Constitution in France and the Netherlands, in May and June 2005, and led to the creation of the Treaty of Lisbon in December 2007. However, what appears more indicative is the fact that the Union will not succeed in transforming into a political community characterized by its own (European) identity due to the lack of a common language, tradition and history.

With regard to transnational civic solidarity, Habermas warns that it 'cannot be produced *solely* through the strong negative duties of a universalistic morality of justice', but through open national arenas in which 'a self-propelling process of shared political opinion- and will-formation on European issues can develop above the national level' (Habermas 2006: 80–1). In this view, national differences – language, tradition and history – are of secondary relevance, whereas priority is given to the citizens of Europe, who while taking an active part in European affairs, will focus more on a common European benefit, rather than the national one. However, this involvement largely depends on the institutions of the EU that are responsible for providing space for the genuine citizen participation in public life. Here, Habermas (2006: 81) insists on the relevance of building mutual trust and, as he puts it, 'increasing trust is not only a *result* but also a *presupposition* of a shared process of political opinion- and will-formation' and, therefore, 'the path to a democratic deepening of the Union and to the requisite mutual networking of national public spheres can only proceed via such an already accumulated capital of trust'.

Later, Habermas (2009) continued to discuss the matter, insisting on the link between intellectuals, who have often been excluded from debates about the future of Europe, and the public, when exchanging views about existing concerns such as the global economic conditions, demographic trends and the clash of Western society with the Islamic world. For example, he talks about potential risks as religious communities are capable of influencing the public sphere of secular societies: 'They can influence the formation of public opinion and will by making relevant contributions, whether convincing or objectionable, on key issues' (Habermas 2009: 64). In order to prevent discords and conflicts, Habermas is in favour of greater inclusion and tolerance regarding minorities. Once acknowledged, tolerance will become a norm for a well-functioning political community where both diversity and freedom to become active participants in the greater community are appreciated.

With 2008 earmarked as the European year of intercultural dialogue, the European Parliament and the Council agreed that 'a fundamental step is promoting the participation of each citizen, men and women on an equal footing, of each member state and of European society as a whole in an intercultural dialogue, in particular through the structured cooperation with civil society. It contributes to creating a sense of European identity, by embracing differences and shaping the various aspects of belonging to a community' (EU Council 2006). Later, the White Paper on Intercultural Dialogue confirmed some of these notions and further clarified: 'If there is a European identity to be realized, it will be based on shared fundamental values, respect for common heritage and cultural diversity as well as respect for the equal dignity of every individual' (Council of Europe 2008). In this way, intercultural dialogue was seen as a mechanism to manage 'multiple cultural affiliations in a multicultural environment. It is a mechanism to constantly achieve a new identity balance, responding to new openings and experiences and adding new layers to identity without relinquishing one's roots' (Council of Europe 2008).

Nonetheless, official documents and conclusions about the year of intercultural dialogue did not say much about European identity.[4] I identify three possible reasons for such omission. First, the multicultural environment can hardly generate identity balance at the EU level. As already noted, the concept of European identity was introduced when European officials realized that having an exclusively Christian democratic polity was not possible and that an unexpected influx of immigrants of non-European descent needed to be addressed. Some post-Maastricht debates concerning Muslim headscarves in Europe have reconfirmed that culture is part of identity, capable of affecting identity balance.[5] This is where the main dilemma emerges: if the advocates of a European identity favour cultural diversity, then where are the problems with headscarves coming from? In his study, Anthony Smith sees culture as a relevant point of departure and notes that cultural identity is connected to national identity but, more importantly for our analysis here, underlines that a collective cultural identity incorporates three distinct features: a shared *continuity*, shared *memories* and a common *destiny* (Smith 1992: 58). These features, taken individually or as a group, represent an ever-growing challenge within a substantially enlarged EU, thus being much more difficult to deal with today than they were in the 1970s or 1980s.

A second possible reason for largely overlooking the notion of European identity during the year of intercultural dialogue is concerned with the very nature of the European Union. Every new enlargement adds new layers to identity formation, thus further challenging and complicating work that is already in progress. The enlargements of 2004 and 2007 are particularly indicative of this trend: the EU welcomed some countries from Central and Eastern Europe, simultaneously provoking a re-emergence of well-rehearsed debates about their backwardness.[6] Therein it is only Western Europe that is seen to be marked by fully democratic societies, while the

4 See EU Council (2008a). In addition, see EU Council (2008b).

5 On the headscarf issues, see Joppke (2009), Klinkhammer (2006), Wallach Scott (2007).

6 On the backwardness debate, see Chirot (1991), Janos (2000), Wolff (1994).

rest of the continent is yet to go through transitions (or Westernization), often encouraging an exclusionary institutional approach. Smith's study lessens this gravity by believing in the European 'family of cultures' and the different involvement and contribution of its constituent parties: although 'Europeans differ among themselves as much as from non-Europeans in respect of language ... territory ... law ... religion ... and economic and political system ... *as well as* in terms of ethnicity and culture', still 'there *are* shared traditions, legal and political, and shared heritages, religious and cultural. Not all Europeans share in all of them ... But at one time or another all Europe's communities have participated in at least *some* of these traditions and heritages, in some degree' (Smith 1992: 70). Smith is right to argue that differences and efforts did manage to bring the parties together at some point in the past in order to enjoy mutual benefits of collaboration and peaceful coexistence. However, these ideas are still dominated by the term 'shared' and not 'common' and it is this missing transfer that provides space for further questions about the possibility of having a common European identity. In fact, while thinking about the nature of European integration, Smith himself insists that

> [i]t is important here to distinguish between families of culture and political or economic unions. The latter are usually deliberate creations; they are consciously willed unities, rationally constructed sets of institutions, the kind of frameworks that some European states are trying to hasten and others to delay. Families of culture, like a lingua franca, tend to come into being over long time-spans and are the product of particular historical circumstances, often unanticipated and unintentional. Such cultural realities are no less potent for being so often inchoate and uninstitutionalized. Thus the sentiments and identities that underpin the Islamic *umma* or community of Muslims are no less significant than any official Islamic social and political institutions. (Smith 1992: 71)

Achieving a common European identity is much more complicated than creating a political or economic union. Apart from requiring more time and effort, the responsibility for a common identity lies in the hands of the EU citizens, thus it is the French, the Swedes, the Bulgarians and many more who are expected to ignore or at least put on hold their national identity for the sake of a common European one. At the same time, this process would be even more problematic for large non-Christian minorities, many of whom have struggled with policies of acculturation, assimilation and integration within the host society. Often, these minorities prefer to continue cultivating their own, imported identity and therefore would have to go through two phases of identity formation, a first one focused on the acceptance of the national identity of the host country and a second one focused on the switch from a new national to supranational, thus European identity. In his 2009 book, Christopher Caldwell questions whether Europe can be the same with different people in it. He argues that the initial idea of a united Europe did not take immigration into consideration: in the 1950s and 1960s, 'European tolerance of other cultures was sincere, particularly among elites, but not even they anticipated that such tolerance would mean the establishment, entrenchment, and steady spread of a foreign religion on European soil' (Caldwell 2009: 91). Indeed, for a long time, Europeans were busy with their ever-expanding European project, primarily inspired by economic cooperation and further progress, whereas religious aspects of the Community were ignored. As noted earlier, Muslims were allowed to come to Europe based on various bilateral agreements, but as soon as their help was not needed, the host countries across Europe expected them to leave. Although this did not happen, Caldwell notes that even 'when Islam became Europe's main religious problem, almost nobody dared to say so' – an aspect that gains even fuller relevance when thinking that the importance of Islam in Muslim communities in Europe seems to be on the rise: 'In France, 85 percent of Muslim students describe their religious beliefs as "very important", versus 35 percent of non-Muslims. In Germany, too, religiosity is more widespread among Muslim immigrants than among natives – 81 percent of Turks come from a religious background, versus 23 percent of Germans' (Caldwell 2009: 161, 143).

A final possible reason why the year of intercultural dialogue did not come with any serious discussions of European identity has to do with solidarity and tolerance. I agree with William Sweet's separation of the two terms: while tolerance 'suggests the existence of important differences among individuals (as in the notion of religious tolerance)', solidarity 'implies that what differences exist among the individuals concerned are not important – that there is a recognition of common interests, and a willingness to engage in actions with others, even if it involves sacrifices on our part' (Sweet 2003: 216).

However, answering two questions – 'How far should tolerance go?' and 'Is solidarity possible?' – is not an easy task. In regard to the former, the present European Union obviously struggles with tolerance. For example, apart from seeing the *burqa* as a symbol for 'the repression that women can suffer in Islam' and a threat to 'security, sexual equality and secularism', some European governments would like to see it banned, although 'banning it altogether would be an infringement on the individual rights which their culture normally struggles to protect' (*The Economist* 2010: 18). Such an approach shows that these governments are ready to express intolerance towards their Muslim minorities. In regard to the question of solidarity, without a good record of tolerance, it is impossible to achieve solidarity on a large scale and across the different barriers that characterize the enlarged EU.

Following the 2004 enlargement of the European Union, the Brussels officials optimistically noted that 'if the counties are to grow together into a viable political union, the people of Europe must be prepared for a European solidarity. This solidarity must be stronger than the universal solidarity ... European solidarity – the readiness to open one's wallet and to commit one's life to others because they, too, are Europeans – is not something that can be imposed from above. It must be more than institutional solidarity. It must be felt by Europeans as individuals' (Biedenkopf, Geremek and Michalski 2004: 9–10). This sound statement suggests that the concept of European solidarity rests heavily on the willingness of the citizens of Europe. Contrary to the intolerance that is often caused by official decisions, thus from above, solidarity is expected to develop and strengthen as a grass-roots phenomenon. This discrepancy is due to the fact that notions of (in)tolerance are primarily relevant for discourses about the relations between 'original' Europeans and European otherness, whereas solidarity is mainly embodied in discourses about cooperation amongst the original Europeans only. Still, even this kind of solidarity can be questioned by looking at how, for example, Italians perceive a growing influx of Romanian nationals.[7]

Thus, the path towards a European identity faced various obstacles from the very beginning. Talks about tolerance, the first link in the chain, are often dominated by discussions of different acts of intolerance that further complicate the viability of European solidarity. This solidarity, as correctly warned by Tzvetan Todorov, is a true prerequisite for the European identity project. However, in his assessment of the situation across the enlarged EU, Todorov notes that '[n]obody wants to die so that customs barriers can be lowered, and nobody willingly parts with some of her income if she doesn't feel she has anything in common with those who will benefit from her contribution. Now the European peoples do not have the impression that they have a common democratic life; so everyone simply looks after herself' (Todorov 2010: 186). These words do not strengthen the concept of European solidarity, but rather point out its limitations. As he goes on to suggest, 'solidarity cannot come into being without the people feeling a sense of solidarity for each other, and this feeling comes in turn from democratic participation, from the common choice of a destiny' (Todorov 2010: 186).

## Conclusion

In his remarkable account, Jacques Delors, former president of the European Commission, defined a united Europe as a 'grouping that is unique in the density and quantity of its commercial exchanges, a comparative oasis

7 See, for example, Kington (2007); 'Immigrant Crime Poisons Italy-Romania Relations', <http://www.euractiv.com/en/enlargement/immigrant-crime-poisons-italy-romania-relations/article-179703> accessed 30 May 2011; 'EU: Italy Targets Romanian Immigrants with Plan to Suspend Schengen', <http://www.unhcr.org/refworld/country,,RFERL,,ITA,,482a97a31,0.html> accessed 30 May 2011.

of monetary order and even of financial equilibrium, and a considerable reserve of internal growth. It possesses a demographic, historical and cultural wealth, homogenous even in its extreme diversity, which, doubtless, no other region of the world can claim' (Delors 1992: 17). Apart from acknowledging the dominance of the economic dimension in the process of European integration, this definition indicated the existence of strong ties that link all Europeans and dominate existing diversities. Accordingly, the idea of 'united in diversity' became the official motto of the EU in 2000. As clarified, '[i]t signifies how Europeans have come together, in the form of the EU, to work for peace and prosperity, while at the same time being enriched by the continent's many different cultures, traditions and languages' (EU 2012).

In contrast to the official optimistic pronouncements and wishes, academic scholarship has continued to question the entire notion of European unity and of a common European identity. While some of the available opinions have continued to believe that '[a]ny attempt to reduce contemporary Europe to a single idea is bound to fail' noting that 'Europeans differ about almost everything imaginable' (Rose 1996: 2), others have decided to give European identity a chance to flourish: 'In reality, identity resides not in diversity itself, but in the status accorded to it. In this way, a purely negative and relative trait is transformed into an absolute positive quality; difference becomes identity, and plurality unity … In this sense, European unity can be assumed by the European Union and contribute to the reinforcement of its project' (Todorov 2010: 180).

As outlined throughout this chapter, since the introduction of the concept of European identity in 1973, Europe has been exposed to various challenges, economic, political and social with the potential of questioning the essence and survival of such an ambitious concept. Economically, in times of crisis, the overarching power of European identity is often ignored, with states being concerned more with their individual or intergovernmental performance, rather than their commitment to supranational ideals. In fact, the 2008 financial crisis has reconfirmed the differences in capacities and implemented approaches between richer and poorer EU members. Politically, it is not entirely clear how the concept of European identity is supposed to advance further if the states that are expected to promote it do not share the same, or at least similar, standpoints with regard to crucial issues relevant for EU stability. For example, the discrepancies characterizing the official rhetoric of individual EU member states about the independent status of Kosovo (with twenty-two members who recognize it vs. five who reject it) have contributed to the delay of the overall settlement of the Kosovo question. Finally, in the field of social dilemmas, and this is where the concept of European identity seems to have been mainly considered and evaluated, numerous questions with regard to Europe's capacity to accommodate and tolerate different cultures and religions have continued to dominate academic and non-academic debates alike. Although the growing influx of Muslim immigrants from the Balkans into the EU during the mid-1990s did not face any serious obstacles and Turkey was officially granted candidate status for EU membership in 1999, the debates about the growing presence of Islam in Europe (largely initiated in the 1960s when Muslims were welcomed to rebuild the post-Second World War Europe) and its impact on European identity have remained highly polarized.

The fact that we are not talking about Europe in terms of the United States of Europe, but rather in terms of the role and goodwill of individual EU member states has made the existing attempts to promote European identity in every possible form – no matter whether by various European representatives and respective official documents or the public – open to speculation and, depending on occasion, abuse. With this in mind, the question of whether the European elites, European citizens and European others will ever manage to speak with a single voice remains a valid one.

## References

Allott, P. (1992). 'How to Cross the EC Pain Barrier', *Wall Street Journal*, 4 March, p. 2.

Biedenkopf, K., Geremek, B., and Michalski, K. (2004). *The Spiritual and Cultural Dimension of Europe: Concluding Remarks*. Brussels: Directorate-General for Research <http://cordis.europa.eu/documents/documentlibrary/104214451EN6.pdf> accessed 12 May 2012.

Caldwell, C. (2009). *Reflections on the Revolution in Europe: Immigration, Islam and the West*. London: Penguin Books.

Checkel, J. T., and Katzenstein, P. J. (2009). 'The Politicization of European Identities'. In J. T. Checkel and P. J. Katzenstein (eds), *European Identity*, pp. 1–25. Cambridge: Cambridge University Press.

Chirot, D. (ed.) (1991). *The Origins of Backwardness in Eastern Europe: Economics and Politics from the Middle Ages until the Early Twentieth Century*. Berkeley, CA: University of California Press.

Council of Europe (2008). 'White Paper on Intercultural Dialogue: Living Together as Equals in Dignity', 2 May <http://www.coe.int/t/dg4/intercultural/Source/White%20Paper%20final%20EN%20020508.pdf> accessed 10 May 2012.

Delors, J. (1992). *Our Europe: The Community and National Development*. London: Verso.

Derrida, J. (1992). *The Other Heading: Reflections on Today's Europe*. Bloomington, IN: Indiana University Press.

*The Economist* (2010). 'Banning the Burqa: A Bad Idea', 15 May <http://www.economist.com/node/16108394> accessed 13 September 2012.

Esman, M. J. (2009). *Diasporas in the Contemporary World*. Cambridge: Polity Press.

EU (2007). 'Declaration on the Occasion of the Fiftieth Anniversary of the Signature of the Treaties of Rome' <http://www.eu2007.de/en/About_the_EU/Constitutional_Treaty/BerlinerErklaerung.html> accessed 10 May 2012.

—— (2012). 'The EU Motto' <http://europa.eu/about-eu/basic-information/symbols/motto/index_en.htm> accessed 5 December 2012.

EU Council (2006). 'Decision No. 1983/2006/EC of the European Parliament and of the Council of 18 December 2006 concerning the European Year of Intercultural Dialogue (2008)', *Official Journal of the European Union*, 30 December, L 412/45.

—— (2008a). 'Council Conclusions on the Promotion of Cultural Diversity and Intercultural Dialogue in the External Relations of the Union and its Member States, 20 November 2008' <http://www.interculturaldialogue2008.eu/fileadmin/downloads/documents/240-officialdocuments/081120_Council_Conclusions.pdf> accessed 10 May 2012.

—— (2008b). 'Notices from European Union Institutions and Bodies: Council Conclusions of 22 May 2008 on Intercultural Competences', *Official Journal of the European Union*, 7 June, C141, 14–16.

European Communities (1973). 'The Copenhagen Summit Conference: Declaration on European Identity', *Bulletin of the European Communities*, December, No. 12, 118–22.

Ezli, Ö. (2007). 'The Development of Turkish Islam in Germany' <http://www.aicgs.org/analysis/c/ezliapr07.aspx> accessed 1 July 2012.

García, S. (1997). 'European Union Identity and Citizenship'. In M. Roche and R. van Berkel (eds), *European Citizenship and Social Exclusion*, pp. 201–12. Aldershot: Ashgate.

Gerolymatos, A. (2004). *The Balkan Wars: Conquest, Revolution and Retribution from the Ottoman Era to the Twentieth Century and Beyond*. Staplehurst: Spellmount.

Guibernau, M. (2009). 'Towards a European Identity?' In A. Gamble and D. Lane (eds), *European Union and World Politics: Consensus and Division*, pp. 274–90. Basingstoke: Palgrave.

Habermas, J. (2006). *The Divided West*. Cambridge: Polity Press.

—— (2009). *Europe: The Faltering Project*. Cambridge: Polity Press.

Hollifield, J. F. (1992). *Immigrants, Markets and States: The Political Economy of Postwar Europe*. Cambridge, MA: Harvard University Press.

Janos, A. C. (2000). *East Central Europe in the Modern World: The Politics of the Borderlands from Pre- to Postcommunism*. Stanford, CA: Stanford University Press.

Joppke, C. (2009). *Veil: Mirror of Identity*. Cambridge: Polity Press.

Kastoryano, R. (2004). 'Religion and Incorporation: Islam in France and Germany', *International Migration Review*, 38 (3), 1234–55.

Kington, T. (2007). 'Italy Tells Romania: We Don't Want Your Roma', *The Guardian*, 26 June <http://www.guardian.co.uk/world/2007/jun/26/italy.international> accessed 5 July 2012.

Klinkhammer, G. (2006). 'Recent Debates on the Headscarf in Europe and Their Meaning for Religious Pluralism'. In M. Pye, E. Franke, A. T. Wasim and A. Ma'sud (eds), *Religious Harmony: Problems, Practice and Education*, pp. 279–88. Berlin: Walter de Gruyter.

Lucarelli, S. (2000). *Europe and the Breakup of Yugoslavia: A Political Failure in Search of a Scholarly Explanation*. Leiden: Brill.

McAllister, R. (1997). *From EC to EU: A Historical and Political Survey*. London: Routledge.

Monnet, J. (1978). *Memoirs*. Glasgow: Collins.

Radeljić, B. (2012). *Europe and the Collapse of Yugoslavia: The Role of Non-State Actors and European Diplomacy*. London and New York: I.B. Tauris.

Robyn, R. (2005). 'Introduction: National versus Supranational Identity in Europe'. In R. Robyn (ed.), *The Changing Face of European Identity*, pp. 1–16. Oxon: Routledge.

Rose, R. (1996). *What Is Europe? A Dynamic Perspective*. New York: Harper Collins.

Smith, A. D. (1992). 'National Identity and the Idea of European Unity', *International Affairs*, 68 (1), 55–76.

Sweet, W. (2003). 'Solidarity and Human Rights'. In W. Sweet (ed.), *Philosophical Theory and the Universal Declaration of Human Rights*, pp. 213–32. Ottawa, ON: University of Ottawa Press.

Todorov, T. (2010). *The Fear of Barbarians: Beyond the Clash of Civilizations*. Chicago, IL: University of Chicago Press.

Wallach Scott, J. (2007). *The Politics of the Veil*. Princeton, NJ: Princeton University Press.

Wolff, L. (1994). *Inventing Eastern Europe: The Map of Civilization on the Mind of the Enlightenment*. Stanford, CA: Stanford University Press.

PART ONE

# Revisiting the Ideas

NICK STEVENSON

# 2 European Freedom and European Memory

In the summer of 2011, a sense of crisis pervaded Europe's media. The economic crisis in Greece, Spain, and Portugal, Italy and Ireland and the responsibilities of fellow Europeans dominated the headlines. The banking and now broader financial crisis led to the slashing of the public sector, privatization and economic uncertainty across Europe. Demonstrations across the continent pictured ordinary citizens and grass-roots social movements seeking to preserve their way of life and standard of living. This situation was made even more precarious with rising fuel, energy and food prices encouraging many citizens to take to the streets. However, this crisis has been taken by many to indicate evidence of the faltering European project. Many are now proclaiming the future heralds the break-up of the European Union and the return to nationalist politics and more aggressive free-market capitalism (Kettle 2011: 35). In addition, there are also fears that the Greeks (and others) may default, leading to the end of the Eurozone. As the German tabloids have been asking, why, indeed, should their citizens pay for the pension plans of Greek public sector workers (Lancaster 2011: 3–7)?

The idea of a social Europe that seeks to correct the excesses of globalization while granting citizens a common citizenship, employment, job security and strong welfare states is increasingly under pressure. Across Europe, right-wing political parties have promoted neoliberalism, increasing inequality and the fear of immigrants. It is this more regressive vision of Europe that currently seems to be dominant. If the broader sense of crisis reminds many Europeans of its internal reconstruction at the end of the Second World War, then we need to maintain a sense of perspective. According to historian Mark Mazower (2011: 12), during the 1940s state planning and international aid (the Marshall Plan) enabled post-war prosperity, but today's politicians are more used to a world run by the market. Europe currently seems to have little sense of an 'alternative' to the dominant policies of neoliberalism that involve privatization, job insecurity, increasing inequality, a reduced public sector, and anti-trade-union laws. If we add to this a growing sense across the continent that multiculturalism has been a failure, and the ending of the Schengen Agreement that allowed free mobility across borders, then clearly we are in a period of transformation. The European financial crisis is not purely about economics but involves social and cultural dimensions as well. If there are deep anxieties within political elites and some publics about Europeans being outflanked by the rising economic powers of China and India there are other perhaps more pressing dangers. David Marquand (2011: 52) has caught the dominant mood by arguing that European societies currently risk descending into 'a big pool of resentment'. This resentment has a mobile focus against the poor, immigrants, Muslims, rich people, politicians and the European Union. If the post-war development of the European Union, national democracy, and treaties on human rights were meant to address the problems of ethnic nationalism then we currently seem a long way from the dream of the inclusive European citizenship of the post-war era.

The historical emergence of European cultural identity has been the subject of a considerable amount of debate (Delanty 1995; Mikkeli 1998). Indeed, the idea of Europe first emerges through the notion of Christendom as opposed to non-civilized barbarians. The idea of Europe as an essentially Christian civilization is, of course, still with us today but makes little sense in the context of more contemporary forms of cultural and religious pluralism. However, the historian Jacques Le Goff (2005), building on the scholarship of Marc Bloch (1961), has argued that the common experience of European feudalism made Europe imaginable as an idea in the Middle Ages. This was a Europe built upon the dominance of the Church and village life, the power of the nobility and a warrior class as well as ideas of chivalry, monogamy and courtly love. However, twelfth-century Europe could also be seen as an intolerant and hateful society given Christianity's role in persecuting heretics, Jews and Muslims in the Crusades. We can see perhaps that this idea (albeit in a reinvented form) lives on today in the rise of right-wing anti-immigrant and especially anti-Muslim political parties after 11 September 2001. The classical sociologist Max Weber (1958) argued, however, that it was Protestantism that was to lay the foundations for European distinctiveness. The dominance of science and technical rationality and states governed by law and bureaucratic procedures were mostly enhanced within the European setting. Weber argued that the rationalism of Western culture had religious origins within ascetic Protestantism. The European Reformation, then, did not end the influence of religious ideas within Western modernity but instead helped develop a particular ethic that was necessary for the development of capitalism. This ethic rejected the enjoyment of life and hedonism more generally for devotion to work and accumulation. These features are recognized as 'cultural' by Weber and were used to dislodge the 'leisureliness' of traditional business practices (Weber 1958: 67). The spirit of capitalism (as it developed within the European context) was driven less by consuming and more by earning. The Protestant ethic could be recognized through a 'job well done', honesty, and a lack of ostentation. These characteristics, which are of course still in evidence today, demanded that citizens attach themselves to the duty of work and rational calculation. If more postmodern times have made us critical of master-narratives like those provided by Weber, he continues to remind us of the central importance of both capitalism and religion to any wider ideas of European modernity (Turner 1994). We might equally remember that mediaeval European societies can be characterized as 'the rigorous economic subjection of a host of humble folk to a few powerful men' (Bloch 1961: 443). Ideas of rank, hierarchy and control of the lower orders (that stopped short of slavery) were all marked features of the mediaeval world. These features, as we shall see, are every bit as significant in shaping European modernity as Weber's notion of the Protestant ethic.

The idea of democracy and human rights in the European setting has done a great deal historically to contain what Dennis Smith has described as 'the honour code' (Smith 2006: 28). This is the capacity of elites to use their power to inflict their will upon others, to bring them to submission and to humiliate them. We are humiliated and generally feel deep resentment when we lack freedom, are denied agency, and feel insecure while being dismissed as a second-class citizen. If European imperialism was the source of the first wave of humiliation then the second has been provided by globalization. As Hannah Arendt (1986) has argued 'race' thinking is characteristic of European imperialism and totalitarianism. If imperial and totalitarian rule could be justified by refusing to recognize the humanity of the other then the honour code can be found alive and well in imperial and totalitarian Europe. However, it suffered a setback in post-war society given the emphasis placed upon human rights, social justice and democracy. These advances have been thrown into question more recently as neoliberal forms of globalization have helped foster a culture of humiliation, disrespect and resentment amongst ordinary people. If democracy, human rights and social justice offer the possibility of building humane European societies then neoliberal forms of globalization have brought this into question. The sociologist Pierre Bourdieu (1999) has accurately recognized the extent to which neoliberal globalization arises less through the opposition of economics and the state than through state policy. Globalization, then, is less the rule of corporations, than through the changing dynamics of capital and state power (Kovel 2002: 70). The retreat of the social state since in the 1980s, the development of part-time and temporary employment, the downgrading of trade unions, and the encouragement of more flexible labour markets have all helped shape the social and economic conditions for the humiliation of the working-class population (Gray 2004). Here European workers are increasingly being told not only that they are in competition with locations that do not place social restrictions upon the operation of capital and that there is 'no alternative' to this state of affairs. European welfare states in this setting are increasingly being reconstructed through ideas of employability and activation. This has meant a situation where citizenship is less of a status than a contract that is built upon the responsibility to take an enterprising view of the self. The public sphere, in this setting, is no longer simply a place where views are exchanged, but also where behavioural norms are modified in ways that stress individual responsibility to secure employment (Borghi 2011). Missing from this contract is any discussion of the kinds of employment being made available, the persistence of poverty, unemployment and inequality, skill and wage levels and employment conditions more generally.

Globalization has acted as the justification for neoliberal policies that aim to produce an insecure and anxious citizenry in an increasingly unequal world (Bourdieu 2003). If the liberal socialism of the post-war era is currently in retreat, it continues to exist as a social memory for many European citizens. In particular, Western European societies after the end of the Second World War experienced a different kind of politics that aimed to construct a society that connected the virtues of both freedom and security. Here I want to argue that it is imperative that historians and sociologists become involved in a critical politics of memory. If it is an exaggeration to argue that postmodern consumer culture seeks to institute a culture of the 'perpetual present', it undoubtedly places any alternative social movement at a considerable disadvantage (Jameson 1998: 20). In the context of this chapter, I want to actively remember the politics of this period in terms of its hopes and aspirations. This is not because I think social science should be involved in producing objectivist history, but because of the need to expand the horizons of the present. This is to recognize along with Gadamer (1976) that any excursion into history is necessarily a means of attempting to form an interpretative dialogue between past and present. Further, it recognizes that the temporal tension between past and present can be a source of moral creativity as we seek to explore the possibility of different narratives and alternatives emerging in the future (Wall 2005). The dialogue with the past is essentially a poetic encounter where different identities and existential possibilities may begin to emerge.

## Remembering European Liberal Socialism

The historians Donald Sassoon (1997) and Eric Hobsbawm (1994) both recall what they refer to as a golden period for capitalism and the development of welfare after 1945. This was partially motivated by a fear of communism, but also recognized that planning was required to save capitalism from its own contradictions. The era of welfare capitalism was both an attempt to rescue capitalism and to provide a bulwark against communism, but also represented a very real victory on the part of organized labour. This was a period when the political left and more generally the labour movement were in the ascendancy. For Norberto Bobbio (1996) the European left wished to reduce inequalities whereas the right has either sought to defend or preserve them. If egalitarians tend to view inequality as socially and culturally created as well as unjust then anti-egalitarians view them as natural or as serving other values. The left's preference for equality has meant that it has sometimes been involved in complex trade-offs against other values such as freedom and liberty. However, one of the twentieth century's most powerful ideological forces pressed the case for equal rights for citizens while seeking to expand both equality and liberty for all. For the left equality and liberty go together as they have historically been motivated to find an alternative to the massive social divisions created by unregulated capitalism. If the left has not been exclusively concerned with class relationships it has historically sought to struggle for a society where capitalism did not dominate. Geoff Eley (2002) argues that since the 1850s this search has involved ideas of citizenship that preferred a society built on cooperation rather than competition and where a genuine democracy could only take root if the power of private property was regulated. In the European setting, the left were to progressively abandon a revolutionary model of social change for one that sought to utilize state power to follow egalitarian ends. Instead of seeking to replace society with the state, the left sought to connect an egalitarian society with a deeper model of democracy. Socialist politics after the Second World War was built upon the labour movement, but this began to falter after the 1970s as it became clear that the old working class was in decline. This was not a society where class did not matter, but where the fragmentation of identities, the rise of the new right and the decline of class solidarities plunged notions of the left into a long crisis. While the left was built on the ideals of public service, trade union power and the idea of progressive improvement, these were all increasingly subject to scepticism during the 1980s. After the assault of neoliberalism and the decline of the labour movement the left suffered a crisis of identity that continues today.

There are, of course, disputes about the extent to which liberal socialist parties in power were able to deliver a programme of increased democratization and equality, but these were undoubtedly part of the aims of the

Western European labour movement. If socialists gradually gave up on the idea of ending capitalism, the democratic socialist model of development was often strongly contrasted with the United States, which endured higher levels of inequality and many more of the social problems evident with unrestrained capitalism, such as higher levels of infant mortality, crime and drug addiction (Sassoon 1998). While unregulated capitalism gave rise to a form of barbarism by producing extreme inequality, competition and commodification, the left could present itself as a force for civilization.

However, missing from these recollections is the argument that liberal notions of socialism also sought to expand the freedom of the whole community. These ideas can be traced back to the European Enlightenment that sought to question the established ideas of traditional hierarchies. In particular, the Enlightenment sought to emphasize the rule of law, constraints being placed upon power and individual autonomy. The extent to which liberal versions of socialism were connected to the Enlightenment could be traced through ideas of progress. Here 'reason' was to be used to question authority, criticize dogmatic beliefs and promote critical reflection. If the notion of progress seems out of date after postmodernism, the holocaust and imperialism, it did not seem that way to many of the liberal socialists of the period. As both Stephen Bronner (2004) and Tzvetan Todorov (2010) argue, the critical spirit of the Enlightenment is best captured by the demand for democratic and discursive forms of inquiry rather than the legitimation of totalitarianism. This tradition, then, is better understood through a discussion of the history of liberalism rather than the shoring up of more authoritarian regimes. It was the liberal emphasis placed upon universal rights, law, and of expanding freedom more generally that meant it could not be equated with totalitarian rule. For democratic socialists, the liberal tradition was more than simply the rule of elites, but instead offered the possibility of bringing similar freedoms to the working-class population that had been enjoyed previously by those elites. For example, the Italian socialist Carlo Rosselli argued in the 1930s that the European social democracy emerging across Europe was actually a renewed form of liberalism (Rosselli 1994: 84). This is not the Marxist struggle for a utopian society without a state, but the attempt to build a society on a rights-based citizenship that emphasizes individual freedom. Rosselli's vision is of a society where citizens are free to develop themselves, no longer 'enslaved' by the daily humiliation of poverty and inequality. For Rosselli (1994: 86), 'socialists postulate the end of bourgeois privilege and the effective extension of the liberties of the bourgeoisie to all'. This meant that it was the labour movement who were the heir to liberalism as only they had the capacity to spread the principles of individual liberty throughout society. Later, Bobbio (1987) would similarly argue for a liberal version of socialism that was built upon the rights of the individual and the democratization of society more generally. Like Rosselli, Bobbio sought to redefine socialism as concerned with the spread of liberty and democracy throughout society, thereby offering a distinctive vision to that offered by Soviet Marxism. The Italian liberal socialism of Rosselli and Bobbio was born out of the fight against fascism while at the same time wishing to criticize ideas of direct democracy. The defining ethos of liberal socialism being the combination of the values of liberty, democracy and equality holding in check the power of elites from below through democratic processes and procedures (Bobbio 1987: 60).

If Rosselli and Bobbio identified the Italian problem as one of allowing ordinary people the possibility of experiencing a life of liberty then, as I have indicated, this has its historical roots in the European Enlightenment. For Bronner, the liberal legacy of the Enlightenment offered the working-class movement a dual purpose. This was the struggle for citizenship whereby they were able to reconcile the idea of liberty for all with social rights. Progressive liberalism was precisely the tradition that would be rejected by totalitarian regimes. Tzvetan Todorov (2003: 14) identifies totalitarian thought as being evident where 'the *I* of the individual must be replaced by the *we* of the group'. Totalitarian thought in both its Nazi and Soviet form seeks to cancel the freedom of the individual. The deliberate dehumanization of the enemy and disavowal of pluralistic ideas are also evident here. It was the liquidation of the capacity of the individual for dissent by the totalitarian state that inspired many liberal socialists. If unregulated capitalism produced massive inequalities and unfairness, then the state was capable of crimes against humanity and of producing a mass society.

George Orwell's liberal socialism can be seen as operating along these contours (Orwell 1999). The nightmare vision of a state-controlled society that has eliminated memory, authenticity and dissent is issued as a warning. However, Orwell's liberal socialism sought to connect liberty and justice in new ways. Like many in the liberal socialist tradition, a great deal of emphasis is placed upon the role of education. A free society depends on people who are not afraid to be free. Freedom is unlikely to be experienced as a value if the education system is reduced to training for employment, but by engaging with unusual ideas individuals are offered the possibility of developing a questioning and critical life. Orwell (2001: 437) hoped that such democratically inspired individuals would be unlikely to be satisfied with a society that was overly totalitarian or 'organised like a beehive'. Ultimately, for Orwell, this did not mean a perfect or utopian society but rather one where economic security and liberal freedoms could be preserved while keeping more overtly authoritarian solutions to social problems at bay. Similarly, Dewey (1916) and Tawney (1961) place a great deal of emphasis upon education as the place where freedom could be learned. Freedom here is less an idea and more a learned practice that needs to be apparent in our daily lives. The idea that education is the place where we learn to be authentic by developing our own ideas and identities can, of course, also be traced back to Enlightenment ideals (Berman 1970).

The liberal socialist tradition in the context of totalitarian Europe sought to extend the idea of liberty to everyone, not simply through the formal expression of rights but by making liberty part of everyday life and curbing the worst excesses of capitalism. The collapse of capitalism in the 1930s and the state control of 'actually existed socialism' not surprisingly made this tradition of thinking one of the major benefactors of the post-war settlement within Europe. However, this 'golden period' of Western European socialism was to come to end in the 1980s. Western European liberal socialism had largely been based upon the recognition by the state of working-class institutions like trade unions and the need to build a progressive public culture (Moschanos 2002). Social-democratic citizenship was a compromise between capital and labour that helped support a politics that gave expression to the establishment of the welfare state and the idea that all citizens were entitled to develop the self through education. The political parties of this period were more than election-winning machines and were largely based upon the progressive middle class and the organized working class. Of course, not all of the parties and citizens of this period could be described as liberal (more conservative strains of thought were certainly evident); however, my argument is that it was an important strain within the internal debate. For example, many of the films and much of the literature about British working-class life in the 1960s demonstrate a sense of both rising expectation and of citizens wanting to experiment with the new freedoms of class mobility and artistic expression. Freedom here was not simply a means of earning more money, but crucially was understood as an opportunity to expand educational horizons and to improve the self (Hoggart 1958). Such a project of self-education was built through alternative organizations as well as dominant institutions and reflected a new confidence amongst many working-class people. If Orwell (2001) had wondered whether intellectual freedom would ever be valued as much as job security by working-class people, an affirmative answer was beginning to be felt by the end of the 1960s. The liberal socialist struggle for a civilized society could be broadly understood as the struggle for a dignified life for everyone. As Tawney (1964: 168) argued, if 'to lead a life worthy of human beings is confined to a minority, what is commonly called freedom would more properly be described as privilege'.

Of course, we would need to recognize that liberal socialism was indeed dependent upon a world when capital was more rooted to the spot than is currently evident. Here I do not simply argue for the reaffirmation of the politics of a previous period or that globalization is wholly a myth. However, there is a need to remember the politics of a previous period where it seemed reasonable to connect a politics of the state not simply to enhanced rationalization and bureaucratization but to a project of democratization and enhanced liberty for ordinary citizens. This is a project that can be recast in new times.

## The European Dream?

Jeremy Rifkin (2004) has sought to identify what he calls the European dream that rivals the American dream. This dream provides an alternative to the dysfunctional cut-throat capitalism of the United States and instead emphasizes welfare provision, well-being and quality of life. While this dream might be more distant from reality in light of the recent economic crisis, we need to remember that the European Union contains a high degree of social and cultural variety, from the relatively egalitarian and strong welfare states of the Scandinavian countries to some of the small-state, low-taxation countries located in Eastern Europe. Indeed, Perry Anderson (2009) and Pierre Bourdieu (2003) argue that many intellectuals have failed to grasp the reality that Europe is more responsive to business elites than it is to democratic pressures from below. If the European Union began as soldering together human rights, democracy and prosperity, it might today more accurately be said to resemble a neoliberal club. This is the Europe of a central bank and bureaucracy that offers little in the way of democratic accountability. By expanding EU membership into Eastern Europe it has allowed European capital access to the low-wage economies of the East. Here we find the gradual erosion of the difference between so-called free-market America and a social Europe. If Europe ultimately failed to stand up to the United States in respect of the 'war on terror', the same might be said in respect of the neoliberal evolution of poor wages, poverty and social exclusion. European imperatives to 'reform' nearly always mean a retrenchment of the welfare system and usually the opposite of the initiatives that led to the setting up of the social state after the Second World War. Here we are compelled to ask what has changed? Why did liberal European socialist ideals that seemed so compelling in the middle of the twentieth century now risk being overtaken by events? Here we might point to the development of a new kind of capitalism more driven by technological change, less tied to particular places and the internationalization of the capitalist economy more generally. This has pushed individual nation states to focus on supply-side economics, seeking to make themselves attractive to large conglomerates and inward investment.

Further, we might also talk of the transformation of what Max Weber (1958) called the 'spirit' of capitalism. If European capitalism was built upon a Protestant spirit devoted to accumulation rather than enjoyment, this is no longer the case within the context of consumer-oriented societies. Zygmunt Bauman (2004) argues that the dominant ethos of the system is no longer the refusal to engage in hedonistic activity. A meaningful life is now a life built around the desire for commodities and consumption. These dimensions had been previously outlined by the sociologist Daniel Bell (1976), who argued that the Protestant ethic originally identified by Weber had been replaced by a world of credit cards and instant gratification. If the dominant character structure of the nineteenth century depended upon restraint and self-discipline then by the 1960s this was being replaced by a restless ethic of consumption. In terms of citizenship, the duty to sacrifice for the good of the community has been replaced by the individual right to pleasure. The central contradiction of capitalism today is between a workplace culture that demands hard work and a consumer culture that emphasizes hedonism and play. If Weber found the origins of the spirit of capitalism in religion, from where did the consumerist ethic emerge? In other words, and to return to Weber's problem, if we can argue that the structures of the capitalist economy have moved from a mostly national-based level to a globally organized consumer economy based upon disposability and fast turnover, this posits a suggestion as to why people wish to consume. This question is not really dealt with even if we recognize the increasing value that is placed upon the design process, niche markets and branding more generally (Lash and Urry 1994). Colin Campbell (1987) argues that the answer to this puzzle lies less within the rationality of the Enlightenment than within Romanticism. The mostly pleasurable associations of consumption that place emphasis on the imagination and fantasy can be located within the Romantic movement. The desire for new sensations, novelty and fashion begins with a change in Christianity in the seventeenth century and ends with the Romantic emphasis that beauty and the imagination are the main principles of life. The Romantic emphasis upon the right to pleasure and upon emotionality become the central features of consumer capitalism.

More recently, Boltanski and Chiapello (2005) argue that the new 'spirit' of capitalism is not simply focused upon consumer 'rewards' but that work itself takes on the language of creativity. The 'spirit' of capitalism is now provided by management gurus and the idea of the enterprising self. The Romantic ethic is no longer opposed to the capitalist system but has systematically been incorporated into its structures. However the 'downside' of this more flexible and innovative world (for some) is the fear of being rejected as a market failure. Intense feelings of anxiety and uncertainty in a world of short-term commitments inevitably undermine the bonds of solidarity necessary for citizenship. The idea of the global market produces a world of frantic information workers all looking over their shoulders, surviving in a world without the security of a decent welfare state. Here exclusion takes on a new meaning in that being excluded from the labour market is not simply to be looked down on as a second-class citizen, but also means to be excluded from the world of consumption through which many modern citizens imaginatively live their lives. If the everyday world of consumer capitalism can be said to have 'democratised luxury' then any attempt to curtail the rights and freedoms to enjoy this world of consumer pleasure begins to sound like a return to more puritanical attitudes (Williams 1982). This is perhaps important in the current context, for if social liberalism is to be revived then a renewed emphasis will need to be placed upon social responsibility as well as freedom. The call for freedom has become the freedom to consume and enjoy lifestyles of hyper-consumption that can be easily connected to the rise of neoliberalism and reluctance to pay high levels of tax. The moral commitment to a shared community and the common good as well as freedoms beyond those of consumption need to be at the fore of creating a new European liberal socialism. While some of the literature on responsibility has simply dismissed concerns with freedom as exemplifying capitalist individualism, it seems that a new contract between freedom and responsibility is required at this juncture (Smart 1999: 180). The balance between the freedom to follow a life of your own choosing while maintaining a sense of responsibility for children, nature and vulnerable others is a good place to start. The ethical life then needs to recognize the mutual importance of both freedom and responsibility in the European setting. Nevertheless, we need to be careful and should not simply follow a number of communitarian writers in insisting upon the rules of community as opposed to liberty of the self (Etzioni 1997). Here there is a tendency to suggest that 'bad behaviour' is the result of the breakdown of the social order and morality more generally. Along with globalization and neoliberalism there comes a renewed emphasis on the moral policing role of the state and anti-liberalism more generally. However, as I have argued, in seeking a renewed emphasis upon morality (which has a tendency to become repressive and illiberal), communitarianism neglects some of the broader economic and social transformations necessary to understand European modernity.

Globalization, on this reading, has been good for capitalism but disastrous for the creation of the common bonds of citizenship. Deindustrialization, regime shopping, outsourcing, anti-trade-union laws and labour market flexibility are amongst the features that have promoted a new culture of capitalism. If the old welfare capitalism needed to keep workers ready and able to work, then flexible capitalism can either import workers from abroad or find new investment opportunities. Further, the development of right-wing political parties since the 1980s has appealed to moderately affluent voters by offering to slim down taxes, cut welfare bills and, of course, to restrict the flows of immigrants. All of these aspects have effectively played upon the fears of voters and ended up demonizing the poor. The possibilities for the cultural development of working-class people have been severely restricted during this period. While the 1960s was a period of rising levels of optimism and inclusive citizenship, this has largely been replaced by uncertainty, consumerism and the use of vicious stereotypes. Entrenched poverty has been dealt with through much tougher penal policies and welfare-to-work schemes that are aimed at forcing the unemployed into increasingly poorly paid forms of employment (Wacquant 2004).

The new capitalism also has implications for the culture of politics more generally. Richard Sennett (2006) has argued that the more uncertain world of global competitiveness, consumerism and supply-side economics undermines the careful 'craft' of citizenship. Firstly, political platforms appear to be increasingly similar, being pro-business and anti-immigrant, which in itself leads those in charge of 'spinning' political messages to overstate the differences between the parties. Also, there is an increasing amount of emphasis placed upon 'character' and questions of 'competence', which again serves to mask the basic similarities between the political parties. Politics has become more consumerist with the demand for 'instant' changes, in which a sense of disconnection amongst the electorate means that increasingly smaller numbers of people follow and participate within the broader democratic culture. While these changes from the past can be overstated and are more in evidence in some countries than others, they are clearly not without relevance. In more general terms, Colin Crouch (2004) describes this condition as post-democratic. Here the formal rituals and procedures of citizenship are in place but are increasingly controlled by powerful business elites. As the egalitarian emphasis of liberal socialism has gone into decline so capitalism has increasingly gained control over the political process. It is under the conditions of post-democracy that the common bonds of citizenship are downgraded, trade unions are marginalized, and the poor are treated with contempt. Citizenship becomes generally weakened as elites have enhanced their control of the political process and the meaning of life is redefined by harsher labour conditions, consumerism and a slimmed-down welfare state. If, in the past, European democracy was contrasted with European totalitarianism, today this comparison has fallen into disuse. If under liberal socialism the aim was the construction of a relatively egalitarian society and individual freedom, then today we are more likely to hear of the moral failings of the poor and the need to create a new entrepreneurial spirit amongst the population more generally. Instead, the most common contrast drawn is between those states that have managed to successfully 'modernize' their welfare regimes and those that remain bureaucratic and uncompetitive.

Finally, as we have seen, liberal socialism placed a great deal of emphasis upon the need to educate the self. This was not only a matter of gaining educational qualifications, but of discovering the authentic path of the self. The idea that all citizens have their own unique potential and that the point of life is to discover our own direction dominated the educational philosophies of that period (Stevenson 2011). This emphasis has now been displaced by league tables, teaching to test and other features all used to focus attention on results. The market here has not, however, reversed the considerable educational inequalities and advantages of middle-class children. If, in the past, the concern was with educational freedom, then in the current setting, freedom in relation to schooling is more concerned with the promotion of private institutions and the break-up of the state. Here my argument is that while accepting the considerable pleasures of consumption, these are mostly (although not all) fleeting and are no match for discovering more 'authentic' passions of the self. The problem is that as consumer culture has grown it has converted education into the means to market success, thereby displacing some of the troubling questions that educators sought to pose. As Erich Fromm (1994: 127–32) knew all too well, more authentic ideas of freedom actually sit uncomfortably with ideas of market freedom. The freedom of the self is more concerned with 'being' than it is with 'having'. Such a view can be traced back to the Enlightenment and beyond and suggests that we are only truly awake when we are realizing our own unique selves in a supportive community.

Therefore, in this context, can we still speak of a European dream that is distinct from the rise of a consumer society and the promotion of free-market individualism? Manuel Castells (1998) has argued convincingly that the European project is now perhaps best understood in the context of globalization. The fact that most European trade remains within the European Union means that more socially progressive reactions to neo-liberalism remain a possibility. An alternative European identity would need to be found beyond mostly technocratic elites and the considerable appeal of reactive racism and nationalism. What Castells (1998: 333) refers to as a 'project identity' would, of course, need to complement rather than replace national, local and regional identity. However, the massacre of Norwegians by a right-wing extremist in the summer of 2011 highlighted the continuing threat from an explicitly European far right. Anders Behring Brevik's mission was widely reported as being to 'save' Europe from Muslims and cultural Marxist supporters of multiculturalism. Here, the concern is perhaps less that there may be others like him, but more that the rhetoric he used on his web pages of indignation, intolerance and hatred closely mirrors that of the more mainstream European right (Reid-Henry 2011).

Whether Europeans still have the capacity to imagine a more inclusive social and cultural identity (a genuine 'project identity') remains to be seen. The new world of informational capitalism (of globalizations both real and imagined) has yet to pursue a political project of the substance similar to that which has allowed capitalism to transform itself in the age of technology and consumer identities. As Anthony Giddens and Ulrich Beck argue, if the European Union is to remain one of the most significant and successful pieces of institution building since the end of the Second World War then it needs to be reimagined in the context of the present (Giddens and Beck 2010: 336–8). It can only do so, however (a point not made by Beck and Giddens), if it recognizes the threat of a new fundamentalism.

## Market Totalitarianism?

If the transition of citizenship has come from above in respect of business and political elites rather than due to pressure from below, what does this tell us about the ways in which European citizenship is being remade? Michael Mann (1987) has convincingly argued that the social citizenship of the post-war period reflected the balance of power between ruling elites and the organized working class. If this balance of power has now shifted (as it seems to have done) how might we understand the emergent form of citizenship in the European context? What remains important about Mann's reflections is the importance he places upon the power of elites, but also how their rule needs to be negotiated through compromise, consent and other features. For the historian Tony Judt (2010a), the European social democracy of the post-war period was built upon the idea that the state and citizens had a responsibility for each other and that this could be demonstrated through access to common services, public provision and inclusive notions of community. The welfare state required relatively high rates of taxation, but became legitimate to the extent to which it delivered a more equal society and bound members of society together in a common community. However, since the 1980s, the idea of there being a common good has come under pressure as notions of the public became devalued. The rise of gated communities, the privatization of space and consumerism, and the downgrading of welfare have all pushed society in a more market-driven direction. For Judt, the left needs to reject radicalism for a progressive conservatism that becomes focused on questions of security, prudence and stability. While this argument can be pushed too far, it is true that questions of freedom and security need to be held in balance. Notable in Judt's account is the emphasis placed on the discursive aspect of politics and how this has been reconfigured (Judt 2010a: 34). One of the major achievements of social democracy through the welfare state was the bonding of both the middle and working class to democratic institutions. In other words, Judt's account recognizes the extent to which ideological constructions need to relate to class positions more generally. For Judt, this retreat from common forms of citizenship is especially evident in the idea that a sense of progress and upward mobility, experienced by many in the 1960s, was dependent upon the state. As Zygmunt Bauman (1998) comments, the welfare state is partly a victim of its own success in producing generations of well-looked-after citizens who no longer think they need a safety net. The poor become the 'other' in the consumer society precisely because they are a constant reminder of what can happen in our insecure world.

Elsewhere, Tony Judt (2010b) goes as far as to argue that the dominance of market-driven solutions currently grips the common sense of elites and intellectuals in a similar fashion to the way that Marxism dominated the minds of many intellectuals in the 1930s. Here Judt refers to the classic work of Polish intellectual Czeslaw Milosz, *The Captive Mind*. Milosz's text describes how a generation of intellectuals across Europe became gripped by a 'new faith' (Milosz 1981: 3). These intellectuals were largely motivated by a doctrine that aimed to produce a perfected mankind arriving at some point in the distant future. Doctrinaire Marxism offered a kind of anti-Enlightenment culture as it was driven by a desire to regulate and control thought. Herein the liberal traditions of the West were dismissed as doctrinaire, evil, elitist and hostile to the needs of ordinary people. The book stands as a criticism of leftist authoritarianism and has a great deal in common with the earlier warnings that Orwell had made in respect of a form of Marxism that knew more about doctrine than it did of the truth. For Judt, the contemporary market-like authoritarian Marxism has a circle of true believers, is dogmatic, and produces a certain blindness to its shortcomings; as Judt argues 'the thrall in which an ideology holds a people is best measured by their collective inability to imagine alternatives' (2010b: 179). The critical component of Judt's historical thinking is quite simply to reveal that in recent times Europeans have seen a world quite different from that of the present, where politics was mainly concerned with developing security and freedom for all after the market failures and authoritarian politics of the 1930s. The introduction of market rationality not only corrodes a shared sense of fraternity and community but also feeds a more general sense of resentment. A common form of citizenship only becomes possible if we learn to rethink the state as the only mechanism available to reduce the power of markets and act in the common good.

Missing from Judt's account is the role played by political elites in justifying the status quo and the war against social citizenship. In general, Judt's account places too much on the liberation struggles of the 1960s, which are read in an overly conservative manner. For Judt, it was the rampant individualism of the 1960s that led to the rampant individualism characteristic of market-driven societies. While there is perhaps a flicker of truth in this account, it should have been more carefully located in some of the problems experienced by social-democratic governments in the 1980s. Further 'progressive' social movements, including feminism, black politics, ecology and gay rights, all emerged out of the 1960s. Judt is nonetheless right to argue that market rationality is becoming the new political common sense amongst European elites. Here we perhaps need to consider the role of elites and questions of symbolic power. Returning to the sociological analysis of Pierre Bourdieu, if globalization is often used as a cover for a top-down strategy of neoliberal domination, then we need to understand how this particular view of reality has become imposed on the citizenry. Judt is partially correct in seeking to remember when ideas of freedom were understood somewhat differently during social-democratic periods of dominance, but we need to understand more precisely how this definition of common sense has come to dominate the political field. With this in mind, Pierre Bourdieu and Loic Wacquant (2005: 178) argue that neoliberalism acts as a form of cultural imperialism. By this they mean that it 'has the power to universalise particularalisms linked to a singular historical tradition by causing them to be misrecognised as such'. Neoliberalism as a form of cultural logic grew up in the context of the United States and is fast becoming a global logic that aims to judge, assess and ultimately displace other modes of development like social democracy. This should be recognized as an export from a particular world region (namely the United States) that addresses not only the interests of global elites, but has built into it a set of historical understandings that take the experience of the United States as the norm. The effect of this migration of ideas not only de-historizes other traditions like European social democracy, but creates a false universalization through ideas of Westernization. The West becomes the site of multiple forms of development that historically have attached themselves to different territories, and in different ways.

If neoliberalism acts as a particular form of symbolic domination then it should be understood as a form of class power. Michael Mann (2003: 178) argues that wherever neoliberal policies are implemented they end up favouring the wealthy. This does not mean, however, that they are simply the expression of the global business class, although these interests tend to be the 'back-seat driver' (Mann 2003: 49) and can nudge or cajole the driver of the vehicle (the political class) in a particular direction, but they are not in full control of the direction of travel. However, as I have argued throughout, if the global economy can push policy in this direction, it is ultimately the state that makes or breaks neoliberalism. It has been the considerable symbolic power of political elites that have normalized these policies. Here we need to develop what might be called 'a political economy of symbolic violence' (Wacquant 2005: 134). We need a cultural sociology that seeks to explain how systems of media and education solidify the rule of elites through the construction of knowledge and information. We could also point to the role that education plays in constructing elites while trying to pass off their success through ideas of a meritocracy. Further ruling elites are granted other symbolic resources through the increasing domination of European media by a limited number of conglomerates. Much of the scholarly talk of 'globalization' has served to mystify the extent to which particular media patterns are largely the result of state policy (Hafez 2007). The decline of public service broadcasting and the arrival of more commercial television systems across Western Europe have gathered apace since the 1980s (Williams 2005). The growth in the dominance of television as a provider of news and entertainment (despite the arrival of the internet) has concentrated power in the hands of private corporations that seek to control the media for reasons of profit and influence (Bagdikian 2005). This then hands considerable power to elites to press particular views of 'reality' that go increasingly unchallenged in a world where the labour movement has lost power. While the circuits of elite power are inevitably more complex and contradictory than this argument suggests, they remain historically unprecedented.

Neoliberalism, then, is not only a set of practices but is equally a form of symbolic domination. Critical intellectuals and social movements have a special responsibility to interrupt the educative project of neoliberalism by talking of its hidden costs, but also to provide alternative interpretations and means of understanding. For Bourdieu (2003), what is required in the first instance is a cultural politics that recognizes 'the social costs of economic decisions' in terms of the development of inequality, uncertainty and humiliation along with widespread indignation, fear of losing status and, of course, outright resentment. The other call is to try and defend the social aspect of the state by improving health care, reducing working hours and improving social protection more generally. The problem is, however, that all of these features are likely to take a profound battering because of the downsizing of the social state and the politics of privatization that has broken out across Europe due to the impact of the broader financial crisis with which my argument began.

## The Search for Utopia?

In this setting we need to ask what a feasible alternative might look like? In terms of the critical politics of memory I am advocating here, that question might be reconstituted through the issue: what do Europeans need to remember to avoid the problems of the past? If part of the 'hidden' costs of globalization is a downward spiral of social protection, increased competition and uncertainty then what can be done to address these issues? Here Europeans should be urged to remember some of the historical consequences of living in a society where many saw themselves as victims. Omer Bartov (2000) argues that it was a widespread sense of humiliation, defeat and victimhood that historically brought so much destruction in its wake. The sense of being a victim tends to blunt citizens' sense of their own destructiveness. Victimhood encourages citizens to focus upon their own pain and troubled circumstances. This is a social setting that does not encourage citizens to take responsibility for the other or the wider community. The totalitarian regimes of Europe's past sought to get rid of unwanted others often by blaming 'minorities' for past humiliations and defeats. This was a Europe of suffering that, according to historian Timothy Snyder (2010), saw totalitarian regimes murder 14 million people between 1933 and 1945. Indeed, most of these victims did not die in the camps, but were more often the result of state-driven policies of deliberate starvation. Europeans need reminding that the feeling of humiliation and defeat can lead to the need for revenge and hatred. The Europe after the end of the Second World War followed a path of human rights, democracy and social responsibility designed to contain (or at least constrain) these destructive feelings by building a world where everyone's freedom and security mattered. If a socially liberal society could be built based upon rising levels of prosperity, economic security and rights to self-development, while always likely to be imperfect, then this would hold in check some of the destructive politics of the past that were forged on the anvil of war and economic misery. This is the European story that needs to be remembered in the context of the present.

Such a memory would require a more cosmopolitan set of coordinates than usually exists when it comes to viewing the past. From this we may take a sense of history as aiding public self-reflection to apply critically to a changing sense of the present. Indeed, such features have been argued to be one of the central characteristics of European modernity (Delanty 2009). Here there have been three main intellectual avenues pursued to save Europe from the indignation that dominated the past and threatens to be revived in the future. The first is Habermas's view of a social Europe, in which European integration is deepened in order to prevent European nations from descending into vicious forms of nationalism (Habermas 1999: 51–7). The state here is caught in a dilemma that if it raises taxes to underwrite programmes of welfare and inclusion, increasingly footloose capital can more easily move elsewhere. The problem with such a solution, of course, is that it seems increasingly unrealistic in the context of the present. Anthony Giddens's (1998) idea of a progressive third-way agenda for Europe's centre left parties, which places as much emphasis upon responsibilities as rights, has lost ground in the global recession due to its failure to develop a sufficiently critical language of the market. In practice, the third way often tends to emphasize the responsibilities of the poor rather than the wealthy and more elite interests. However, in the context of the present, the aim to rethink the liberal socialist tradition while recognizing the importance of ideas of responsibility cannot be overestimated. Finally, there is the idea that Europe requires a European-wide grass-roots movement from below seeking to construct a people's Europe (Mathers 2007). However, European citizens, despite considerable resistance, have yet to display the appetite for the social struggles that might turn these aspirations into a reality.

Here we need to remember that the prospects for a social and liberal Europe were bolstered by the collective experience of catastrophe. The need to construct a Europe based upon freedom and social solidarity undoubtedly had its roots in the politics of the 1930s. The reshaping of the continent was both a European as well as a national form of politics. While Anthony Smith (1995) has argued it is only nations that have memories, here it is important to point to more cosmopolitan constructions of the past. Such views are at best misleading if we follow Ulrich Beck's (2000) ideas about the possibility of a second modernity. If the first stage of modernity was one of self-contained nation states, then globalization moves into a contemporary era with a more enhanced sense of interconnection. While this does not necessarily bring with it a more developed sense of being European, or, indeed, of European responsibilities as the recent debt crisis bears out, cosmopolitanization at least introduces the possibility of memories that flow across previously established borders of nationhood. If the routes towards a social Europe are less than certain, we are at least granted the imaginative possibility of talking about differences and similarities across cultural borders. If Europe is now the site of an insecure and increasingly anxious citizenry who fear downward mobility without the protection of the social state, then perhaps now is the time to have a closer look at our shared history. Given the continued power of the nation state, the argument here is that there cannot simply be a post-national social Europe. National identities, despite the problems of the past, and as the histories of liberal socialism demonstrated, are for many one of the few remaining sources of solidarity. Here we need to give up opposing cosmopolitanism and nationalism and look for ways in which they might work together (Calhoun 2007). As we have seen, cosmopolitanism in the case of the European Union is not necessarily more progressive than nationalism. The recovery of the idea of bringing liberalism home for the majority of citizens is not one that can be exercised exclusively at the national or post-national level. There is nothing exclusively European about liberal socialism, yet we do need to think quite carefully about how the historical gains of a previous (and now fading) period can be held onto and revived in the increasingly indignant culture of the present.

These problems are enough to cancel any idea of the end of history or the equally misleading idea that human societies (like human beings) can escape their own pasts. Instead, the remembered past is part not only of our collective experience, but also of the cultural resources that we will need to face the challenges of the future. The attempt to dispense with the past (or even put it on hold) only risks storing up problems for us in the near future. Globalization in this sense is one part fiction (justifying neoliberal reform) and one part reality pointing to new challenges to Europeans hoping to keep the memories of their progressive solutions alive. As Norman Birnbaum

(2001: 380) argues, most of the children who have benefited from the social reforms of the past (both European and American) lack any sense of what this has given them. The development of the media of mass communication as the dominant educators of the consumer age can hardly be relied upon to communicate this sense. If European socialist parties continue to argue for the protection of the public reforms that increased the quality of our common lives, they have perhaps not paid enough attention to their own history. The question remains: how are the hopes of citizenship to find a sense of moral purpose outside of the lessons of history? Could the citizens of today find new meanings in the present through an engagement with the politics of the past? Unless we are prepared to sacrifice collective ideas of freedom and security to the uncertainties of the market, then the past contains lessons to learn. This does not, of course, mean that all of our answers can be found by simply returning to the philosophical and political traditions of the past. As I have indicated, questions of globalization and the ecological crisis should be enough to persuade us that there are genuinely new challenges for European modernity. However, a return to the past could yet encourage us to remember not only European tragedy and suffering, but a sense of hope as well.

## References

Anderson, P. (2009). *The New Old World*. London: Verso.

Arendt, H. (1986). *The Origins of Totalitarianism*. London: Andre Deutsch.

Bagdikian, B. H. (2005). *The Media Monopoly*. Boston, MA: Beacon Press.

Bartov, O. (2000). *Mirrors of Destruction: War, Genocide and Modern Identity*. Oxford: Oxford University Press.

Bauman, Z. (1998). *Work, Consumerism and the New Poor*. Buckingham: Open University Press.

—— (2004). *Europe: An Unfinished Adventure*. Cambridge: Polity Press.

Beck, U. (2000). 'The Cosmopolitan Perspective: Sociology of the Second Age of Modernity', *The British Journal of Sociology*, 51 (1), 79–105.

Bell, D. (1976). *The Cultural Contradictions of Capitalism*. London: Heinemann.

Berman, M. (1970). *The Politics of Authenticity*. London: Verso.
Birnbaum, N. (2001). *After Progress: American Social Reform and European Socialism in the Twentieth Century*. Oxford: Oxford University Press.
Bloch, M. (1961). *Feudal Society*. London: Routledge and Kegan Paul.
Bobbio, N. (1987). *The Future of Democracy*. Cambridge: Polity Press.
—— (1996). *Left and Right*. Cambridge: Polity Press.
Boltanski, L., and Chiapello, È. (2005). *The New Spirit of Capitalism*. London: Verso.
Borghi, V. (2011). 'One-Way Europe? Institutional Guidelines, Emerging Regimes of Justification, and Paradoxical Turns in European Welfare Capitalism', *European Journal of Social Theory*, 14 (3), 321–41.
Bourdieu, P. (2003). *Firing Back: Against the Tyranny of the Market 2*. London: Verso.
Bourdieu, P. *et al.* (1999). *The Weight of the World: Social Suffering in Contemporary Society*. Cambridge: Polity Press.
Bourdieu, P., and Wacquant, L. (2005). 'The Cunning of Imperialist Reason'. In L. Wacquant (ed.), *Pierre Bourdieu and Democratic Politics*, pp. 178–98. Cambridge: Polity Press.
Bronner, S. E. (2004). *Reclaiming the Enlightenment*. New York: Columbia University Press.
Calhoun, C. (2007). *Nations Matter: Culture, History, and the Cosmopolitan Dream*. London: Routledge.
Campbell, C. (1987). *The Romantic Ethic and the Spirit of Modern Capitalism*. Oxford: Blackwell.
Castells, M. (1998). *The End of the Millennium*. Oxford: Blackwell.
Crouch, C. (2004). *Post-Democracy*. Cambridge: Polity Press.
Delanty, G. (1995). *Inventing Europe: Idea, Identity, Reality*. London: Macmillan.
—— (2009). 'The European Heritage: History, Memory and Time'. In C. Rumford (ed.), *The SAGE Handbook of European Studies*, pp. 36–51. London: Sage.
Dewey, J. (1916). *Democracy and Education*. New York: The Macmillan Company.
Eley, G. (2002). *Forging Democracy: The History of the Left in Europe 1850–2000*. Oxford: Oxford University Press.
Etzioni, A. (1997). *The New Golden Rule*. London: Profile Books.
Fromm, E. (1994). 'The Humanistic Credo'. In R. Funk (ed.), *The Erich Fromm Reader*, pp. 127–32. New Jersey, NJ: The Humanities Press.
Gadamer, H. (1976). 'The Historicity of Understanding'. In P. Connerton (ed.), *Critical Sociology*, pp. 117–33. London: Penguin.
Giddens, A. (1998). *The Third Way*. Cambridge: Polity Press.
Giddens, A., and Beck, U. (2010). 'Open Letter on the Future of Europe'. In C. Lemert *et al.* (eds), *Globalization: A Reader*, pp. 336–8. London: Routledge.

Gray, A. (2004). *Unsocial Europe: Social Protection or Flexploitation*. London: Pluto Press.
Habermas, J. (1999). 'Crossing Globalization's Valley of Tears', *New Perspectives*, 17 (4), 51–7.
Hafez, K. (2007). *The Myth of Media Globalization*. Cambridge: Polity Press.
Hobsbawm, E. (1994). *Age of Extremes: The Short Twentieth Century*. London: Michael Joseph.
Hoggart, R. (1958). *The Uses of Literacy*. London: Chatto and Windus.
Jameson, F. (1998). *The Cultural Turn*. London: Verso.
Judt, T. (2010a). *Ill Fares the Land*. London: Allen Lane.
—— (2010b). *The Memory Chalet*. London: William Heinemann.
Kettle, M. (2011). 'The Nationalists Have Won: Europe's Dream Is Over', *The Guardian*, 24 June, p. 35.
Kovel, J. (2002). *The Enemy of Nature*. London: Zed Books.
Lancaster, J. (2011). 'Once Greece Goes ...', *London Review of Books*, 33 (14), 3–7.
Lash, S., and Urry, J. (1994). *Economies of Signs and Spaces*. London: Sage.
Le Goff, J. (2005). *The Birth of Europe*. Oxford: Blackwell.
Mann, M. (1987). 'Ruling Class Strategies and Citizenship', *Sociology*, 21 (3), 339–54.
—— (2003). *Incoherent Empire*. London: Verso.
Marqland, D. (2011). *The End of the West: The Once and Future of Europe*. Princeton, NJ: Princeton University Press.
Mathers, A. (2007). *Struggling for a Social Europe*. Aldershot: Ashgate.
Mazower, M. (2011). 'Any New Marshall Plan Will Founder in the Minds of Europe's Hesitant Leaders', *The Guardian*, 6 July, p. 12.
Mikkeli, H. (1998). *Europe as an Idea and an Identity*. Basingstoke: Palgrave Macmillan.
Milosz, C. (1981). *The Captive Mind*. London: Penguin.
Moschanos, G. (2002). *In the Name of Social Democracy*. London: Verso.
Orwell, G. (1999). *Nineteen Eighty-Four*. London: Secker and Warberg.
—— (2001). 'The Intellectual Revolt'. In P. Davison (ed.), *Orwell and Politics*, pp. 416–19. London: Penguin.
Reid-Henry, S. (2011). 'Norway: The Mourning After', *New Statesman*, 1 August, pp. 23–5.
Rifkin, J. (2004). *The European Dream*. Cambridge: Polity Press.
Rosselli, C. (1994). *Liberal Socialism*. Princeton, NJ: Princeton University Press.
Sassoon, D. (1997). *One Hundred Years of Socialism: The West European Left in the Twentieth Century*. London: Fontana Press.
—— (1998). 'Fin-de-Siècle Socialism: The United, Modest Left', *New Left Review*, No. 227, pp. 88–96.

Sennett, R. (2006). *The Culture of the New Capitalism*. New Haven, CT: Yale University Press.
Smart, B. (1999). *Facing Modernity*. London: Sage.
Smith, A. D. (1995). *Nations and Nationalism in a Global Era*. Cambridge: Polity Press.
Smith, D. (2006). *Globalization: The Hidden Agenda*. Cambridge: Polity Press.
Snyder, T. (2010). *Bloodlands: Europe Between Hitler and Stalin*. London: Bodley Head.
Stevenson, N. (2011). *Education and Cultural Citizenship*. London: Sage.
Tawney, R. H. (1961). *The Acquisitive Society*. London: Collins.
—— (1964). *The Radical Tradition*. London: Penguin.
Todorov, T. (2003). *Hope and Memory*. London: Atlantic Books.
—— (2010). *The Fear of Barbarians: Beyond the Clash of Civilizations*. Cambridge: Polity Press.
Turner, B. S. (1994). *Orientalism, Postmodernism and Globalism*. London: Routledge.
Wacquant, L. (2004). *Punishing the Poor: The Neoliberal Government of Social Insecurity*. Durham, NC: Duke University Press.
—— (2005). 'Symbolic Power in the Rule of the State Nobility'. In L. Wacquant (ed.), *Pierre Bourdieu and Democratic Politics*, pp. 133–50. Cambridge: Polity Press.
Wall, J. (2005). *Moral Creativity: Paul Ricoeur and the Politics of Creativity*. Oxford: Oxford University Press.
Weber, M. (1958). *The Protestant Ethic and the Spirit of Capitalism*. New York: Dover Publications.
Williams, K. (2005). *European Media Studies*. London: Sage.
Williams, R. H. (1982). *Dream Worlds: Mass Consumption in Nineteenth Century France*. Berkeley, CA: University of California Press.

ADAM F. KOLA

# 3 European Identity, Minor Transnationalism and a Semi-Peripheral Perspective

'When you are in the family ... you have more rights than when you are asking to join and knocking on the door', said French President Jacques Chirac in February 2003, thus before the biggest enlargement of the European Union (EU), scheduled for 2004, and at the time when some additional countries, like Romania and Bulgaria, were discussing their EU membership. In his words, '[T]hey missed a great opportunity to shut up!' – an anger inspired by the new members' decision to support the United States (US) involvement in the war in Iraq (Chirac 2003). Apart from the discussion about the equity of this intervention, Chirac's words reverberated in all Central and Eastern European (CEE) countries, because they highlighted semi-peripheral presentiments about Czech, Polish and others' place in or, in fact, outside the European club. However, those words provoked determined opposition and debate about the real presence and role of CEE countries in a common Europe. Chirac's attitude towards the other nations inspired ideas about a Europe partitioned into a better and worse Europe or, as US Secretary of Defense Donald Rumsfeld put it in January 2003, into Old and New Europe, distinguishing between Western supremacy and Eastern complexes (Chirac 2003). The proof of the (il)legitimacy of that supremacy and those complexes was, amongst other things, the European story of the 2008 global crisis and subsequent recession (with a relatively strong Polish economy) or European presidencies of such countries as the Czech Republic or Poland. Such situations have demonstrated that New Europe can adjust to new situations and it can, on the one hand, fight for its own businesses and economic performance, as well as cooperate on behalf of the common European good, on the other.

If a rough but effective institutional and political coexistence of Western and Eastern Europe is possible, what about European identity, especially if we take a look from a semi-peripheral and minor transnational perspective? Can we find any new thoughts and approaches in this New Europe or do we just have to shut up, as Jacques Chirac said, and obediently follow our older brothers and sisters from old European democracies? This chapter will explore these questions by focusing on two crucial dimensions, namely the issue of European roots and the related problem of identity. In semi-peripheral gazes such questions are indissociable, because identity is not only a project for the future but usually is deeply rooted in the past.

The idea for the then European Community (EC) and the present European Union was based on utopian dreams about a better future. It was a project that opposed the negative past and the history of European divisions, conflicts and wars, and built on some well-defined basic values. I would argue that alongside economic reasons, a certain set of principles, according to the founding fathers of the EC, was closely related to Western Christian, and especially Roman Catholic, ethics. As a consequence, any debate about the roots of the modern European identity mentions the following three elements: Greek (democracy and philosophy), Roman (law and order) and Christian (ethics and humanism) traditions. However, if we take into account the practice of European coexistence and controversies, all those noble ideals disappear and are replaced by ordinary political games, in which a win–win strategy does not always apply. More precisely, what becomes obvious in times of crisis very often predominates over slogans about a common Europe, integrity, solidarity, etc. And what is even more important, and is peculiarly visible in New Europe, is that we can find many traditions that are treated as even more valid in the present discourse.

Hence, it could be difficult or even impossible to find any straight translation from current political life into the world of ideas (and vice versa). For the reasons which will be explored in this chapter, in Central and Eastern Europe, the second perspective – ideas – is more appropriate and better represented than the strictly political debate on the roots and identity of Europe.

All attempts directed towards a precise definition of the roots of Europe are bound to fail. Yet, a glance at a variety of concepts that have appeared in Poland, the Czech Republic and other Central and Eastern European countries leads towards a new interpretation of the multifaceted nature of European roots and even of the concepts of European identity. These concepts also make us look with favour at all ideas that do not hide in the narrow peripheries of basic categories and simplified schemes and do not copy truisms (like the already mentioned and oft-repeated Greek-Roman-Christian trinity), but which, on the contrary, point at new questions, not studied until now. From this perspective, minor Europe(s) offer(s) a more innovative and interesting opinion about Europe as a united political project and Europeanism as a new (still only potential?) identity. Hence, the main aim of the chapter is to provide a survey of Central and Eastern European literature (academic, political, historical, belles-lettres) and, on that basis, to elaborate critically whether the proposition of Europe without domination and hegemonic politics nowadays is still only a project. Could it be something more than another utopia? Is the destiny of Europe analogous to that of Atlantis?

From this perspective, experience of migration and/or cosmopolitan experience is very important and in many ways formative for the proposed ideas, especially if we take into consideration exiled intellectuals, for whom this simultaneously double, core and semi-peripheral perspective is approachable. Accordingly, some of the intellectuals that will be considered include Leszek Kołakowski, Krzysztof Pomian, Jan Zielonka and Pope John Paul II. We could also find interesting voices from non-emigrants, like Václav Havel or Karol Modzelewski; however, in these cases the ideas presented are created by people related to the opposition in the communist period, and in that sense we can call those dissidents in internal exile. Nevertheless, we should look at those voices as an exemplar indicating possible way of thinking.

Looking back into the history of European integration at the Copenhagen European Summit in 1973, when the frames of common identity were proposed (Radeljić 2012), we get the impression that this document was unknown in Central and Eastern Europe (except among experts in topics concerning the EC/EU), and that discussions about

European identity were far from those arrangements. Semi-peripheral debates on European identity were based on intellectual speculations and historical investigations of the history of the Old Continent, but only to some extent on the history of real European integration. Hence, the Union's practice was omitted. There are several reasons for this situation. In the discourse on European identity, two dimensions are interspersed: on the one hand, European identity is strictly presented as EU identity and, on the other hand, European identity goes beyond the EU frame, thus relating to Europe itself. In Central and Eastern Europe, those two perspectives are very often confused. When we want to talk about the first approach, in fact we are talking about the second. This is partly connected to the fact that those countries did not take part in forming and formulating the frames of European institutions and – all the more – identity, and in the post-war era were isolated behind the Iron Curtain and were functioning in a different political system. In consequence, at the beginning of the twenty-first century, when the integration of Central and Eastern European countries with the EC/EU started, common structures and ideas were already shaped and completed. To be precise, the process of enlargement of the EC/EU undeniably changes the form of the Union. A clear sign of this shift-in-progress is hesitation about the future place of Turkey in the EU. Nevertheless, the basis and foundations for European identity were framed before the enlargement at the beginning of the twenty-first century. Hence, Central and Eastern European countries did not take part in its definition. At the turn of twentieth century, all those nations were catching up with the Union's 'backwardness',[1] without, however, real references to the older European documents and without common knowledge about the paths leading to the final solutions. This is, on the one hand, a real danger and weakness in the dialogue with Western Europe, because those two (Western and Eastern) narrations about Europe and their common identity pass each other; on the other hand, it could be a chance for the

1 I do not use this term with a pejorative, disparaging or evaluative meaning, but in a descriptive sense of not being a part of European integration till the turn of the century.

EU to take a fresh look at the topic in question and to find solutions that will take into consideration the needs of all members of the EU.

The story told here about complementary features focuses on the problem of the extending and opening-up of Europe, in more or less chronological order. The extending and opening-up of Europe, in both historical and synchronic dimensions, is one of the most important aspects of constructing a European identity based on historical roots from the semi-peripheral perspective and minor transnationalism. Apart from the basic trinity – Greek, Roman and Christian traditions, which is also repeated in Central and Eastern European discourse – we can find a few constituents that are either idiosyncratic or based on local cultures associated with the Old Continent. However, locality is not the only (one) formula for Central and Eastern European authors, because very often they transgress regional borders and follow universal indications. I will argue that due to the comparable cultural constellations and analogous historical background and experiences (including intellectual and political) of Central and Eastern Europe, we can point out similarities that make relevant (but not essential or substantial) the difference between Eastern and Western perceptions of Europe. I propose to call this viewpoint 'minor transnationalism', as suggested by François Lionnet and Shu-mei Shih (2005).[2] In addition, three aspects or ways of conceptualizing the problem of European roots and identity are taken into consideration, each of them different in scope: the diversity of Europe, European peripheries and borderlands and, finally, modern European history.

2 This term is not axiomatically marked here but used in a descriptive sense. Analogously, the category of 'semi-periphery' is adopted from Immanuel Wallerstein's world-systems theory (2004), but used rather as a catchword, without theoretical and ideological background.

## Europe Came from Asia[3]

Czech religious studies specialist and philosopher, Břetislav Horyna, in his 2001 book *Idea Evropy: Pohledy do filosofie dějin* [*The Idea of Europe: Insight to the Philosophy of History*] defines Europe by negation. Accordingly, Europe is not 'only a place, empire [*říše*], space or geopolitical and political science category' (Horyna 2001: 9). On the contrary, it is 'in the first place: a paradigm, sign, style, subject, idea and simultaneously it still remains a place, empire and the space of wasted subjects, lost paradigms, forgotten styles, fading thoughts, signs, which we still are able to read, but which we no longer understand' (Horyna 2001: 9). Similarly, Leszek Kołakowski emphasizes that Europe is something more than simply 'geography'. In his text *Czy Europa może zaistnieć?* [*Can Europe Arise?*], referring to Winston Churchill's speech at the University of Zurich on 19 September 1946 titled *Let Europe Arise!*, he claims: 'So, strictly, if Europe is a geographical category, it cannot be evidently the base of any idea; but when it is supposed to have a cultural definition, this definition must be formed beforehand, hence we know what Europe is' (Kołakowski 2002).

Horyna (2001: 11), following the trace of genealogical-historical explanations, states that 'Europe was born in Asia and it came from Asia'. During the Greek–Persian wars, the geographical category which Europe had belonged to at that time changed into a political category. Greek identity had been constituted as non-Asian and in this meaning it can be associated with Europeanism. But, as Horyna (2001: 16) underlines 'that identity was not the work of Greek people, its creation and in consequence, creation of Europe should be attributed to Persian people'. European identity understood in such a way does not belong to Europe, does not have an inner source in European culture, as is mistakenly believed by many authors writing

3 Some of the examples and quotations presented in this section can be found in my 2011 book, published in Polish as *Europa w dyskursie polskim, czeskim i chorwackim: Rekonfiguracje krytyczne* [*Europe in Polish, Czech and Croatian Discourse: Critical Reconfigurations*].

about European roots, but this identity is Asiatic in its origin. Therefore, in the process of seeking our identity and roots we cannot limit ourselves to boundaries indicated by stereotypes and prejudices about traditionally apprehended Europe. We are committed to dialoguing with non-European cultures, or even more: when we are debating European identity we should also take into consideration all those traditions and ideas, which are not, at first blush, European at all, because in fact they describe considerably ourselves and tell the truth about us. The problem of the (post)colonial heritage is probably the best example.

Václav Havel's texts and speeches also contain motifs indicating the Asian roots of Europe. In his speech to the Italian Senate on 4 April 2002, he said that 'progenitors of our contemporary nations came to these lands from Asia, and that the name Europe itself depicts a presumably Asian perspective – the word means "West" and looking from the East, Europe is of course situated in the West, over which the Sun sets every evening' (Havel 2002). He observed further that 'behind Europe, i.e. West of it' there was nothing more, only the ocean and emptiness, abyss and the end of the world, 'a grave, the kingdom of shadows'. Inevitably, the association with the land of the dead or simply with the end of the earthly wandering of a man must appear in this place. In addition, '[a]s it is known, one could wander around the world long and with great hope in the heart, but only as long as one reached the place, where the possibility of farther voyage or farther retreat ended definitely, that is, when he got to the place, where the world itself, with all its innate earthly expectations ended'. It is an undeniable fact that this is a horrifying perspective, therefore 'ancient Europe's inhabitants could have had disheartening and even claustrophobic thoughts as to their existence: from one side, the pressure of great ancient Asian states and also so-called barbarian nations or tribes approaching from the East, and from the other side, darkness, nonentity and void' (Havel 2002). Havel concluded that 'in accordance with some thinkers, European civilizations regard the attitude towards some key "othernesses", such as Asia and nonentity as exceptionally important'. It is hard to say if Horyna's book was an inspiration for Havel – it is not even important. For the author of the famous essay *Moc bezmocných* [*The Power of the Powerless*] neither geography nor history is the most important factor in defining the Old

Continent. He is conceptualizing Europe from the human perspective of individuals – and in that sense he is the heir of the tradition and ethos of the First Republic and its president Tomáš Garrigue Masaryk and Čapek's brothers, Karel and Josef. However, he also recognized Asia as a source of European roots, a territory which was recognized, available and foreseeable. On the other hand, the Atlantic Ocean was too big and terrifying, impossible to overcome. Asia was settled by people, whereas the ocean was a place of the unknown and was the background for myths and legends.

This is similar to the works of one of the most important Polish historians, Karol Modzelewski, who was, like Havel, a dissident in the communist system. He invokes Jacques Le Goff and emphasizes that the ancient and Mediterranean roots of Europe were not homogeneous. Apart from Greek and Roman elements, classical culture was created by 'Hellenistic civilization, which transferred elements of the despotic traditions of the ancient East to the late Roman Empire and particularly to Byzantium and the Byzantine Church' (Modzelewski 2004: 6). It is no longer a sphere of myths and legends, but of real historic mechanisms. If we invoke ancient Greece, we should regard the East of the Old Continent as part of the European canon, because it is easier to find ancient elements in 'Byzantium, than in the states of Charlemagne or Otto I' (Modzelewski 2004: 6–7). In European culture, the division corresponding to the Latin and Hellenistic partition the East–West schism is, in Le Goff's and Modzelewski's opinions, the deepest and most tenacious division within the Old Continent. The multiplicity of historical aspects in presented propositions is pivotal and underlines that even in unquestionable references, which are, by and large, treated as a base for European roots, as in the case of the Greek, Roman and Christian tradition, things are in fact not so simple and unequivocal.

Sociologist and philosopher Zygmunt Bauman, quoting Krzysztof Pomian's thoughts, regards in turn that 'Europe came to be the birthplace of a *transgressive* civilization – a civilization of transgression' (Bauman 2004: 7). Europe endures imprisonment in the narrow borders of the Old Continent and opposes every constancy and finitude. It insistently aims at trespassing boundaries. The essence of European culture is – with both positive and negative consequences – expansiveness. In this context, Czech intellectuals like Václav Černý, Miroslav Vlk and Tomáš Halík use the term 'to evangelize', which is also understood beyond its religious context as a metaphor that refers more or less to Bauman's intuitions).

## *Barbaricum*

Krzysztof Pomian, the author of *L'Europe et ses nations* [*Europe and its Nations*] and the Director of the Scientific Committee of the Museum of Europe in Brussels since 2001, referring to Montesquieu, defines the beginning of Europe as in the fifth century, when the barbarians crossed the *limes* and settled down in the Roman Empire. The fusion of three horizons occurred: the cultural unification of Rome, barbarity and Christianity. The consequence of this process was the arising of Europe. As he puts it, '[t]he barbarians learnt Christianity, they learnt Latin, to read and write as they had not been able to' (Pomian 2002). And, as the Roman Empire was closely related to the Mediterranean basin, so Europe expanded in northern and eastern directions. The borders of Roman and Christian civilization moved to the North and Baltic Seas.

However, thoughts that are marginal in Pomian's deliberations are crucial concepts for Modzelewski's project. He is mainly interested in traditions of barbaric peoples and is opposed to the strangulation of European tradition to the Mediterranean circle. What is essential from the present perspective, 'not recognizing those roots, however, it is impossible to understand either the complex history of Europe or its cultural diversity as it exists today' (Modzelewski 2004: 8). It is not true that Hellenistic, Roman or Christian cultures diminished barbaric peoples and made them a reflection of their own ideals; quite the contrary – assimilation and acculturation occurred amongst the particular peoples in diversified ways in time and space. This process was different amongst Celtic, Germanic, Slavic and Baltic peoples (Modzelewski 2004: 7). Those differences and the diversity that arose as a result have been present up to this day and are a factual background to European identity.

In the context of European integration, Modzelewski's *Barbarzyńska Europa* [*Barbarian Europe*] has one more important dimension – methodological, but understood in terms of the categories used in engaged humanities and social studies, that is, not only as an academic problem but as a socio-political one, too. In this sense, the methodological dimension has philosophical, ideological and even political implications. Modzelewski, following Reinhard Wenskus, opposes using and overlapping the ethnolinguistic categories that arose in the nineteenth century in research on barbarian peoples. Borrowing ideas and interpretational schemes from cultural anthropology, Modzelewski is trying to overcome the dependence on historiography and archaeology in explaining nationalisms and segregation. Wenskus 'emphasized [as early as in 1974], that areas characterized by similarities of social-system structures do not coincide with areas of language communities' (Modzelewski 2004: 12). He noticed similarities between Celtic, Germanic, Slavic and Baltic peoples, and he treated them as one cultural circle, which, as already mentioned, in different ways responds to the process of acculturation with Mediterranean traditions.

Modzelewski's project surpassed pure and simple historiography and is a distinct voice in the debate about European roots, and also, as a consequence, about construction of European identity. As observed, the '[b]arbaric cultural heritage is, in addition to those of Rome and Byzantium [but not Greek in its ancient meaning], an essential component of a complex European identity' (Modzelewski 2004: 464). It co-creates unity and verifies it at the same time, as '[t]he balance of mutual influences between classical culture and traditional cultures of *barbaricum* is expressed in a very different way and this diversity is present in contemporary Europe' (Modzelewski 2004: 464).

## The Two Lungs of Europe

The Christian heritage of Europe is emphasized by intellectuals connected with the Church, especially priests. They usually refer to the authority of the pope. In Central and Eastern Europe in the time of the disintegration of communist regimes and integration into NATO and the European Union, the central figure was John Paul II, who perceived union not only in economic and political dimensions, but also in the realm of the spirit. For John Paul II, Christian values, which are universal, should be a base for European integration and such a standpoint is fully understandable. However, we have to remember his cold relations with Eastern Christianity, especially with the Orthodox Church in Russia or Serbia. Even if we agree that behind his ecumenical activity, in the whole of the Western Christianity machine was hidden a new version of Christianization (or evangelization), that is, a conflict between two religions, we should mention one aspect of his intercultural project. He was crucial in reviving the idea of Eastern Christianity as foundational for European identity. For him, the most important role in this process was played by the brother saints, Cyril and Methodius, Christian missionaries amongst the Slavic peoples, who were declared – beside St Benedict of Nursia – the patrons of Europe.[4] John Paul II was talking about two lungs of the Church, Eastern and Western, which the Church should breathe with. Radosław Zenderowski, based on Grzegorz Przebinada's remarks, underlines:

> One fact seems to be worth attention, that the allegory of 'the two lungs' of Europe, associated inseparably with John Paul II, was adopted by the Pope from a Russian poet and thinker – Vyacheslav Ivanov (1866–1949). The metaphor of organic connection of both continent parts comes from Ivanov's letter to Charles du Bos, from 1930, John Paul II referred to it in public for the first time one year after taking a seat of the Holy See … Ivanov in turn, drew this idea from an eminent Russian theologian and ecumenical activist, Vladimir Solovyov (1853–1900), whose output John Paul II frequently refers to. (Sowiński and Zenderowski 2003: 30)

The two lungs of Europe were mentioned in an analogical way by the Roman Catholic priest, cardinal and Jesuit, Tomáš Špidlík, Czech by origin, an expert of Orthodox theology. He combined in ecumenical

4 In 1999, John Paul II declared also as co-patrons of Europe Saint Catherine of Siena, Bridget of Sweden and Edith Stein (Teresia Benedicta of the Cross). This gender and geographical balance is an interesting and usually unnoticed aspect – even by its own representatives – of Catholic social teaching.

perspective Eastern and Western Christianity and emphasized these dual roots of the Old Continent (Špidlík 2007). Speaking about the roots of Europe, John Paul II directed attention to Cyril and Methodius, because they 'had preached the Gospel in the name of non-divided Church' (John Paul II 1985: 208, 2005: 96), from before the Great Schism period. Thus is important from the ecumenical perspective of the rapprochement of the two Churches and their religious traditions on equal rights and positions, without domination of either side.

However, we should remember that a fully ecumenical project could be put into practice only in religious dialogue and in the space of private beliefs, not between two religions (some representatives of the Roman Catholic Church also agree with this) (Halík 1997, 2002; Kola 2011: 191–6), or on the secular dimension of legal cooperation in a democratic environment, as is the case with the EU (de Lazari 2009: 19–37). Religious ecumenism is impossible as long as Christian churches lay claim to be universal. If all churches are universal, no church can really be ecumenical. In fact, behind such declarations about peaceful cooperation and coexistence, we can find the domination and hegemony of one side. However, in the case of the enlargement of the EC/EU, combined with the churches' endeavours to expand European roots also along the Eastern tradition, we can find attempts to describe our identity better and in more appropriate ways.

Next, we can observe that extending European identity as understood traditionally is a necessary condition of building European unity from a semi-peripheral perspective. Nevertheless, it is still a big challenge for the Old Europe.

John Paul II (2003: 217) underlined that the roots of European civilization should be seen in antiquity, especially in Greek and Roman tradition. He added that Europe takes much 'from Celtic, Germanic and Slavic sources as well as Christianity' and that 'there are various languages, cultures and legal traditions of those nations, regions as various are their institutions'. Moreover, he also remarked that despite historical and political differences, 'in comparison with other continents, Europe is perceived as a unity' (John Paul II 2003: 217). This unity was his aim both under communist power in Eastern and Central Europe and after the collapse of communism and the beginning of full European union.

## The First European Integration: Real Unity?

For Polish historian Jerzy Kłoczowski the crucial moment for European integration does not come until the tenth to eleventh centuries. In that time, the fundamental shift or displacement from the Mediterranean world to the north took place. It was defined, on the one hand, by relative stability of the Western part of the continent and, on the other, by a rise of the younger Europe (Kłoczowski 1998). As he later put it, '[c]ountries of Central and Eastern Europe, situated between the Adriatic and Baltic seas – Croatia, Czech Republic, Hungary, Poland and Scandinavian countries ... succeeded in the 10th century, particularly in its second half, officially accepting Christianity from Rome' (Kłoczowski 2004: 44). This was a period of deep changes in social structure and agricultural production, but also in art, architecture and town planning.

In the book *L'Europe et ses nations*, Pomian distinguished three European integrations. The first one took place in mediaeval times and is more or less related to Kłoczowski's position, presented above. However, the beginning is moved forward, because it started in the twelfth century, while the fourteenth century is the end of this first European community. According to the author, 'since the 12th century Europe has been an actual unity ranking with overlapping Christian and Latin communities' (Pomian 2004: 40). He simultaneously accentuates that it is a new quality in the Old Continent, but not including politics: '[the] Latin area remains a mosaic of territorial units of various sizes and subjected to authorities of various scope, joining or dividing as a result of dynastic combinations and which mutual relations cannot be defined in any general formula' (Pomian 2004: 40). The author distinguishes three elements, three cultures creating this first community. They were: scholastic culture, chivalric culture and burgess culture, 'and rather the culture of urban oligarchy, principally from northern Italy, Flanders and Rhineland' (Pomian 2004: 46). Those three cultures were different and separated from each other, but together they created *christianitas*. Scholastic culture is not identical with the monastic culture from the early mediaeval times, which was crucial for Kłoczowski to distinguish European integration. It is similar to chivalric culture, which is not equal to the earlier culture of warriors, and especially to the traditions of barbarians.

Pomian notes that '[m]onastic culture had to face the warrior culture', while '[s]cholastic culture co-exists with chivalric culture, which transforms into the nobility' (Pomian 2004: 45). Accordingly, he underlines one important feature of those cultures: in creating a common Europe they were elitist and exclusive, and in fact were in a minority. The majority was the fourth culture – peasant, which was deep-set in locality, and based on pagan (or barbarian in Modzelewski's view) beliefs and customs. It is valid even in those areas where Christianity had been present for a millennium. Recapitulating the first period of European integration, Pomian, with a big dose of anthropological sensitivity, states: 'Each populace lives therefore in many cultures. In European clergy culture; in chivalric culture – stretched between European extremity and national extremity being just in a shaping process; in burgess culture, limited to their own town, but simultaneously opening to the world; and in peasant culture, solely ethnic and local. In written and oral cultures. In "high" cultures, although not equal, as well as in "low" culture' (Pomian 2004: 47–8).

## The Second European Integration: Autopoietic Scriptworld

The second European integration started at the beginning of the sixteenth century. It was called by Krzysztof Pomian the *Respublica Litteraria*, where the privileged position was held by the francophone or, in fact, 'francoscript', *La République des Lettres*. The author states that the expression meant 'people, who would be identified today as intellectuals, perceived collectively as an environmental group' (Pomian 1992: 145). It was a guild of the people of the pen, the republic of letters (Pomian 1992: 145–96, 2004: 72–80), and I would call it an autopoietic scriptworld.[5]

This culture was supranational and contained the whole of Europe. The Latin language was official and common, enabling communication within the Old Continent. Scholars were legates of mediaeval scholastic culture and the humanistic tradition of the Renaissance. *Respublica Litteraria* contained both Catholic and Protestant areas, but at that time the Orthodox space was outside this newly born culture. However, we should remember that from the beginning of the eighteenth century, Russia would be a part of a united scholars' world. Erasmus became its luminary, 'a protagonist and the highest authority, what makes Basel, where he lives, the centre of international humanism'. The centre declined with his death. This was when religious wars in France finished, and Paris once more became the intellectual capital of Europe. However, that religious freedom finished at the end of the seventeenth century. In that period 'Huguenots expelled by Louis XIV, settle down in the Republic of the United Netherlands, in England, Prussia and Scandinavian kingdoms' (Pomian 2004: 72–3). Like Erasmus, who played the crucial role in the first period, this time Pierre Bayle is 'the leader as its [*République des Lettres*] theoretician and legislator' (Pomian 2004: 73). Pomian, based on Bayle, defines the Republic; although without boundaries, it is a land of

> freedom identified with the autonomy of individuals towards everything, what is particular, temporary and local. It is supposed to be a society of national beings, which citizenship can be obtained only of an individual's own will, divesting oneself of passions and all other bonds with communities, to which one belongs due to his birth or external constraint … [T]he only hierarchies respected there result from the differences between the contributions of particular individuals into common

5 'Autopoietic' refers to the Humberto Maturana and Francisco Varela concept used in biology or, in fact, to Niklas Luhmann using that term in his systems theory, whereas 'scriptworld' refers to David Damrosch's ideas. For Damrosch (2007: 195), 'scripts … achieve a global reach far beyond their linguistic base, with profound consequences for … cultural in general … A global script forms the basis of a broad literary system – what we might call a "scriptworld" – in which works that use that script are composed'.

> creation ... Values left outside include: religious denomination, loyalty towards the country, nation and even a family, identified with all what is temporary, particular, local, what means non-constitutive for a human being in itself; contrary to reason, which ... represents what is common, inevitable and global. (Pomian 2004: 73–4)

This supranational republic of scholars was multidisciplinary and took into account political writings and belles-letters, natural science and philosophy, mathematics and historiography. Simultaneously, qualitative change happened. Ancient authorities were no longer the most important source in searching for truth, but permanent doubting, scepticism, experiments and empirical research were fundamental to scientific thinking. 'New science and new philosophy initiate together the most radical drift away from tradition, which took place in European history since Christianity introduction' (Pomian 2004: 77). Nicolaus Copernicus, Galileo Galilei, René Descartes, Thomas More, Isaac Newton and Pierre Simon de Laplace were members (or rather citizens) of this republic. New forms of organization were visible signs of new science: informal research groups, academies, journals, scientific societies, etc. In the eighteenth century, those informal structures were institutionalizing and were depending more and more on state foundations, where those personal contacts and exchanges of ideas were less and less important. Regional versions of the *République des Lettres* occurred, such as *Republic of Learning*, *Republica dei Letterati* or *Gelehrtenrepublik* (Pomian 2004: 80). However, the disappearance of the *République des Lettres* in the eighteenth century was connected with the processes of nation-state building. In consequence, in the nineteenth century, national universities arose in East and Central Europe, on the model proposed by Wilhelm von Humboldt.

On the one hand, if we compare this nineteenth-century model with the ideals of the founding fathers of the *République des Lettres*, the academic world changed its character and modes of functioning. On the other hand, some of the basic rules created in that time are still effective now and the privileged position and social status of science and scholars in the Euro-American world is very high.

In Pomian's conception, the eighteenth century brought the end of the common, supranational European project. In other approaches, the

Enlightenment is the beginning of European civilization. One of the best examples from Central and Eastern Europe is a book *Spór o dziedzictwo europejskie* [*Dispute on European Heritage*] by Ewa Bieńkowska (1999). She is not original in such a perception of the eighteenth century and the way traditional philosophy treats the Enlightenment as a peak of human intellectual development and critical thinking; hence, the (semi)peripheral debate about this period is a reflection of the core's dispute on the topic in question. But from a Polish perspective, the Enlightenment is perceived beyond Western, and especially French, atheistic tradition, and, on the contrary, it is bound in coexistence with religiousness. Bieńkowska is, of course, not the first or only one to write about that period from such a perspective and, what is more obvious, she is not the first or only one who underlines this sacred–profane complex and its role in creating European identity. For example, Jan Patočka, one of the most important and famous Czech philosophers, was convinced that 'contemporary Catholicism is not inevitably supposed to be in conflict with the enlightened mind and its liberalism' (Baluch 2001: xv). Bieńkowska, in similar spirit, notes: 'I can imagine the situation, when Catholicism too discovers for itself astonishing religious treasure of that epoch, concealed in lay thought as well, and what is worse, in anticlerical one; when it becomes interested in intuitions flowing out from a common source' (Bieńkowska 1999: 10).

Leszek Kołakowski underlines that we cannot treat Christianity as the only force in the Old Continent's integration (it is connected with searching for European roots, the world views of the modern founding fathers of European community, as well as with building European identity). But if we are to respect different opinions in multicultural and pluralistic Europe, in agreement with all its founding traditions, we have to take into consideration those traditions that are not connected with the Christian tradition, or, even more, which are in opposition to it. Kołakowski says:

> And is there anyone who would dare to claim that Jews, who had never accepted Christianity, but influenced European culture in an amazingly effective manner, do not belong to this culture? Does not the non-Christian belong to this culture, i.e. great areas of the age of Enlightenment, great areas of socialistic movements and liberal movements, great parts of Freemasonry? Do not Spinoza, Hobbes, Voltaire, Kant, Diderot, Sartre, and dozens of the most outstanding writers and thinkers, who

> were either indifferent or adverse towards Christianity or else were condemned by the Church, belong to Europe? Someone could say that all those people had been Christians automatically, inside their hearts, but this would have to be proved. The Roman Church is cosmopolitan in its mission, and the pope frequently emphasizes the necessity of spiritual foundations of the movement that would unite Europe; however, it is necessary to define where and how to situate the cultural boundaries of what is 'European'. (Kołakowski 2002)

Kołakowski avoids simplification. Many authors, when talking about the non-Christian roots of Europe, underline only the ancient traditions of Greek philosophy and Roman law. However, the author of *Główne nurty marksizmu* [*Main Currents of Marxism*] is not writing about antiquity, but about times when creating a common European (intellectual) space was less controversial. He underlines that there exists a whole secular tradition, or one connected with non-Christian religions (like Islam or Judaism), which are undoubtedly a part of European roots. Obliviousness to these histories is contradictory to the European spirit.

On the other hand, modern Western philosophy and the Enlightenment is blamed for all disasters that have touched Europe from the eighteenth century to today: the terror of the French Revolution, (post-)romantic nationalisms, wild capitalism, colonialism, twentieth-century totalitarian systems (fascism, Nazism, communism), to the late capitalistic atomization of societies and idiosyncratization of culture, and finally to the development of science, technique and technology, and industry and the consequential ecological pollution and disaster. A counter to those negative effects of the Enlightenment and modern European philosophy and intellectual life (beyond the rightness and legitimacy of such a statement and critique) can be seen as an idea for a future Europe as a unity (such as the protection of the environment in Břetislav Horyna's (2001) concept), which would allow the Old Continent to take a lead in global competition in primacy over the other powers.

## The Third European Integration: A Neo-Mediaeval Utopia?

Thinking about the future through the prism not only of the more or less distant past, but also of the present times is also a way of creating European identity. A critical approach is undoubtedly needed. However, Europe should be seen also as a project. In this case, all utopias – philosophical, literary and political – although based on imaginative and persuasive elements (but when put into effect in life can be a curse, like a communist utopia), seem indispensable for every community. This is intended to include not only the utopias which preserve the existing *status quo* and emphasize the potential threats of anti-utopias, but also to draw on a new utopia that may indicate a possible direction for further development. Hence, 'minor Europe' can offer courageous solutions in the process of building a European community, not as an exclusive model but, on the contrary, as an inclusive one. This seems especially important in the case of enlargement of the EU (the case of Turkey is instructive) or in the face of the growing numbers of immigrants. The ideas presented herein should be taken into account in discussion about a potentially real, inclusive European identity that, on the one hand, breaks the hegemonic, Western viewpoint within the European community, while, on the other hand, goes beyond established borders (including intellectual ones).

The third European integration, according to Pomian, concerns the post-war era, the second half of the twentieth and the beginning of the twenty-first century. He emphasizes that this integration is intentional, planned and effectively accomplished. The author stands for this project, as in his opinion, the sense of Europe is to go beyond one particular nation, language, state, culture, confession, and *ipso facto* transgress towards universal values. Hence, it is a very Eurocentric approach, not taking into account non-European cultures, and its universality should be seen in that light. Pomian's project is politically and engaged in outlook, but it is worth protecting, because it brings us more good (peace, democracy, development, integration, wealth) than bad (chaos, conflicts, disorder, war).

Other propositions of Central and Eastern European intellectuals also construct a future European identity and shape the community. But if some of them present a soft and very likeable vision of the Old Continent, the others directly formulate the project of Europe from a hard political perspective – as an empire. In soft political categories, Europe is an intellectual construct, more or less precise and finished, whereas in hard approaches it is a defined concept ready to be applied to socio-political reality. In that sense, the second group of propositions, understanding Europe as an empire, is more interesting, because it is more invasive into our lives.

In addition, I would like to emphasize three additional reasons why these approaches are important from the European perspective. First of all, Europe as an empire should be seen as a purely European concept. It does not refer to the model of the United States of America and in consequence it does not project the United States of Europe. On the one hand, for the younger Europe, the American dream is still an ideal to which Central and Eastern European countries and their nations uncritically aspire. On the other hand, some European countries and especially their elites – each for different reasons – are anti-American. What is the reason for such a transatlantic scepticism? The United States was created as a philosophical project formulated in opposition to the Old Continent, against intolerance, religious persecutions, nationalisms, social and class inequalities, wars and conflicts. Polish philosopher Andrzej Szahaj describes this situation in the following way: 'America was supposed to be an exception in many cases, the Promised Land for the oppressed and injured, the Real New World, in which the sins originating from a European past could have been censured so successfully that nobody would have been tempted to repeat them again' (Szahaj 2004: 11). The Unites States was supposed to uncover European weaknesses and failings. From such a perspective, integrated Europe does not want to be the new United States of the old world but wants to find a new solution, a new way of supranational integration based on its own tradition. Empire could be a good example and model.

The second reason why an empire of the Old Continent is popular as a solution has to do with the mediaeval background of the first European integration. Moreover, and this is the third reason, this idea is reinterpreted in the model of new mediaevalism or neo-mediaevalism. In his

2007 book, *Europe as Empire: The Nature of the Enlarged European Union*, Jan Zielonka explores this idea in the most innovative and persuasive way. What is more, Zielonka does not limit his project to deliberation about Europe as an idea, but rather talks about Europe, or the EU as a practice. Efficient organization and smooth functioning of the communion is his aim, because Zielonka is aware of technocratic dangers. It is symptomatic that Central and Eastern European intellectuals' weakness of focusing on the historical aspects of European identity is therein used pragmatically in a project for better functioning of the EU today and tomorrow.

The mechanism of pragmatic return to the ideas of mediaeval times is described by Jacek Czaputowicz. He discusses the influence of globalization on the nation state and underlines the issue of sovereignty. In mediaeval times, two levels of human dependence existed: internal or minor, implying loyalty to the feudal lord, and external or major, implying loyalty to the pope and Church. The opinion of Hedley Bull, claiming that in the Middle Ages 'none of the rulers or state were sovereign in the sense of being equipped with supremacy over a particular territory', is paid attention to (Czaputowicz 2001: 32). When the nation state arose, this stable system changed. The inner circle has extended, whereas the external has shrunk. Both have met in the idea of nation state. Globalization leads to the inverse of this process. Sovereignty of the nation state is dispersed in two directions: external and internal. In Czaputowcz's model, the external direction is broken into two paths: integration (with regional but supranational organizations, like the EU) and globalization. Internal direction – fragmentation – is related to transfer of some part of authority to the regional and local powers. As he puts it, '[i]n this system, just like in the Middle Ages, the dependence relationships do not run vertically, towards clearly geographically separated states, but horizontally – in accordance with functional criteria' (Czaputowicz 2001: 33). In that sense, while referring to Bull, the use of the term 'neo-medievalism' is legitimated (Czaputowicz 2001: 32).

The notion of 'an Empire' is conceptualized in a different way by Michael Hardt and Antonio Negri. They note, that '[t]he decline of sovereignty of nation-states … does not mean that sovereignty as such has declined', but that 'sovereignty has taken a new form' (Hardt and Negri 2000: xi–xii). They call that an empire, but in fact it shares a lot of features with neo-mediaeval approaches. Furthermore, '[i]n contrast to imperialism, Empire establishes no territorial center of power and does not rely on fixed boundaries or barriers;' thus, 'it is a decentered and deterritorializing apparatus of rule that progressively incorporates the entire global realm within its open, expanding frontiers' (Hardt and Negri 2000: xii). What is particularly important with regard to the question of identity is that 'Empire manages hybrid identities, flexible hierarchies, and plural exchanges through modulating networks of command' (Hardt and Negri 2000: xii–xiii). The authors conclude their description of such an empire by noting that '[t]he distinct national colors of the imperialist map of the world have merged and blended in the imperial global rainbow' (Hardt and Negri 2000: xiii). Following this route, sociologist Jadwiga Staniszkis (2004: 127) insists that 'Empire is a motion, and rather – a whirligig, attracting all the time new areas into the orbit of its logic'.

Even if empire in Hardt and Negri or Staniszkis's understanding is a global idea, whereas in Zielonka's proposition it is closely connected with European space, the mechanics of its functioning are similar. An analogous way is followed by others, both from the core (for example, Michael Oakshott's division into *universitas* and *societas*, based on mediaeval times) and semi-peripheral nations (as discussed by Marek Cichocki). Cichocki underlines the decentralization of power in the Middle Ages and the diversity of socio-political structures, which overlapped each other: local administrative units, seigneurial domains, tribal communities, huge territorial units, like counties, principalities, kingdoms, but also cities, professional guilds, clergy or knighthood. Despite political and functional heterogeneity, they were all united with one another and 'the areas of authorities penetrated one another, creating one great unity defined as *Republica Christiana*' (Cichocki 2007: 311). Accordingly, '[in] political-social meaning various societies, local units, corporations and confederations made great completeness as *societas civilis*' (Cichocki 2007: 311). From this perspective, analogous to Czaputowicz's arguments, the Middle Ages is not only one of the basic sources for our common European identity or the roots of the Old Continent, but – and it should be emphasized here – a proposition for a new model of European community; to clarify, in the Middle Ages, the state order was not perceived 'in our territorial and static meaning', but as a 'varied and dynamic order of authority between diversified subjects and diversified authority levels' (Cichocki 2007: 310).

When interpreting these references to the Middle Ages it is important to realize that the modern nation state with a defined territory is based on the Westphalian system starting in 1648, but fully developed, especially in Central and Eastern Europe, in the nineteenth century, and as such, it is a historical creation that could decompose or change. What is more, for Cichocki, the neo-mediaevalism of Jan Zielonka or Peter Koslowski is not only a new model for European integration, but it is also an alternative to all the federalists who dream about the United States of Europe, that is, one uniform European super-state. It enables us to describe '[t]he Union as more dynamic, complex and internally heterogeneous structure … which means rather distanced from the model of a homogeneously functioning state' (Cichocki 2007: 326), a nation state in the spirit of the Westphalian treaties. This fact gives preference to abandoning the paradigm of territorial homogeneity and the definitive character of the borders. It enables us 'to describe the increasingly hybrid nature of expanding Union identity' (Cichocki 2007: 326).

For Jan Zielonka, who is 'one of the more flamboyant cavaliers' in the field of European studies (Dannreuther 2007: 118), the EU '[b]ecomes a polycentric polity penetrating rather than controlling its environments', in which 'multiplicity of various overlapping military and police institutions is likely to remain the norm' (Zielonka 2007: 1). Furthermore, it possesses a 'multilevel governance system of concentric circles, fuzzy borders, and soft forms of external power projection resembling the system we knew in the Middle Ages, before the rise of nation states, democracy and capitalism' (Zielonka 2007: 1).

The author notes that even if the European Union's system is complicated for European citizens, due to its multifaceted and polycentric aspects, the neo-mediaeval paradigm is there to 'help the Union to maintain peace and security in Europe' (Zielonka 2007: 171). For him, this model of European coexistence is better than the Westphalian nation state model transferred on the supranational level and then aimed at building a European super-state in the sense present during the last two hundred years in the forms of modern empires, like the United Kingdom or the United

States. What is more, for him, it is a real alternative to the ineffective and costly present-day European Union with its technocratic machinery. In Zielonka's opinion, the EU 'can function as a sort of "meta-governor": a governing body that distributes decision-making competence between multitudes of territorially and functionally defined self-governing actors' (Zielonka 2007: 190). Simultaneously, it is important for the Union 'not to try to impose tight hierarchical control', instead, it should take up a position of a 'mediator between various European networks and as a facilitator of continuous communication, cooperation and compromise between such networks' (Zielonka 2007: 190). In accordance with the neo-mediaeval paradigm, EU boundaries should be 'flexible and open to those neighbours who embrace the basic set of liberal values' and rules compulsory for this kind of political organism (Zielonka 2007: 190). It is obvious for him that dissolution of the EU and a return to the nation states is also not a solution, because in global competition even the biggest and the richest states are too weak. Only Europe as an empire can compete with other world powers like the USA or China.

In the final part of Cichocki's text, apart from indicating basic differences between the mediaeval and neo-mediaeval models (different values being the grounds of each, freedom and security problems, and so on), a dose of support for a national state seems to be observed, which, in the author's opinion – contrary to the neo-mediaeval, unclear network structure – provides security and stabilization 'within the range of fulfilling economic and social rights, functional solidarity, judicature, democracy and human rights' (Cichocki 2007: 327).

The problem of identity should be examined taking into consideration the above-outlined perspective. Paradoxically, the neo-mediaeval paradigm could help us to save our own, especially local and regional, identities in the process of building a supranational European identity. In the processes of decentralization and deterritorialization, the nation state level is, or rather, can be, enfeebled. But in fact, in a multi-level and multilateral structure, all those levels can be preserved: local, regional, national, European. There is no contradiction between them, as has been presented in the nationalistic ideologies of nineteenth- and twentieth-century political thoughts. The neo-mediaeval paradigm focuses on the structural level of political functioning, whereas our individual or collective identities can be shaped freely. But the open question is whether this paradigm will deepen the disproportions between Old and New Europe or, conversely, will it lead to the equalization of differences?

## Conclusion

It is clear that in projecting the shape of the EU (does that mean also Europe per se? I would not be so sure) Eastern and Central European intellectuals are able to dialogue with core thinkers and leaders without any complexes, and – against Chirac's will and threat – are not to be shut up. It is true that very often they are looking into the past, but they know how to learn from history. One of the visible achievements is a multi-paradigmatic interpretation and explanation of the problem of European roots and projects of European identities, which corresponds to local traditions, *mentalité*, cultures, without, on the one hand, surrendering to the quasi-colonial domination of the Western, core countries, and on the other hand, sinking into triviality, insignificant for modern Europe's references to the trinity of its Greek-Roman-Christian background.

This voice of self-satisfied Old Europe, even in times of crisis, must be blunted due to the not-so-commendable historical moments. And this is not just about the distant past, as was presented above. It is enough to listen intently to post-Yugoslav feminists, like Dubravka Ugrešić or Svetlana Slapšak, for whom the post-Yugoslav wars in the 1990s were possible in the context of European connivance and inactivity or inefficient and selective (not)aid. In her 1998 book *The Culture of Lies*, Ugrešić writes that such a culture is not characteristic only of the reality of post-Yugoslav states, but also of Europe. In Central and Eastern European discourse we can find more of such critical and bitter words addressed to the West.

In conclusion, we should try to answer one fundamental question: is it necessary to look into the distant past in building European identity, even if we go beyond the canonical trinity? I would take a risk and hypothesize that all those debates are in fact games in the intellectual field, a clash of symbolic orders, where accumulated symbolic capital could determine the real supremacy. However, from a social perspective, the more burning questions, and still very painful, are issues from the recent past, which are a part of cultural and social memory. What is more, different nations focus their memory on separate events from the past, like Katyń in Poland, the post-Yugoslav wars in the Balkans, and so on. From the perspective of the history of Western connivance and inactivity, the whole post-war era, based on the order of and emerging as a consequence of the Yalta Conference, is troublesome. The Iron Curtain and the structural asymmetry between East and West in Europe as a result of the Cold War order have created semi-peripheral identities. In this perspective, what is (could be?) common for a whole European identity? The end of this identity-building process is still a distant future, it is a work in progress, with a final hazy outline somewhere on the faraway horizon.

## References

Baluch, J. (2001). 'Czeski esej współczesny'. In J. Baluch (ed.), *Hrabal, Kundera, Havel… Antologia czeskiego eseju*, pp. v–xxv. Kraków: Universitas.

Bauman, Z. (2004). *Europe: An Unfinished Adventure*. Cambridge: Polity Press.

Bieńkowska, E. (1999). *Spór o dziedzictwo europejskie. Między świętym a świeckim*. Warszawa: WAB.

Bull, H. (1977). *The Anarchical Society: A Study of Order in World Politics*. London: Macmillan.

Chirac, J. (2003). 'Chirac Lashes Out at New Europe', *CNN World*, 18 February <http://articles.cnn.com/2003-02-18/world/sprj.irq.chirac_1_french-president-jacques-chirac-eu-leaders-romania-and-bulgaria?_s=PM:WORLD> accessed 18 February 2013.

Cichocki, M. A. (2007). 'Nowe średniowiecze', *Nowa Europa: Przegląd natoliński*, 1 (5), 310–29.

Czaputowicz, J. (2001). 'Globalizacja – wpływ na państwo narodowe', *Polska w Europie*, 4 (38), 21–34.

Damrosch, D. (2007). 'Scriptworlds: Writing Systems and the Formation of World Literature', *Modern Language Quarterly*, 68 (2), 195–219.

Dannreuther, R. (2007). 'Review of Jan Zielonka's *Europe as Empire*', *European Foreign Affairs Review*, 12 (1), 118–20.

Halík, T. (1997). 'Ptal jsem se cest', interview given to J. Jandourek, *Praha Portál*.

——(2002). *Co je bez chvění, není pevné. Labiryntem světa s vírou a pochybností*. Praha: Nakladatelství Lidové noviny.

Hardt, M., and Negri, A. (2000). *Empire*. Cambridge, MA: Harvard University Press.

Havel, V. (2002). 'Speech to the Italian Senate', Rome, 4 April. Polish translation by T. Grabiński, in *Gazeta Wyborcza – Gazeta Świąteczna*, 7 June.

Horyna, B. (2001). *Idea Evropy: Pohledy do filosofie dějin*. Praha: Argo.

John Paul II (1985). 'Wyzwanie dla ewangelizacji Europy', homily from 13 October. In J. S. Gajek and L. Górka (eds), *Cyryl i Metody: Apostołowie i nauczyciele Słowian*. Vol. 2: Dokumenty, pp. 206–9. Lublin: KUL.

—— (2003). 'Speech to the Parliamentary Assembly of the Council of Europe', Strasbourg, 8 October 1988. In S. Sowiński and R. Zenderowski (eds), *Europa drogą Kościoła: Jan Paweł II o Europie i europejskości*, pp. 216–23. Wrocław: Zakład Narodowy imienia Ossolińskich – Wydawnictwo.

——(2005). *Pamięć i tożsamość. Rozmowy na przełomie tysiącleci*. Kraków: Znak.

Kłoczowski, J. (1998). *Młodsza Europa: Europa Środkowo-Wschodnia w kręgu cywilizacji chrześcijańskiej średniowiecza*. Warszawa: PIW.

——(2004). *Europa: Chrześcijańskie korzenie*. Warszawa: Stentor.

Kola, A. F. (2011). *Europa w dyskursie polskim, czeskim i chorwackim: Rekonfiguracje krytyczne*. Toruń: Nicolaus Copernicus University Press.

Kołakowski, L. (2002). 'Czy Europa może zaistnieć?', *Tygodnik Powszechny*, No. 43 <http://www.tygodnik.com.pl/apokryf/18/kolakowski.html> accessed 18 February 2013.

Lazari, A. de (2009). *Polskie i rosyjskie problemy z rosyjskością*. Łódź: University of Lodz Press.

Lionnet, F., and Shu-mei, S. (eds) (2005). *Minor Transnationalism*. Durham, NC: Duke University Press.

Modzelewski, K. (2004). *Barbarzyńska Europa*. Warszawa: Iskry.

Pomian, K. (1992). *Przeszłość jako przedmiot wiedzy*. Warszawa: Fundacja Aletheia.

——(2002). 'Jak tworzyła się współczesna Europa', interview given to P. Wroński, *Gazeta Wyborcza*, 11 December.

——(2004). *Europa i jej narody*. Gdańsk: Słowo/obraz – terytoria.

Radeljić, B. (2012). 'On European Identity: Origins, Challenges and Prospects', *The Review of International Affairs*, Vol. LXIII (1145), 7–23.

Sowiński, S., and Zenderowski, R. (2003). *Europa drogą Kościoła: Jan Paweł II o Europie i europejskości*. Wrocław: Zakład Narodowy imienia Ossolińskich – Wydawnictwo.

Staniszkis, J. (2004). *Władza globalizacji*. Warszawa: Scholar.

Szahaj, A. (2004). *Zniewalająca moc kultury. Artykuły i szkice z filozofii kultury, poznania i polityki*. Toruń: Nicolaus Copernicus University Press.

Špidlík, T. (2007), *Chrześcijańska tożsamość Europy: Dwa płuca*. Kraków: Bratni Zew.

Ugrešić, D. (1998). *The Culture of Lies: Antipolitical Essays*. University Park, PA: Pennsylvania State University Press.

Wallerstein, I. (2004). *World-Systems Analysis: An Introduction*. Durham, NC: Duke University Press.

Zielonka, J. (2007). *Europe as Empire: The Nature of the Enlarged European Union*. Oxford: Oxford University Press.

EMMA DE ANGELIS

# 4 The EU's Historical Narrative and Enlargement to Eastern Europe

The European Parliament (EP) is a key actor in the construction of an identity for the European Union (EU). As the only directly elected institution within the EU's structure, and the largest conglomerate of politicians within the European arena, ever since its inception it has strived to give voice and shape to ideas about Europe, the nature and goals of the process of European integration, and the identity and values on which this process is based. This quest for the construction of a European identity was especially evident in the EP's debates of subsequent enlargement rounds, when the need to justify the entry of new members into the European 'club' also provided a unique opportunity to actually define and refine the criteria for entering the club – not just in terms of the actual, practical criteria imposed by the EU as a whole, but also in terms of the ideational foundations of the project.

Over four decades of enlargement debates, the EP developed a strong identity discourse based on political, historical and cultural elements.[1] The debates on the enlargement to Central and Eastern Europe, which were held regularly between 1999 and 2004 as part of the EP's increased involvement in the enlargement process, were characterized above all by the construction of a strong historical narrative to strengthen the legitimacy of eight new countries that had, until barely a decade before, been on the opposite political and economic side of the Iron Curtain. They provided an opportunity for the members of the European Parliament (MEPs) to reflect upon and articulate their ideas about Europe and about

1 For a discussion of the EP's enlargement discourse and identity construction with regard to Eastern Europe, see De Angelis (2011).

its historical identity, and were in this sense much more about the existing (largely Western) members of the EU and their shared project than about Central and Eastern Europe per se. The constructed historical narrative was therefore a Western European narrative – and the extent to which it actually resonated with Central and Eastern Europeans, and if they would actually subscribe to it during or after the enlargement process, is a question that will also be addressed towards the end of this piece.

## On Historical Narratives and Collective Identities

The European Parliament's enlargement debates in the post-Cold War period gave prominence to new themes alongside that of political identity. The debates on the fifth enlargement, in particular, were characterized by the presence of a strong historical narrative that flanked the existing political features of the European identity constructed by MEPs in the previous three decades. In articulating this historical narrative and inserting it alongside political values in their legitimization of the accession of ten new countries between 1997 and 2004, MEPs attempted to go beyond a purely political identity in their construction of Europe: this article explores the contents of this narrative, its use in parliamentary discourse, and its limits within the wider enlargement debate.

It is widely accepted in social identity theory that history, or rather shared historical narratives, constitute a fundamental element in the construction and reconstruction of collective identities. The past is often mobilized in order to justify or legitimize the present, and it is interpreted and understood in the function of contemporary concerns and needs. This interpretation and reinterpretation of the past constructs 'myths' that give meaning to the present and provide a shared framework for political debate (Straub 2005; Stråth 2000).

Myths can be defined as 'a special kind of story about the past that symbolises the values of a group and legitimates their claims' – as, for instance, does Peter Burke (2001) in his work on European memory. Such myths are largely produced by political and cultural elites and are based on the construction of historical narratives that are then used as a frame of reference for political debate. They provide a source of political legitimacy, not necessarily based on historical continuity, but also, potentially, a legitimacy founded on a 'sharp break with the past due to traumatic experiences or policy failures' (Müller 2002: 26). In this sense, historical events (or a specific selection of historical events) are interpreted and constructed into a historical narrative that shapes collective memory. History, memory and identity are thus inexorably interconnected to the extent that the meaning constructed through a historical narrative provides political legitimacy and cohesion to a community (Stråth 2000). Historians have a long tradition of looking at the role of myths and collective memory in the foundations of national identities. For instance, George Mosse (1990) analyses the creation of the 'Myth of the War Experience' in post-First World War Europe, and Germany in particular, as the attribution of meaning to a hitherto meaningless experience by taking it through a process of memorialization, institutionalization, and even trivialization that transforms a recent historical experience into a key element of political culture. Henry Rousso's (1991) analysis of the way the French have remembered, or removed, their Vichy past, provides a further example of how history and memory have played out in a selective form of remembering a troubling past through different phases of French public life. The role of history in the construction of collective identities is therefore well documented, and it may not come as much of a surprise that a historical narrative of Europe did in fact also emerge in the European Parliament's identity discourse on enlargement.

European Parliament discourse developed a strong historical narrative that provided legitimization for the process of European integration as undertaken by the European Union: this discourse emerged most clearly during the debates on the fifth enlargement, after having been present but largely understated and never fully articulated in previous enlargement debates. The striking difference between the second and third enlargements as opposed to the fifth was, of course, the end of the Cold War, which greatly affected the way in which MEPs elaborated their historical narrative in the second half of the 1990s and early 2000s. If 'history' was mainly used as the spectre of past conflict and in order to justify cooperation amongst former enemies as a new political course during the Cold War, in what some authors referred to as Europe's past being Europe's 'other' in the construction of European identity (den Boer, Bugge and Wæver 1993), after the conclusion of the Cold War the order of the previous fifty years was called into question and the need to revisit the European Community's (EC) role in this history arose. This development manifested itself in many ways throughout Europe. The end of the Cold War opened a Pandora's Box of contested histories between different nationalities in prospective member states, from the Baltic states to the former Czechoslovakia and to the bloody conflict in the former Yugoslavia, while at the same time redefining the terms within which the existing members had previously been able to define the EC's place in history. The European Parliament's discourse on the fifth enlargement reflected this reality by articulating not a single historical theme, but a variety of historical references that, reprised by different actors at different times, formed a complex and heterogeneous narrative. Whether these themes can be seen to constitute a 'historical narrative of Europe', much along the lines of historical narratives that are the basis of the construction of collective identities (Blanco Sío-López 2010), will hopefully be clearer at the end of this analysis.

## Opening the Gates: The End of the Cold War and the Challenge of Redefining 'Europe'

The sudden collapse of the Iron Curtain brought back to the surface continent-wide historical debates that had thus far remained dormant within the discursive frame provided by the Cold War. The year 1989 represented a watershed in the political, military and security, economic, and ideological organization of the continent, unravelling the geopolitical order that had shaped Europe in the post-war era and ushering in new period of uncertainty, as well as opportunity, for the countries of both Western and Eastern Europe. Debates in the European Parliament reflected the climate of confusion that characterized the months immediately following the Eastern European revolutions of 1989–91, and the soul-searching that defined much of the 1990s up to the turn of the twenty-first century.

The EC was to a large extent a product of the post-war order: it may have claimed to represent 'European values' that reached beyond the Iron Curtain in time as well as space, but its exclusively Western European membership and its political and economic orientation placed it firmly and conclusively within the West. The USA encouraged the integration process from its inception and the EC's political self-image was firmly opposed to the Eastern European dictatorial system – as exemplified by the emphasis on democracy and human rights in the development of the Community's political identity. When Eastern European peoples tore down their communist regimes and the new democratic governments started clamouring for their nations' right to 'return to Europe' and queuing up for EC membership, the EC had to suddenly come to terms with German reunification, the 'moral obligation' to open its doors to its 'lost' neighbours, and the need to maintain economic and political stability within its own borders and, hopefully, across the continent.[2] The very concept of a 'return to Europe' used by Central and Eastern European intellectuals from the late 1980s, claiming that their countries' rightful historical place was amongst the countries of Western Europe rather than with the non-European East, challenged the division into Western and Eastern Europe in the name of a prior shared history (Garton Ash 1986; Kundera 1984). Gorbachev's Common European Home rhetoric, although not directly quoted by MEPs, may also have facilitated the emergence of a strong discourse based on the idea of a 'united Europe'. Moreover, the wars in Yugoslavia acted as a powerful reminder of a pre-Cold War European history of national and ethnic conflict and reawakened fears of Europe falling back into its historical

2 Ulrich Sedelmeier (2005) also highlights the idea of a moral obligation towards Eastern Europe. In addition, see Pocock (1997).

pattern of confrontation and war.[3] The re-emergence of such concerns with historical legacies of the pre-Cold War era would become an important feature in the EP's discourse on the Eastern enlargement.

The membership requests from the countries of the former Eastern bloc flowed into the existing debate on the rationale and goals of the European integration process. After the revival of the Single European Act in 1986 and the Maastricht Treaty in 1992, the Union had already entered a phase of introspection and self-questioning, brought on by the economic challenges of rising unemployment and coping with globalization, combined with the strategic and geopolitical challenges of the end of the Soviet Union and Europe's role in a changing global arena. Previous considerations for further integration and institutional reform within the EC itself would manifestly need to be adjusted to the new circumstances. The 1990s were therefore to a large extent a decade of soul-searching for the newly named European Union, which faced dealing with new institutional developments and further plans for reform via the Maastricht, Amsterdam and Nice Treaties, while at the same time finding itself called to respond to complex political developments, with the violent breakdown of Yugoslavia and the consequent European debacle as perhaps the most symbolic example of the new challenges facing the EU. The preparation from 1997 to 2004 of the most numerous enlargement ever experienced by the Union was an important catalyst for a new reflection on the deeper meaning of European integration, which accompanied the development of the Union well into the first decade of the new millennium until the accession of ten Eastern and Southern European countries in 2004, and its coda three years later with the entry of Bulgaria and Romania (Fuchs and Klingemann 2002).

The European Parliament debated what would become the fifth enlargement round at length, not just in discussing the yearly Commission Progress Reports on each candidate country starting in 1998, but also in

3 See, for instance, Ulpu Iivari, Party of European Socialists (PSE), Finland, 'EP Debates: Europe Agreement with Slovenia', 23 October 1996.

preparatory discussions before and after Council meetings[4] or 'State of the European Union' debates.[5] This enlargement would become a defining issue for the European Union, and MEPs explored both the broader political aspects of accepting so many countries that were new to democracy and market economics, and the minute details of accession, from fisheries to agricultural subsidies, to the candidates' overall readiness to implement the *acquis communautaire*. The EP also pushed for negotiations to start with all the candidate countries at once and for the date of accession to be set for 2004 and was keen to highlight how the Council and Commission later adopted its suggestions, as German European People's Party (EPP) representative and future EP President Hans-Gert Pöttering proudly pointed out on 9 April 2003, during the debate on the ratification of the accession treaty:

> It was our House that demanded a timetable for the negotiations – which the Commission and the Nice Summit accepted – so that they could be completed in time, enabling the countries capable of doing so, and their people, to take part in the 2004 elections to the European Parliament. It was our House that did that! That is what we should be telling people, and it is something of which we can be proud, for it helps to make democracy real in Europe and to give the people of the ten countries the opportunity to send freely-elected representatives to the European Parliament. Let us rejoice in that!

With the acceleration of the enlargement process after the beginning of accession negotiations, the EP's related activities also increased: debates were more frequent, meetings with the representatives of the parliaments of the candidate countries intensified, and the EP's presidents visited the candidate countries increasingly often.

Discussions of the fifth enlargement also intensified because at the turn of the millennium it was becoming more necessary than ever to explain enlargement to EU voters: disillusion with European integration, increasing talk of the EU's democratic deficit, and widespread preoccupation with

4 See, for instance, debate on 'Preparation of European Council Meeting in Cardiff', 27 May 1998.

5 See, for instance, debate on 'State of the European Union', 18 September 1996.

the citizens' disaffection with the Union all highlighted, in the minds of their European representatives, the need to strengthen the legitimacy of the integration process in general and of enlargement in particular in the eyes of the European public.[6] There was, amongst MEPs, a perceived need to justify the intake of ten new Eastern European countries. A renewed recourse to history and Europe's past was a means for providing just such legitimization.

Throughout the fifth enlargement debates, the 'return to Europe' slogan resonated with European parliamentarians and fuelled their reflections on the idea of Europe, intended as the project of European integration but also more broadly as a community of peoples that shared the European geographical, political and cultural space beyond the borders of the EU. Enlargement provided new stimuli for this debate: perhaps more than any other enlargement round before it, the enlargement round of 2004 provided the context for a prolonged and open-ended discussion on the origins, progress and ultimate aims of the process of European integration embodied by the EU.

The historical themes that emerge more frequently in European parliamentary discourse form a series of interconnected myths: the first is the myth of the 'founding fathers' and of European integration as reconciliation, which is elaborated in opposition to a broader, negative foundation myth of Europe's heritage of conflict and bloodshed prior to the first integration initiative of 1950. These myths are very closely intertwined and constitute the basis for legitimization of the European Union as a whole – and have been present in parliamentary and Community discourse ever since the launch of the Schuman Plan in 1950 (Anta 2007; Gilbert 2008). Furthermore, in order to justify widening this process to the countries of Central and Eastern Europe, MEPs emphasized a new set of historical references in their enlargement debates: the idea of a common European

6 See, for instance, the debate of 3 October 2000, especially contributions by Pat Cox and Miguélez Ramos (PSE) on the need to engage with the public on enlargement. MEPs also discussed polls on public attitudes towards enlargement in September 2001.

heritage and an undivided Europe before the Cold War trumping the 'artificial' separation superimposed by the post-Second World War confrontation between East and West.

## The Myth of European Reconciliation and Its 'Founding Fathers'

European Parliament discourse after the end of the Cold War was characterized by ubiquitous references to the history of European integration and to the 'founding fathers' of the European Union. Besides the official commemorations such as the anniversaries of the Schuman declaration, MEPs often referred to the 'founding fathers' when they wanted to stress the positive moral, idealistic and yet pragmatic and innovative origins of the process of European integration. This was a recurrent need when debating the fifth enlargement. For instance, during the December 1997 debate on Agenda 2000 and enlargement, similar references were made by speakers on behalf of all the main party groups: Dutch Liberal Democrat Gijs De Vries highlighted that 'the historical responsibility for our generation is to do for the whole of Europe as the generation [of] Adenauer, Beyen, Monnet and Spaak did for France and Germany: to build one communal house, a joint framework within which power is subordinate to the law'.[7] He was echoed to the right of the political spectrum by Italian Alleanza Nazionale MEP Gastone Parigi: '[T]he coming enlargement is the direct and logical consequence of that revolutionary act which was the foundation of the construction of Europe – I refer to the Schuman Plan – revolutionary because it has weakened the nationalist culture which had been laid down over the centuries, east and west of the Rhine, giving rise to

7 Gijs De Vries, Liberal Democrat, Netherlands, 'EP Debates: Enlargement – Agenda 2000', 3 December 1997.

wars and tragedies with monotonous regularity'.[8] This even resonated with those on the left, as reflected by the German socialist, and former European Parliament President, Klaus Hänsch: '[A] final point which I shall phrase in very general terms: the generation of politicians of the 1950's had the courage and the foresight to remove the thousand-year-old antagonism between France and Germany in a European Community. Our generation of politicians will have to develop the courage and foresight to give the whole continent, for the first time in a thousand years, an organization of peace and cooperation'.[9]

Irrespective of the different political affiliations, policy prescriptions and nationalities of the three speakers, they all referred to the founding fathers of the European Union in a remarkably similar way: they credited them with creating a community for European nations on the Western side of the Iron Curtain and for having extraordinary vision in finding a creative and peaceful solution to conflictual relations amongst former enemies. The lexicon associated with the myth of the founding fathers always revolved around 'vision', 'courage', 'foresight', 'inspiration'.[10] These references to a 'generation of leaders' constituted part of a positive myth that was accepted by MEPs from mainstream political groups across the political spectrum.[11] Moreover, when speaking to outside audiences on behalf of the EP, presidents have used this myth whenever they needed to emphasize the 'rightness' of the European project, its implied 'moral superiority' over what came before, and its unique place in history. Pat Cox, for instance, spoke repeatedly of the 'generation of European leaders ... who had the

8 Gastone Parigi, Non-Attached (Alleanza Nazionale), Italy, 'EP Debates: Enlargement – Agenda 2000', 3 December 1997.

9 Klaus Hänsch, PSE, Germany, 'EP Debates: Enlargement – Agenda 2000', 3 December 1997.

10 Maria Martens, EPP, Netherlands, 'EP Debates: European Council in Vienna – Austrian Presidency', 16 December 1998.

11 There were, of course, exceptions to this consensus, mainly on the far right and far left of the political spectrum, who are against integration per se. See, for instance, Bruno Gollnisch, Non-Attached (Front National), France, 'EP Debates: Enlargement – Agenda 2000', 3 December 1997.

courage of their European convictions',[12] of the 'vision' and 'indispensable' leadership of Monnet, Schuman, Adenauer, de Gasperi and Spaak.[13] The general thrust of his references to the founding fathers is well condensed in this extract from a speech he delivered on 5 February 2004 in front of the Cercle Gaulois on '2004: Towards a Union of 25, Towards a European Constitution, Towards the European Elections':

> In Western Europe, with the Second World War barely over, certain individuals had the courage to think big. People like Konrad Adenauer, Robert Schuman, Jean Monnet, Paul-Henri Spaak, Alcide de Gasperi and others, who took the time, who had the authority, the will and the political and personal determination to think in the long term and to think big: not to lose themselves in mean-minded trivia, but to pull themselves out of the ashes and ruins of war, and see hope where there was despair, see an opportunity in the midst of economic collapse, and see the European project in terms of the ideal of reconciliation: a project which offered possibilities which would make those men a generation different from any other generation that Europe had ever known.[14]

His predecessors in the role of European Parliamentary President also used similar sets of references. In 1998, José María Gil-Robles Gil-Delgado quoted directly from Jean Monnet's memoirs in his speech entitled 'The Europe We Are Building' to legitimize the 'new philosophy' of cooperation above national interest, which he saw as the underpinning of the integration process.[15] Nicole Fontaine also referred to the founding fathers as examples of extraordinary leadership: 'What the founding fathers of the European Economic Community achieved with six states in the wake of the defeat of Nazi Socialism, we are now prompted by contemporary developments

12 Address by Pat Cox (Liberal Democrat Group, Ireland) on the occasion of the solemn opening of the Convention on the Future of Europe, Brussels, 28 February 2002.

13 Address by Pat Cox to the Irish Business and Employers Confederation (IBEC) Conference on 'Our Future in Europe: Nice and Beyond', Dublin, 20 September 2002.

14 Speech by Pat Cox to the members of the Cercle Gaulois on '2004: Towards a Union of 25, Towards a European Constitution, Towards the European Elections', Brussels, 5 February 2004.

15 José María Gil-Robles Gil-Delgado, 'The Europe We Are Building', Madrid, 1998.

in the world to achieve in our turn, and for the same reasons, for the whole of the continent of Europe'.[16] Klaus Hänsch used very similar words during the enlargement debate of 9 April 2003:

> I am cautious about drawing historical comparisons, but it is appropriate to do so today. A generation of politicians in the Fifties – Konrad Adenauer, Robert Schuman, Jean Monnet, Alcide De Gasperi, Paul-Henri Spaak and others – had the courage and the vision to establish a European Community that would overcome a thousand years of antagonism between Germany and France and begin the unification of Europe in the West. We, the present political generation, have the opportunity, for the first time in a thousand years, to bring the continent together by peaceful means and on a voluntary basis into a European Union, a union of freedom, peace and prosperity. If we do not seize this opportunity, we will be failing in our historic mission.[17]

The allusion implied in Hänsch's words remains fairly vague: it is in fact unclear whether the thousand years he refers to pertain to the Holy Roman Empire, to the Roman Empire, or perhaps to Charlemagne – a figure often considered a precursor of attempts to unify Europe. Nevertheless, the quote is exemplary of the way in which MEPs used historical references when discussing 'Europe' during the fifth enlargement: the abundant allusions to an unspecified historical time when Europe was allegedly unified served as one of the legitimizing arguments for the 're-unification' of the continent, lacking any chronological specificity but creating a sense of historical inevitability that permeated much of the fifth enlargement discourse.

The myth of the founding fathers greatly emphasized the idealistic aspect of the integration process. It was often embedded in an interconnected and yet wider theme of European integration as 'reconciliation' and as a 'peace process'. European integration was described as a 'communal

16 Nicole Fontaine, speech at 'The 12th meeting of the President of the EP with the Presidents of the Parliaments of the Countries Participating in the Enlargement Process', Brussels, 5 December 2001.

17 Klaus Hänsch, PSE, Germany, 'EP Debates: Enlargement', 9 April 2003.

house'[18] based on principles of 'solidarity'[19] and 'cooperation'[20] between former enemies. The MEPs deemed it 'the only concrete idea for achieving peace and prosperity'[21] in Europe, based on 'the brilliant, but historically unusual, idea of bringing people together at the negotiating table instead of through trench warfare'.[22] This was an image of Europe as the historical embodiment of new values – 'peace as our rule and a shared destiny as the solution'.[23] The idea of reconciliation was extended to the Eastern and Southern European candidate states during the highly symbolic 'extraordinary debate on enlargement' held by the European Parliament with the representatives of the candidate countries on 19 November 2002. Therein MPs from the ten candidate countries due to accede in 2004 participated in a session of the EP and sat with their future colleagues in their respective political groups. The debate itself was meant as a symbol of how reconciliation finally embraced Eastern Europe, marking 'a truly continental-scale act of reconciliation and healing'.[24]

Members of the European Parliament gave little or no consideration to figures who had developed ideas about European integration before 1950, such as Aristide Briand or Richard Coudenove-Kalergy. The history that they chose to speak about was very much the history of the Europe embodied by the European Union, with its treaties and its institutions. MEPs were concerned with legitimizing a specific conception of 'Europe' realized in the institutional system originated by the Treaties of Rome in 1957, and not with alternative conceptions of Europe or any might-have-beens.

18 Gijs De Vries, Liberal Democrat Group, Netherlands, 'EP Debates: Enlargement', 9 April 2003.

19 Klaus Hänsch, 'Rekindling the European Flame', speech given at Leyden University, 21 February 1996.

20 Staffan Burenstam Linder, EPP, Sweden, 'EP Debates: Enlargement – Agenda 2000'.

21 Otto von Habsburg, EPP, Germany, 'EP Debates: Applications for EU Membership', 14 April 1999.

22 Cecilia Malmström, Liberal Democrat, Sweden, 'EP Debates: Progress report on enlargement', 28 November 2002.

23 Enrique Barón Crespo, PSE, Spain, 'EP Debates: Enlargement', 9 April 2003.

24 Pat Cox, Liberal Democrat Group, Ireland, 'EP Debates: Introductory Remarks – Extraordinary Enlargement Debate', 19 November 2002.

The founding fathers thus became the principal characters in the wider positive myth that underpinned the discourse on European Union: the myth of the inherent moral 'goodness' of the integration process, intended as a historical process of reconciliation amongst former enemies. Moreover, enough time had passed between 1950 and the first decade of the twenty-first century that any partisan allegiances to Christian democracy or socialism, Atlanticist or non-Atlanticist tendencies, or even to nationalities to which Schuman or Monnet may have made politically charged references, were effectively neutralized. Referring to more recent figures such as Helmut Kohl or François Mitterand, whose role in European politics and within the Community could have been considered just as significant, would have been much more likely to introduce an unwelcome partisan or national element to a discourse whose goal was essentially the construction of a common interpretation of the origins and evolution of the European Union of the present. The 'founding fathers' thus became more than merely the political leaders who initiated the integration process: whether their choice to initiate the integration process aimed to meet the geopolitical or economic needs of their nation states was no longer an important or determining factor in the way they were portrayed five decades later. What mattered instead was the fact that politicians working at the heart of the integration process in the 1990s used their very names, words and choices as a legitimating myth for the continuation of that process, and that by doing so they chose to emphasize the ideals underpinning the process rather than national interest per se.

This narrative of reconciliation as the historical uniqueness of European integration reverberated throughout the fifth enlargement discourse and inherently legitimized both the need to continue along this path of integration and the necessity of allowing candidate states to become involved in it as full members. The possibility of referring to a generation of leaders that had initiated this process five decades earlier gave this theme the strength of a historical myth: in the 1990s, European integration was no longer a new initiative but a reality whose fifty years of institutional existence and success guaranteed its place in European history. The fact that this was a particular kind of integration based on the establishment of common institutions and that other ideas had existed, for instance, in the interwar years, and still floated around about different methods of integration, remained largely outside of parliamentary debates. On the other hand, the figures who had launched this particular kind of integration in the 1950s had in some cases, for instance, Jean Monnet's, already acquired a 'larger than life status' within the 'integration story': Monnet had a whole education programme dedicated to him in 1989, which included the establishment of Jean Monnet chairs and Centres of Excellence for the study of European integration – this meant that their names could be used to provide the European Union with a set of wise figures from the past. Moreover, at the turn of the twenty-first century, with arguably four decades of successful integration under the Union's belt, MEPs were no longer talking just about a recent political phenomenon with an uncertain future. They could now claim that what had been born as a risky political initiative had consolidated its rightful place in history over four decades of institution building. By the time the enlargement process to the Central and Eastern European countries began in earnest in 1999, the integration process itself was ripe for use as a myth in itself, and was the source of legitimacy for continuing along the path indicated fifty years earlier by the founding fathers.

## 'Breaking with History': The European Project Defies Historical Legacies

The European Parliament's historical narrative of Europe inserted the positive myths of the founding fathers and of reconciliation highlighted above into a wider narrative depicting Europe's history as a negative and dark past that needed to be contrasted and overcome through an integration process whose primary aim was to 'break with Europe's history' (Wæver 1996: 121–2). The idea had in fact been present in European discourse since the inception of integration. However, in the late 1990s and early 2000s, this came to form the tenets of a complex historical narrative in which the old negative myth of conflict was interwoven with the newer myth of reconciliation embodied by the European Union as a primary theme in the legitimization of the fifth enlargement. This historical narrative was based on the claim that Europe must reject its history prior to 1950: the negative myth of Europe's long-term historical experience provided a broad frame for the positive myth of reconciliation and cooperation. Europe's dark past served to legitimize the integration process as the only tool capable of providing reconciliation amongst European nations and cooperation as the basis for peace and prosperity. While the reconciliation myth was essential for the legitimization of the European Union and for its enlargement to the wider European continent, its essence was entirely rooted in the historical legacies of Europe's experiences prior to the launch of the integration process in 1950.

The discourse of the European Parliament presented the idea of reconciliation and of European integration in general as a 'break with history', a 'historical absurdity ... that was gradually consolidated and came to change the face of history',[25] a project initiated to defy Europe's historical legacy and to 'go against' history. Europe's past of war and violence culminating in the two world wars is the negative historical myth that underpins the whole European construction. Paradoxically, it was this very historical myth that legitimized the idea that in order to achieve peace and prosperity Europe must free itself of its historical legacy and project its political vision into the future, denying a past that had led to so much bloodshed.

Throughout the fifth enlargement debates, MEPs and EP presidents acknowledged that the roots of European integration were to be found in war, underlining that '[o]ut of the ashes of destruction and hate of two world wars came a Union of the European peoples. War between the member states, despite centuries of rivalry and conflict, is now unthinkable. Europe can be a force of peace throughout the continent',[26] and 'the original challenge was twofold: first, through close cooperation, to subdue

25 Enrique Barón Crespo, PSE, Spain, 'EP Debates: Enlargement – Agenda 2000', 3 December 1997.

26 Klaus Hänsch, PSE, Germany, 'Address to the National Assembly of Slovenia', Ljubljana, 2 April 1996.

an historic hostility which tears our continent apart in order instead to build friendship and understanding, and secondly to provide political and economic strength and thus the confidence in our system based on democracy and market economy, which was necessary to be able to resist the external threat which the Soviet Empire posed on the dark horizon. Through its successes the EU has changed the path of world history'.[27] Yet the historical roots of European integration also meant that Europe needed to break away from its past and create a new system that was to be completely detached and opposed to the previous one: not just to 'overcome history' but 'not to allow a triumph of the dead over the living not to let history dominate our future'.[28]

The myth of post-war Europe as a 'peace process'[29] based on reconciliation and cooperation was thus based on a mirror historical narrative of the violence and nationalist antagonism that dominated Europe until the culmination of the Second World War. Many MEPs emphasized how historical attempts to unify Europe had been carried out by force and how only the European Union embodied the peaceful and voluntary unification of the continent:[30] for instance, in 1996 Italian EPP representative Antonio Graziani argued, referring to historical legacies and the rights of minorities in Slovenia, that a Europe assigning blame for past events 'would not be a Europe of today, far less of tomorrow, but the Europe of the civil wars of the recent and more distant past'.[31] A year later, his Danish colleague in the EPP Frode Kristoffersen, speaking in his role as *rapporteur* for Lithuania, also talked about the need to bring Europe together after

27 Staffan Burenstam Linder, EPP, Sweden, 'EP Debates: Enlargement – Agenda 2000', 3 December 1997.

28 Klaus Hänsch, 'Address to the National Assembly of Slovenia', Ljubljana, 2 April 1996. This was both a reference to national antagonisms that had led to conflict and world war and to the resurgence of nationalist conflict in the former Yugoslavia.

29 Pat Cox, Liberal Democrat Group, Ireland, 'EP Debates: Enlargement', 9 April 2003.

30 Cecilia Malmström, Liberal Democrat, Sweden, 'EP Debates: Enlargement', 9 April 2003.

31 Antonio Graziani, EPP, Italy, 'EP Debates: Europe Agreement with Slovenia', 23 October 1996.

centuries of violent struggle: '[T]he idea is to get this Europe repaired and bind it together again. A characteristic of this part of the world is that for centuries, at regular intervals, we have bashed each other over the head, and time and again Europe has been dismembered ... but now at the end of this century the important thing is to organise relationships in this part of the world and to repair the damage that was done in the first half of the century'.[32] Spanish socialist and former EP President Enrique Barón Crespo argued on 19 November 2002 that enlargement would finally bring an end to the shameful trail of war and blood left by the twentieth century and that Europe would go back to being a geographic union and would be born again as a political unit:

> Con ello [enlargement] conseguiremos, simbólicamente en Grecia, que Europa se liebre del rapto del Minotauro, que la ha tenido tanto tiempo presa. Porque, cuando en 2004, se abran las puertas para los nuevos socios, Europe volverá a ser una union geográfica desde el Atlántico hasta el Báltico y desde la Laponia hasta Chipre, y atrás quedarán las ignominies de un siglo XX en el que las guerras y repartos de botín rasgaron los Estados, destrozaron a los pueblos y trazaron fronteras a sangre y fuego ... Europa ... renacerá como una unidad política.[33]

Swedish Liberal Democrat Cecilia Malmström reiterated during the enlargement debate of April 2003 that 'for the first time, we are uniting almost the whole of the continent by peaceful means – through agreements, compromises and treaties, rather than through war and conquest'.[34]

32 Frode Kristoffersen, EPP, Denmark, 'EP Debates: Enlargement – Agenda 2000', 3 December 1997.

33 Enrique Barón Crespo, PSE, Spain, 'EP Debates: Extraordinary Debate on Enlargement', 19 November 2002 ('With this we will achieve, symbolically in Greece, that Europe free herself from the Minotaur's abduction, which kept her prisoner for so long. When in 2004 the doors open for the new members, Europe will return to being a geographical union from the Atlantic to the Baltic and from Lapland to Cyprus, and so the ignominies of the twentieth century will cease, the wars and booties that tore apart states, strangled peoples and traced frontiers with blood and fire ... Europe ... will be reborn as a political unit'.).

34 Cecilia Malmström, Liberal Democrat, Sweden, 'EP Debates: Enlargement', 9 April 2003.

Pat Cox came back to this idea time and again in his speeches in front of the Parliaments of the candidate countries: 'For the first time in millennia on the continent of Europe, we are creating a common space of prosperity, reconciliation and peace. We are not creating that space at the point of a sword or from the barrel of a gun, but as I said earlier, by the free will of a free people. It is that which gives the depth and strength to the European process of reconciliation'.[35] This negative foundation myth was predicated on the need to break with history, by creating and advancing a new, 'ahistorical' principle of organizing political and economic relations amongst the peoples of Europe and thus breaking free from the dominant legacy of the past. The image of Europe constructed through the use of these historical narratives was therefore one in which Europe, intended as the contemporary framework of supranational institutions and close cooperation between member states, was the child of a unique generation of leaders who decided to reject the legacy of Europe's past and on the basis of this rejection created a new system of relations based on the shared commitment to reconciliation. Europe, in this sense, is therefore to this day a historical process of reconciliation – one that stemmed from the history of this continent and yet projects its identity into the future and rejects the image of Europe embodied by the past.

This historical narrative had at its very heart a contradiction that could in the long term undermine the whole construction of a historical foundation myth for the European Union. By selecting only a very specific and very short historical experience as the positive foundation of the modern European polity, and attributing a wholly negative connotation to the course of European history before 1950, the European Parliament effectively denied legitimacy to historical references attempting to go further back in time to the much richer and longer history of Europe before 1950. Moreover, in identifying the experience of European integration after the Second World War with the only positive historical experience that Europe

35 Address by Pat Cox, Liberal Democrat Group, Ireland, to the Saeima's Plenary Session (Latvian Parliament), Riga, Latvia, 28 May 2002. He used the word 'reconciliation' twenty-eight times in his speeches over his two years as EP President.

could refer to in constructing its identity and advocating the need to break with all previous history, parliamentary discourse attributed a positive value to an experience that had been shared only by Western European countries on the basis of economic integration and, to a much smaller extent, political cooperation. This created problems on two levels: it excluded Central and Eastern European countries from the Union's positive historical narrative and it deprived even Western Europe itself of the possibility of finding positive shared experiences beyond the beginning of the integration process – rejecting as part of that negative past cultural and political experiences that could otherwise have provided additional content to a positive foundation myth. It excluded centuries of shared political, cultural and social experiences that were actually considered by many Europeans as the most important aspect of their common heritage. In light of the division between East and West during the Cold War, the MEPs' choice of founding their historical narrative on the exclusion of the experiences prior to the Second World War is in fact quite puzzling: justifying the fifth enlargement would entail a difficult balancing act between a double narrative of recent exclusive experiences and previous, unspecified common experiences of alleged European unity before the Cold War.

## Justifying the Fifth Enlargement: A Common History Before the Cold War

The European Parliament's debates on the fifth enlargement saw MEPs engaging with the double challenge of providing legitimacy to the European integration process as a whole, and justifying the expansion of membership to the countries of Central and Eastern Europe that throughout the East–West bloc confrontation had constituted the Community's political 'other'. Geopolitical and economic reasons were of course paramount, yet a historical theme also came into play: Central and Eastern European countries had the right to be part of the integration process because, according to the historical narrative of 'Europe', before the Cold War had forced them on the 'wrong' side of the Iron Curtain, those countries were part of Europe and thus shared a long, if at times far from peaceful history with Western European countries. The theme of 'breaking with history' was vividly used in the justification of enlargement, when it was combined with the idea of the Cold War as the historical 'kidnapping' of the Eastern half of the European 'whole'.[36]

Before the end of the Cold War, Western Europe had defined itself politically in stark opposition to the communist dictatorships of Eastern Europe. After 1989 its political identity could not be changed – in fact, it was strengthened by an increased emphasis on 'European' values such as democracy, human rights and the rule of law.[37] Enlargement to Central and Eastern Europe was predicated on the need to support these countries' political reorientation towards adherence to these same politico-cultural values.[38] However, this in itself was not sufficient to legitimize enlargement. After all, none of the former Warsaw Pact countries were yet fulfilling the political and economic criteria of membership nor would they come close to Western European standards throughout the 1990s.

With the fifth enlargement, however, MEPs clearly felt the need to go beyond the traditional political identity to provide a historical one alongside it as a foundation myth of the European integration process embodied by the EU. The European Parliament largely justified widening EU membership to Central and Eastern European countries on the basis of a moral duty stemming from a twofold reading of history as having 'robbed' these countries of their 'rightful place' in Europe through the Cold War and

36 See, for instance, Jean-Louis Bourlanges, Liberal Democrat, France, 'EP Debates: Enlargement – Agenda 2000', 3 December 1997.

37 That such values may just as accurately be deemed to be 'Western' did not seem to alter the course of MEPs' words much: only a few individuals pointed this out, or tried to engage with the prickly question of what can in fact be deemed to be the difference between the 'Europeanness' and the 'Westerness' of certain political values.

38 The Copenhagen Criteria were established in 1993 <http://ec.europa.eu/enlargement/enlargement_process/accession_process/criteria/index_en.htm> accessed 10 November 2012.

of an earlier, shared historical heritage cutting across the Iron Curtain. This shared history made the accession of Central and Eastern European countries 'natural'.[39] The fifth enlargement would bring together centuries of common 'history, culture and art' and overcome the division imposed by Yalta and Munich.[40] These two historical moments symbolized the two different aspects of the historical division of Europe: Munich was considered by many to be the moment in which Western Europe had abandoned Eastern Europe to National Socialist aggression, and Yalta was seen as the imposition of an artificial geopolitical and ideological division that would then be cemented by the hardening of the Cold War. In both cases, MEPs claimed that the way in which these countries had been abandoned to their fate now imparted upon the European Union a 'moral obligation' to accept their membership applications.[41] Enlargement would mark the final end of the Cold War division and 'ensure that the old iron curtain is not replaced by a velvet one, excluding part of the continent from the benefits of belonging to the European family'.[42] It was also 'an act of moral justice: European countries, countries which are just as European as those which are already part of the Union but which, by a twist of fate, found themselves, through no fault of their own, on the wrong side of an artificial line drawn across our continent, are coming back to Europe, coming back to us'.[43] The lexicon in sentences such as the one above moreover shows how by using 'history' as a somehow external or superior force that imposed the Cold War division, MEPs also partly absolved Western European countries and

39 Nicole Fontaine, 'Speech to the European Conference', Sochaux, 23 November 2000.

40 Enrique Barón Crespo, PSE, Spain, 'Extraordinary Debate on Enlargement', 19 November 2002.

41 Otto von Habsburg, EPP, Germany, 'EP Debates: Applications for Membership', 14 April 1999. He was referring specifically to the Baltic states.

42 Peter Truscott, PSE, UK, 'EP Debates: Enlargement – Agenda 2000', 3 December 1997. For other examples, see also Frode Kristoffersen, EPP, 2 December 1998, and Klaus Hänsch, PSE, Germany, 'Progress towards Accession by the Twelve Candidate Countries', 3 October 2000.

43 Jas Gawronski, Liberal and Democratic Group, Italy, 'EP Debates: Enlargement', 9 April 2003.

their most powerful ally, the USA, from responsibility for the division of the continent.

Europe had, of course, never been unified in the first place, and so such talk of 'reunification' constituted at best a very benevolent view of European history before the world wars and the onset of the Cold War. Larry Wolff's (1994) study of the invention of the idea of Eastern Europe in the eighteenth century provides but one example of the fact that the distinction between East and West had already been present in the European consciousness for centuries, and that Western Europe had a long tradition of excluding Eastern European countries from its political and even 'civilizational' self-image. The concept of Mitteleuropa is another instance of the many different concepts of 'Europe' and potential ways of subdividing its countries and peoples by grouping them according to different cultural, political and geographical criteria – and one that did not really make an appearance in parliamentary enlargement discourse (Stirk 1994). Furthermore, what the MEPs' alleged 'common history' actually amounted to was never specified. While this was pointed out by some MEPs,[44] such remarks remained isolated and did not influence the main thrust of parliamentary discourse. European parliamentarians seemed, on the contrary, to prefer instead a reading of history that was more in line with that put forward by East-Central European intellectuals in the 1980s, from Kundera to Havel. In fact, Vaclav Havel himself became an important point of intellectual reference for many MEPs, who quoted his words time and again during plenary debates. His ideas about the 'dream' of uniting the European continent made their way into the enlargement discourse of the European Parliament and EP President Pat Cox constantly quoted Havel's 1990 speech to the EP when visiting the candidate countries: 'Without dreaming of a better Europe we shall never build a better Europe. To me the twelve stars of the European flag do not express the proud conviction that we will build heaven on this earth – there will never be heaven on earth – I see these twelve stars as a reminder that the world could become

44 See, for instance, André Brie, Confederal Group of the European United Left, Germany, 'EP Debates: Progress Report on Enlargement', 19 November 2002.

a better place, a better place that in time and from time to time if we had the courage to look up at the stars'.[45]

Increasingly, MEPs and EP Presidents talked not merely of 'enlargement', but of 'reunification': the word reunification appeared sixteen times in the October 2000 enlargement debate, twice in September 2001, eleven times in the 19 November 2002 debate (not the extraordinary debate of the morning, but the standard debate on the progress by the candidate countries in the afternoon), and nine times in the final enlargement debate before the official accession of the new member states on 9 April 2003. Pat Cox used the word 'reconciliation' sixty-three times in the official speeches he gave outside plenary over his two-year term as EP President between 2002 and 2004.

Parliamentary discourse on the fifth enlargement also built upon the idea of the European project as a break from history by defining the need for enlargement as the need to 'amend history'[46] and to 'finally turn the page'[47] on the 'cruel division of Europe'[48] imposed by the Cold War. The accession of the Eastern European countries was therefore also the symbolic closure of the period of division and signified that the Berlin Wall had finally been torn down.[49] Enlargement was thus 'an opportunity

45 Pat Cox was referring to the speech by Vaclav Havel to the European Parliament, 16 February 2000. Speech by Pat Cox to the Estonian Parliament (Riigikogu), Tallinn, Estonia, 15 April 2002.

46 As Enrique Barón Crespo put it: 'As citizens of the European Union we now have the historic opportunity to transcend Munich – to reverse the events of 1939 when the people of central and eastern Europe were abandoned – and this must be done on the basis of what we have built. I think it is a question of amending history, and we should welcome the opportunity to do so' (Enrique Barón Crespo, PSE, Spain, 'EP Debates: Enlargement – Agenda 2000', 3 December 1997).

47 Jean-Claude Pasty, Union for Europe, France, 'EP Debates, Enlargement – Agenda 2000', 3 December 1997. Even though Pasty had a very different, right-wing, political position from the speaker preceding him, he still made use of the same set of references.

48 Ursula Stenzel, EPP, Austria, 'EP Debates: Enlargement', 9 April 2003.

49 Address by Pat Cox, Liberal Democrat Group, Ireland, at the European Council in Brussels, 25 October 2002.

because it [was] an occasion to reunite what the tragedies of recent history had torn apart'.[50] The mere use of the word 'reunification' provided the fifth enlargement with significant historical and moral legitimization: '"enlargement" itself is not the correct name – it is the coming together again of our old continent of Europe, it is a reunification, a re-birth of sorts, a renaissance of the European idea'.[51] Upon the signature of the Accession Treaty on 16 April 2003, Cox stated that the history had finally been corrected and its legacy overcome: 'Today we consign our fractured past to the history books'.[52]

The narrative constructed by MEPs remained fairly superficial and the rhetoric highlighted above was really the whole extent of their elaboration of a historical discourse. They refrained from trying to define the actual contents of this alleged common history and created a narrative that could perhaps work within the specific circumstances and emotional connotations of the fifth enlargement, but would prove difficult to extend to other cases.

## Contested Histories: Unresolved Debates on the European Past

The dominant historical narrative of parliamentary discourse on the fifth enlargement remained fairly general and rarely touched upon unresolved debates about the past that were still relevant for contemporary politics in the acceding states. A compelling illustration is provided by the way

50 Catherine Lalumière, European Radical Alliance (ERA), France, 'EP Debates: Enlargement – Agenda 2000', 3 December 1997.

51 Pat Cox, Liberal Democrat Group, Ireland, 'Speech to the Estonian Parliament (Riigikogu)', Tallinn, 15 April 2002.

52 Address by Pat Cox, Liberal Democrat Group, Ireland, President of the European Parliament at the Ceremony of the Signature of the Treaty of Accession, Athens, 16 April 2003.

in which the European Parliament tried to tackle the issue of the Beneš Decrees, the controversial piece of Czech legislation at the centre of the debate on the political requirements for EU enlargement. MEPs were not in agreement over the interpretation of the Beneš Decrees in history and eventually a consensus emerged not to discuss them as a historical issue, which would have led to a much wider debate on reprisals and possibly on forced migration throughout Central and Eastern Europe at the end of the Second World War. Instead, they mainly confined them to the realm of the past, as exemplified by the words of German EPP representative Jürgen Schröder: 'This is not some sort of attempt to rewrite history on our part. There is no question of that. It is Today and, more importantly, Tomorrow, which are at stake'.[53] In addition, his fellow group member Elmar Brok stressed: 'Our task is not to examine the past from a legal perspective, but to ensure that no discrimination arises as a result of the current application of the law … there is no attempt to use issues of history as new combat instruments in the European Union; instead, we must ensure that we learn from history to prevent the suffering, expulsions, murders and wars which occurred in the past from ever happening again'.[54] British PSE member Simon Murphy was in agreement: 'Questions of history are important but questions of history are exactly that, historical questions … they are not conditions for accession to the European Union'.[55] As was fellow British and Liberal Democrat Graham Watson: '[The] Liberal Democrats deplore the abuse of enlargement negotiations to reopen old wounds and animosities. The infamous Beneš Decrees are a good example of this. It serves no useful purpose to inflame tensions on this issue'.[56]

The European Parliament, however, remained divided on its judgment of the Beneš Decrees and, more broadly, on how to address and deal with certain consequences of the Second World War in candidate

53 Jürgen Schröder, EPP, 'EP Debates: Applications for EU Membership', 14 April 1999.

54 Elmar Brok, EPP, Germany, 'EP Debates: Enlargement of the Union', 12 June 2002.

55 Simon Francis Murphy, PSE, UK, 'EP Debates: Enlargement of the Union', 12 June 2002.

56 Graham Watson, European Liberal Democrat and Reform Party (ELDR), UK, 'EP Debates: Enlargement of the Union', 12 June 2002.

countries. Many MEPs eventually argued that the controversy was unnecessary because the decrees were a historical occurrence and should bear no consequence for Czech eligibility for EU membership, as entry would project this country into a common future and a 'community of justice'[57] that would ensure the respect of human and minority rights. They also argued that the Czech willingness to comply with the Copenhagen Political Criteria was evidence enough of their allegiance to the principle of reconciliation, the 'moral foundation of integration'.[58] Reconciliation was thus used as a blanket concept that could also include the Czech case: by joining the EU the Czech Republic would embrace the principle of reconciliation as the founding principle of European integration, and other EU members would in turn extend this 'spirit' to the Czech Republic and ensure, as a community, that the discriminatory nature of the Beneš Decrees would remain confined to the past.

This was a means to overcome the obstacle without dealing with the deeper historical issues inherent in the adoption and maintenance of the Decrees in the Czech legal system. It allowed the MEPs a way out of the debate on the treatment of minorities in Central and Eastern Europe after the war, and it also allowed for the continued use of the general narrative of integration as reconciliation, glossing over the more controversial aspects of the past and its consequences, without delving into the actual complexities of specific historical events, and even relegating them to a past that was 'closed' and far away as opposed to a past that still had contemporary relevance. Even if references to such events may have been more relevant to contemporary politics and hence could arguably have stimulated greater interest and possibly identification amongst Europe's citizens, there could be no agreement across the political spectrum and national divides on the 'correct' interpretation of such histories, and thus they were left out of the dominant narrative.

57 Jürgen Schröder, EPP, 'EP Debates: Enlargement', 9 April 2003.

58 Ibid.

## Conclusion

The EP's historical narrative for the fifth enlargement followed many strands, weaving together the three historical myths: that of the founding fathers and reconciliation, that of Europe's dark past, and that of a shared history prior to the Second World War and the Cold War – all the while using the idea of reconciliation as a common thread. Parliamentary discourse built up these myths within its debates. In the EP's image of Europe, the European Union itself became the embodiment of the myth of the European peace process, and was presented in constant opposition to the historical tradition of violence. The recent positive myth was anchored in the myth of the long history of conflict and legitimized as a decisive rupture with Europe's historical legacy and as the dawn of a new era. In justifying the fifth enlargement, however, Parliament also reintroduced the idea that there was in fact a positive shared history between the countries of Western and Eastern Europe and that this constituted the basis of a 'reunification' of the continent: enlargement was thus transformed into the rightful return of the kidnapped East to the common European fold.[59]

To what extent, however, did this narrative resonate with those very Central and Eastern Europeans who were acceding to the EU and for whose accession the narrative was developed? Did they, entirely or in part, buy into the historical identity discourse articulated by MEPs, refer to the same foundation myths or at least use similar historical references?

The first encounter between MEPs and representatives of the Central and Eastern European candidate countries, on the occasion of the November 2002 debate in which the doors of the EP were opened for participation to colleagues from the future member states, seems to suggest that there was little if any desire amongst the latter to share the historical narrative developed by MEPs. The myth of the founding fathers was used by some of the candidates' representatives, with a Slovak speaker referring

59 On this issue, see Helene Sjursen (2002).

to Schuman as 'the father of Europe',[60] Slovenia's representative referring to both Schuman and Adenauer, but the overwhelming majority did not refer to them, or indeed to any other elements of the historical narrative developed by MEPs thus far.

The absence of a common historical discourse upon this occasion, however, may well have derived from a preoccupation on the part of the candidates with the very real political and economic requirements of membership, trumping for the time being the need for a full development of a common identity beyond compliance with formal entry requirements. The question that remains is whether there was in fact a convergence onto a common discourse, and specifically a common historical narrative, in the enlarged European Parliament after the new countries' entry in May 2004. This would show that new MEPs from Central and Eastern Europe shared the same interpretation of the EU's historical identity, or at the very least that they were socialized into a common way of thinking and talking about Europe and European identity. The persistence of this discourse would also show that the historical narrative developed to justify the fifth enlargement could in fact be applied to other circumstances, rather than remain confined to a very specific time and context and thus failing to provide a universally, or at least more widely usable basis for a shared identity.

A preliminary exploration of enlargement debates between 2004 and 2007, when the enlarged EP debated the accession of Bulgaria and Romania, does not, however, seem to corroborate this hypothesis. On the contrary, very little mention was made of historical references, and the potent historical discourse that permeated enlargement debates between 1999 and 2004 was largely absent between 2004 and 2007. The idea of reconciliation, for instance, which was at the heart of the narrative before 2004, was mentioned once in the December 2004 debate on Romania's

60 Ján Figel, EPP, Slovakia, 'Extraordinary Debate on the Future of the European Union after Enlargement', 19 November 2002. Cyprus representative also referred to the myth of the founding fathers, namely Jean Monnet and Robert Schuman, as 'visionaries'.

progress towards accession, in relation to the 'historic reconciliation between Romania and Hungary'.[61] The immediately subsequent discussion on Bulgaria did not even have that token reference – although the German Van Orden did state that 'the European Union's enlargement to the east and south-east marks a momentous change in Europe. We have finally put an end to the hostilities and the divisions of the Cold War'.[62]

The debate on both Bulgaria's and Romania's accession on 12 April 2005 fared slightly better: Hungarian Socialist MEP Dobolyi stated: 'We are ready to welcome the people of Bulgaria into the association to which they have always belonged, since they share our history, culture and values. In so doing, we mark the end of an artificially created break, just as in the case of Romania'.[63] Her Polish colleague Libcki also recalled the idea of the artificial division imposed upon Europe during the Cold War: 'The accession of these two countries will mean that the divisions created by the Yalta agreement, and that ran counter to European culture, tradition and justice, will at last be totally erased from the map'.[64]

These were meagre offerings, however, for the nearly three years that passed between the enlargement of May 2004 and its completion with the accession of Bulgaria and Romania on 1 January 2007. Debates over this enlargement were held every few months, and yet no other examples of MEPs reprising the historical narrative of the previous five years were present. This may have been the result of a very simple change: as eight Central and Eastern European countries had already joined the EU in 2004, the urgency to justify the mere fact that they had in fact the right to join had lost most of its potency – and this would reflect on the debate on Bulgaria and Romania, whose accession could largely be seen as an

61 Csaba Sándor Tabajdi, PSE, Hungary, 'Romania's Progress towards Accession', 15 December 2004.

62 Geoffrey Van Order, European Conservatives and Reformists Group, UK, 'Bulgaria's Progress Towards Accession', 15 December 2004.

63 Alexandra Dobolyi, PSE, Hungary, 'Application for Accession of Bulgaria and Romania', 12 April 2005.

64 Marcin Libcki, Union for Europe of the Nations (UEN), Poland, 'Application for Accession of Bulgaria and Romania', 12 April 2005.

extension of the 2004 enlargement. However, this seems only a partial explanation for the sudden disappearance of a discursive strand that had until then been so pervasive – indeed, the Bulgarian and Romanian accessions would have been the perfect occasion for reiterating and consolidating this discourse, and showing its applicability beyond the specific circumstances of the fifth enlargement. This, however, was not the case. There is therefore another reason that strikes the observer as the root of history's disappearance from the enlargement discourse: the narrative developed prior to 2004 was not shared by the new post-communist states that had joined the EU. The strong Western European slant with which the historical construction had been drawn made it exclusive, rather than inclusive, because it justified the entry of Central and Eastern European countries on essentially Western terms.

Members of the European Parliament had shaped their historical discourse in the image of their own historical experiences and contemporary political concerns. MEPs in the 1990s were widely concerned with the public's increasing disaffection with the European project. They were also aware that recourse to images of war and bloodshed risked not having any resonance with the new generations of European citizens: precisely because the reconciliation process had been so successful, MEPs in the 1990s grew increasingly aware of the fact that young Western Europeans had only ever experienced 'peace and prosperity'.[65] Images of war in Europe no longer worked in the same ways as they had in the Cold War decades: despite the outbreak of war on European territory with the prolonged conflict in the former Yugoslavia, crucially, the new generations did not have any direct experience of the world wars and nor, increasingly, did their parents. The European Union had made the idea of war amongst the member states such an alien concept that it now became difficult to conjure up the myth of reconciliation as the primary factor of legitimization for the Union. At the same time as they were constructing this myth, MEPs were also increasingly aware of the fact that it would not be sufficient to stimulate

65 See, for instance, Gunilla Carlsson, EPP, Sweden, 'EP Debates: Progress Towards Accession by the Twelve Candidate Countries', 3 October 2000.

strong allegiances to the enlarged European Union amongst its citizens: the myth of reconciliation may have been consolidated during the fifth enlargement debate and used to justify the accession of Central and Eastern European countries, but whether it would survive as a legitimating tool for the future remained open to question.

Almost as significant was the fact that the myth of European integration was constructed on the basis of largely superficial, and even artificial, historical references: MEPs rarely, if at all, chose to venture into the complexities of European history, nor did they seek to provide an accurate understanding of the intricacies of the common historical experiences that they referred to. This was due to the very nature of their historical discourse, which revolved around the creation of a foundation myth for the contemporary needs of their political project. Their political use of history was part of a rhetorical arsenal aimed at defining 'historical' Europe in terms of the concerns of contemporary European politics: a simplified version of history was essential to the successful creation of a legitimizing myth. To an extent, the intricacy of European history, both in terms of its divided and violent nature and in terms of the political, cultural and social interconnection of European societies dating back long before the beginning of political and institutional integration defied the attempts by Europe's elected representatives to provide a simplified version of 'the common European history' that could be fully convincing to its citizens and to future member states. The European narrative remained composed of different myths and the need to justify the fifth enlargement compelled MEPs to bring back references to yet another set of pre-war experiences to overcome the Cold War division. This undermined the coherence of the myth of post-war integration, and the attempt to use 'reconciliation' as the key concept bridging the gap between Western and Eastern Europe fell short of its target when Cypriots failed to resolve their own division. The controversy surrounding the Beneš Decrees in the Czech Republic also remained frozen and both countries joined the European Union in May 2004 without any progress on these issues.

The fact that the historical narrative was largely absent from enlargement debates post-2004 does not necessarily mean, however, that the EP's identity discourse abandoned history altogether. On the contrary, the late 2000s were characterized by a surge in activity within the European Parliament on questions of memory and history, exemplified, for instance, by the adoption of resolutions on the occasion of anniversaries such as the end of the Second World War or the Schuman Declaration, the designation of 23 August as the European Day of Remembrance for Victims of Stalinism and Nazism, and of 11 July as the Day of Commemoration of the Srebrenica Genocide. The EP also took the highly controversial decision in December 2008 to set up a 'House of European History' in Brussels, a museum whose mission is 'to bring Europe's history alive … and help promote an awareness of European identity'.[66] History and memory thus remained very much at the heart of EP activities and discourse, and their absence in the 2004–7 enlargement debates is not therefore an irrefutable indication of the end of the EP's historical narrative. What the absence did mean, however, was that the legitimating function of the historical narrative applied to the fifth enlargement was not easily transferable to other enlargement rounds.

The historical narrative of reconciliation remained limited to the unique circumstances of the Eastern European enlargement. More importantly, it was based on a Western European experience of the post-war years that was not, and could not be, shared by the Central and Eastern European partners – and their reluctance to even broach the subject after their entry was evidence of the gulf in both the experience and perception of history.

66 European Parliament, 'EP Bureau Decides to Set Up a "House of European History"', 16 December 2008.

## References


Anta, C. G. (ed.) (2007). *Les pères de l'Europe: sept portraits*. Brussels: PIE-Peter Lang.

Blanco Sío-López, C. (ed.) (2010). 'European Memories and the Construction of a Collective European Memory', Special Issue of *Richie Europa Newsletter*, Issue 8.

Burke, P. (2001). 'Foundation Myths and Collective Identities in Early Modern Europe'. In B. Stråth (ed.), *Europe and the Other and Europe as Other*, pp. 113–22. Brussels: PIE-Peter Lang.

De Angelis, E. (2011). 'The European Parliament's Identity Discourse and Eastern Europe, 1974–2004', *Journal of European Integration History*, 17 (1), 103–16.

den Boer, P., Bugge, P., and Wæver, O. (1993). *The History of the Idea of Europe: What is Europe?* Milton Keynes: Open University.

Fuchs, D., and Klingemann, H.-D. (2002). 'Eastward Enlargement of the European Union and the Identity of Europe', *West European Politics*, 25 (4), 19–54.

Garton Ash, T. (1986). 'Does Central Europe Exist?', *The New York Review of Books*, 9 October, 45–52.

Gilbert, M. (2008). 'Narrating the Process: Questioning the Progressive Story of European Integration', *Journal of Common Market Studies*, 46 (3), 641–62.

Kundera, M. (1984). 'The Tragedy of Central Europe', *The New York Review of Books*, 26 April, 33–8.

Mosse, G. L. (1990). *Fallen Soldiers: Reshaping the Memory of the World Wars*. Oxford: Oxford University Press.

Müller, J.-W. (2002). 'Introduction: The Power of Memory, the Memory of Power and the Power over Memory'. In J.-W. Müller (ed.), *Memory and Power in Post-War Europe: Studies in the Presence of the Past*, pp. 1–37. Cambridge: Cambridge University Press.

Pocock, J. G. A. (1997). 'Deconstructing Europe'. In P. Gowan and P. Anderson (eds), *The Question of Europe*, pp. 297–317. London: Verso.

Rousso, H. (1991). *The Vichy Syndrome: History and Memory in France since 1944*. Cambridge, MA: Harvard University Press.

Sedelmeier, U. (2005). *Constructing the Path to Eastern Enlargement: The Uneven Policy Impact of EU Identity*. Manchester: Manchester University Press.

Sjursen, H. (2002). 'Why Expand? The Question of Legitimacy and Justification in the EU's Enlargement Policy', *Journal of Common Market Studies*, 40 (3), 491–513.

Stirk, P. (1994). *Mitteleuropa: History and Prospects*. Edinburgh: Edinburgh University Press.

Straub, J. (ed.) (2005). *Narration, Identity, and Historical Consciousness*. New York: Berghan Books.

Stråth, B. (2000). 'Introduction: Myth, Memory and History in the Construction of Community'. In B. Stråth (ed.), *Myth and Memory in the Construction of Community: Historical Patterns in Europe and Beyond*, pp. 19–46. Brussels: PIE-Peter Lang.

Wolff, L. (1994). *Inventing Eastern Europe*. Stanford, CA: Stanford University Press.

Wæver, O. (1996). 'European Security Identities', *Journal of Common Market Studies*, 34 (1), 103–32.

FRAN CETTI

# 5 Europe and the 'Global Alien': The Centrality of the Forced Migrant to a Pan-European Identity

During the last decades a radical shift has taken place in Europe's common immigration and asylum policy: many forced migrants,[1] previously able to enter the region on a work visa or to claim asylum in one of its member states now risk criminalization if they attempt to cross its external borders. More often than not they are characterized as 'illegal migrants' – particularly if they come from impoverished countries and regions of conflict in the Global South. The European Union's (EU) external borders themselves have become increasingly securitized[2] and detached from their territorial remit, guarded by the technologies of surveillance and interception and extended far beyond the region into the high seas and deep into other continents. As a consequence, the forced migrant is regarded, pre-emptively, as harbouring the intention to cross into Europe illegally long before they reach the actual geopolitical borders. They carry their label of illegality with them wherever they happen to be in the world.

1 I use the term 'forced migrant' to refer to those individuals who are driven by circumstances such as repression, war, poverty or fear of poverty to seek personal safety or greater economic security in a richer, more stable country. This covers a wider range of people than the more narrowly defined terms 'refugee' or 'asylum seeker', which have specific legal meanings.

2 'Securitization' refers to the introduction of practices beyond the norm (as in emergency legislation), in response to an existential threat. 'Securitized' borders, therefore, are sites where security measures of the sort normally only applicable in exceptional situations (such as militarized policing, intensive electronic surveillance and biometric controls) have become normalized and routine.

Their designation as universal 'outsiders' positions them in binary opposition to the region's 'insiders', the populations of its nation states, who are thereby encouraged to regard themselves as the bearers of a privileged cultural identity that marks them out as specifically 'European'. Yet, as a cohesive and unitary set of supranational cultural attributes, European identity is a concept that appears to lack purchase amongst the region's heterogeneous, increasingly cosmopolitan populations. This can be seen most clearly when economic and social crisis throws the fault lines of the European project into stark relief. Such circumstances, however, incite even greater attempts by Europe's political leaders to create a normative, '*hyper*-nationalist' pan-European identity – an identity that recognizes itself only in the presence of what it is not: the ubiquitously 'illegal', culturally 'alien' forced migrant.

## The Nation State and the 'Disruptive' Forced Migrant

Although globalization would appear to undermine the raison d'être of the nation state, there is a fundamental connection between nationalism and the global capitalist system (even in its neoliberal form). Capitalism generates nationalism as the condition of its continued existence as a system based in the global network of interlinked, but competing and often antagonistic, nation states that serve as its local conduits. Nationalism is therefore embedded within capitalism's ideological processes, and it implies a complex of further interrelated narratives (including that of national security: the necessity to defend the nation and its citizens against external, existential dangers), which together naturalize a state-oriented imagination of the world. It simultaneously generates, as Soguk (1999: 32) points out, 'the specific vocabularies, significations and classifications through which [the] stories [of the forced migrant] are written, circulated and incorporated' into popular discourse. It is the characterization of the forced migrant as the 'alien' figure in the national stories of today's European nation states that lends coherence to the understanding of what it means to be a national citizen, but it holds an even greater foundational significance for the more inchoate concept of a pan-European identity.

Although national identities appear timeless and static, they are forms of social life. As such, they are – just as the nations within which they arise – historically specific formations; the fashioning of national identities is an ongoing socio-historical process. Bhabha (1990) describes this as the process of 'people production', what he calls 'narrating the nation', emphasizing that the citizen is not a natural or even self-evident presence but must be repeatedly produced. However, for the most part, this process is routine and invisible, taking place below the radar of individual awareness. National culture as a cognitive structure is embedded in the everyday narrative of social life, encoded in the web of social consciousness, and thus it takes on quasi-biological overtones: people appear to be born with a cultural identity. This emotional, subconscious identification suppresses the reality of the complexities of social being, disguising its inherently mutable nature, through an essentialized understanding of national belonging formed in opposition to the essentialized characteristics of those who fall outside the national frame. 'We' represent normality as opposed to 'their' deviations from it.

The realities of the life of the forced migrant, however, challenge the apparently hegemonic discourse of nationalism by cutting across what Soguk (1999: 54) calls 'the cartographic logic of the territorial state and its privileged sites of identity'. Displaced by the effects of a system of radical global inequality (violence, poverty, and economic and social dislocation), and forced into the global circuits of survival migration, their very mobility blurs the boundaries between 'insiders' and 'outsiders', destroys the notion of an impermeable barrier between the security of 'here' and the apparently dangerous and volatile world 'out there', and threatens to fragment the common-sense view of the world as naturally separated into national territories. Their presence erodes the national narrative. As Appadurai (2006: 45) puts it, '[t]heir movements threaten the policing of borders. Their financial transactions blur the lines between national economies and between the legal and the criminal. Their languages exacerbate concern about national and cultural coherence'.

Capitalist economic globalization, therefore, unleashes forces that challenge the exclusive claims of the nation state over the lived reality of its populations, yet these forces simultaneously offer it new resources in the form of the forced migrant. Soguk notes that the figure of the forced migrant has 'paradoxical implications for the practices of state sovereignty'; the forced migrant is 'both disruptive and recuperative', a 'problem' to be addressed and a 'resource' to be used 'in the service of the discursive ... social and political practices of representation' that naturalize the nation state (Soguk 1999: 15). Through its insertion into the daily narratives of national belonging that underpin the common-sense understanding of the world, the figure of the forced migrant can be recruited to serve the ideological needs of the most economically powerful nation states even as it threatens to disrupt their processes of naturalization.

Although construed as marginal, this figure is a vital component in both the discursive and material processes of inclusion and exclusion – that is, in the practice of making and remaking the nation state and the national citizen. The nation state secures its coherence – its sovereignty and its right to exist – only insofar as it can successfully claim to both represent and to defend its citizens, its domestic 'national community', from existential dangers. The daily practices of statecraft must therefore '*incite* popular and institutional discourses of problems and dangers ... and *regiment* them in terms that privilege a statist imagination of world' (Soguk 1999: 40). The presence of the forced migrant is problematized as a potential threat in order to privilege the national citizen and thus the identity and very reality of the nation state itself. Equally, as citizenship is shorthand for legitimacy, it is only through reference to the nation state and its national citizens as concrete, territorialized identities that the concept of a homogeneous 'illegal migrant' is constructed out of a mass of individuals, each with a unique personal history, cultural attributes and life trajectory.

## The Creation of a 'Hyper-National' European Identity

Soguk (1999: 4) remarks that there is no 'intrinsic paradigmatic refugee' and no commonality to their experience, save the experience of displacement, as there are as many reasons for moving as there are forced migrants. The fact that each forced migrant has an individual story, formed in particular circumstances, was to a certain extent recognized by the terms of the 1951 Refugee Convention, in which the individual circumstances of the asylum seeker was laid down as the litmus test for national decisions over granting refugee status. During the 1990s, Europe's increasingly harmonized, region-wide immigration and asylum regime still paid lip service to the Convention. However, by the time the war on terror was made manifest in a security regime that included not only the 'rendition' of putative Islamic terrorists to regimes of torture, but also the deportation of forced migrants back to the dangerous situations they had originally fled, violating the Convention's principle of 'non-refoulement',[3] it had already been hollowed out by the declarations of European politicians that it was outdated, and was all but abandoned in practice.[4]

The political environment of heightened security allowed Europe's common immigration and asylum regime to openly assert the mandate it had implicitly adopted during the course of the 1990s: to intercept forced migrants before they reach its external borders and gain access to the asylum procedures of member states. The securitization of the immigration and asylum process (Bigo 2008; Huysmans 2006; Squire 2009) has retrospectively given its transformation a rational gloss: the forced migrant is redefined as 'illegal' by branding unregulated attempts to enter the region as

3 The Refugee Convention forbids the return of asylum seekers to countries where they would be in danger of death or inhumane treatment.

4 In the United Kingdom, for example, former Prime Minister Tony Blair outlined in 2001 his intentions to 'reform' the Refugee Convention. Subsequently, in 2009, the then immigration minister Phil Woolas proclaimed he wanted to restart the debate about the Convention and its enshrinement of the individual's right to asylum from state persecution (*The Guardian*, 10 January 2009).

criminal acts endangering national and regional security. The identity goes before the intention – to be poor and globally mobile is to be labelled and treated as an 'illegal migrant' (and thus denied the chance to claim asylum), even before crossing Europe's external borders.

Such radical new forms of exclusion, which result in the increasingly frequent denial of a legal identity (or any form of identity vis-à-vis the nation state bar that of 'illegal migrant'), mean that those forced migrants who do manage to (illegally) circumvent the barriers to entry into the European Union become 'voiceless' and stateless figures within the national/regional space itself. For this reason, Fekete speaks of two Europes existing side by side: a visible Europe and a shadow Europe, the latter comprising what she calls a new 'underclass' of stateless, rightless forced migrants subsisting on the margins of society (2009: 190). The very ontology of the region is informed by these insider/outsider dynamics; an understanding of what it means to be a European national is framed by the binary discourse of national belonging versus marginality or exclusion. The figure of the forced migrant is therefore a politically produced figure: their concrete marginality is the effect of a set of governmental policies and practices that are animated by a discourse that first effaces them by evacuating their complex experiences of individual and political content, thereby exiling them from the possibility of the national populations' imaginative identification with their situation, and then reconstructs them as a figure solely defined by the vocabulary and imagery of security. This discourse invests the technologies, administrative systems and personnel tasked with border control with the power of designating individual forced migrants as illegally mobile bodies. In the process, as figures of illegality, they become the ideological prism through which the image of the regional bloc of nation states as a unified entity – its internal coherence – is reflected.

This enforced marginality is thus a vitally productive resource: in a seemingly paradoxical move, the marginalized figure becomes central to the constant work of validating a specific pan-European identity. This is especially the case at a time when the region itself appears more divided than ever. As Europe's nation states face the effects of widespread financial and economic crisis, national politicians have turned to an increased reliance on the timeless and habitual categories of nationalism. Despite the obvious contradictions in a regional cluster of nation states adopting a strategy tailored to the individual nation state itself, the nationalist template is further employed by the political managers and ideologues of the European Union in the attempt to invest Europe itself (a region fractured by inequalities and competing capitals) with an emotional legitimacy – a 'felt' understanding of its populations of themselves as 'European'. This entails its daily reproduction through multiple acts of exclusion and marginalization.

The political necessity to negate the consequences of the fractured nature of the European Union arises from the fashion in which it has developed. Its formation as a regional alliance of nation states has been driven by certain identities of interest amongst its nationally based capitals – the desire for mutually supportive economic growth in order to compete successfully on the global economic stage. The pressures of the globalized financial markets and the emergence of new, globally competitive economic powers such as China and India have continued to focus some sections of the region's elite on the need for Europe to evolve into a quasi-territorial unit. However, the EU appears to lack of a sense of genuine legitimacy or moral authority amongst the populations of its member states. Its adoption of a neoliberal agenda (albeit with national variations), under the disciplinary tutelage of an unaccountable European Central Bank, gives added weight to Anderson's (2011) argument that it has developed as an elite, financially driven project, with little or no democratic accountability, subject only to the constraints of the market. It appears far from the vision of popularly endorsed federal unity. The desire for a European 'super-state', when viewed against the reality of it as a conflicted, hierarchical entity, highlights the contradictions lying at the heart of the European project.

Even the global forces that propel the move towards regionality simultaneously undermine it: uneven capital and labour flows between the nation states accentuate uneven development. Competitive international pressures generated by the global economic system have helped forge a hierarchy of nation states within the regional bloc. Disputes about state spending were already rife throughout Europe before the onset of financial and economic crisis, with increasing friction between the wealthy centres and their hinterlands. What Traynor (2007) calls 'the rich peoples' rebellion' spread to a pan-European level as the expansion of the European Union from fifteen states to twenty-seven widened disparities in wealth. With the European Union now comprising over 500 million people, the wealth gap grew proportionately; by 2007, for example, the richest corner of Europe, inner London, was generating three times the wealth of the European Union's national average, in comparison to north-eastern Romania, which produced barely a quarter.[5] The subsequent crisis in the Eurozone exacerbated the economic divide. Reacting to pressure from the global stock markets, the EU imposed strict austerity measures on struggling southern European economies, bringing penury to large sections of their populations, with the inevitable accompaniment of social unrest and the diversion of this unrest into a strident anti-immigrant racism, fuelled by the nationalist rhetoric of both far right and mainstream politicians. The EU, as a regional alliance, appears as riven by conflicts as are its component states.

Hence Europe faces a crisis of representation. The coherence of the European Union partially rests on its ability to legitimize its existence as a beneficial super-identity to its various groups of national citizens. However, these citizens are divided by the chronically unequal effects of neoliberal policies, the implementation of austerity programmes and the consequent (re)validation of bitterly competing national narratives. For example, a self-serving narrative has arisen in northern Europe of southern European profligacy and corruption, which is countered by an equally virulent one of an inherent German desire for European hegemony. That these stereotypes have appeared at such a time is of little surprise, but they also indicate that the idea of a unified European identity has always contained an inherent weakness: 'Europeanness' is regarded by many of the region's national populations as an abstraction of dubious authenticity that appears to carry little in the way of a coherent social, cultural and historical narrative. It does not possess the emotional heft of national identification, particularly

5 This statistic illustrates the situation before the 2008 financial crisis. However, there is little reason to believe that these percentages differ greatly today. According to the European Commission's statistical body, Eurostat, in 2013 Luxembourg was the wealthiest country in terms of GDP, compared with Romania and Bulgaria whose GDPs were less than half the EU average. For figures, see http://epp.eurostat.ec.europa.eu/statistics_explained/index.php/National_accounts_-_GDP.

at times of national stress. However, in search of a corrective, the political ideologues of the EU have turned to what Anderson, in his seminal book on nationalism, calls the tried-and-tested 'political-biographical narrative of the realm' (1991: 175) – but one enlarged to encompass the idea of a European identity. The nation state's initial formation out of vast polyglot empires entailed the engineering of profound changes of consciousness through the construction of 'a narrative of identity' (Anderson 1991: 175). In a similar fashion, crisis today calls forth a reiteration not only of national narratives but also of a sort of hyper-nationalism, placed within the context of a global redistribution of privilege and deprivation. The ongoing process of constructing and reconstructing a discourse of European belonging (with its nationalist narratives of inclusion and exclusion) is constantly recalibrated at an ever higher pitch.

As a part of this hyper-nationalism, the region's internal conflicts and divisions have been translated into a discourse of opposition between the concepts of 'cultural unity' and 'cultural heterogeneity' – what Balibar (2004: 12) calls 'code for the idea that, on the margins, "European" cultures are permeated and overlap with "non-European" influences, which could obstacle the process of the "Europeanisation of Europe"'. The reality of Europe, however, is of a region *within* which languages, religions and cultures co-exist and mix in dynamic interaction. As Balibar insists, Europe as a region is a 'series of assembled peripheries' – 'each region of Europe is made of overlapping peripheries, each of them open to influences from other parts of Europe and from the whole world' – so an essentialized Europe can only consist of constructed identities (2004: 12). It is this primary contradiction inherent in the European project that threatens to expose the ideological nature of the political pursuit of a unified, essentialized European identity. However, it also fuels the sense of urgency behind the incessant (re)construction of a common-sense supranational narrative through the discourses and practices of inclusion and exclusion: the making of European citizens through the creation of 'aliens'.

## European Citizenship and the 'Illegal Migrant'

European citizenship, however, is in itself is a problematic concept. As it can only be created through nationalist tropes, this can militate against the perception of a regional cultural unity. Dauvergne points out that each move to make supranational European citizenship more meaningful inscribes increased sovereign power to the member states: 'formal citizenship ... sheds its geographies while shoring up the embattled sovereignty of nations beleaguered by the onslaught of globalization' (2007: 506). European citizenship is derivative: no one is solely a citizen of the European Union, since European identity is based on citizenship of one of its constituent nation states. The European member states are the 'gatekeepers' to citizenship of the entire European Union (Dauvergne 2007: 504). To counteract these contradictory elements, the designation of the forced migrant at the European border as a potentially 'illegal' and culturally alien presence in whichever member state they happen to be, or whichever they wish to enter, endows European citizenship with a greater sense of coherence.

This is accomplished in a number of ways. As Dauvergne (2007) remarks, although citizenship has become more flexible for nationals of the European Union's member states, for those already outside the narrative of national belonging, citizenship law is becoming increasingly exclusionary. In combination with the erosion of *jus soli* (citizenship by virtue of birth within the territory of the nation state), many nation states are emphasizing the link between citizenship and a hereditary ethnic 'national community' with the unspoken reassertion of *jus sanguinis* (citizenship by 'blood', that is, through the possession of an ancestor of that nationality). This means the status of a forced migrant deemed to be illegally present in a member state, and all the deprivations and injustices such a status entails, will be passed down the generations – 'children may inherit a status of legal transgressor at birth' (2007: 507). It allows a migration of inclusion/exclusion away from the regional border and into the heart of Europe itself by labelling part of Europe's population as inherently 'alien' and 'illegal', complementing the shift of border policing far beyond the physical borders into other countries and regions as part of an increasingly unified migration/security regime, dedicated to the interception of the pre-defined 'illegal migrant'.[6]

Underlying the emergence of the European citizen as a new historic figure, therefore, lies the introduction of what Balibar (2004) calls the concept of 'security-identity': 'The material constitution of Europe oscillates ... between ... a *violent process of exclusion* whose main instrument ... is the quasi-military enforcement of "security borders", which recreates the figure of the *stranger as political enemy*, pushing the European construction ... into the language of culture wars and clashes of civilisations, [and] a *"civil" process of elaboration of differences*, which involves ... issues concerning ... Europe's "identity" and "community"' (Balibar 2004: 14).

The encoded signifier in this citizenship discourse is 'cultural compatibility'. The dissemination of a sense that a European identity, and its apparently inherent democratic values, is under siege from the 'alien' cultures of non-European 'outsiders' entails taking the necessary measures to secure its survival. Hence, the extraordinary rigour with which the regional borders are reinforced through enhanced exclusionary activities, accompanied by a quotidian discourse of cultural difference.

## The National Identity Debate

The belief in an inherent national identity is a crystallization of the idea of cultures as unchanging, closed totalities; any sense of their essentially protean, permeable nature is erased by their characterization as immutable. By promoting this particular understanding of national identity, Europe's politicians and political ideologues are able to translate the politics of inclusion and exclusion, with their implicit racial undertow, into a cultural

6 This is enabled by the extended reach of surveillance technologies, patrols in international waters and around the coasts of neighbouring countries, and the outsourcing of border control to global security companies and third-party states.

narrative of national belonging, naturalizing the polarized relationship of 'insider'/national citizen and 'outsider'/'illegal migrant'. The individual is relegated to one or the other category 'not according to what one does or what one believes, but on a "common sense" basis, on account of who one "is"' (McNevin 2006: 137).

In each European country the national identity debate has taken on nationally specific themes, but in ways that assert their essential 'Europeanness', defining more exclusively what it means to be a national citizen by reinforcing the identity of the unwanted 'outsider' and the idea that such individuals carry within them a threat to what are presented as core European values. The figure of the forced migrant represents, at the very least, the danger of cultural dilution. Although it undoubtedly impacts the 'illegal migrant' most profoundly, the resurgence of openly nationalist discourses also creates an increasingly hostile environment for so-called 'legal' migrants, non-nationals with some form of temporary residency status, and established migrant communities within Europe. Such discourses animate, and are disseminated through, the administrative technologies of citizenship reforms, integration policies, cultural codes of conduct, and securitized asylum and immigration laws. For example, in the United Kingdom, the 2002 White Paper, *Secure Borders, Safe Havens*, with its introduction of citizenship tests, language tests and oaths of allegiance, intended to inculcate a 'shared sense of belonging and identity' and 'cultural cohesion', heralded a definitive break with an official tolerance of cultural diversity (or 'multiculturalism') (Seymour 2010: 81). This was reinforced by the appeals of politicians and cultural commentators alike for the privileging of nationalism and 'British values' and the demand for integration.

Throughout Europe, equivalent demands have continued to be reinforced over the last decade by a succession of punitive measures. Those who refuse to take or who fail such 'integration' tests have been threatened with expulsion (Austria), with fines and having their social security payments cut (the Netherlands), or their residence rights removed or curtailed (France) (Fekete 2011). In 2004, former Dutch immigration/integration minister Rita Verdunk felt empowered enough by the mainstreaming of the ideology of a superior European culture to even float the idea of 'integration badges' (although this was a step too far for the majority of her fellow politicians: it was too redolent of the Nazis' introduction of the yellow star for European Jews). In Germany, meanwhile, the debate has focused around the role of the *Leitkultur* [leading culture] and the necessity of migrants to officially recognize its primacy through overcoming a number of state-enforced hurdles to entry and residence.[7]

In keeping with the mood of exclusionary nationalist rhetoric and policies, the European Commission issued a directive to the European Parliament in 2011, entitled 'The European Agenda for the Integration of Third-Country Nationals', which called for 'more efficient and effective integration policies' and introduced 'a flexible European toolbox … allowing Member States to choose the measures which are most likely to prove effective in their context' (European Commission 2011). The force behind this injunction may be veiled in neutral official language, but given the context in which it is deployed and the heightened sense of nationalist feeling that the very term 'integration' is imbued with, it could scarcely fail to be taken as an endorsement of the adoption of punitive measures against those who are deemed to fall short of the radically unequal standards of national belonging, and who are therefore characterized as unwilling to integrate into the 'national community'. Indeed, in Germany, as Fekete (2011) points out, a new word '*Integrationsverweigerer*' [one who refuses integration] has entered the racially inflected lexicon of negative descriptions of migrant identity.

The issue of language as the touchstone of cultural homogeneity has become a recurring theme. In relation to migrants and migrant communities, the debate about language is couched in terms of a 'language deficit', and this particular aspect of cultural identity has found a new level of urgency in the rhetoric of politicians at a time when governments are administering deep cuts to public welfare, including the near-uniform

7 Fekete (2011) quotes German philosopher Jürgen Habermas, who senses that behind this debate lies a relapse into an 'ethnic understanding of our liberal constitution … With an arrogant appropriation of Judaism – and an incredible disregard for the fate the Jews suffered in Germany – the apologists of the *Leitkultur* now appeal to the "Judeo-Christian tradition" which distinguishes us from foreigners'.

withdrawal of funding for provision of precisely the sort of language courses the Commission appears to recommend. The Council of Europe has reiterated this demand: 'Clearly, language teaching and language testing have a central role to play in any adequate response to the challenges of migration and the integration of migrants into the host society' (2011: 6), at the same time as acknowledging that 'some countries that set language requirements … do not offer language courses, so that candidates have to turn to the private market' (2011: 12). The fact that the legal standard is set, but the means to reach it are placed beyond the financial reach of many migrants, lends credence to the suspicion that such policies and pronouncements have an ideological (and populist) rather than practical motive.

Fekete (2011) uses examples from Germany and Austria to illustrate how language has become a tool in the ongoing process of marginalization: at the same time as the Association for German Languages was attempting to insert an acknowledgement of the primacy of the German language into the German Constitution itself, the neighbouring Austrian government was introducing pre-entry integration language requirements and proposing legislation that would decree the deportation of those migrants whose German does not attain a certain level of competence within their first few years of residence. It is now a routine legal requirement for migrants to reach a set level of language competency not only in Germany and Austria, but also in Denmark, the Netherlands and the United Kingdom, in order to be granted citizenship or permanent residence and, in some cases, to be admitted to the country in the first place (Council of Europe 2011: 20). Although all these various 'integration' requirements are an assertion of the superiority of specific national cultures, as is obviously the case with rules of residence and entry based on the ability to speak the national language, they are linked to a belief that the populations of each member state are naturally attuned to certain cultural mores and values that could be collectively described as 'European' and, as such, they reflect a more fundamental pan-European agenda.

## Security Politics, Islamophobia and European Identity

It is no accident that the 'cultural turn' in European politics,[8] with its emphasis on a renewed spirit of national pride in cultural and historical identity, has accompanied the entry of an overt anti-immigration politics into the political mainstream. The cover afforded by the language of culture has helped divest its progenitors of the charge of racism. Žižek claims that the mainstream political parties of Europe have 'cut the umbilical cord [attaching this theme] to the far right fringe parties' (2009: 35), adopting and legitimizing their rhetoric. The inherent violence of the language of national culture when used as a tool of social control is seen not only in its concrete outcomes – in increasingly restrictionist policies, for example, and the rise in racist attacks – but also in its ability to strip individuals down to an abstract 'cultural essence'. As Žižek (2009: 57) comments, 'verbal violence is not a secondary distortion ... the image overdetermines the way I experience real [people]', and guides and justifies the actions that flow from this experience. It 'inserts [the designated figure] into a field of meaning which is ultimately external to it' (2009: 52).

This 'field of meaning' is currently that of security. Although there may be no logical connection between 'illegal migration' and the creation of an integrated European security system whose overt rationale is defence of the region against 'global terrorism', this disconnect is obscured. The spread of an increasingly dominant security discourse throughout the polity of the European Union has given the link between the prevention of forced migration into the region and its defence against terrorist attacks an emotional coherence. The definition of Islamic terrorism is situated

8 This refers to the adoption by mainstream European politicians of the rhetoric of the far right. Extremist politicians had been using this type of 'cultural' discourse in their anti-immigrant and anti-Islamic drive since the 1970s. From the late 1990s on, however, this language has become a convenient alibi for the politicians of mainstream parties. In many respects, the political agenda of the European Union has become contaminated by radical nationalism – this has been particularly so as many far right politicians have become part of local and even, on occasion, national administrations.

on a continuum, and the security measures are able to stretch out along it to include not only members of European Muslim communities and migrants from Muslim-majority countries, but forced migrants per se. The underlying drive behind the discourse of national security, however, has less connection to the prevention of terrorism or 'illegal migration' than it does to the need to ensure legitimacy for Europe's neoliberal political system by infusing its disparate populations with a sense of belonging to a common pan-national community through the manifestation of external threats to the existence of a specifically 'European' culture and way of life.

The securitized, hyper-nationalist discourse prevalent in Europe summons up older, more deeply entrenched ideological boundaries of race. As Passavant (2004: 153) says, this discourse is 'hegemonising the field across national boundaries ... [and] to the extent that governing practices are superseding national state sovereignty, they are functioning according to the biopolitical logic of race'. The racially defined figure of the globally mobile, universally threatening 'alien' has a long historical track record, dating from the aggressive, outward push of Western European nation states in the first wave of globalization in the late nineteenth and early twentieth centuries, when it was used to characterize the Jewish immigrant from eastern Europe and Russia. This racialized image has resurfaced time and again (finding its most focused and virulent form in Nazi Germany); it may develop new attributes over the years, and be less visible at some times than at others, but the tropes are embedded in the structure of Europe's nation states. As the security agenda gains dominance within the European Union, and economic recession promotes the reassertion of an openly nationalist discourse, these tropes lie close to hand. Earlier traditions of cultural racism, therefore, have provided a rich store of vocabulary, imagery and generalizations, which lend the polarization between different cultures and societies the status of a generally accepted, common-sense 'truth'. An interlocking system of specific modes of expression and intellectual currents of thought transforms the ideas of superiority/inferiority and inclusion/exclusion, indicative of a racialized understanding of the world, into seemingly natural phenomena (Brennan 2007).

Within such an environment, the argument espoused by Caldwell (2009), for example, that large-scale immigration (in particular, immigration from Muslim-majority countries) is transforming a weak, ageing, under-confident Europe, loosening the bonds of national allegiance and eroding its social cement, appears to be gaining the status of orthodoxy amongst European politicians. As it does so, it helps essentialist assumptions to move from the political margins into the mainstream. The reiteration of such themes as the demographic advance of an antagonist Muslim culture in Europe through migration and high fertility rates has taken on an increasingly aggressive expression. The historian Niall Ferguson (2004), for example, has spoken of a 'youthful Muslim society to the south and east of the Mediterranean' poised to colonize a 'senescent' Europe, and warned of 'creeping Islamicization'. The idea that multiculturalism has been used as a cover for reactionary 'non-European' cultural practices has taken root not only in the United Kingdom, but has been echoed in France, the Netherlands, Switzerland, Denmark and Germany. Incorporated into the agendas of Europe's mainstream political parties, particularly in countries where ultra-right-wing nationalist parties mobilize a high share of the popular vote, the political manipulation of such a highly racialized discourse provides a well-worn route that national politicians often follow in times of crisis.

The image of Islam as incompatible with 'Europeanness', added to a discourse that presents both European Muslim communities and forced migrants from Muslim-majority countries as a threat to European national integrity (culturally, by virtue of their 'alien' way of life, which is presented as founded upon so-called 'backward' religious beliefs and practices, and demographically through migration and high birth rates) has spawned the concept of 'Eurabia'. This apocalyptic vision of a Europe dominated by its Muslim presence, although not openly avowed by mainstream European politicians, has been subsumed into the political quest for a pan-European identity. This is due to the fact that Orientalism, as Said (1991: 7) says, 'has never been far from the idea of Europe'. It has been used many times over the years to cement a collective notion of 'us' Europeans through the identification of the 'other' non-Europeans – the sense of an overarching European identity has been consistently derived negatively. The conversion of individuals into ideological bearers of a region's values, ideas and culture enables the discursive production of European identity by conveying a sense of absolute 'difference'. Europe is defined in the shadow of the threat of a supposed universal, univocal Islamic identity. Taking their cue from Huntington's (1998) idea that the 'cultural wars' of Europe presage a Fourth World War (he describes the Cold War as the third global conflict), which will usher in an 'era of barbarism', proponents of the idea of 'Eurabia' view Europe as the new front line in a battle to decide the future of the region's identity (Kundnani 2008).

Although these themes have been rehearsed many times over recent decades, especially since the end of the Cold War, the war on terror appears to have been the catalyst for their projection into mainstream political discourse. The attack on multiculturalism and cultural diversity, and the assertion of a common European identity, cannot be divorced from the global franchising of the war on terror. In their most current form, these tropes are manifest in cultural disguise, what Balibar (1991) calls a 'racism without race'. The war on terror added a further dimension to the pan-European project, providing it with a military discourse, imbuing the structures of national security – which are inextricably connected to Europe's 'global asylum regime'[9] – with a culture of xenophobia and Islamophobia. The call for a 'new crusade', in the form of a strident reassertion of so-called 'liberal' values and national identity, has taken hold – one that presents itself as both a cultural and ideological response to the imminent threat to an essential 'Europeanness'. Whether they be established communities in Europe, forced migrants from Muslim-majority countries, or the populations of these countries themselves, particularly those in North Africa, at the edges of Europe, Muslims are portrayed as a threat, representing the implantation of an 'alien' culture in the heart of Europe – one that threatens to engulf the continent both demographically and culturally (Carr 2010a).

In distinction to such emotive rhetoric, however, the reality is that by 2011 Muslims only constituted around 19 million out of a 504 million-strong

9 The European Union officially adopted the 'Global Approach to Migration' as the basis for its 2009 Stockholm Agreement. This is a five-year plan for 'European justice, freedom and security' running from 2010 through to 2015 (Council of the European Union 2009).

population in the European Union (Pew Forum 2011); many are underprivileged and marginalized, internal 'outsiders', struggling against racism and lacking access to civil rights. They are often subject to the disciplinary measures of national governments in the form of profiling and invasive surveillance. Those forced migrants who also happen to be Muslim often live a precarious existence within Europe, particularly as the new strain of open anti-Muslim racism has further legitimized the securitization of the EU's common immigration and asylum regime. The belief that radical Islam is carried into the heart of Europe by migrants from Muslim-majority countries has combined the twin security preoccupations in one. Hence the security agenda has linked anti-terrorist measures into Europe's common immigration and asylum processes, ensuring that its victims are for the most part not global terrorists but forced migrants. Raids against undocumented migrants and irregular workers, and arrests for infringement of immigration laws, justified by recourse to the discourse of security, effectively criminalize the struggle by 'illegal migrants' to survive. Fekete (2004: 16–17) comments that those already within a member state are 'vulnerable to the awesome power of the European state and to the repressive reach of their countries of origin'. Yet it is through the translation of such marginalized figures into an obsessive security preoccupation that the image of an embattled European identity has gained its power and coherence.

## The Border and European Nationalism

The defining motif of such policies and pronouncements is that of the border. It arises in this context with Younge's (2010) concept of 'identity gatekeepers', in the dual shape of those delegated to maintain European border controls against so-called culturally 'alien' 'outsiders' and those mandated to police the increasingly exclusionary citizenship criteria. In Younge's (2010: 105) words, '[t]he gatekeepers adjust the rules of entry according to the political, economic and social demands of the time, even as they insist they are authenticating a timeless truth'. The creation of a Ministry of Immigration and National Identity in France symbolizes in its very name the intimate connection between securitized borders and cultural assimilation policies. Between them, the material function of globally extensive border controls and the ideological function of internal 'identity borders' perform a triangulation of the forced migrant, trapping them in the no-man's land of an 'alien', 'illegal' status.

Borders are the crucial *sine qua non* of the nation state. Torpey maintains that the invention of the passport as the validation of an individual's identity, and hence their right to cross the national border, was a crucial moment in the formation of the modern European nation state. It represented a key technology with which the state could attempt to control mobile or 'ambiguously defined' populations: '[T]he state system [does not] *effectively* control all movements of persons, but it has monopolised the *authority* to restrict movement' through the creation and control of the technologies of identification (Torpey 2000: 5). Europe's current security discourse – one that produces the figure of the 'illegal migrant' – is also embedded deep within the twenty-first-century technologies of identification and control: 'The capacity of security discourse to shape government is not simply the symbolic capacity of defining dangers but also the technological and bureaucratic capacity of structuring social relations through the implementation of specific technological devices (closed circuit TV, electronic walls, passports, visas, fingerprints) in the context of specific government programmes' (Huysmans 2006: 85).

Movement across Europe's external borders is not only policed by security personnel but also managed through surveillance and tracking equipment, mass databases, data warehouses and data-mining technology. The technologies of exclusion rolled out across Europe, including the Schengen Information System (SIS II), Eurodac and the Visa Information System (VIS),[10] all rely on searchable biometric databases. Border con-

10 The Schengen Information System is a Europe-wide database of 'unwanted' third-country nationals – a biometrically updated version, SIS II, is due to start operation in 2013. Eurodac, introduced by the Dublin agreement (2004), is a complementary

trols increasingly comprise sophisticated techniques for identifying and categorizing 'illegal' activities and individuals by reference to a nexus of transnational external dangers (global terrorism and 'illegal migration', which are discursively linked to human trafficking and international organized crime). These threats are presented as not only endangering citizens' lives, but also threatening to overwhelm the integrity of member states' economies, social norms, welfare systems and national culture.[11] The profoundly political question of European identity, who is and who is not to be regarded as 'European', who is and who is not 'illegal', is woven into all the various technologies and administrative processes; the discourse of security rationalizes these exclusionary processes through reference to the key trope of national identity – who belongs and who does not.

The European Union's securitized asylum and immigration regime helps validate a belief in the integrity of its external borders as boundary and defence of an essential, specifically European identity. Its legal and administrative policies, administrative measures, surveillance technologies, border policing, joint deportations and ever-expanding detention estate (see Migreurop's 2013 map of detention camps) disseminate an ideological narrative in which 'illegal migrants' attempting to enter Europe constitute a grave threat. This is particularly so when, in economically straitened

---

central register of the fingerprints of all who claim asylum at the borders of member states. It has since been updated into a vast database recording and storing other biometric details. The technology that enables the collection of personal data in the SIS II database was extended to visas in 2007; VIS stores the biometric fingerprints of all those who apply for visas to Europe.

11 For example, David Goodhart, former editor of *Prospect* and now director of the think-tank Demos, asks in a 2004 *Prospect* article: 'Is there a "tipping point" somewhere between Britain's 9 percent ethnic minority population and America's 30 percent, which creates a wholly different US-style society – with sharp ethnic divisions, a weak welfare state and low political participation?' The integrity of the British welfare system, he argues, is threatened by immigration from the Global South, which he characterizes as the arrival in the UK of 'people from poor parts of the developing world with little experience of urbanisation, secularism or western values'. He has more recently reiterated (and elaborated) this argument in his 2013 book, *The British Dream*.

times, each national government within the regional bloc needs to secure its role as guarantor that radically reduced public services and increasingly marginal opportunities for employment will only be granted to those who are included within its definition of 'the nation' or 'the European nation' – although the latter is a conception that reveals its own contradictions when hostility is channelled towards migrants to the wealthier economies from the poorer European nation states, as witnessed in recent populist rhetoric in the United Kingdom directed against the right of Bulgarians and Romanians to live and work in the country as full European citizens.

However, despite securitized border controls, and in contradiction to the European narrative of exclusive belonging and national security, many so-called 'illegal migrants' continue to be employed in key economic sectors. The agricultural and food-processing, catering, service and construction industries in many European countries rely heavily on their labour (Anderson and Rogaly 2005; Andreas and Synder 2000; Sassen 2003; Shelley 2007). They constitute what Davis terms a 'stealth workforce' (2006: 178), linked to the formal economy through a web of subcontracting networks. In this way, they are silently embedded in the political community as economic participants but endowed with the status of 'illegal workers', open to extremely high levels of exploitation through their invisibility, lack of rights and precarious position, always vulnerable to detection and deportation. They are policed as 'outsiders' even as they are economically incorporated through the informal labour markets. As McNevin (2006: 136) notes, '[t]heir ambiguous position reflects the incorporation of states and individuals into the global political economy and its patterns of privilege and marginalisation'.

## The Manufacture of the 'Global Alien'

This apparently contradictory situation illustrates one of the many ways in which the processes of capitalist globalization set in train movements of peoples across national boundaries into the global cities of the central regions of global capitalism, where multiple allegiances and modes of identity threaten to unravel the nationalist narrative. The wider global context that nation states are forced to engage with and operate in brings into being multiple dimensions of belonging. The pressures and demands of integration into a global economy, therefore, expose the contradictions within the discourse of national identity; simultaneously, however, they lead to its amplification into a European supranational identity in order to neutralize their impact. In the face of economic and social crisis, the heightened rhetoric of nationalism carries with it implicitly racialized classifications that trigger an instantaneous emotional response and possess the potential to naturalize the concept of an exclusive and unique 'Europeanness'.

In a globalized environment, however, these categories increasingly assume the universal, cultural guise provided by various interpretations of Huntington's (1998) 'clash of civilisations' discourse. Those excluded from the narrative of national belonging are criminalized by means of the nationalist tropes of inclusion/exclusion but in fundamentally global terms, universally cast outside the law, regardless of which nation they enter or try to enter. As Dauvergne shows, the 'migration law–national identity' relationship has evolved, creating the novel concept of the forced migrant as somehow *being* 'illegal' and the ubiquitous use of the term 'illegal' as an identity in and of itself, apparently divorced from any national provenance: 'The migration law–national identity coupling is not new ... [However], what is emerging at the outset of the 21st century in response to the growing forces of globalization is a new twist on this relationship, the nub of which is encapsulated by the idea of people "being really illegal"' (Dauvergne 2004: 87). Those compelled to cross the borders of the rich economies by way of the increasingly criminalized circuits of forced migration are endowed with this identity, as though the term 'illegal' possessed 'a fixed meaning' and was not simply 'an adjectival description'. The label 'illegal' is empty of content: 'illegals are transgressors, and nothing else, by definition' (Dauvergne 2004: 87). The formerly widespread acceptance of an understanding of the forced migrant as a 'refugee' – a legal identity framed by the discourse of human rights – has therefore been all but subsumed by a ubiquitous illegality. This has helped engineer a global understanding of 'insiders' and 'outsiders', but one that still carries a racial code in its polarizing terminology.

The globally applicable identity of the 'illegal migrant' is intimately related to the central paradox the European nation state confronts as it struggles to assert new forms of legitimacy as part of a globalized system. As the current financial and economic crisis shows, the policies that the politicians of member states pursue in order to accommodate global economic interests and channel the flow of global finance into their national economies, consistently override the welfare of their national citizens. Their sources of legitimation are consequently diminished until they appear to be mainly grounded in the assertion of control of their population and its defence against existential threats. The idea of a global threat from beyond national borders displaces the responsibility for systemic failures and crises onto those carrying its visible marks; displaced individuals forced to flee the consequences of violence and wrecked or dismembered economies are portrayed as endangering Europe's identity, cultural integrity and internal coherence. They are implicitly imbued with the character of global representatives of an alien world 'out there', one that is portrayed as a backward hinterland, the site of anarchic wars, violence, terrorism and scarcity (Kaplan 1994).

Carr describes how a new genre of dystopian military/security futurology has emerged that sees threats to the European way of life as emanating 'not only from rogue states, weapons of mass destruction and terrorism, but also from … conflicts over dwindling resources, migration, disease, organized crime, abrupt climate change and the emergence of "failed cities" where social disorder is rife' (Carr 2010b: 13). The idea of an 'arc of instability' from North Africa to Southeast Asia which threatens to disintegrate into an 'arc of chaos', precipitating the 'collapse of governing authority, migrations, societal collapse and social disorder' (Carr 2010b: 19), has generated an emphasis on military terminology in official European discourse. As asylum policy has now become expressed almost solely in terms of security, this discourse has infected the way the figure of the forced migrant is constructed. Kaplan (1994) portrays them as carrying the 'virus' of this anarchic world to the very borders, and even into the heart, of the nation states of the Global North: '[A]s refugee flows increase … national borders will mean less ... the real borders are the most tangible and intractable ones: those of culture and tribe ... Whatever the laws, refugees find a way to crash official borders, bringing their passions with them, meaning that Europe and the United States will be weakened by cultural disputes' (Kaplan 1994: 7). This idea may have been voiced two decades ago, but it appears to continue to exercise influence over the outlook and policies of Europe's political, military and security elite (Carr 2010b).

As a result, the forced migrant has become the most vulnerable victim of a securitized system of control and exclusion – ostensibly targeted at the global terrorist – that now openly defines Europe's global regime of asylum and immigration. Although the cultural racism that fashions these figures and drives the asylum regime appears rooted in national concepts, it is not bounded by national borders, but has instead become a spatialized politics of identity (De Genova 2010). The quality of being 'alien' is stripped of social location and sourced solely in the cultural essence of the forced migrant, a quality they carry around with them whichever borders they cross. It is one that is mirrored by the concept of 'Europeanness' – in its sense as the bearer of an overarching, universal canon of values. This universalist discourse conceals a specifically nationalist one. Europe's supranationalism is based on the assumed cultural integrity of the region, and what it defines as superior cultural (and therefore universal) qualities are 'concentrate[s] of qualities that belong to [certain] nationals "as their own"' (Balibar 1991: 59).

The insistence on universality, however, lends the legal and administrative application of 'global migration control' the appearance of an instrument that, while responding to the everyday concerns of national citizens, exists in a realm guided solely by abstract principles, above and beyond the taint of everyday, nationally specific political demands. The forced migrant can therefore be dehumanized and reduced to an ideological abstraction through the imposition of a universally applicable 'alien' identity. This is compounded by the implicit interweaving of the forced migration discourse with an Islamophobic one, where Islam is assumed to hold a claim to a rival universalism that strives to negate the spread, and threatens the existence, of European cultural values. By virtue of placing Europe's perceived antithesis (situated on a continuum that runs from the historical 'Islamic enemy' through to forced migrants) in a similar trans-temporal, global category, the marshalling of nationalist impulses has the effect of producing, as Said puts it, a 'coercive framework' that reduces human plurality into 'two terminal, collective abstractions' (1991: 55).

The global figure of the 'illegal migrant' has therefore become a crucial component in the construction of a supranational European identity. Its ideological function as the negative substrate of the idea of 'Europeanness' entails that the forced migrant must be visibly identified and rejected; they are caught in a relentless political focus that *includes* them in the national picture through its strategy of *exclusion*. The ideological creation of the figure of the forced migrant as a 'global alien', contrary to the abstract universality espoused by the system that fashions this racialized figure, is infused with state power and pushed onto the central stage of European politics; it becomes the ideological pivot for the normalization of a neo-liberal system of capitalist globalization as it is manifest in its national and regional form. As access to the national space is predicated on national belonging, the question of national identity (and consequently the struggle to embed a hyper-national European identity amongst Europe's disparate populations) relies on the policing of a constructed division between what it means to be 'European' and what is defined as 'non-European'. Hence, Europe's external borders are imbued with political content: the cross-referential instruments of border control acquire the authority to determine the boundaries of legitimacy. In so doing, the border becomes midwife to the birth of a putative pan-European identity that is manufactured out of its binary opposition to the forced migrant, who is portrayed as the threatening global representative of an 'alien' culture and way of life. The figure of the forced migrant has become a political tool used in the bid to instil a cohesive sense of 'Europeanness', and to thus normalize the adoption of a neoliberal pattern of politics within a region that has been profoundly fractured by its divisive effects.

## References


Anderson, B. (1991). *Imagined Communities*. London: Verso.

Anderson, B., and Rogaly B. (2005). 'Forced Labour and Migration to the UK'. Study prepared by COMPAS in collaboration with the Trades Union Congress. Oxford: COMPAS <http://www.compas.ox.ac.uk/fileadmin/files/Publications/Reports/Forced%20Labour%20TUC%20Report.pdf> accessed 29 November 2012.

Anderson, P. (2011). *The New Old World*. London: Verso.

Andreas, P., and Snyder, T. (eds) (2000). *The Wall Around the West: State Borders and Immigration Controls in North America and Europe*. Lanham, MD: Rowman & Littlefield.

Appadurai, A. (2006). *Fear of Small Numbers: An Essay on the Geography of Anger*. Durham, NC: Duke University Press.

Balibar, E. (1991). 'Racism and Nationalism'. In E. Balibar and I. Wallerstein (eds), *Race, Nation, Class: Ambiguous Identities*, pp. 37–67. London: Verso.

—— (2004). 'Europe As Borderland'. The Alexander Humboldt Lecture in Human Geography. Netherlands: University of Nijmegen <www.ru.nl/socgeo/colloquium/Europe%20as%20Borderland.pdf> accessed 13 April 2008.

Bhabha, H. (1990). *Nation and Narration*. London: Routledge.

Bigo, D. (2008). 'Globalised (In)Security: The Field and the Banoptican'. In D. Bigo and A. Tsoukala (eds), *Terror, Insecurity and Liberty: Illiberal Practices of Liberal Regimes After 9/11*, pp. 11–48. London: Routledge.

Brennan, T. (2007). 'Settling Scores: the Orientalists Strike Back', *Race & Class*, 48 (3), 94–113.

Caldwell, C. (2009). *Reflections on the Revolution in Europe: Immigration, Islam and the West*. London: Allen Lane.

Carr, M. (2010a). 'Review: Reflections on The Revolution in Europe: Immigration, Islam and the West by Christopher Caldwell', *Race & Class*, 51 (3), 81–7.

—— (2010b). 'Slouching Towards Dystopia: The New Military Futurism', *Race & Class*, 51 (3), 13–32.

Council of Europe (2011). 'Language Requirements for Adult Migrants in Council of Europe Member States: Report on a Survey' <www.coe.int/t/dg4/linguistic/Source/Mig-ReportSurvey2011_EN.doc> accessed 13 March 2012.

Council of the European Union (2009). 'The Stockholm Programme – An Open and Secure Europe Serving and Protecting the Citizen' <http://register.consilium.europa.eu/pdf/en/09/st17/st17024.en09.pdf> accessed 23 January 2013.

Dauvergne, C. (2004). 'Making People Illegal'. In P. Fitzpatrick and P. Tuitt (eds), *Critical Beings: Law, Nation and the Global Subject*, pp. 83–99. Aldershot: Ashgate.

—— (2007). 'Citizenship with a Vengeance', *Theoretical Inquiries in Law*, 8 (2), 489–507.

Davis, M. (2006). *Planet of Slums*. New York and London: Verso.

De Genova, N. (2010). 'The Deportation Regime: Sovereignty, Space, and Freedom'. In N. De Genova and N. Peutz (eds), *The Deportation Regime: Sovereignty, Space, and the Freedom of Movement*, pp. 33–65. Durham, NC: Duke University Press.

European Commission (2011). 'The European Economic and Social Committee and the Committee of the Regions: European Agenda for the Integration of Third-Country Nationals: Communication from the Commission to the European Parliament, the Council' <http://ec.europa.eu/home-affairs/news/intro/docs/110720/1_EN_ACT_part1_v10.pdf> accessed 15 March 2012.

Fekete, L. (2004). 'Anti-Muslim Racism and the Security State', *Race & Class*, 46 (1), 3–29.

—— (2009). *A Suitable Enemy: Racism, Migration and Islamophobia in Europe*. London: Pluto Press.

—— (2011). 'Understanding the European-wide Assault on Multiculturalism', London: Institute of Race Relations <http://www.irr.org.uk/2011/april/ha000021.html> accessed 3 June 2012.

Ferguson, N. (2004). 'Eurabia?', *New York Times*, 4 April <http://www.nytimes.com/2004/04/04/magazine/04WWLN.html> accessed 8 October 2009.

Goodhart, D. (2004). 'Too Diverse?', *Prospect*, 20 February <http://www.prospect-magazine.co.uk/magazine/too-diverse-david-goodhart-multiculturalism-britain-immigration-globalisation/#.Uc74Aq6FImV> accessed 15 March 2009.

—— (2013). *The British Dream: Successes and Failures of Post-War Immigration*. London: Atlantic Books.

Huntington, S. (1998). *The Clash of Civilisations and the Remaking of the World Order*. London: Touchstone Books.

Huysmans, J. (2006). *The Politics of Insecurity: Fear, Migration and Asylum in the EU*. London: Routledge.

Kaplan, R. D. (1994). 'The Coming Anarchy', *Atlantic Monthly*, 273 (2), 44–76 <http://www.theatlantic.com/doc/199402/anarchy> accessed 22 February 2013.

Kundnani, A. (2008). 'Islamism and the Roots of Liberal Rage', *Race & Class*, 50 (2), 40–68.

McNevin, A. (2006). 'Political Belonging in a Neoliberal Era: The Struggle of the Sans-Papiers', *Citizenship Studies*, 10 (2), 135–51.

Migreurop (2013). 'Principle Spaces of Detention' <http://www.migreurop.org/IMG/pdf/Carte_Atlas_Migreurop_8012013_Version_anglaise_version_web.pdf> accessed 3 March 2013.

Passavant, P. A. (2004). 'The Paradox of Human Rights'. In P. Fitzpatrick and P. Tuitt (eds), *Critical Beings: Law, Nation and the Global Subject*, pp. 137–58. Aldershot: Ashgate.

Pew Forum (2011). 'The Future of the Global Muslim Population: Projections for 2010–2030'. Washington, DC: Pew Research Center <http://www.pewforum.org/uploadedFiles/Topics/Religious_Affiliation/Muslim/FutureGlobalMuslimPopulation-WebPDF-Feb10.pdf> accessed 23 March 2013.

Said, E. W. (1991). *Orientalism: Western Concepts of the Orient*. London: Penguin.

Sassen, S. (2003). 'Global Cities and Survival Circuits'. In B. Ehrenreich and A. R. Hochschild (eds), *Global Woman: Nannies, Maids and Sex Workers in the New Economy*, pp. 254–74. London: Granta Books.

Seymour, R. (2010). 'The Changing Face of Racism', *International Socialism*, Issue 126, 65–94.

Shelley, T. (2007). *Exploited: Migrant Labour in the New Global Economy*. London: Zed Books.

Soguk, N. (1999). *States and Strangers: Refugees and Displacement in Statecraft*. Minneapolis, MN: University of Minnesota Press.

Squire, V. (2009). *The Exclusionary Politics of Asylum*. Basingstoke: Palgrave Macmillan.

Torpey, J. (2000). *The Invention of the Passport: Surveillance, Citizenship and the State*. Cambridge: Cambridge University Press.

Traynor, I. (2007). 'Wealth Gap Grows and Solidarity Fades as Rebellion of the Rich Spreads Across the EU', *The Guardian*, 11 June <http://www.guardian.co.uk/world/2007/jun/11/business.spain> accessed on 11 June 2012.

Younge, G. (2010). *Who Are We – and Should It Matter in the 21st Century?* London: Viking.

Žižek, S. (2009). *Violence*. London: Profile Books.

# PART TWO

# European Identity in Times of Crisis

BO STRÅTH

# 6 The Idea of a European Identity as an Escape Forward: A Historical Perspective on the Present Euro Crisis

The intensified discussion about Europe over the last thirty years has, to a large extent, been organized around the concept of identity. As such, it is a debate about a concept charged with a highly ideological content. European identity is usually seen in relation to national identity, either in tension-filled opposition to it, that is, as an alternative which might replace the nation, or in a relationship where it overlaps and supplements the nation. The structure of national identity is 'projected' onto the European identity, and this projection has an ideological underpinning, for no projection is ever disinterested/non-ideological (Schulz-Forberg and Stråth 2010; Stråth 2010 [2000]).

The formal definition of identity is the state of being equal or identical. Identity means sameness. This can only make sense as a belief, a myth, or an identification with something, that is, as a projection of the ego onto something else and the symbolic representation of this 'something else'. European identity is not a phenomenon in an essentialist sense, in which the task would be to investigate its content and forms of expression. Rather, European identity was discursively shaped in a specific historical situation, and the task is to investigate under what circumstances this formation took place, and to reflect on the fact that an obsession with 'integration', the buzz word in the 1950s and 60s, was replaced in the 1970s, and increasingly from the 1980s, by the obsession with 'identity'.

With reference to identity, Europe is connected to an idea and normative centre rather than a precisely formed territory. Europe is a discourse which is translated into a political and ideological project. Europe does not have an essence beyond one that is shaped by language. If Europe has a meaning, it is as a political programme. In this sense the Declaration on a European Identity at the European Community (EC) Summit in Copenhagen in 1973 was very successful, although the development of the concept took directions different from those envisaged by its architects. A political programme does not mean *the* political programme. It is, rather, something under continuous negotiation and re-negotiation. Both as politics and ideology, Europe must be seen in the plural, always contested and contradictory.

Luisa Passerini (1998) has argued for Europe as a cultural, intellectual and even emotional programme, as opposed to a political project. Her Europe is an imagined territory, which is the *locus* of shortage, absence and doubt, critical to pompous and declamatory versions. Europe is also ambivalent, in her view. In order to create this Europe considerable intellectual energy of constructive criticism must be invested. In this way the painful historical connections between Europe and violence will not be forgotten but dismantled and uprooted. Luisa Passerini's emphasis is in her approach on Europe as a self-reflecting critical culture of identification and not identity.

Identity is a problematic and fuzzy concept. If taken literally, it means equality, sameness, the quality of being identical. It is a concept used to construct community and feelings of cohesion and holism, a concept to convey the impression that all individuals are equal in the imagined community. The launching of the idea of a European identity occurred in a situation of an experienced lack of such a phenomenon. Utopian dreams of community, cohesion and holism, which are all contained in the concept of a European identity, were mobilized precisely in a situation where there was a lack of such feelings. Identity thus becomes a problem when there is *no* feeling of cohesion and community, and this is particularly the case in situations of crisis and turbulence, when established ties of social cohesion are eroded or broken down. Political management of economies ('political economy') went unquestioned during the first decade of European integration, and the idea of a European identity no more came to mind than the idea of unemployment. At that time, European integration in political practice was understood in terms of the political coordination of national economies rather than as an identity project. The EC did not stand for the

European Community but for 'Communities' in the plural. Integration was the concept of the 1950s and 1960s which was used in the Cold War context to conjure up images of European unity. At that time, integration was the key concept for translating Europe into a political project. It was when integration failed as an instrument of mobilization that identity came to be promoted.

In what precise situation, then, did the idea of a European identity become politically mobilized? In 1970, with the experience of the previous European deadlock in the 1960s through de Gaulle's obstruction politics and veto against British membership of the European Economic Community, and against the backdrop of growing tensions with the United States after 1965 in financial, security and political terms, the second generation of European leaders rose to the occasion when de Gaulle had been forced to step down in 1969. They saw the possibility to once more raise the horizon of expectations through decisive institutional steps towards a federal Europe. The federalist language became more concrete with a clear institutional design. As soon as de Gaulle had been forced to step down, the decision was taken at the summit in The Hague in December 1969 both to intensify (tighten, deepen) cooperation in the fields of security politics and economic and monetary politics, and to enlarge the membership from six to nine. Deepening implied the drawing of outlines of an economic and monetary union, based on both economic and monetary politics as the basis of a shared currency, and a security and political union: the Werner and Davignon Plans. The Werner Plan was brave in its architecture since it attempted to merge the economic and the social. It was a clear step in a federal direction. The Werner Plan was ambitious in seeing the economic and monetary controls given wholly over to the aegis of Community-level government.

A major problem was that the federal budget and financial capacity outlined in the Werner Plan, besides the monetary dimension of European economic and monetary union, necessarily brought the question of a European democracy to the fore. Initially, the European integration project, as it was designed in the Paris Treaty in 1951 on a European Coal and Steel Community and in the Rome Treaty in 1957 on a European Economic Community, was not thought of in terms of a European democracy. On the contrary, the experience that marked the European leaders after 1945 was the fact that democracy could be dangerous. Nazism had seized power within a democratic order. The aim of Konrad Adenauer, Robert Schuman, Alcide de Gasperi, Jean Monnet and the governments of the Benelux countries was to create an organization that kept them safe from excesses in the name of democracy. What later became the Commission was in the Paris Treaty called the High Authority and had a capacity to impose its will on the member states of the community. The High Authority was a supranational body standing above the member-state governments rather than being the sum of them. European integration was meant to place constraints on nation-state democracy, in order to keep them democratic, through unelected European institutions (Müller 2011a).

European integration on the basis of the Paris and Rome treaties functioned as a distribution of labour between European and national levels. Brussels was the guardian of the market order based on free trade within a customs union which would provide economic wealth for the member states to distribute in order to buy allegiance and legitimacy in the electorates. The Community level was responsible for economic integration and the member-state level for the social issues and the distribution of the yields from the growing economy. Integration historian Alan Milward (1992) called this distribution of labour the European rescue of the nation state.

The emerging model was a substitute for the more ambitions US plans after the Second World War in order to make the European continent more peaceful. These plans laid out the United States of Europe (USE) according to the blueprint of the USA. The European leaders in the late 1940s objected to the American intentions vehemently. What emerged from the negotiations were the Treaties of Paris and Rome.

Ideologically, the emerging distribution of labour between the European and the national levels was underpinned by two political scientists who had escaped Nazism through emigration to the USA in the 1930s: Karl Deutsch and Ernst Haas. Their neo-functionalist theory described how integration would become ever tighter, through the spread from the customs union for commodities to ever more areas of cooperation, such as communication and labour markets. There was an implicit understanding of development towards a final federal goal, although the precise way there was not outlined. The imagination of a self-propelling machine towards ever higher levels of European integration was propagated. The Werner and Davignon Plans in 1969 should be seen in this framework.

The Werner Plan for a European Economic and Monetary Union and the Davignon Plan for a European Security and Foreign Political Union were launched in December 1969 as a response to de Gaulle's blockade of European integration under the label of *l'Europe des patries*. However, they were also in a sense a fulfilment of de Gaulle's politics, more precisely his politics vis à vis the USA. In the 1960s he had built up a growing tension with the USA in the area of monetary and security politics. The US dollar hegemony was challenged and doubts became ever stronger that the USA would be prepared to protect Europe under its nuclear weapon umbrella in the case of a war with the Soviet Union. De Gaulle's solution to this situation was a strong Europe dominated by France. The solution by the European leaders after de Gaulle was a strong Europe through new steps of integration.

In August 1971 the dollar collapsed and the international order established at the end of the Second World War at Bretton Woods broke down. Against the backdrop of the Vietnam War, US financial burdens made commitments about the stability of the dollar and the guarantee of its value in relation to gold impossible. The oil-price shock in October 1973 emphasized the continued breakdown of the international order. This could have been a European moment in which the tension-ridden relationships with the USA since the 1960s could have been transformed into a more independently performing Europe with the Werner and the Davignon Plans as instrument.

The Declaration on European Identity looks at first glance like a brave new step in a federal direction after the Werner and Davignon Plans, but the framework of the statement hinted rather at the limits of the federal step. Caught between the Yom Kippur War and the oil-price shock, the initiatives from December 1969 began to lose momentum. Already in April 1973, the Commission warned that the dynamics were evaporating from the two plans. This was before the oil-price shock. The determined commitment to establish a European alternative to the American global hegemony in financial and military political terms was easier in argument than in action.

Jean Monnet, now 85 years old, felt that the principle of delegation of national competences to the supranational institutions was fast approaching its limits. In the summer of 1973, he proposed to Edward Heath and Willy Brandt, his old companions, and to Georges Pompidou, that the chiefs of government and state of the Nine form a provisional European government committed to implementing the Paris Declaration from 1972, with the aim of establishing a European Union with a European government and a directly elected parliament. Heath and Brandt supported Monnet's idea, but Pompidou did so only in part. In particular, the French president was against a European government. Under the imperative of the oil-price shock, Monnet increased his pressure on the three leaders and proposed a small meeting between them and their six colleagues of the EC Nine before the end of the year. Monnet had in mind an informal meeting without a formal agenda at which all questions could be brainstormed without protocol, prestige and final communiqué. The Commission and the prime ministers of the smaller member states, as well as their foreign ministers feared being sidestepped and Monnet's idea was transformed into a big formal summit meeting.

Monnet's plan for a very small inner circle of leaders to take decisive steps failed. The summit in Copenhagen in December 1973 failed to agree on anything, including the periodicity of the summits. In this situation the idea of a European identity came in as a face-saving tool. The declaration on a European identity was an escape route, nothing more and nothing less (Knipping 2004: 204–5).

The idea of a European identity was introduced as an instrument to stabilize the situation after the breakdown of the international order and to support the Werner and Davignon Plans. The idea of identity was based on the principle of the unity of the Nine – this was just after the first enlargement – on their responsibility towards the rest of the world, and on the dynamic nature of the European construction. The meaning of 'responsibility towards the rest of the world' was expressed in a hierarchical way. First, it meant responsibility towards the other nations of Europe with whom friendly relations and cooperation already existed. Secondly, it meant responsibility towards the countries of the Mediterranean, Africa and the Middle East. Thirdly, it referred to relations with the USA, based on the restricted foundations of equality and the spirit of friendship. Next in the hierarchy was the narrow cooperation and constructive dialogue with Japan and Canada. Then came détente towards the Soviet Union and the countries of Eastern Europe. At the bottom of the list came China, Latin America, and, finally, a reference was made to the importance of the struggle against underdevelopment in general (Passerini 2000). The fact that the USA was mentioned after the Middle East must be understood in the framework of the prevailing oil-price shock and the fact that President Nixon had refused since 1971 to let the dollar guarantee the Bretton Woods order. Refused is perhaps not the right word. He could not. The Vietnam War had overstretched the dollar to the edge of collapse, but even before then de Gaulle had begun to undermine confidence in the American substitute for the gold standard by his repeated threats to change his dollar reserves for gold.

The identity concept was, despite its nine tiers, vague and full of diverging interpretations. It was not quite new at the time of the Copenhagen Summit in December 1973 and had been discussed for some time. The Paris summit in October 1972 had agreed that Europe must be able to make its voice heard in world affairs and affirm its own views in international relations. François-Xaviers Ortoli, the newly appointed President of the Commission, argued in a statement to the European Parliament in February 1973 that the Paris agreement meant a decision to establish a European identity, which needed to be comprised of 'a heartfelt desire, shared by all our peoples, to differentiate ourselves from the rest of the world' (Ortoli 1973a). A few weeks later, Ortoli gave a speech in London entitled 'Towards a European Identity' where he defined the concept: Europeans are a people [sic! in the singular, BS] who have a common cultural background, a history often divided, who react more or less the same way before events, who have more or less the same mode of life, the same level of development (Ortoli 1973b).

The outline of the identity concept referred, by implication, to Western Europe. It was made in a time which still did not know the European motto of unity in diversity. In April 1973, Henry Kissinger, the US Secretary of

State, suggested a Year of Europe in a speech in which he lamented the perceived European practice of each country asserting its autonomy whenever it was to its benefit and invoking unity to curtail the independence of others. He argued for a new balance between self-interest and common interest. The Nine had not been consulted by the Americans before the Year of Europe was launched and the European leaders did not conceal that they would have preferred an American approach that was less precipitate, dramatic and demanding. The EEC foreign ministers met in July in an effort to establish a common European approach and a common identity when dealing with the USA. In September three draft papers by the British, Irish and French governments were discussed at a committee meeting in Copenhagen.

The British paper was entitled *The Identity of the Nine vis-à-vis the United States*. The paper discerned two alternative approaches. One would be to identify the common values and historical heritage of European civilization and distinguish those which are shared with the Americans. The second approach would consider the identity of the Nine in terms of the specific issues likely to be foremost in the discussion with the USA during the coming months. The paper emphasized the second more pragmatic approach and found it difficult to distinguish between European and American identities apart from the fact that historical associations linking Europe with the Middle East, Africa and other overseas territories and Europe's lack of raw materials would require her to seek special relations with these countries. The Irish paper emphasized the difference between a European identity and a Community Identity. The latter was only part of the wider European identity. As in the British paper, the main reason for drawing attention to a European Community identity was linked to the American Year of Europe initiative and the anticipated visit to Europe by President Richard Nixon towards the end of 1973 (which never occurred, however). The Irish paper concluded that the Community should adhere to the present dimension of its identity, thus its competences under the Treaty and its progress so far in political cooperation. To go further would be an error. Finally, the French paper went exactly in the direction that the Irish memorandum warned against, striving to direct the European identity toward the rest of the world and not just the USA. In contrast to the British and Irish papers, the French paper had no difficulty in describing Europe's differences with the USA. The Nine were the inheritors of a common civilization that expressed itself in a rich variety of national cultures. They were aware of sharing in common a certain number of legal, political and moral values that they wanted to preserve. As in the British paper, emphasis was placed on the role of Europe's natural resources. Europe had interests that derived from its history, its geographic position, its state of natural resources and its exchanges with the rest of the world. The French paper placed not the USA but the African and Mediterranean peoples first in its discussion of identity in terms of external relations.

The attempted leap ahead in Copenhagen in December 1973 developed the neo-functionalist understanding of Europe as a self-propelling machine in new directions towards a federation based on a European demos rather than economic and political integration. Neo-functionalism had lost credibility under de Gaulle at the cost of new theoretical understandings of European intergovernmental integration. Through the identity concept, neo-functionalist thoughts about a final federal goal came back.

The identity language underpinned a mythical imagination of a European progressive teleology. The idea of a European identity and a European demos led to the question of a European democracy. The question emerged as to how democratic power could be transferred from the member states to the European level. This was the question about the democratic deficit. Such a transfer would mean a clash with the ideas of the founding moment of the post-1945 European project, ideas which had received intentional expression in the High Authority.

The European Parliament got a new setting in 1979 when for the first time it was elected directly by the national electorates. However, this innovation was not the solution to the problem of the European democratic deficit that it might have pretended to be. In its self-understanding, the directly elected parliament was the expression of the will of a European people that did not, however, exist. The problem was not the way in which it was elected but its role in the institutional framework in Brussels. The enactment of a people's will in democratic societies emerges not in terms of consensus, as is so often erroneously argued, but through contention, debate and compromise (compromise is enforced rather than voluntary consensus).

Since the French Revolution political conflict has been measured along a right–left scale. The social issue is thereby a key dimension. This right–left dimension is the core axis that has been institutionalized in national parliamentary democracies. In the European Parliament, however, it is much less developed. The institutional setting from the early 1950s is, in this respect, still in operation. National sovereignty was not transferred to the European Parliament but to the High Authority/European Commission. The years since the introduction of direct elections to the European Parliament in 1979 have certainly meant an expansion of its prerogatives under growing contention with the Council (Pollak 2007: 159–64). However, the point of departure has been a kind of consensus in the European Parliament in an institutional confrontation with the Council and the Commission much more than a legitimating political confrontation about various alternatives *within* the Parliament. Therefore, the European Parliament is different from the national parliaments of the member states.

Instead of a politicization of the European Parliament, a step was taken in the opposite direction when a government conference was called to prepare a new integrative step under the presidency of Jacques Delors. The deeper integration meant the expansion of the customs union for commodities to an internal market with free movement also for capital, services and persons. The intergovernmental conference ended up in the Single European Act about the internal market in 1987. The idea formulated in Milward's expression 'the European rescue of the nation state' was reinforced. European politics was about economic integration, whereas social problems in the wake of economic integration were referred to as issues within the member states.

Instead of a linkage of the idea of a European democracy to social achievements and guarantees of certain social standards, as in the national democracies, the idea of a European democracy implicit in the identity language was connected to the European market with individual European citizens as the intermediaries. From now on, the identity discourse shifted meaning from more homogeneous understandings of a European demos through a European identity. The free and sovereign European citizens with driving licences, a European anthem and other symbols would reinforce the internal market and through feedback be reinforced as citizens. The market was made compatible with a European people. It was not like in the member states wherein the state provided the framework of democracy and citizenship, and the core of European democracy was not about guaranteeing social standards. The market would solve the problem of the democratic deficit and provide the European institutions with the missing European people. In retrospect, this was a bypass operation around the real problems, those concerning the connections between the economic and the social, but the effects of this circumvention only became fully visible twenty years later.

The collapse of the Soviet empire and the end of the Cold War in 1989–91 provided incitements for new integrative steps. Even before the fall of the wall in November 1989, plans for an economic and monetary union had been elaborated as an extension of the internal market. These plans gained momentum when the question of German reunification emerged on the political agenda. French President François Mitterand was frightened by the reunification perspective, and he had good historical reasons to be so. However, his resistance could not break the American and British preparedness to accept the *Wiedervereinigung*. In that situation he saw a common European currency as a guarantee. In a similar vein to the way in which Jean Monnet and Robert Schuman, in the Paris Treaty of 1951 on the European Coal and Steel Community, had used coal and steel as the instrument to reinforce West Germany and at the same time control its strength, Mitterand used the German mark by transforming it into the euro.

A common currency was an integrative dimension which also had a clear link to the identity language. The Maastricht Treaty was about a monetary union, amongst other things, and the name shift from the European Communities to the European Union, signed in December 1991, again conjured up imaginations of a European federation. However, due in particular to British resistance, the Treaty did not contain as strong a social dimension as Jacques Delors wanted. And as to the monetary dimension, which the United Kingdom refused to enter, it did not want like the Werner Plan of twenty years earlier to contain a fiscal dimension. Instead of strong institutional instruments for common financial politics, the Growth and Stability Pact with a lower legal status was signed. The lack of a financial capacity to match the monetary focus and the large productivity differences between north and south in the euro area has today become an existential problem that threatens the whole integration project. At the beginning, the problem was ignored in the general market euphoria and the new globalization and end-of-history language that followed on the collapse of the Soviet system. The market would, in the long run, provide the European federation and the European identity that the name shift from community to union suggested. The market became the motor of the self-propelling European machine. European democracy would emerge through the market. The problem of social disintegration in the wake of economic integration, which had been the major issue and bone of contention in nineteenth-century nation-state building, and which had erupted in the Great Depression of the 1930s under the name of national socialism, was played down or ignored.

However, instead of a European people unified in a supranational European Union managed by a strong Commission, as the Maastricht Treaty and the shift of name from European Economic Community to European Union indicated, the European political practice with the aim of establishing an internal market, as it developed after Jacques Delors' powerful leadership, meant a migration of power from the centralized level of the Commission to the member-state governments assembled in the Council. The enlargement from EU 12 to EU 15 in 1995, with Austria, Finland and Sweden inaugurated as new members, hardly increased the commitment for a deeper integration of Europe. Two kinds of accelerating tensions reinforced one another: one between federal European Monetary Union and European Political Union rhetoric in the wake of Maastricht and the institutional cover of this rhetoric, and the other between deepening and enlargement. Here, quite obviously, was a parallel to the 1970s. The regulative framework from the 1950s based on compelling directives, with the pretension of a supranational law *sui generis*, was gradually being transformed into intergovernmental agreements in the so-called open method of coordination process. Instead of a tighter political union and a higher level of integration, in comparison to the economic free trade unification, the trend since the 1990s has been towards a looser kind of intergovernmental cooperation and coordination, from hard law to soft law and from harmonization to coordination. The European summits in

Luxembourg 1997 and Lisbon 2000 outlined this transformation from the image of a Europe beyond the nations to a Europe of the nations. High politics in Europe had to recognize that the nation had returned on the European scene and had to find political responses to this fact. Not even modest claims and expectations of intergovernmental coordination of the responses to the collapse of the financial markets in 2008 were redeemed.

Against the backdrop of the breakdown of the general market euphoria initiated by the fall of the Soviet system, the concept of European identity no longer serves a purpose. The image of a European people, as it was designed in the framework of the Cold War and as it was re-designed through the market linkage after the end of the Cold War, seems to be more distant than ever. The political agenda today deals with national identity, nationalism and populism. The present state of the common currency, which potentially could have been a strong instrument of identification, underpins this disintegrative development. Germany and Greece have become symbols in the growing nationalistic language used to refer to the euro crisis. Mitterand's euro strategy of controlling the strong German economy through a common currency seems to have failed.

The problem with the identity concept, however, began before the 2008 financial collapse. The European distribution of labour between the economic and the social, between the European centre in Brussels and the member states, got new problematic preconditions in 2004. The non-binding identity language was against the backdrop of the enlargement from EU 15 to EU 25 transformed by a new key concept: the constitution. The insight grew that the enlargement required an institutional consolidation and a stronger legal framework which would set the rules for majority decisions in a number of policy areas. The squaring of the circle in the political implementation of the growing insight dealt with the small-state claim that all member states were equal and the big-state claim that the size of the population must be considered. For example, Luxembourg and Cyprus could not have the same vote weighting as Germany. It was easy to agree on the principled justification of these two claims but much more difficult to translate them into figures and degrees of influence. Owing to this, the Nice summit in December 2000 ended in a fiasco. The intergovernmental constitutional convention decided in Laeken one year later nevertheless managed to find a formula that solved this and other problems. This was elaborated on to become a constitution which was signed in Rome in October 2004 and in the following ratification process became the subject of referenda in each of the member states. The European Constitution was the tool that would give the identity language legal and institutional coverage and substance.

The signing of the Constitution and the referenda occurred just after the big enlargement to EU 25 on 1 May 2004, which provoked strong feelings about dramatically growing social inequalities between the old and the new member states. Here is not the place to discuss the material substance of such feelings. The mechanism that worked was the *perceptions* of growing inequalities and of threats of social dumping when cheap labour flooded the labour markets in the West and the industry moved to the East. The Polish plumber who took jobs from domestic workers played an important role as a symbol that personified these perceptions in the French referendum campaign. The no-votes by the French and the Dutch electorates in May and June of 2005 shook Europe. The European left had failed to imagine and build up a European solidarity, but continued to think and act in national terms when it came to social politics and welfare arrangements. This failure brought the market escapism and the dreams of an identity without a social dimension to an abrupt end.

The financial crisis in 2008 and the euro crisis in 2011, which quite obviously are connected into one major global crisis with an epicentre in Europe, have triggered debates in two different directions: more nationalism and populism versus a stronger European capacity to react politically to what is argued to be the dictates of the market forces. Here the fact that viewing market forces as a dictator reduces the perceived scope for political action must be appreciated. The idea of a European identity has disappeared in these processes and the same is true for the dreams of a European constitution. The present more narrow debate deals with the question whether and how the complex Lisbon Treaty, decided in December 2007 and rejected by the Irish voters in a referendum in 2008, thought of as a substitute of the failed constitution, can be amended. This debate is closely connected to the question whether the EU will split between its euro core and the rest. In substantial terms at the end of 2011, there seem to be two alternative solutions to the economic problem: first, to let the European Central Bank act as a lender of last resort and issue Eurobonds (favoured by most countries but opposed by Germany) and, second, to impose discipline in order to avoid inflation and to prevent the imposition of south European economic politics in the euro area.

In the wake of the search for a viable political strategy in response to the ongoing financial crisis since 2008 the democracy question has replaced the identity question. What does democracy mean when the financial authority of the nation parliaments is undercut repeatedly and systematically? Is it possible to imagine a European democracy as a compensation for the national democratic deficit? Would a European democracy based on the power of coordinated financial politics require a federal solution? What would the implications for the question of a European identity be?

The prevailing economic crisis is as much a political crisis. The arguments for a political Union with a fiscal capacity have grown, but hardly the political will to implement them. Moreover, the question that remains unanswered so far is how a political union can gain democratic legitimacy. The conventional view since the 1990s has been that the Commission in Brussels must be controlled by the national governments and parliaments as the only way to reconcile the requirements of European integration with democratic legitimacy. The current crisis is likely either to stretch such understandings of democracy or to over-stretch the euro. However, the German drive for a stronger fiscal rigidity aims at discipline with automatic sanctions of infringements, which does not provide a scope for politics. If this solution is passed then there is a high probability that the euro will face the same destiny as once did the gold standard in the 1930s, when social protests overruled the political attempts to maintain monetary rigidity. Only with a considerable scope for European fiscal politics can legitimacy and popular support be expected.

The stretch of the prevailing understandings of democratic legitimacy means that Europe is in a situation where what Joseph Weiler (1999) has called 'constitutional tolerance' has become problematic. The term refers to a broad European culture of compromise where member states have voluntarily submitted to an expanded EU law and at the same time been tolerant of exception clauses or even vetoes when some members have felt that vital national interests or even identities have been at stake. The financial crisis requires concerted action in more determined forms by all members of the Eurozone.

The problem here is that this approach will probably split Europe between the actual and the candidate member states with the euro and those who prefer to remain outside the common currency, in a complex mix of European law and conventional international law. On the other side, the crisis might provide the European constitutional moment, which quite obviously was not there in 2005, although it might be a constitutional moment for only a limited number of EU member states.

Jürgen Habermas (2011) proposes the idea of transnationalization of popular sovereignty against the backdrop of the massive resistance against a European federal super-state. Individual European citizens and member states would divide constituent power equally and should understand themselves as co-authors of a new European constitution. Habermas understands democratic sovereignty in Europe as being located in two interdependent and asymmetric fields of sovereignty: the individual sovereignty of each citizen and the collective relations between the citizens in a nation state. The two fields check and delimit one another. This kind of curtailing self-restriction is inherent in democratic constitutions but has a much longer history that goes back to political theories by Jean Bodin, Thomas Hobbes and others. The point that Habermas is making is that these two fields can expand separately institutionally as well as politically, and that this is what is happening within the EU. In the EU, the citizens of Europe are unified in two different participating roles, as individual Union citizens and as national members of the member states. As individual EU citizens they directly elect the European Parliament, as citizens of the member states they indirectly control the 'executive federalism' of the EU located in the Council rather than the Commission. On this basis, the democratic division of sovereignty is also true of the EU. The dual sovereignty constitutes not only the member states but also the EU. The EU is the ideal typical continuity of the national democracies by other means, in the view of Habermas. However, this continuity is so far only an ideal type when the question of how far this is from the constitutional reality of the Union is legitimately posed. The conclusion of Habermas, on this ideal typical ground, is that the solution must not necessarily be perceived in terms of a federal United States of Europe, but that the member states can remain as democratic nation states. The interplay of the two citizen roles, the individual European and the collective national, provides the transnational equilibrium between the asymmetric sovereign parts.

The planned fiscal pact no doubt encroaches upon the European sovereignty concept, but not because it can enforce rigid budget rules against the national parliaments, but because the coercive measures are not covered by a real fiscal union. Only if the tax, social and economic politics were sufficiently coordinated at the EU level, as in the never-realized Werner Plan, would fiscal interventions into the member states be legitimate. Integration rather than discipline is the key to the democracy question in the framework of the euro crisis.

This does not mean that other answers to the crisis could not be conceived from the viewpoint of democracy. Influential voices argue for reinforcing nation-state-based legitimacy while at the same time restricting the freedom of nation states. By contrast, political theorist Jan-Werner Müller argues that a grand constitutional bargain, with meaningful participation from European publics, seems preferable. However, much will depend on the details, and the smaller member states are unlikely to be happy with an even more democratic Europe, which they equate with being outvoted by the more populous countries. What might look like a real continent-wide democracy on paper, as in the theory of Habermas, could exacerbate the democratic disconnect within Europe: people might accept supranational democracy in theory, but cannot see it as part of their lives, and particularly not when it comes to the democratic substance of hard fiscal realities. Alternatively, for Müller (2011b), Europeans might come to see the crisis as the moment when they were forced to realize what has been true for some time: they really do share each other's fate. The special nature of the EU could well remain political union without overarching statehood. But Europeans might ultimately push harder for true fiscal integration, which could include a genuine European treasury.

The idea of a European identity was launched as an attempt to hide the failure to link the social and the economic in the Werner Plan. It was an escape from political action and responsibility in a situation of economic and political crisis in the 1970s. The escape meant an investment of hopes and expectations in the European project as a self-propelling machine towards a distant federal goal, circumventing the question of political management for reconciling the tension between economic integration and social disintegration. The European teleology continued in new forms in the 1990s when the identity concept was, in a biased way, linked to the economic internal market language. The European identity and the subsequent European demos would emerge through European citizens performing on and driven by the market. Social cohesion would occur automatically through the new market economy. The emerging identity through the market would provide the preconditions of a European demos and a European democracy. Historically, in the nineteenth-century construction of national identities, the core dimension was as much social integration as it was economic. But economic integration did not automatically mean social integration. Often the relationship was the opposite. The omission of the social became a major problem with the major EU enlargement in 2004. Today the concept of a European identity has lost meaning due to the neglect of the social.

One potential solution for the future, which more than ever stands out in bold relief against the solution of the 1970s, would be immediate political action for a democratic response to the market terror, where the issue of identity is seen in a more relaxed way and its importance is played down. This insight is becoming widespread and escapism today by means of the identity concept would be an existential threat to European integration. Escapism with the identity language today occurs in the member states, where nationalism grows. This nationalist escapism is a serious threat to European integration. Democracy and political management of the economy, the economy as a polity, is the issue at stake, not identity. There certainly exists a connection between politics and identity, but this time the sequence must be the opposite and therefore more realistic: political action first and then *possibly* an emerging European identity. This is an optimistic scenario. The pessimistic version of collapse is no less realistic.

## References

Habermas, J. (2011). *Zur Verfassung Europas. Ein Essay*. Frankfurt/Main: Suhrkamp.

Knipping, F. (2004). *Rom, 25. März 1957. Die Einigung Europas*. Munich: DTV.

Milward, A. (1992). *The Rescue of the European Nation State*. London: Routledge.

Müller, J.-W. (2011a). *Contesting Democracy: Political Ideas in Twentieth Century Europe*. New Haven, CT: Yale University Press.

——(2011b). 'A Shared Fate: The Political Implications of the Eurozone', *Boston Review* <http://www.bostonreview.net/BR36.6/jan-werner_mueller_european_union_crisis.php> accessed 21 December 2011.

Ortoli, F.-X. (1973a). 'Address by President Ortoli to the European Parliament', 13 February. Brussels: EU Commission Historical Archives.

——(1973b). 'Towards a European Identity'. Speech delivered by President Ortoli at Chatham House, London, 23 February.

Passerini, L. (1998). *Identità culturale europea: Idee, sentimenti, relazioni*. Firenze: La nuova Italia.

——(2000). 'The Last Identification: Why Some of Us Would Like to Call Ourselves Europeans and What We Mean by This'. In B. Stråth (ed.), *Europe and the Other and Europe as the Other*, pp. 45–65. Brussels: PIE-Peter Lang.

Pollak, J. (2007). *Repräsentation ohne Demokratie: Kollidierende Systeme der Repräsentation in der Euorpäischen Union*. Vienna: Springer.

Schulz-Forberg, H., and Stråth, B. (2010) *The Political History of European Integration: The Hypocrisy of Democracy-through-Market*. London: Routledge.

Stråth, B. (ed.) (2010) [2000]. *Europe and the Other and Europe as the Other*. Brussels: PIE-Peter Lang.

Weiler, J. H. H. (1999). *The Constitution of Europe. 'Do the New Clothes Have an Emperor?' and Other Essays on European Integration*. Cambridge: Cambridge University Press.

DORA KOSTAKOPOULOU

# 7 Political Alchemies, Identity Games and the Sovereign Debt Instability: European Identity in Crisis or the Crisis in Identity-Talk?

Is it possible to talk about European identity amidst the turbulence the Eurozone faces? If it is, what kind of meaning would one attribute to European identity now that questions of 'survival' – be they related to foiling the fragmentation of the Eurozone, overcoming countries' worsening economic performance and/or recession, or even safeguarding citizens' dreams for a decent future for themselves and their families – have made the pursuit of existential quests a luxury? And further, why is it that European identity, which was supposed to be a shield against not only events threatening to destabilize the EU but also cycles of popular enthusiasm and disenchantment, has not been mobilized? I believe that any observer of the unfolding events in Europe would find it interesting that questions of economics (taming sovereign debt without undermining economic growth), politics (possible models for enhancing fiscal supervision in the EU and enshrining this in primary law and further political union) and the price of the lack leadership (Europe's politicians have not acted promptly and decisively), have completely overshadowed what may be termed 'identity-talk'.

If in such periods of turbulence or, to use the institutionalist language, at such critical junctures (Hall and Taylor 1996; Steinmo, Thelen and Longstreth 1992), European identity appears to be almost irrelevant both to political protagonists and to ordinary people, the question that needs to be raised is whether it has ever really been relevant at all, notwithstanding its prominence on discursive agendas and in policy priorities at both the supranational and national levels since the late 1970s.[1] This question has important implications for the future, too, since any reappearance of identity narratives would not escape the critique that they may be just veneers seeking to mask or to promote certain political claims which may, in fact, be unrelated to identity issues.

The relevance of European identity is my main focus in this chapter. True, readers may find my quest for the explication of the role and political functionality of European identity deeply problematic. While the latter would be understandable given the innumerable pronouncements that have been made as well as the efforts, policies, discourses and research programmes that have been devoted to it during the last two decades, critics would hopefully agree with me that this question has not been asked very often and that the absence of European identity claims in the present era is puzzling. In this respect, it may be interesting to go beyond questions such as 'What is Europe's identity?' or 'How can a European identity be more than a thin overlay of deeply rooted national identities?' or 'What is the meaning of European identity?', and to instead examine why political arguments are framed in ways that prioritize European identity at time *t*, while disregarding it at *t*+1. In other words, what does 'European identity' do when it is invoked and validated by certain political actors or forces at a certain historical and political conjuncture?

Before proceeding to address these questions, it should be stated at the outset that I distinguish between subjective identifications with the EU, which are invariably evolving and shifting in the same way that any personal self-identification evolves, changes and develops in response to events and the external environment (the personal world), and the collective

1 The concept of identity appears in social science in the second half of the twentieth century. Its appeal has much to do with Erik Erikson and Fromm's psychoanalytic work on individual personality. Erikson was concerned about the crises of 'personal identity' in the post-Second World War era and influenced by Freudian ideas and cultural anthropology which became entangled with American national policy in the 1950s and 1960s and the development of 'area studies', designed to map the 'national character' of countries, in American universities. For a wonderful explication of the origins of 'identity' and 'identity theory', see Mackenzie (1978).

'projects' about European identity formation that have public and institutional manifestations and political consequences (the political world). The subsequent discussion centres on the latter, thereby leaving room for perceptions about 'Europe', in general, or the European Union, in particular, to exist freely as states of mind and for individuals to weave their personal stories and identifications concerning fellow Europeans or the European institutional configurations without any impediment. Subjective identification with Europe is thus disentangled from public narratives and political claims relating to European identity and projects for Europe or the member states in this chapter.[2]

The subsequent discussion explores the above-mentioned questions on the basis of five steps. First, I examine the dichotomy of national identities and European identity that has dominated the academic literature and the public agenda in an attempt to uncover the political functions of this dichotomy. I question whether the conditions are right for the possible emergence of a European identity given that the view that the EU allegedly lacks the homogenizing elements that have underpinned the formation of national identities has been in the main a 'home-made' (i.e. member state) distinction. Accordingly, it projects concerns and political arguments existing in the member states. Secondly, I discuss ways of conceptualizing the EU and the possible types of European identity. This discussion leads me to argue that the relation between national identities and European identity is not conditioned by the identifiable qualities or meanings entailed by these two distinct entities, as is often assumed in the literature, but by discursive constellations which are time and space specific. In other words, contradictory or symbiotic relations are projections of specific discursive articulations (Step 3). This is attested by the Eurozone turbulence and the present constellation (Step 4). If European identity, as produced in and by historically specific articulations for certain political purposes and functions, should be the main focus of our attention, then

2 Margaret Somers (1994) has distinguished between public narratives and self-understandings that are shaped by stories that may or may not be shared.

the question is what is left, if anything, of European identity. This question is examined in the last section of the chapter.

## Step 1: On Identity Games, Politics and Imperfect Equilibria

Having set out the foundations and the regulative framework for the common market and against the background of political battles and the demise of the Bretton Woods system in 1971, the European Community was searching for a new vision in the 1970s. A narrative on European identity seemed to be the missing ingredient that could reinvigorate European integration by eliciting people's interest in and support for European affairs. The Werner Report on European Monetary Union in 1970, and the launch of European Political Cooperation in the same year, had provided impetus to the political development of the Community, but the latter process, unavoidably, needed 'Europeans', too. And 'Europeans' would only lend support to the political development of the Community if 'market Europe' became transformed into 'a people's Europe' (Kostakopoulou 2001). Accordingly, the 1973 Copenhagen Summit furnished a Declaration on European Identity which was to be built by coordinated action, both internally and externally. The internal face of European identity required a predominantly political public narrative which would champion critical legal and political principles, such as respect for the rule of law, social justice, human rights and democracy, as well as the award of special rights for Community citizens, while the external one would highlight the role and responsibilities of the nine member states vis-à-vis the rest of the world.[3] In December 1974, the Paris Summit Conference endorsed the declaration and laid down the foundations for direct elections to the European Parliament and the incremental development of a citizens' Europe. Leo Tindemans, the Belgian Prime Minister, who was instructed by the Paris

3 Annex 2 to Chapter II, 7th General Report EC, 1973.

conference to articulate concrete proposals for strengthening citizens' rights, produced a report which advocated the protection of fundamental rights in the EU, consumer rights for European citizens and the protection of the environment. The establishment of common European rights would bring 'European close to its citizens' and create a feeling of identification with the Union as a whole, in order to make 'a people's Europe' a reality.

Nevertheless, Tindemans' report did not capture the national executives' political imagination, its recommendations did not have sharp edges; they merely furnished the basis for a soft identification with the EU. The proposed reforms cannot be viewed as undermining the national frames of reference or threatening the member states' sovereign powers in the fields of citizenship and migration regulation, thereby upsetting their categorizations and established identities. Unlike the Tindemans report, however, the Commission's invocation of the concept of 'a passport Union' in its report on 'Towards European Citizenship' (1975), which included the adoption of a uniform passport, harmonization of the rules affecting aliens and the abolition of controls at internal frontiers, entailed the prospect of changing radically political realities, framing perceptions and shaping citizens' orientations.[4] The replacement of national passports by a uniform passport was seen by Community institutions as establishing a definite connection between individual Europeans with the Community and ensuring equality of treatment for all passport holders by non-member countries, irrespective of their nationality. But member states detected in this proposal the questioning of their powers of categorization of the population under their jurisdiction. And by 'confirming the Community as an entity vis-à-vis the rest of the world' and eliciting popular feeling of belonging to that entity, it appeared to clash with national identities and feelings of belonging to distinct nation states.

Further reforms at the turn of that decade, such as the first direct elections to the European Parliament in 1979,[5] the introduction of the uniform passport in 1981, the prospect of the abolition of internal fron-

4 Bulletin EC, Supplement 7/1975.

5 *Official Journal of the European Communities*, 278, 8 October 1977.

tier controls coupled with the Commission's draft directive on residence of Community nationals in the territory of host member states in 1979, and its proposal to grant local electoral rights to Community nationals residing in host member states,[6] appear to recast established conceptions of community membership and intra-Community migration away from the member states' classificatory and regulatory matrix.[7] The discourse of European identity served to legitimize such developments in the same way that the discourse on national identity had served to legitimize state-building in the previous century. Community officials tapped into historical processes of state-building and sought to utilize the symbolisms and 'consciousness raising' initiatives (such as a European flag, a European anthem, stamps and so on) that had accompanied the formation of nation states (Kostakopoulou 2001: 44–7). By borrowing existing tools, resources and established mythomoteurs, they foreclosed the possibility of innovative solutions and pre-empted antagonistic reactions by the member states.

The member states opposed the relaxation of the national citizenship requirement for franchise in the 1970s, thereby forcing the Commission to shift its attention from political rights to establishing local consultative councils for migrant workers in the host member states. And, in the mid-1980s, although, in addition to local electoral rights, the Adonnino Report[8] explicitly recommended voting rights at European Parliament elections in the member state of residence as well as a number of other reforms designed to strengthen citizens' involvement in and identification with the Community, the member states continued to remain unconvinced. Yet, the 'people's Europe' problematique was gaining momentum and the absence of progress in the grant of special rights to mobile Community citizens was seen to undermine attempts to construct a European identity by making European decisions and affairs relevant to the lives of ordinary Europeans and the developing practice of European citizenship (Wiener 1998).

6 Bulletin EC, 10/1972.

7 The latter term is borrowed from Brubaker (2010).

8 Pietro Adonnino chaired the ad hoc Committee for a People's Europe in line with the mandate given to it by the Fontainebleau Council in 1984.

The narrative about the formation of European identity and the political reforms that sustained it clearly created interference patterns in national executives' regulatory and governmental powers. They also threatened to superimpose a different notion of citizenship upon the prevailing notion of national citizenship, since in the 1970s and 1980s Commission officials did not merely see the emerging notion of Community citizenship to be simply additional to national citizenship but envisaged that the latter would eventually become subordinate to the former.[9] The gestures towards the creation of a soft identification with the EU were gradually seen to implicate a harder European identification narrative which would have an internally equalizing effect since Community nationals would be assimilated to state nationals and enjoy complete equality of treatment and a coercive external categorization.

The Draft Treaty on the European Union (DTEU) proposed by the European Parliament in 1984 echoed Spinelli's belief that the Second World War had reduced 'the habitual respect of citizens for their states and their myths and opened the way to the united European transformation' (Spinelli cited in Maas 2007: 120) and recommended the formal establishment of European Union citizenship conditioned on the possession of member-state citizenship. Although the draft treaty did not have a formal institutional impact in the sense of its provisions finding their way into the concrete articles of the Single European Act, it did, however, provide important normative and ideational resources which would be utilized at Maastricht and beyond. In fact, it may be argued that the DTEU's provisions on Union citizenship, the Adonnino Committee's work[10] coupled with the Commission's determination to expand the personal scope of free movement beyond active economic actors, which was also reflected in the 1985 Paper on Completing the Internal Market,[11] and the formal adoption of the three 1990 Residence Directives (on students, pensioners and self-sufficient European citizens provided that they had medical

9 Bulletin EC, 12/1972, point 1104; Bulletin EC, Supplement 7/1975.

10 Bulletin EC, Supplement 7/1985, pp. 9–14.

11 COM(85)310.

insurance and sufficient means so as to avoid becoming a burden on the welfare system of the host state),[12] led to the constitutional framework on Union citizenship at Maastricht. And although the European citizenship discourse had somewhat subsumed the European identity narrative in the late 1980s, with emphasis placed on citizens as participants in politics at Community and national levels, the latter was resurrected in the early 1990s as national delegations were justifying their approval of Union citizenship on the grounds that it would enhance feelings of belonging to a single entity (Maas 2007: 47–8), thereby enhancing the creation of a citizens' Europe.

The Maastricht Treaty gave constitutional status to Union citizenship by pronouncing 'every person holding the nationality of a member state a citizen of the Union' and supplementing the pre-existing Community rights to free movement and residence (Article 8a EC) with local and EP electoral rights in the member state of residence, consular and diplomatic protection when travelling abroad and non-judicial means of redress, such as the right to petition the European Parliament and to apply to the Ombudsman. It is true that the Maastricht framework included a limited set of rights and many of the Commission's proposals were omitted from the final text. It is also true that the normative potential of Union citizenship was not fully appreciated at that time. Its predominant concerns were about making Europe a tangible reality in the lives of European citizens and thereby increasing the Union's social legitimacy by promoting identification with it as well as addressing its democratic deficit. Indeed, the Commission successfully linked the progressive implementation of the citizenship agenda with the enhancement of democracy in the EU, which would in turn lead to the reinforcement of the political dimension of the Union, while national executives preferred to view 'Europeanness' or European identity as a key

12 Directives 90/364, 90/365 and 90/366, which were replaced by Directive 93/96. The European Parliament and Council Directive of 29 April 2004 *on the right of citizens of the Union and their Family Members to move and reside freely within the territory of the Member States* (2004/38/EC), which repeals the above mentioned Directives, introduces three separate categories of residence rights and establishes an unqualified right of permanent residence after five years of continuous legal residence in the host Member State (OJ L 158/77, 30 April 2004).

step towards a more coordinated foreign policy.[13] However, European identity politics was not wholly subsumed by the discourse on democratic participation and the social legitimacy deficit of the EU.[14]

## Step 2: Point, Counterpoint

The establishment of the new institution of Union citizenship gave rise to the prospect of the dilution of national citizenship and fears about divided loyalties and allegiances in some national arenas. While the Commission and the European Parliament welcomed innovative templates on citizenship and membership which superseded troubled national pasts and national loyalties and granted non-national EU citizens political rights in national arenas, certain member states were concerned about what they saw as the narrowing of the parameters of national states' policy choices. This was the case in spite of the fact that the Maastricht Treaty explicitly affirmed that the Union is obligated to 'respect the national identities of its Member States, whose systems of government are founded on the principles of democracy' (F.1 TEU) and must contribute to the flowering of the cultures of the member states while also respecting their national and regional diversity (Article 128 EC) at that time. Similarly, in an attempt to appease national sensitivities and anxieties, the Declaration on the Nationality of a member state, annexed to the Final Act of the Treaty on European Union, expressly stated that 'the question [of] whether an individual possesses the nationality of a Member State shall be settled solely by reference to the national law of the Member State concerned'. Similar declarations were adopted by

13 See the TEU's Preamblic reference (9) to 'reinforcing European Identity' in the context of defence policy.

14 Compare Wiener's (1998: 295) insight that the citizenship discourse in the early 1990s showed that 'the focus shifted from creating a feeling of belonging to establishing the legal ties of belonging'.

the European Council at Edinburgh and Birmingham. The Birmingham declaration confirmed that, in the eyes of national executives, Union citizenship constitutes an additional tier of rights and protection which is not intended to replace national citizenship – a position that found concrete expression in the amended Article 17(1) at Amsterdam.[15]

Notwithstanding these pronouncements about the 'added value' and enriching character of EU citizenship, however, the promise of constructive politics entailed by Union citizenship unsettled national political actors. Denmark decided to opt out of the TEU's Union citizenship provisions, stating that 'nothing in the TEU implies or foresees an undertaking to create a citizenship of the Union in the sense of citizenship of the nation-state. The question of Denmark participating in such a development does, therefore, not arise'.[16]

On the discursive chessboard of the 1990s, European citizenship and the construction of a European identity were not merely portrayed as 'dangerous supplements' (Kostakopoulou 1999), but also as part of 'either (European)/or (national)' dualisms. Although such a discursive articulation reflected nationalist preferences for overriding and undivided national-statist loyalties and deeply rooted state-centred identities which were resistant to change, it was, nevertheless, premised on questionable assumptions and politics as well as on misinformation about European developments. As we shall see below, it also foreclosed the promotion of more collaborative, open and inclusive practices of citizenship at both national and European levels in the 1990s. The new function of a reconstructed discourse about a super-added European identity, as a threat to national identities, was to shield domestic rules, policies and practices from unwanted change and to stifle a debate about their adaptation to new circumstances and developments (processes of Europeanization) by cultivating anti-European sentiments amongst the population.

15 Bulletin EC 10/1992. The Amsterdam Treaty added the statement that 'Union citizenship shall complement national citizenship' to Article 8(1) EC (Article 17(1) on renumbering).

16 Danish Declaration, OJ C348/4, 31 December 1994.

The national identity game unfolded in the 1990s and exhibited three distinct patterns: first, it was used to sustain implicitly or explicitly a reifying view of national identities and citizenship practices since it simply asserted their historicity, primacy and importance without mentioning their continuing change and adaptation to the realities of a globalized economy and a more mature and multifaceted European Union decision-making process. Second, it focused on the 'thingness' of national identities, that is, their existence and reification, and not on their substance, that is, their meaning and consistency, which are often quite difficult to define. Third, it served to reinforce the simplistic view of European integration as not only entailing the eventual demise of the state, which had to be resisted, thereby ignoring the complex realities of everyday permeation of European laws and judicial decisions into national arenas and multi-level governance, but also as deficient, since it lacked the 'ethnic mythomoteurs', that is, the myths, symbols, memories and tradition that had been instrumental to nation-state building (Smith 1981, 1986, 1991). The European identity/national identities dichotomy was thus a discursive articulation which moved progressively backwards and thrived on essentialism and the selective remembering of a past, thereby ultimately thwarting a debate about weaknesses in democratic representation, inclusive and equal political membership and citizenship policies at both the national and European levels. Oddly enough, the alleged clash of identities seemed to be mutually reinforcing of established nationalities at the domestic level and of the alignment of the novel institution of European Union citizenship to such standards of nationality, thus effecting no change to the cognitive template of citizenship-cum-nationality.

The flawed fiction about the opposition between a European identity and national identities was entirely 'home-made', that is, constructed in national arenas. English nationalism underpinned the Conservative Party's opposition to TEU's 'ever closer Union'; as Wallace (1995: 50) wrote, 'the Conservative Party's discourse is instinctively that of national identity'. British Eurosceptics argued that national sovereignty and identity had to be defended against a 'Federal Europe' seeking to undermine democracy and erode the sense of nationhood of the member states. Fears about the prospect of a European federation were also expressed in France, despite the fact that the two intergovernmental pillars of the Treaty on European Union confirmed the crucial role of the member states in determining the pace of the European integration process. To such fears, Hoffmann added the prospect of 'a Baroque or Gaudiesque construction, multilevel and multispeed, manipulated above all by Germany' (Hoffmann 1993).

Through such narratives member states sought to validate domestic arrangements, reassert statist power and galvanize popular opposition to 'Europe', thereby stifling political dynamics for change at the European and national levels. Realities such as 'system interaction' and 'system change' through the everyday processes of policy-making at European level, the European Court of Justice's expanding case law which ensured both the amplification of the four fundamental freedoms (free movement of goods, persons, services and capital) and the member states' implementation of Community legislation were conveniently ignored by circumstantialist political discourses. The terminology and symbols associated with a language of the past were used in order to reassert the nation state as a relevant organizational concept and to react against perceived threats of erosion of state power owing to the shift to qualified majority voting in certain areas, the increase in the competences of the EU, the establishment of EU citizenship and the abolition of internal border controls. National identity-talk invoked unspoken assumptions and qualities that were meant to merit our automatic approval thereby transfiguring issues and developments into matters of survival of 'what we hold dear'.

Academic writing at that time seemed to lend support to such narratives either by positing system effectiveness at the European level as being antithetical to democracy which was aligned to national governance in a perfect and unquestionable way (Dahl 1994: 23), or by pointing to the absence of a 'European demos' that would sustain the construction of a European polity (Weiler 1991) and the embryonic stage of a European public sphere and lack of the deeply rooted myths and memories required for the formation of collective identities. By pinpointing the 'impossibility' of constructing the European Union polity and the improbability of generating a sense of pride, trust and a shared identity amongst the peoples of Europe, they sought to highlight the validating logic of statism, thus reaffirming the homogenizing impulses of national identities and providing self-justificatory strategies for ideological and political positions. The issue of national identity and its continued survival in light of the trends towards greater and deeper integration and globalization became the foreground for the generation of interests and political claims, while in reality the maintenance of these interests and claims was the reason for the appearance of the national identity discourse and the alleged threat that a singular 'Europe' posed. The success of this narrative hinged on its ability to project national identity as the main reason for national worries and concerns – as opposed to a veneer camouflaging vested interests. This was a clever move since the main focus would have to be on understanding and taking into account identity issues and not on analysing the deeper interests and the political claims involved in 'national-identity talk'. Accordingly, the desired resolution would have to be based on an acknowledgement by European officials of the resilience of national identities and on less 'Europe', in the sense of a less active Commission and a less active court (Horvath 2008: 78–82). By starting from an a priori assumption about deep-rooted national identities that provided the ultimate locus of political authority, the home-made dualism between national and European identities thus obtained a symbolic force that therefore precluded an engagement between the democratic credentials of the forces invoking it and the substantive merits of their claims.

## Step 3: Disconnecting the Dots

The oppositional discourse on identities was underpinned by two tactics, namely, treating identities, be they national or European, as unified concepts and simplifying what such categories might stand for. In this respect, they left very little room for individuals' multiple identifications or the shifting meaning and importance that each of them might acquire in certain contexts. Reflecting the ideology of nationalism, national identities were depicted as unambiguous, integrated, monistic and overarching, thereby overlooking the shared interests that might exist amongst citizens belonging to different countries with respect to certain issues as well as individuals' propensity to prioritize an identity other than their national one in certain situations. The abstraction of the nation could not accommodate multiple identifications and the individual's freedom to shift in and out of subject positions and to call upon different identity options in different contexts for different purposes (Wallman 1983: 70). Yet people cultivate affinities and identify with groups, communities and organizations which extend beyond and across state borders and it is this journeying in multiple worlds that makes us who we are and creates political options for us. In other words, 'I' is the product of many 'We's' (Mackenzie 1978), and a given political identity is simply one narrative to realize a sense of common purpose.

Interestingly, the fixity, monism and inflexibility characterizing national identities were also grafted onto the European level without any attempt to rethink and adjust the theory of identity to the institutional peculiarities of the Union and the historical as well as political indeterminacy of Europe. As regards the latter, a cursory look at the literature can reveal the many 'faces' of Europe or the many 'Europes' within Europe: the Europe of Greek mythology, the Hellenistic Europe, the Roman Europe, the mediaeval Europe, the Christian Europe, the Europe of Enlightenment, the Colonial Europe, the racialist Europe, the capitalist Europe, the 'kidnapped' Europe (Kundera 1984), the brainwashed Europe which was able to redeem its cultural identity after the fall of communism, and so on. Indeed, all the above narratives circulated in the public space in the later 1980s and 1990s. In addition, right-wing discourses have always appealed to a selective 'European heritage' and have ignited racism and xenophobia by culture-baiting ethnic and religious minorities as 'others' and threats to the alleged relative ethnocultural homogeneity of Europe. Indeed, GRECE (Groupement de recherche et d'études pour la civilisation européenne), the cultural wing of the French 'New Right', sought to empty Europe of the 'Judeo-Christian elements of egalitarianism' and notions of humanism and universalism in an attempt to revive an 'original' European identity which would not incorporate the European Union's migrant and multicultural population (Kostakopoulou 2001: 26–7).

As regards the institutional peculiarities of the European Union, Habermas (1992a, 1992b) identified the possibility of severing ethnos and demos and fashioning a political identity at the European Union level which would promote the flourishing of equally legitimate cultural forms of life. On this account, democratic citizenship would be the integrating device of the new polity and the foundation for the formation of a European public sphere that would be separate from the national spheres. Constitutional patriotism would thus complement national patriotism without displacing it. Weiler (1997) and Bellamy and Castiglione (1997) articulated variants of the Habermasian approach, seeking to accommodate 'non-rational political loyalties' that exist at national level and to gradually correct them. In addition to a 'corrective European identity', functional and constructive European identity options emerged as candidates for the formation of a European political identity within a system of nested and interacting tiers of governance. By creating a diverse map of European identity pathways, the above accounts showed that Eurosceptic discourses about the incompatibility between national and European identities completely concealed what has always been so, that is, the reality of multiple identities, and what might have been, the symbiosis amongst identities.

The discussion thus far has sought to sketch out the multiple games implicated in the invocation of a European identity for more than three decades and the modalities of power involved. One cannot but be impressed by the variety and diversity of the political configurations of European identity and the political strategies underpinning them. Although it has not been my intention to construct an all-encompassing theory of European identity that would account for all of them, the discussion has intimated that we need a more thorough investigation of the various uses of European identity or of the politics of 'European identity' talk.

In this respect, it would be incorrect to view European identity as antithetical to national identities. For such an opposition, i.e. an either/or dualism, is not the by-product of a relation amongst two distinct entities having their own intrinsic qualities and differing implications, but the artificial projection of a process as well as a context seeking to justify certain political claims and arguments by depicting them as antithetical. Crucially, as the discussion has unfolded, this process and the context on which it is based were conditioned by the time and the discursive games played by political actors. And discursive games at any given time are a function of circumstances, perceptions, information and prevailing political interests. It is thus the constellation of time, space and discourse within which nodes of power operate that determine both European identity and national identity 'talks'. One could easily envisage a different constellation of time, space and discourse in which the same relation (European and national identities) could be depicted quite differently or could even be seen to be of no relevance at all. Hierarchies of power or forces of antipower may or may not have an interest in making 'identity' a central issue or in combining identities in so many different ways that enhance the pluralization of individuals' energies and their channelling into processes of democratic transformation.

## Step 4: Instability in the Eurozone

We have seen that the dualism between a European identity (A) and national identities (B) was not essentially an issue of the relation between A and B, since A and B as well as their relation (AB) were projections of context C which infused them with particular meanings designed to justify political claims and/or to motivate or limit political action. This process has been time bound; it is the political context in time *t* that gives A and B, as well as AB, their specific meanings and fixes their relation. For it is plausible that in time *t*+1, the same relation which was depicted as antithetical (A*v*B) could be perceived to be symbiotic (AB) or could even be downgraded to an unproblematic or irrelevant relation (-AB). By choosing the Eurozone crisis as the crucial *t*+1 moment, I wish to reveal the contingency, artificiality and inherent limitations of claims concerning identity and thus the unavoidable plasticity (Unger 1987) characterizing all political contexts and discursive configurations.[17]

Interestingly, one would have expected a proliferation of identity claims in a period such as this which requires sacrifices on the part of some members for the interest of the whole; after all, identification with a polity, be it at a national or a European level, is meant to elicit popular support in times of crisis. In this absence of sustained attention to European identity and its relation to national identities since 2009, I discern not only the artificiality of the debate on national identities and European identity, but also the possibility of less ideological politics sustained by the realization that what was taken for granted in the past was the by-product of a set of historically situated political choices and a circumstantialist environment that was receptive to such choices.[18]

It is noteworthy that when the extent of Greece's debt exposure was revealed and austerity measures contemplated, the population did not feel the pull of national identity in order to rally behind the government. Instead, discord, narrow party-political interests, opportunistic agendas by party leaders and strategies of blame attribution and shifting predominated. Indeed, events not only in Greece, but also in Spain, Portugal and Italy during the last two years have shown that the presence of an allegedly strong sense of collective identity does by no means make people less critical of the status quo and more willing to support it in times of crisis. National identities have little to offer when it comes to concrete and acute economic

17 Rogers Brubaker and Frederick Cooper (2000) have sketched the emergence of the identity focus in the academic literature in the early 1950 and its proliferation in the 1970s and 1980s following the turbulence of the 1960s and the weakness of class politics in the USA. In addition, see Ely (1997). Also, Gleason (1983) has noted that the 1930s *Encyclopedia of Social Sciences* (New York: Macmillan, 1930–1935) did not have an entry on identity, but the 1968 *International Encyclopedia of the Social Sciences* (New York: Macmillan, 1968) did have one on 'identity, psychosocial', written by Eric Erikson.

18 My argument here differs from path-dependent theories which see present outcomes and developmental paths as the product of past choices and decisions taken at critical junctures that shape the contours of future developments. For a more detailed discussion, see Pierson (2000) and Thelen (1999).

problems. While populist forces may seek to exploit the former in order to mobilize the people against the EU, there is a widespread acceptance that the sovereign debt problem is 'home-created' and that their governments would still have to put their own economic affairs in order, whether the country is within or outside of the Eurozone.

Similarly, high levels of 'Europeanness' in specific countries provide little guidance in terms of predicting whether a particular country will welcome a fiscal Union or be prepared to grant bailout packages to its debt-ridden European neighbours. This is not only because people's subjective identifications fluctuate so unpredictably that being a winner or a loser at time *t* provides almost no guarantee that one will display a positive or negative attitude towards European integration at time *t*+1 (Kostakopoulou 2011). It is also due to the fact that valuations change, identifications evolve and even fade away, and this is the result of a range of endogenous as well as exogenous factors. This is, perhaps, one of the important lessons we have learnt from the sovereign debt crisis in the Eurozone area. Despite being winners, German citizens did not welcome further bailout packages in the Eurozone or the French proposals for a closer economic union, with a centralized authority coordinating taxation and expenditure, even though they are aware of the severe economic – as well as political – costs associated with either the collapse of the euro or the fragmentation of the Eurozone (Fleming 2011: 39).

Similarly, the EU has finally embarked upon a closer economic and fiscal union because this is seen to be the only credible option to solve the economic crisis in an effective way and to avert a euro collapse that would endanger European integration in its entirety. In a speech delivered on 28 November 2011, the Polish Foreign Minister, Radoslaw Sikorski, reminded Germany that it has been the biggest beneficiary of the single currency and thus has a responsibility to display leadership in resolving the crisis (Sikorski cited in Cavendish 2011: 35). Accordingly, not only does the sovereign debt crisis make notions of national or European identity less relevant, it also shows that 'Europeanness', indexes of Europe's populations, may have very little to offer in particular settings which require concrete measures, imaginative solutions and credible policy ideas in order to respond to crises effectively. In such circumstances, people's loyalty cannot be assumed; it has to be earned by political leaders. And trust in politicians, institutions, systems, be they political or economic, is not an objective quality brought about as a result of the tag of nationality we all carry, but it has to be cultivated, nurtured and sustained through the adoption of the right policies, credible attempts to root out systemic problems, corruption and irresponsible spending, and the avoidance of inefficient policy-making decisions. As the details of the new European fiscal contract are being negotiated, 'Europe' has finally come once again to the 'rescue' of the state (Milward 1992), that is, of its solvent and financially undisciplined members. Seen from this perspective, further and closer European integration does not appear to be consonant with winning 'game, set, and match' for either national identities or a European identity, but with the very preservation of a political experiment that enables such identifications to be invoked and reconstructed, to circulate, flow and to interact.

The present economic crisis thus exposes the fallacy of a normative commitment to identity as an end goal that holds state polities together or the glue that will unite the European Union. It also demonstrates the optionalist or circumstantialist character of invocations of identity, be it national or European. For instance, UK Prime Minister David Cameron's decision to shield the city of London from the unwanted European financial transaction tax can hardly be amenable to claims about a shared national identity, given popular discontent about the banking elite that is held responsible for the 2008 economic crisis and Britain's public sector debt. At the same time, a European identity cannot be mobilized at a time when Europe has been so deeply divided about identifying comprehensive solutions to the economic crisis, be they permanent rescue funds and the issuing of joint Eurobonds or measures to regain market confidence, as well as the institutional pathways of implementing them. At the present conjuncture, therefore, national identities cannot be mobilized to construct subjects and/or electors for states. Nor can European identity be utilized in order to prop up the euro. Political elites can derive neither arguments nor answers from them that suit them. They know this as well as that European publics are in an anti-'politics as usual' mood.

## Step 5: What is Left of European Identity? Mapping Possibilities

Identities, be they personal or collective, are stories, that is, narrative constructions which enable us not only to make sense of our existence within, and entanglement with, particular social worlds but also to take part in them as political actors as well as subjects. They are thus necessarily situated in time; they belong to time and are subject to the waves of change. Constructivist perspectives have convincingly demonstrated that, contrary to primordialist and ethnocultural accounts of nationalism, national identities are not expressions of timeless essences (Anderson 1983). Being historically conditioned, but also constructed, narrated and reinterpreted in myriad ways, identities are infinitely plural and complex. The same realization should accompany the examination of their relations (which often take the form of oppositions) to other identities, be they subnational or European. This relation, too, is the product of political imagination and history and is thus subject to differing articulations and interpretations. In this respect, it is important to refrain from bracketing identity issues from the historically specific political context and ideological tableau within which political actors invoking them act. Seeking to find ontological realities would not be a wise pursuit. The same applies with respect to European identity, and the discussion above charted its emergence and evolution during almost three decades (1970–95) as well as its fading in the era of the sovereign debt crisis. National and European identity constructions have an almost fractal quality and are made salient or less relevant depending on the political context, while claims about clashing identity dualisms being seemingly more prescient than games of simplification can camouflage political claims and assumptions. Therefore the question that needs to be addressed at this point is: what is left of European identity? Should we abandon it as a concept and category of analysis? Or could it be utilized in progressive ways to foster or accentuate political developments in the European Union that enhance human welfare?

Evidently, the above question refers to European identity as a collective narrative. For individuals in the EU remain free to use it as subjective identification which could be made to fit with so many rich, complex and diverse personal experiences. It is thus bound to remain a floating resource entering individuals' lives intentionally or unexpectedly, being subject to cultural or political articulations and rearticulations, being invoked and then set aside as individuals shift in and out of environments in time-specific contexts. In this evolving narrative cycle of self-identification, a European identity can still have an important role to play. But recognizing our freedom to 'draw', 'construct', 'represent' and 'imagine' the world we call 'our own', to choose to remember, champion, forget or make irrelevant our connections with the European space does not give us the licence to worship essentialist constructions of European identity and false dualisms. Subjectivized narratives must be ethical. Individuals have an ethical duty to refrain from severing the European space from the world and the values of humanism by closing off connections, cultivating resentment and hatred towards the other and erecting arbitrary boundaries amongst different nationalities, religions, races and ethnic origins. More importantly, we need to show our distaste and objections to racialist, exclusivist and homophobic notions of European identity which clearly forget that 'creating an ever closer Union amongst the peoples of Europe' has been a project in healing Europe from the evils of cruelty, war and inhumanity, imagining a better world and making it possible since the very beginning.

But what could it be said about European identity as a collective story? Could it be used as the basis of social and political action? Could it nurture progressive collective self-understandings? Or should it be made an appendix? I would argue that an acknowledgement of political uses of European identity does not necessarily make European identity obsolete. It may well provide an argument for less identity-centred politics, but still leaves enough room for identity narratives in politics. In my earlier work I have defended a constructivist option of European identity nourished by an inclusive European Union citizenship and an open and principled European migration and asylum policy. Such a mode of European identity does not rely on hegemonic 'identifiers', that is, political units categorizing, distinguishing and positioning 'ins' and 'outs', but emerges as a result of the institutional openings it creates and the empowering trajectories for co-creating social life it gives rise to. By resisting fixed and essentialist readings, European identity becomes the pure locus of the possible; that is, of writing a different future, opening up opportunities for institutional arrangements that enhance freedom and equality, creating opportunities for new and more enriched life experiences and encouraging multifarious connections amongst peoples and collectivities. European identity could thus be seen as the space of political possibility. A space that is sustained by subversive memory, hope, and a willingness to find solutions to common problems that exist and emerge unpredictably from within as well as from a rapidly changing and volatile external environment. Unlike national narratives, which can only make national identities credible, unified and homogeneous by bracketing the violence associated with the historical matrix that shaped the formation of the nation state and socializing citizens into similar acts of forgetting, European identity relies on memories and the remembrance of the human suffering that has accompanied its past. In this sense, a collective European identity can only be an actionist and subversive identity. By the latter, I mean an identity that utilizes the memories of the past in order to push a vision for humanity forward and that gives freedom to believe that another world is possible. And by constantly reminding us that polities can be built by design and dissimilarity with state formations, that political realities are changed, changing and changeable and that it is possible to transgress the boundaries that have made and make national identities not only visible but also singular and exclusive, it opens up possibilities for modifications in institutions, policies and cultures and for alternatives. In this account, European identity can only be experimental, transformative, enigmatic, diffuse, fluid, transitional and ambivalent. Should this fill us with trepidation? I do not believe so. As Berger, Berger and Kellner observed in 1974 with respect to a different context, 'stable identities (and this also means identities that will be subjectively plausible) can only emerge in reciprocity with stable contexts (and this means contexts that are structured by stable institutions)'. But, as we all know, stability is simply an illusion.

## References

Anderson, B. (1983). *Imagined Communities*. London: Verso.

Bellamy, R., and Castiglione, D. (eds) (1997). *Constitutionalism, Democracy and Sovereignty: American and European Perspectives*. Aldershot: Avebury.

Berger, P. L., Berger, B., and Kellner, H. (1974). *The Homeless Mind: Modernization and Consciousness*. Harmondsworth: Penguin Books.

Brubaker, R. (2010). 'Migration, Membership, and the Modern Nation-State: Internal and External Dimensions of the Politics of Belonging', *Journal of Interdisciplinary History*, XLI (I), 61–78.

Brubaker, R., and Cooper, F. (2000). 'Beyond Identity', *Theory and Society*, 29 (1), 1–47.

Cavendish, C. (2011). 'We're Crippled by a Risk We Can't Even Quantify', *The Times*, 1 December, p. 35.

Dahl, R. (1994). 'A Democratic Dilemma: System Effectiveness versus Citizen Participation', *Political Science Quarterly*, 109 (1), 23–34.

Ely, J. D. (1997). 'Community and the Politics of Identity: Toward the Genealogy of a Nation-State Concept', *Stanford Humanities Review*, 5 (2), 70–95.

Fleming, S. (2011). 'The Devastating Price of Pulling Out of the Euro', *The Times*, 7 September, p. 39.

Gleason, P. (1983). 'Identifying Identity: A Semantic History', *Journal of American History*, 69 (4), 910–31.

Habermas, J. (1992a). 'Citizenship and National Identity: Some Reflections on the Future of Europe', *Praxis International*, 12 (1), 1–19.

—— (1992b). 'The European Nation-State', *Ratio Juris*, 9 (2), 125–37.

Hall, P. A., and Taylor, R. C. R. (1996). 'Political Science and the Three New Institutionalisms', *Political Studies*, 44 (4), 936–57.

Hoffmann, S. (1993). 'Thoughts on the French Nation Today', *Daedalus*, 122 (3), 63–79.

Horvath, E. (2008). *Mandating Identity: Citizenship, Kinship Laws and Plural Nationality in the European Union*, Alphen aan den Rijn: Kluwer.

Kostakopoulou, D. (1999). 'Nested "Old" and "New" Citizenships in the European Union: Bringing Forth the Complexity', *Columbia Journal of European Law*, 5 (3), 389–413.

—— (2001). *Citizenship, Identity and Immigration in the European Union: Between Past and Future*. Manchester: Manchester University Press.

—— (2011). 'On European Identity'. In R. Bellamy and U. Staiger (ed.), *EU Citizenship and the Market*, pp. 16–18. London: UCL.

Kundera, M. (1984). 'A Kidnapped West or Culture Bows Out', *Granta*, Issue 11, 92–122.

Maas, W. (2007). *Creating European Citizens*. Lanham, MD: Rowman & Littlefield.

Mackenzie, W. J. M. (1978). *Political Identity*. Harmondsworth: Penguin Books.

Milward, A. (1992). *The European Rescue of the Nation-State*. London: Routledge.

Pierson, P. (2000). 'The Limits of Design: Explaining Institutional Origins and Change', *Governance*, 13 (4), 474–99.

Smith, A. D. (1981). *The Ethnic Revival in the Modern World*. Cambridge: Cambridge University Press.

—— (1986). *The Ethnic Origins of Nations*. Oxford: Blackwell.

—— (1991). *National Identity*. Harmondsworth: Penguin Books.

Somers, M. R. (1994). 'The Narrative Constitution of Identity: A Relational and Network Approach', *Theory and Society*, 23 (5), 605–49.

Steinmo, S., Thelen, K., and Longstreth, F. (eds) (1992). *Structuring Politics: Historical Institutionalism in Comparative Analysis*. Cambridge: Cambridge University Press.

Thelen, K. (1999). 'Historical Institutionalism in Comparative Politics', *Annual Review of Political Science*, Issue 2, 369–404.

Unger, R. M. (1987). *Plasticity into Power: Comparative Historical Studies on the Institutional Conditions of Economic and Military Success*. Cambridge: Cambridge University Press.

Wallace, H. (1995). 'Britain Out on a Limb?', *Political Quarterly*, 66 (1), 47–58.

Wallman, S. (1983). 'Identity Options'. In C. Fried (ed.), *Minorities: Community and Identity*, pp. 69–78. New York: Springer Verlag.

Weiler, J. H. H. (1991). 'The Transformation of Europe', *Yale Law Journal*, 100 (8), 2403–83.

—— (1997). 'To be a European Citizen: Eros and Civilisation', *Journal of European Public Policy*, 4 (4), 495–519.

Wiener, A. (1998). *Building Institutions: The Developing Practice of European Citizenship*. Boulder, CO: Westview Press.

VICTOR M. OLIVIERI

# 8 The Trajectory and Political Implications of European Identity in a Time of Crisis

The unprecedented institutional development of the European Union (EU) has been accompanied by the equally rare formation of a common European identity, both as a central part of the European project and an emergent phenomenon amongst EU citizens experiencing the effects of higher social mobility. Although its origins can be traced to Greek antiquity, the contemporary form of European identity is unique in the sense that it incorporates, complements and competes with well-established aspects of 'traditional' national and regional identities in a supranational *sui generis* sense. Our unfamiliarity with European identity has unfortunately resulted in the reapplication of conceptualizations and instruments of measurement previously deployed to assess more 'traditional' identity politics at the state level. Just as the ambiguous institutional form of the EU suffers from a lack of familiarity with more 'traditional' forms of political organization and it is often treated as a federal system while others see it as a supranational state or international organization, a strange hybrid creature in motion (McAllister 1997: 7–8), political scientists are also not quite sure how to treat this 'new' European identity. The intertwined futures of European identity and the European project seem uncertain in the midst of a Eurozone crisis, a resurgence of right-wing extremism, and the ongoing call by nationalistic movements for further fragmentation of the nation state. However, much of that uncertainty extends from our unfamiliarity with European identity and its effects on political behaviour.

Although the future of the EU receives considerable scholarly attention from a multitude of viewpoints and approaches, this chapter focuses on European identity from the bottom up, using horizontal interactions at the individual level, in an attempt to highlight aspects of European identity often overlooked, introduce a different 'creature' of sorts in European society, and shed some light on the possible future of the EU. Despite scholarly interest in the role European identity plays in European integration and the national politics of EU member and candidate states, there has been little ethnographic work exploring the individual-level factors leading to variation in the degree of and affinity for European identity. Forms of collective identity have been shown to be a major factor in determining political behaviour, support and participation in EU member states (Carey 2002; Fowler and Kam 2007; Hooghe and Marks 2004; Laffan 1996; McDonough 1995), but European identity remains an elusive concept for political scientists.

The EU is a strange creature by virtue of our unfamiliarity with its institutions. It is a 'work in progress' on account of its embryonic nascent stage and unknown trajectory. European society is also on a trajectory of sorts towards the unknown. It is difficult to establish 'where' it is heading because there are many competing views and actors involved. There is, however, an *emergent behaviour* in European society that follows simple individual rules of alignment, separation and cohesion to avoid conflict between individuals while maintaining the group. These simple rules create complex individual interactions but maintain the group 'on course'. This 'strange creature' operates through individualistic as well as group logics to resemble the behaviour of a flock of birds. The process of migration in this case is the departure from 'traditional' identities at the state level towards a 'new' supranational European identity.

The analogy of European society as a flock of birds is particularly useful in illustrating the findings from my cross-regional ethnographic study between Spanish autonomous communities and countries of the United Kingdom (UK). Likewise, it offers commentary on the methodology used up to this point to assess European identity and its effects on political behaviour: understanding the probabilistic actions of the individual does not explain the flock. This chapter aims to provide a small glimpse into the future of European identity by combining these two strands of analysis to highlight the following findings:

(1) States formed under the rhetoric of the nation state maintain a hegemonic discourse of exclusion and homogenization that securitizes policies concerning ethnic minorities and migrants;
(2) Stateless nations circumvent the state through more inclusive discourses and policies that seek to establish a heterogeneous nation, partly in response to the nation state and partly for the sake of their self-realization as nations;
(3) While both states and stateless nations are becoming more inclusivist, even mutually inclusive, they are moving towards inclusiveness at different speeds at regional and national levels;
(4) The overall trajectory of European society is towards more inclusion, or what one could consider a more European identity, but there are dynamic and imperfect processes that do not always overlap neatly.

The following section briefly summarizes the study of European identity. Its purpose is to provide a background of how and why European identity is viewed as it is today and why a different approach was needed to gain a better understanding. Ultimately, the section will serve as a simple reference point. Flocks travel from one place to another and we must understand where it is headed and, perhaps more importantly, why it is headed there.

## The 'Beginning' of European Identity

Contemporary inquiry into the formation of European identity began in the late 1950s with the arrival of three broad-scale 'grand theories' of European integration: transactionalism, neo-functionalism, and intergovernmentalism. The first major project was *Political Community and the North Atlantic Area* (Deutsch *et al.* 1957), which focused on 'international community' formation through the analysis of ten historical cases and posited Deutsch's notion of 'transactionalism'. Transactionalism argued that

European integration resulted from the interconnectedness produced by the flow of goods, services and people. Deutsch measured mutual sympathies amongst European individuals through survey data as dependent on transaction levels. He found that greater assimilation of individuals into an interconnected common social space increased the prospects of community formation – thus political integration. Reducing his findings to the bare minimum: greater numbers of transactions result in greater 'we-feeling'. The second integrationist project arrived with Ernst Haas's *The Uniting of Europe*, arguing a spontaneous functional 'spillover' would occur due to the cooperation and social integration of technocrats into increasingly political realms (1958). Haas derived four general factors leading to European integration through spillover: well-developed central institutions capable of implementing and lobbying for integration; elite activation around those central institutions; the acceptance and promotion of 'inherently expansive tasks' leading to a cascade of spillover effects from initial to later steps; and the 'continuity of national policy aims' (Lindberg 1963: 7–12). Haas's neofunctional approach to European integration, claiming the primacy of states and their national experiences is instrumental in European integration, became an influential political science research programme in the 1960s by being able to provide explanations of significant developments within Europe (such as Charles de Gaulle's refusal to tolerate further integrative steps laid out in the Treaty of Rome). The third integrationist project was Stanley Hoffmann's 'intergovernmentalism', which provided a major alternative to neo-functionalism by arguing that integration could proceed only as far and as fast as national governments wanted to work together, since national interests would always have primacy over European integration efforts (Hoffmann 1966). Drawing inspiration from realism in international relations theory, intergovernmentalism argued that state economic and security interests would predominate over European interests, especially because they represent core aspects of state sovereignty. European integration efforts that transcended these traditional boundaries of state sovereignty would only antagonize European states and cause them to further limit integration.

The three integrationist projects fell out of favour in the scholarship of the 1970s due to slackening European integration at the time. The demand to answer generalizable questions about integration eroded amidst doubts about the EU experiment. A resurgence of interest had to wait until considerable progress had been made once again. In 1987, the adoption of the Single European Act (SEA) reinvigorated political research on the EU by calling for a single market programme and the abolition of all internal economic exchange barriers by the end of 1992. For example, Sandholtz and Zysman's (1989) analysis of the single market programme is very much consistent with Haas's neofunctional account of EU integration, characterizing the SEA as a series of elite bargains between the European Commission, national politicians and powerful industrialists. Their brand of neo-functionalism blended intergovernmentalism through the argument that EU elites responded to changes in the international economic structure by reorienting traditional state interests towards European integration process. Although most scholars were not as explicit about the involvement of supranational elites as Moravcsik's (1991) perspective, contemporary representations of European integration as 'conventional statecraft' emphasized that states' preferences had clearly been redefined towards supranational integration.

Furthermore, there has been other significant mixing of the three original broad-scale grand theories of European integration. In fact, amalgamation is the norm rather than the exception. Straddling the neo-functionalist–intergovernmentalist divide, Marks (1993) has proposed a theory of 'multilevel governance' attempting to account for the general diffusion of political authority in the EU. Sandholtz and Sweet's (1998) study of the governance of integration has developed along the transactionalist–neo-functionalist line. Moravcsik (1993) re-engaged the debate with a liberal intergovernmentalist approach and created an International Relations forum for the question of European integration. Hix's 'new governance' has been equally inspiring to many new Europeanists, stimulating a new generation of mid-range theories covering matters of institutional theory and governance and a wide range of issues in social construction (Hix 1994, 1998).

Much contemporary EU research is an empirical continuation of the three original 'grand theories' of European integration, but transactionalism, intergovernmentalism and neo-functionalism bring little substance to the question of identity construction because they treat it as by-product of the European integration process despite it being actively promoted in the EU (Jacobs and Maier 1998) and it being a part of the European landscape from Greek antiquity. Further, the study of EU identity still suffers from an incomplete account of the construction of identity, lacking clear hypotheses concerning the relative causal weight of identity in the European integration process (Hooghe and Marks 2008: 23). Transactionalism has been shown to be significant both in the production of a European community and the product of it (Deutsch 1961; Inglehart 1990; Wendt 1994), so we must question: to what extend could it be used to explain the construction of a European identity? (Laffan 1996; Smith 1992). Deutsch's 'community' and 'we-feeling' are relatively close to the notion of European identity, but they are not equivalent. Transactionalism highlights a civic component creating a cultural component of identity but it is underdefined as a mechanism to fully explain community building and 'we-feeling'.

Intergovernmentalist approaches have been used in the EU literature to explain periods of sweeping change and periods of gridlock as coinciding with the complementing or diverging national interests of EU member states (Moravcsik 1993). The only problem with these explanations is that they oversimplify the relationship between individual citizens and their national governments. States are not the only actors in the EU integration process; there are a number of complex and dynamic interactions amongst a variety of actors with their own interests and abilities to affect the discourse of European identity. Of those many actors, people are the most important marker for the success or failure of an identity discourse, for they are the ultimate objective of identity politics.

States and elites might be the drivers of the process of integration, but even before referenda gave popular sovereignty veto power, a type of European cultural identity affected elite decisions and became an important determining factor. The primacy of states and their national experiences might be instrumental in limiting European integration, but only as far as national elites and (now) national citizens have viewed supranational integration efforts as 'foreign'. The unit of analysis in the question of European identity needs to be reoriented away from the state and refocused to take account of the individual and group dimensions; these are the best measures of the success of European identity and hold the key to understanding interests, expectations and political behaviour in the EU.

Although neo-functionalism and its 'spillover' stand opposite to intergovernmentalist approaches to European integration (Garrett and Tsebelis 1996; Ross 1995; Sandholtz 1992) neither mechanism, top-down or bottom-up, seems enough to explain the formation of European identity. While the top-down promotion of a European consciousness and the creation of a European identity has been an explicit policy goal for almost forty years,[1] the bottom-up cultural component of European identity clearly predates the civic component of EU citizenship by twenty years, if not back to Greek antiquity – greatly limiting the neo-functionalist 'spillover' and intergovernmentalist claims. The EU is by far the most successful integration effort in the world, but how can European identity mean different things to different people under different contexts while still symbolically uniting millions of citizens across twenty-seven states, twenty-three official languages and at least a dozen minority languages?

There is a highly pertinent difference between civic identity and cultural identity. Michael Bruter (2003) explored this difference and exemplified how these two conceptually distinct components of European identity respond differently to various cues in the environment. In his view, European civic identity can be understood as the degree to which EU citizens feel they are citizens of a European political system, whose rules, laws and rights have an influence on their daily lives – 'identification with their political system as an institutional frame' (Bruter 2003: 1155–6). Conversely, European cultural identity is best described as the perceptions

1 The early 1970s witnessed leading politicians placing the development of a supranational identity on top of the EC political agenda during debates on the future of European integration (Wiener 1996: 19). The promotion of a European consciousness through public relations campaigns and symbols amongst ordinary citizens remained at the top of the European political agenda during the push for a single economic area in the 1980s and once again in the early 1990s upon the arrival of the single market, the Treaty of Maastricht, and the introduction of EU citizenship as new supranational status.

of individuals that fellow Europeans are closer to them than non-Europeans, as a community or human group, regardless of the nature of the political system (Bruter 2003: 1156).

This civic/cultural divide is pervasive through other conceptualizations of European identity, particularly limiting the Europeanization and integration literatures. Europeanization is a process by which 'states adopt EU rules' (Schimmelfennig and Sedelmeier 2005: 7), but it can also be seen as the construction, diffusion and institutionalization of formal and informal rules, shared beliefs and political practices (Checkel and Katzenstein 2009). The process of European integration has also straddled the civic/cultural divide with implicit functional elements following transactionalism (Deutsch *et al.* 1957) or spontaneous spillover (Haas 1958). Alternative incorporations of European identity include literature on social learning, where states adopt European rules because they perceive them as inherently appropriate and Europeanization is considered domestically legitimate (Checkel 2001). Other scholars also emphasize collective learning, internalization and persuasion to explain compliance after the redefinition of interests that occurs during the process of interaction (Haas 1990; Haas 1992; Ruggie 1998: 867–9).

Whether socialization, persuasion, or habit is the mechanism by which candidate states adopt EU rules over time, the fact that civic interaction precedes the cultural aspect of European identity in all of these literatures should be viewed as a major shortcoming. Since membership in the EU is expected to create a supranational identity that influences policy-making, much of the work on identity and Europeanization has unfortunately focused on the ways European elites and institutions socialize candidate states' identities, their preferences and interests (Checkel 2007; Hooghe 2005; Jupille and Caporaso 1999).

## A New Approach to European Identity

Most scholars find European identity is created from the top down by institutions, elites and the symbols of the EU (Checkel 2005; Kaelberer 2004; Laffan 2004; Risse 2006; Sassatelli 2002; Smith 1992). These scholars follow the neofunctional EU integration literature (Haas 1958) in presenting both the purposeful social engineering to support EU institutions and the unintended 'spillover' as creating European identity in the everyday interactions citizens have with the institutions and symbols of the EU. Whether purposeful or banal interactions, this segment of the literature finds EU citizens embedded in a system of meaning that affects their identification from the top down with little or no effect from the bottom up.

Some scholars find that European identity is created through a bottom-up effect and characterize it either as a pessimistic 'backlash' arising from the perceived loss of national cultural heritage (Checkel and Katzenstein 2009; Fligstein 2008) or as an optimistic European public sphere fostering a European demos (Favell 2008; Risse 2010). These segments of the literature follow intergovernmentalism (as in Hoffmann 1966; Moravcsik 1991) and multi-level governance theories in the European integration literature (as in Marks 1993) to highlight the formation of European identity through bottom-up effects resulting from top-down influences. While it certainly seems likely that the divide between the pessimistic and optimistic branches of the literature signals a division between the development of more or less European identity depending on the context of how it is viewed from the bottom up, recent arguments postulate the possibility that it does not matter whether Europeans have an affinity or distaste for European identity as long as they are immersed in the discourse of European identity (Risse 2010). Banal Europeanization could be just as powerful as staunch opposition to being European because both embed the individual in the European system of meaning-making.

Not realizing the extent to which it is meaningful to be engaged in seemingly non-meaningful ways, the performance of 'being' European has been taken for granted by both top-down and bottom-up conceptualizations.[2] Billions of daily interactions between EU citizens create Europeans through horizontal means much more than the purposeful actions of any group of individuals or institutions. This horizontal mechanism of European identity formation, which has been underexplored, is the central focus of the remainder of this chapter.

Although being European does not mean 'not being nationalistic', it means not being a 'classical' or 'traditional' nationalistic citizen. European identity does not jettison nationalism – it modifies it. What remains is a hybrid of European and national identity, not a mixture of both that can be segmented to have particular portions called upon under specific contexts. 'Being' European means being less nationalistic, in the instrumental and exclusivist aspects of the nation, but self-identifying as European is not necessary to 'being' European because daily interactions with other EU citizens are enough to foster European identity. One does not need to think of oneself as 'European' to 'be' European precisely because the recognition of the self occurs in relation to another in an instrumental sense. It is enough to be less traditionally nationalistic to become more European.

All identity is performative. It is always for someone and for some purpose. While individuals are the ones performing identity, it is also in the context of a group, a specific time period and a particular situation. Although identity seems very fluid and context dependent when looking at the individual level and in the context of a particular situation, it is much more coherent at the aggregate level and within the boundaries of a specific time period. Groups may vary depending of the aggregate level (local, regional, national or supranational), while a meaningful time period is determined by group members appropriating historical and contemporary socio-political events as significant to their identity formation. Not all individuals have the same affinity for a discourse of identity, but patterns can be interpreted in context to assess which aspects of the identity discourse carry the most weight. Individuals do this all the time to assess

2 Although being immersed in the discourse of European identity would certainly fall within the performance of European identity under the bottom-up mechanism.

their place and membership in their imagined community. The performance of 'being' European is an emergent phenomenon in this regard – like the flocking of birds.

Geographic and longitudinal aspects of identity create a mosaic of information for individual EU citizens. On one hand, these patterns 'guide' individual behaviour based on the logic of appropriateness and the logic of consequences, as policed by in-group and out-group behaviour. On the other hand, individuals within a system of meaning, in a particular group in a specific time period, have the ability to change and contest their system of meaning-making, perhaps having an effect on the trajectory of their group identity. European identity has changed old identity patterns to create a reorientation of the trajectory of European society. By changing how individuals view themselves in their system of meaning through the introduction a new logic of appropriateness, the EU has shifted individual behaviour.

However, this is not a simple path-dependent process to European identity formation at the individual level – it is much more interactive and everyone has the power to affect the identity discourse. Some individuals and actors (including elite, state and EU institutions) have greater power to affect the discourse of identity. These actors have very strong effects in the formation of European identity at the aggregate level, especially in appropriating symbols and critical junctures or inflection points in the formation (or demise) of European identity. Although systemic forces (Eurocrisis) also have the ability to shift the trajectory of European society, the most important component is the individual EU citizen.

A flock has a 'mind of its own' in the sense that every bird can change its course at any given time and shift the trajectory of the whole flock. The flock's movements are based on millions of complex interactions every second. It is a living thing itself. In just such a way, European identity is continuously constructed in the billions of everyday interactions that make EU citizens reconsider their nationalistic ties in the most unassuming ways.

## Findings from the Field

Findings from the field are an interpretation of the narratives, meaning-making, and uses of symbols by EU citizens in their daily lives. Comparing and contrasting these semiotics within and across systems of meaning-making can be accomplished by placing them in the context in which they were uttered or displayed, questioning the reasons why they were performed and interpreting the various patterns arising. Significance is found when the reasons behind two types of semiotic performances are the same but the display or discourses are different across regions, but also if the reasons behind the semiotic performances are different but the display or discourses are consistent across regions.[3] Comparing across regions and states provides us with a better 'image' of European identity and helps answer the question 'Where is European society heading?'

One way to provide a more complete and nuanced understanding of European identity and its political implications is a cross-level ethnographic approach that examines EU citizens' semiotic practices through a cross-regional comparative study. The goal of this study was to construct a 'semiotic topography', a detailed analytical tool weaving national and subnational systems of meaning-making to illustrate how contemporary socio-political developments link multiple communities, their historical pasts and present discourses of identity in socio-political competition. This innovative mixed-method strategy for collecting and packaging empirical qualitative data is based on the systematic application of subnational concomitant variation, stratified quota sampling, 'modified' ordinary language interviewing, and the interpretative analysis of semiotic practices.

Spain and the United Kingdom were selected as country case studies based on concomitant variation amongst five key causal factors of European identification: socio-cultural heritage, geopolitical heritage, level of EU involvement, time of EU involvement and intensity of regional

3 This is where modified OLI is particularly useful in cross-checking responses with the three internal robustness checks it provides.

identification (Checkel 2005; Fitjar 2010; Kaelberer 2004; Laffan 2004; Risse 2006; Sassatelli 2002).[4] As the central focus of the research, the regions within these countries and the various research sites within were selected based on the same standards, but also to acquire enough variance in income, education, religiousness, political ideology, community size and social openness. Altogether, the study explored identity politics in twenty-one regions, over a period of fourteen months between 2010 and 2013, before, during and after times of peak identity politics.[5]

Participants in the study were local citizens selected via stratified quota sampling, a mix of stratified sampling (across levels of analysis) and quota sampling (along key demographic factors). This sampling ensured local and regional identification while preserving variance in age, race, gender, education, income, travel and foreign residency, but not with the goal of assembling a completely representative sample because of the focus on semiotic practices.[6] Initial participants were local and regional 'cultural experts' who guided the initial identification of meaningful political cleavages through in-depth interviews and supervised mini-fieldwork exercises in specific localities. Semi-structured interviews and focus groups (ranging from one to four hours) took place in local cafe bars, restaurants, terraces,

4 Concomitant variation in small-N casework is preferred when searching for degrees of magnitude between variables present and outcome to draw inferences, especially when searching for key variables and trying to generate new theories.

5 The Spanish case study covered: Madrid, Catalonia, the Basque Country, Asturias, Galicia, Granada, Malaga, Almeria and Mallorca. The UK case study covered: London, South East England, South West England, East of England, East Midlands, Yorkshire and the Humber, North West England, North East England, Wales, Scotland, Lewis and Harris, Skye, and Northern Ireland. A period of peak identity politics included the 2010 FIFA World Cup victory for Spain, the 2012 London Olympics for the UK, or the Eurocrisis for the EU.

6 While it may be highly beneficial for subsequent empirical research to approximate a representative sample in studying semiotics, it is impossible to 'replicate' ethnographic work of this nature – the best a researcher can do is 'package' the ethnographic accounts collected using a semiotic topography for subsequent analysis by other means.

parks, plazas, community centres and a variety of other social settings providing natural venues for identity discourse.

Prompts tailored to elicit responses emblematic of social cleavages and personal preferences across local, regional, national and supranational levels of analysis were used instead of direct self-identification questions that juxtapose and fractionalize identity to produce unintended value-added responses. These prompts were used in ordinary language interviewing (OLI), which operates by finding judgments, elaborations, logic and confirmations about individual interpretations of a system of meaning (Schaffer 2006). The first step uses judgment questions prompting the participant to express opinions and make discriminations revealing standards implicit in a meaning. Internal logic questions provide the opportunity for the participant to reflect more deeply and sort out their own perception of reality by asking them to relate earlier answers to current or historical topics – making sense of semiotics in context and providing the first robustness 'check' against value-added responses. Restatement questions further confirm understanding and demonstrate that the interviewer is listening, but can also serve as a second robustness 'check' when corroborating previous interviewee accounts with a new participant or within a focus group setting.

The OLI process is repeated by topic with each participant with the sensitivity necessary to understand that not every question will apply to every participant in the same manner, while some will apply for surprising reasons. The last robustness 'check' is performed when previous accounts are corroborated outside of the system of meaning in which they were produced, to elicit the understanding and logic behind meaning-making by an out-group to identify if, in fact, the semiotic performance is recognized and intelligible by outsiders. This last step is a strategic modification to OLI in light of the need to create a semiotic topography across regions and systems of meaning-making. Countless hours of participant observation, the interpretation of spaces and linguistic landscapes, all complement the findings from interviews and focus groups to complete the ethnographic study.

The central finding is that EU citizens become more 'European' the more they engage with other EU citizens and identify with them, thus changing their everyday political behaviour towards more inclusivity and less exclusivity.[7] While this seems commonsensical and unremarkable at the individual level, explaining what this means with 'hard' data and 'real world' examples at the group level becomes increasingly complicated. What it means to be European might be crystallizing into a coherent performance across EU member states through the use of more inclusive attitudes towards others, but regional, national and supranational identities are continuously interacting to shape and reshape identity politics. Knowing how European identity 'works' is prerequisite to understanding contemporary politics in Europe, despite the vast multitude of semiotic practices used to construct, reify and contest identity.

Social identity theory conceptualizes identity as a dynamic process of interaction and comparison between the self and the other by which individuals ascribe themselves to different groups (Reicher 2004; Stets and Burke 2000; Tajfel 1981). The self-conception of in-group membership, group processes and intergroup relations leads to in-group and out-group bias, exhibited as prejudice, discrimination, ethnocentrism, stereotyping, group polarization, crowd behaviour, intergroup conflict, conformity and group cohesiveness (Hogg 2006). While these perceptions affect intergroup relations and political behaviour to reinforce the divide between self and other, Europeans may be more inclusive of other groups for two main reasons: post-materialist individuals have greater levels of cognitive mobilization, the ability to situate the self as belonging in multiple contextual backdrops and affinity for a larger social identity beyond previous confines (Inglehart 1970; Janssen 1991), and EU citizens feel 'European' when they perceive shared traits, values, goals, fates or experiences with other European nationals and view them as part of a supranational in-group (Brewer 2001; Gaertner *et al.* 1993).

Social identity theory explains how Europeans are now part of a larger social group and belonging to that imagined community might lower their

7 The construction of an imagined European community might even have surpassed the material contact with other individuals, to the point that the meaningful social interactions EU citizens have with other Europeans need not be person-to-person – they can be over distance, electronic, through stories, images or even fictional.

out-group bias towards other EU citizens by virtue of in-group membership. However, findings from the ethnographic study highlight how the Europeanization of Europeans goes well beyond the wealthy, educated and socially mobile 'Eurostars and Eurocities' (Favell 2008). They also point out that EU citizens need not self-identify as 'Europeans' to have more inclusive attitudes towards other EU citizens or have a more inclusive view of the EU. This surprising finding accentuates that the Europeanization of Europeans is occurring daily in the most unassuming ways.

Some of the most basic family rituals and routines (such as getting ready in the morning, household meals, evening entertainment) now have a distinct 'European' influence through the increased availability, quality and denomination of goods from other European countries inside the home, despite national borders and seasonal trends. Increased contact with these products in the most private of spheres is reformulating everyday life, reconditioning preferences to be more inclusive of other European nationalities and reshaping political behaviour in the EU.

For example, seasonal fruits and vegetables previously not available or more expensive during winter months in northern European countries are now more available and more affordable due to trade agreements with southern European countries.[8] These goods bear denominational origin stickers on the bag or item itself, increasing the social contact between the individual and other European countries by literally bringing a little piece of the country into their homes and into their bodies. Likewise, the increase of denominational goods, those nominally protected by the traditional geographical origin of products, has greatly increased daily contact with other European countries.[9] These interactions certainly bring a new meaning to the phrase 'you are what you eat'.

There are many more unassuming behaviours that make contemporary EU citizens more European – far too many for this chapter. Since Spain and the UK are currently facing demands for independence from component

8 For example, Portugal, Spain, Italy, Greece and even Turkey.

9 These include wines, cheeses, hams, sausages, seafood, olives, beers, balsamic vinegar and some breads, fruits and vegetables.

nations, right-wing movements throughout Europe are reshaping domestic politics, and allegiance to the European Union is increasingly in question in the midst of a fiscal crisis, the remainder of the chapter will focus on European identity during times of peak identity politics. This section will present a semiotic and discourse analysis across regions of both countries during the 2010 FIFA World Cup (which Spain won), the 2012 UEFA Euro (which Spain also won), and the 2012 London Olympics – all in the backdrop of the European financial crisis. Findings will present how EU citizens in Spain and the UK are behaving more European during these peak times of identity politics despite much 'self-and-other' rhetoric and displays.

Semiotic displays of 'traditional' national identity, which focus on the juxtaposition of self against other, include hanging a Spanish or Catalan flag from a window, displaying an English or Scottish flag instead of a British flag in a pub, chanting 'Yo soy Español, Español, Español!' after a Spanish victory or singing regional folk songs in Scotland. Likewise, wearing traditional attire or not wearing specific colours, having street signs in Welsh, Irish or Basque as well as – or in spite of – an official national vernacular, or protesting the display or lack thereof of national symbols are all semiotic displays of national juxtaposition. Individuals are deeply embedded in the system of meaning-making created and maintained by nationalism.

Conversely, using symbols of the EU and taking part in EU rituals is being European. But when an individual knows the meaning of nationalistic semiotic performances and refuses to engage in them, that individual is also using European semiotic practices. These might include subtle changes to accents, mannerisms and dress, but also more overt displays like choosing life partners and having close relationships with people from other European countries, different ethnic backgrounds and different religions. There are many ways in which EU citizens are becoming more European and semiotic displays can be found in anything from attitudes towards foods of different origin, to entertainment and media, to voicing support towards relaxing immigrant policies and broadening minority rights. Attitudes are difficult to assess, so the 'evidence' provided hereon will focus solely on observable practices and discourses.

Contemporary socio-political events create the opportunity for diverging identity discourses to come head to head. Images of crowds celebrating the 2010 Spanish World Cup victory in the streets did not reverberate throughout Spain, where regional identities are typically strong and the FIFA World Cup caused some to become clearly stronger. When I asked participants 'What are your feelings on Spain's World Cup victory?', I received drastically different responses. Most in the Basque Country did not seem care and dismissed the event as if a foreign country had won. In fact, many people in Bilbao and San Sebastian wore orange for the Netherlands during the final match. These findings are not surprising given that the Basque have long privileged their regional identity over the Spanish, but the extent to which they dismissed the win, as if it had been achieved by another country, is very important. What is most interesting is that a repeat visit to the Basque Country during the 2012 UEFA Euro confirmed the behaviour – I watched as people throughout San Sebastian wore green during the Ireland–Spain match – but those very same people were also cheering for Spain.

The performance of Basque identity in the Basque Country has created a paradoxical situation for many Basque and Spanish citizens living in the region. The social norm is clearly not to support the Spanish national team. This calls for many on both sides of the citizenship question to display allegiances to the other teams by wearing their colours. This insightful view into the self-and-other nationalistic relationship between the Basque Country and Spain is only overshadowed by the observation that many Basque and Spanish support the Spanish national team. Several ways of getting around the Basque social norm were identified by visiting multiple localities and interviewing individuals throughout San Sebastian before, during and after the game: (1) wearing the opposing colours allows one to perform identity without 'being' Basque, allowing both Basque and Spanish people to blend in despite their support for the Spanish national team; (2) going to bars outside their neighbourhood allows individuals to voice and display their support of the Spanish team outside their local system of meaning, skirting any social retribution from neighbours; (3) watching the game at a bar friendly to those unsupportive of the Basque self-and-other relationship with Spanish identity ensures safety in a group setting.

These observations can be combined with countless anecdotes indicating a shift away from self-and-othering in the Basque Country that support the finding that the Basque are becoming more inclusive. For example, a similar anecdote told by a young Basque professional working in a Bilbao hotel revealed considerable insight: 'As children growing up in Bilbao and going to school, we could never wear red as a primary colour on a shirt because the other kids would tease you pretty hard. And forget about wearing anything red and yellow, you might not even make it home, or if you did, you would never forget and do it again'. Encountering a child in a full Spanish national team kit walking home from school with his mother twenty years later, I asked him and his mother if the other children ever gave him a hard time at school. To my surprise, the answer was 'no'.[10]

Beyond semiotic practices, evidence of the increasing inclusivity can be found in the two-level game between institutional policies towards minorities and the social affinity to welcome minorities in the Basque Country. The Basque Nationalist Party (PNV) coalition welcomed immigration through legislation creating a regional citizenship based on residence rather than ethnicity, contrasting Basque values of openness and tolerance against the restrictive nature of Spanish immigration law reforms that were initiated in 2000 (Jeram 2012).[11] This political strategy was designed to encourage immigration to the Basque Country by implementing policies that offered socio-economic and legal incentives to foreigners, including basic housing, monthly stipend, social services, legal services and health care. The nationalist coalition reconceptualized citizenship as a means of deepening democracy and allowing newcomers to actively participate in

10 This finding was corroborated by the observation of children wearing variations of the Spanish team shirt during the time of the 2012 UEFA Euro throughout parts of Bilbao, San Sebastian and Vitoria.

11 The first tangible institutional response by the PNV-led government was decree 40/2002 that created the Department of Housing and Social Affairs and included within that new ministry a Basque Directorate of Immigration. The first Basque Immigration Plan (PVI), passed in a plenary session of the Basque parliament on 3 December 2003, leaves little doubt that it was elaborated in reaction to the restrictive immigration laws put in place by the Popular Party at the state level (Jeram 2012).

society (Jeram 2012). While some of these programmes have been reduced due to political turnover in the region and economic woes in Europe, the effect on Basque society has remained.

Ethnographic findings confirm that the normative aspect of immigrant policies implemented in the 2000s has taken root and a majority of Basque agree that anyone living in the Basque Country should receive the rights and privileges afforded to the Basque. Interviews and focus groups across the Basque Country found the main discourse on immigrants was inclusivist and welcomed integration instead of assimilation or stratification. Notwithstanding some negative views of the relationship between immigrants and crime, the normative view that immigrants should be included and integrated in Basque society speaks volumes. This Basque case is illustrative of a broader trend: stateless nations are incorporating themes of inclusive citizenship into their national imagined communities, in contrast to European states that are opting for tougher distinctions between nationals and non-nationals with aggressive programmes of cultural integration.

The Scottish National Party (SNP) is another proponent of inclusive policies towards immigrants, asserting that more immigrants will be beneficial for Scottish society and its economy, and advocating the devolution of immigration policy from Westminster to the Scottish Parliament.[12] The Scottish government has initiated a series of campaigns and initiatives (such as One Scotland – Many Cultures and Fresh Talent Initiative) to become more attractive to immigrants as an inclusive and multicultural nation (Hepburn and Rosie 2012: 14). Since 2003, the SNP has also focused on a 'better immigration policy' which should be free of racial bias, claiming additional immigration legislative competence and political capital by differentiating Scotland from the United Kingdom (Mycock 2012). This is also clearly a political strategy for the SNP, which has successfully courted votes by including ethnic minorities in the organization

12 The SNP framed its demand for more oversight over immigration by focusing on the rhetorical effect presented by the English dichotomy of 'us versus them' and the Scottish emphasis on 'kindness and compassion' (Hepburn 2009: 521).

and representation of the party and created affiliated organizations like 'Asians for Independence' and 'New Scots for Independence' to bolster grass-roots support.[13]

The SNP addressed immigration in the 1992 manifesto with its vision for a 'multicultural society' and cultural diversity as an enrichment of the region, adding a more direct path to citizenship in 2001, and continuing to implement loosened immigration policies attracting the highly skilled while fighting discrimination and racism.[14] This instrumental approach, however, might highlight that not all ethnic minority groups are treated equally in Scotland, as Hussain and Miller (2006) point out, and that an increase in exclusivity, especially towards English, might be increasing amongst Scottish people, despite the inclusivist rhetoric deployed by political elites. Immigrants with a Pakistani origin, on the other hand, find it much easier to belong to the Scottish region, which has been constructed as a main marker of Scottish identity by the political elites over the last twenty years (Hussain and Miller 2006; Mitchell *et al.* 2012).

While the multicultural Scottish society might not yet be achieved, the normative aspects in Scotland are definitively shifting to a more inclusive discourse. The focus on a civic identity associated with a sense of belonging to the region is pervasive enough to become inclusive of all residing in Scotland in the upcoming Scottish independence referendum. By contrast, and perhaps reifying the Scottish 'other', people of Scottish descent residing in England will not be allowed to take part in the referendum. Hussain and Miller (2006) examine the differentiation between internal and international immigrants in Scotland and show that there is a significant difference between how people with a Pakistani origin and how migrants

13 While speaking at the Pakistan Welfare Trust's 20th Annual Dinner in 2007, Alex Salmond promised that 'over the next four years as First Minister, [he] will do all that [he] can to encourage more ethnic minority Scots to seek representation in parliament, and in all parts of Scotland's national life', concluding that 'different traditions do not undermine our culture – they enhance it' <http://www.scotland.gov.uk/News/Releases/2007/06/04090501> accessed 10 January 2013.

14 The SNP would grant citizenship to anybody living and/or born in Scotland, or to anybody with one parent born in Scotland.

from England are perceived, arguing that Scotland has developed a positive relation between multiculturalism and sub-state nationalism and, in particular, elites are deliberatively inclusive since 'Scottish elites, like Scottish football fans, have been determined to present to the world a better image than their English counterparts. It is part of their national pride' (2006: 198–9). Although the historical role of England as the Scottish 'other' persists, recent ethnographic findings complicate this view.

Many Scots shunned the 2012 London Olympics and opposed the formation of an all-inclusive Team GB football team months before any competition.[15] Scottish identity had crept back into mainstream discourses after the devolution of power, the creation of the Scottish Parliament (1999), and under Alex Salmond's leadership of the SNP. Kilts became popular wear at high-profile events and local weddings, the Saltire (Scottish flag) was worn by politicians and flown on countless banners during sport events, local celebrations and everyday locations (including the side of city buses or local buildings). Scottishness became apparent in everyday life without an overt move by the political elite. However, by the start of the Olympic games, most Saltires had been replaced or overwhelmed by a tide of Union Jacks (the United Kingdom flag). Interestingly, these remained as unassuming reminders until well after the games; bunting, ribbons and the broad influx of red, white and blue paraphernalia remained displayed throughout Scotland.

When I asked participants 'What are your feelings on the Olympics and/or Team GB?', I received surprisingly similar and overall positive responses throughout. At a time of presumed peak identity politics, the exclusive aspect of Scottishness was muted and most identified as Scottish and British. In fact, after the overwhelming influx of British symbols began to recede a month after the Olympics, Saltires and Union Jacks were waved side by side as a triumphant Andy Murray returned to Dunblane after winning the Olympics and the US Open. Scots displayed and voiced their inclusive identification throughout the Olympics and until the conclusion

15 Team GB is the all-nation Great Britain team, including athletes from England, Wales and Scotland.

of ethnographic fieldwork in January 2013. These ethnographic findings supplement policy interpretations to confirm the increasing inclusivity in the Basque Country and Scotland, allowing us to create linkages to other culturally distinct regions in Europe.

This sort of national inclusion was also clearly visible during the 2010 FIFA World Cup in Spain. Moving away from the Basque Country and onto another culturally distinct region in Spain, we can see how the privileging of regional identity in Catalonia was just as strong as in the Basque Country, but carried a vastly different sentiment: Catalans viewed the win as their own. The hinge of the debate was the six Barcelona Football Club players on the Spanish national team, including five starters, the sole goal scorer in the championship game, and the national team's top goal scorer. The obvious follow-up question 'Would you feel the World Cup win belonged to Catalonia if there were just one or two players from Barcelona Football Club?' received incredibly jagged and dismissive responses from Catalans – the overwhelming response in the other regions of Spain was 'Of course not'. While these findings might seem commonsensical, they speak volumes and introduce us to the reconstruction of identities throughout the Iberian peninsula.

Participants in smaller towns throughout the regions sampled privileged their local identity over the regional identity. This tiered organization was particularly evident in Andalusia, where the trend was also present in larger cities. Lower socio-economic status, lower education and less experience with foreign travel/residency have a strong association with local self-identification. Upon close examination in various focus groups, two explanations arise beyond that of local group proximity providing a salience missing from larger groups: participants developed a sense of pride that overwhelmed the perceived out-group bias towards their group as poor, uneducated, uncivilized or lazy; participants have a strong distrust of government at all levels and think of 'the state' as an outsider.

Social and political cleavages were even more pronounced amongst Spanish citizens in the culturally distinct regions when images of the Spanish state were called upon. Responses against the Spanish state as the 'other' – the out-group – included greater regional identification in (descending order) the Basque Country, Catalonia, Galicia, Balearic Islands and Andalusia. Instrumental trends were noticeable outside identity discourse amongst larger and wealthier cities, while smaller and less wealthy cities more easily clung to an identity discourse privileging their in-group over the Spanish other. This trend continues onto the individual level, with the more educated, well-travelled and wealthier study participants better understanding the intricacies and competition over the regional/national discourse of identity than their counterparts, who were more embedded in the processes. It would be a disservice, in fact, to label the contestation of the Spanish state as a uniform part of the national identity discourse when it was made clear in many focus groups and interviews that 'their nation' had nothing to do with the Spanish state.[16]

The inverse was observed when the European economic crisis was brought up as supranational lens. At the regional level, supranational identification was greater in (descending order) the Basque Country, Catalonia, Galicia, Balearic Islands and Andalusia.[17] Larger and wealthier cities yielded much more supranational self-identification, while smaller and less wealthy cities yielded a slightly lower, yet easily appreciable, incidence. Younger, more educated, well-travelled and wealthier study participants also typically had higher supranational self-identification.[18] Instrumental trends were clearly noticeable throughout but the crucial finding seems grounded on existential motivations.

Responses from the level-of-analysis-tailored prompts reveal one significant regional pattern: the stronger the regional identification is in a region, the stronger European self-identification will be as reaction against the 'official narrative' of the state. The image of the state has long been used in tandem with nationalism to evoke a sense of security. Discourse analysis

16 This was primarily so in the Basque Country, Catalonia and, to a much lesser extent, in the other culturally distinct regions where the regional 'national' discourse was not as successfully evoked.

17 The Balearic Islands could be an exception in this pattern because of the large numbers of European tourists that frequent the island. A similar pattern was noticeable in popular tourist destinations in Malaga.

18 One key exception was with younger study participants in smaller, less wealthy, cities and towns, which yielded a higher presence of local and regional identity.

revealed European supranational identification provides another layer of security beyond the state, if not from the state.[19] A remarkably high rate of participants in the Basque Country, Catalonia and Balearic Islands, but also to a lesser extent in Andalusia and Galicia, valued their regional identity above Spanish and European. Participants in these regions overwhelmingly identify with their regional identities first and foremost, but, surprisingly, European identity was the second-most-often cited identity in participants in the Basque Country and Catalonia.

Despite focusing on proxies to identity, all participants used a tiered conception of identity when explicitly asked about their self-identification. It is evident the World Cup had some sort of effect on most, if not all. The Basque and Catalan clearly placed regional identity above national, whereas Andalusians placed local above regional while still embracing the win, but these schemes were not the norm throughout. The epicentre of Spanish self-identification during this peak time of nationalism was focused on Madrid, where respondents overwhelmingly privileged Spanish identity over regional and European identities. Spanish citizens residing in areas of high tourism in Malaga, Granada and Galicia also displayed this disproportional affinity to Spanish identity for a very different reason.[20] This trend was clearly noticeable through discourse analysis but also in the use of symbols.[21]

Regional flags have played an important symbolic role in Spain, even before the Spanish Constitution officially enacted the seventeen autonomous communities in 1978. Today, all communities have a widely recognized

19 This is particularly evident in the most culturally distinct regions.

20 Although Galicia is not often considered a top Spanish tourist destination, Xacobeo 2010, the Holy Year commemoration of 'El Camino de Santiago' pilgrimage, was taking place during the research trip drawing thousands (>270,000) of pilgrims to Santiago de la Compostela. 'El Camino de Santiago' is the pilgrimage to the Cathedral of Santiago de la Compostela that was revived in the 1980s as part of the European cultural experience.

21 A multitude of symbols were used by participants to qualify group identity beyond the display of flags or flag colours, including (but not limited to): language, gastronomy, weather, terrain, music, literary and historical figures, historical events and locales, cities and emblematic buildings, local traditions or rituals, and lifestyle.

and frequently used regional flag that can be found anywhere from people's balconies, to colours on a wristband, cafe sunshades and napkins. This is not surprising given that Spain is one of the most culturally diverse European states and regional systems of meaning are strong. What is extraordinary in Spain today is the changing meaning and use of the Spanish flag. The use of the Spanish flag was very common during the time of my study, but this was definitively not the case in the past. During Franco's oppressive rule, the Spanish flag acquired a black eagle behind the Spanish coat of arms. Known as the 'fascist eagle', the Spanish flag retained fascist connotations long after Franco's death, the removal of the eagle from the flag, and the restoration of democracy in 1978. The Spanish flag was hardly ever used by common citizens and represented a source of tension in official buildings and international events, as an enduring symbol of the repressive regime and those few still yearning for a return to 'better times'.[22]

The Spanish flag received meagre domestic attention before Euro 2008, when it finally arrived on the international stage with a sense of pride after Spain's first major international soccer victory in decades.[23] Participants revealed that this was really the first time the Spanish people had felt 'proud of being Spanish' and displaying the Spanish flag began to become acceptable. Prevalence of this semiotic practice increased slowly for two years, following the successes of Spaniards in various international sports, until the 2010 World Cup presented the opportunity to voice long-silenced discourses with the spectacularly wide use of the Spanish flag. The tipping point in usage of the flag was undoubtedly the 2010 World Cup, or more precisely, the World Cup victory.

Malaga had the highest per capita personal use of the Spanish flag than any other region sampled – even Madrid. Granada and Galicia also had considerably high per capita personal use, especially considering that Granada's coastal towns are much less developed and touristy and that Galicia is one

22 The Spanish government banned all public references to the Franco regime and removed any statues, street names, memorials and symbols associated with the regime in 2007 – it is now illegal to display the pre-constitution crest with the black eagle.

23 UEFA European Football Championship held in 2008, which Spain had only won once before (1964) while still under the rule of Franco and the fascist regime flag.

of the most culturally distinct regions of Spain. The island of Mallorca is one of the most desired tourist destinations in the Mediterranean, attracting thousands of European expatriates, but it did not have a similarly disproportionate per capita use of the Spanish flag. The intriguing finding here is that, unlike other high-tourism areas, residents of Mallorca identify with Mallorca before identifying with Spain, and Spain before Europe.

Considering Basques and Catalans overwhelmingly identify with their regional identity first and European identity second, with Spanish identity being a distant third or not at all present, it was anticipated the Mallorcan scheme would follow suit, as it is also one of the most culturally distinct regions. When the opposite was found it was accompanied by two explanations: the territorial isolation creates an 'island culture' with a strong affinity grounded on key differences from the national culture; the high per capita presence of multiple out-groups (tourists) advances the necessity to identify with the most geopolitically viable identity – the island.[24] These explanations are remarkably applicable to the historically and geographically isolated Basque Country as it entered modernization and the Franco era, when it could no longer viably protect itself or its unique culture. The link between the high-tourism areas is that self-identification occurs along the most salient and powerful identity available; use of the Spanish flag in Malaga, Granada and Galicia and the use of the Mallorcan flag in Mallorca are semiotic responses against out-groups.

The fact that Spanish citizens identify with one political unit over another reveals that identity groupings are discrete visions salient at the subnational level. Nothing could illustrate this better than hanging a flag from your residence's window in Catalonia. Spanish flags were displayed nearly everywhere in Spain during the summer of 2010, including Catalonia – which claimed the victory as its own. The significant observation, however, was not the near 1:1 distribution ratio between the Catalonia flag and the Spanish flag, which could be interpreted as equal distribution amongst

24 A similar island culture effect is seen in the UK, which enjoyed a separation from continental Europe during the period of heavy geopolitical contestation during modern state-building and still sees itself apart from Europe in many respects.

those Spanish citizens residing in Catalonia that identify with Catalonia or Spain. Instead, the significant finding is that there was not a single occurrence of a household displaying both the Catalonian and Spanish flags.

Focus groups and interviews, some with citizens displaying one of the flags from their residences, confirmed that specific behaviour 'would just not happen here'. There was a slight noticeable discontent amongst respondents for those displaying the Spanish flag, even if they were not Catalan and just in the region for work, but the clear message was that one must choose to be either Catalan or Spanish. This self-policing practice specifies that it is acceptable to be Spanish in Catalonia and display your affiliation through the use of the Spanish flag, but it is not tolerable to hold both identities as equal.

The World Cup victory undoubtedly created a source of stress for many citizens in the culturally distinct regions of Spain, but Basque flags could not be used to claim the Spanish victory as their own despite ties to the team.[25] Banners proclaiming 'This is not Spain. This is not France. This is Euskal Herria, the oldest nation in Europe' were instead hung in the streets in Bilbao and San Sebastian to inform tourists throughout the World Cup that they were in the Basque Country.[26] It was illuminating that not a single personal display of the Spanish flag was observed. This was a bit surprising after the presence of so many Spanish flags in Catalonia and when considering that the Basque Country has major industry and banking hubs attracting workers from all over the peninsula and Europe – self-policing was clearly at work.[27] Focus groups and interviews, some

25 Despite having several players originating within the greater traditional boundaries of the Basque Country and three from the Athletic Bilbao, the Basque did not claim the Spanish victory as their own.

26 Stickers and posters carrying the same message were dispersed by baieuskalherriari.org. These messages were most often in English, clearly targeting tourists – not Spanish citizens.

27 Civic project signs bearing the Spanish crest and European flags were also the focus of in-group policing. The Spanish seal was often crossed out with spray paint when these signs were displayed in the culturally distinct regions of Spain, while the European flag remained intact. Some Spanish flags hung by individuals in these regions met a similar fate, having black paint splattered on them. Participants revealed anti-Franquist

with Spanish citizens from other regions and Basque who have considerable experience living outside the Basque Country, confirmed that displaying the Spanish flag would also 'just not happen here'.

The reification, contestation and reconstruction of identities occurs through interactions amongst a multitude of actors with wide-ranging capabilities to affect discourse; the meaning of state identity is no different. Multiple agents are interlocked in an ongoing process that often pins local, regional and national identities against one another. Regional and national agents gain the ability to influence behaviour and beliefs by not only separating the image of the region or state from society but by elevating it beyond, to represent only a particular set of interests (Migdal 2001) – security being most notable.

The use of Spanish and Catalan flags during the FIFA World Cup clearly represent the immediate instrumental value gained at the individual level from the team's victory, but participants in Madrid, Andalusia and the Balearic Islands exposed the event to be the tipping point of a larger movement – the gradual shift of state identity. The state-in-society approach details the link between the Spanish people and the reconstruction of the contemporary Spanish state, which was evoked, reified and contested decades after Franco. The World Cup victory and the new meaning of the Spanish flag together represent a culminating point in Spanish identity and a shift in the referent of identity. The appropriation of the World Cup win by the Spanish people is emblematic of 'We, the people of Spain, have achieved this' instead of 'Spain (the state) has achieved this'.

On the other hand, heirs of cultures silenced and persecuted by the Franco regime viewed the Spanish victory somewhat differently. Catalans, Basque and Gallegos found instrumental value in rejecting Spanish identity through discursive contestations in focus groups, by hanging banners or regional flags and by not displaying the Spanish flag, but they found an existential value in embracing European supranational identity for the

---

sentiment and resistance against the Spanish 'official narrative' as a source for this behaviour. Consequently, European symbols met little or no resistance in these regions.

same reasons their patriotic counterparts embraced the new Spanish identity: the people as referent. This striking similarity was evident in many other cross-level topics brought up during focus groups and interviews (such as the economy, immigration, religion), confirming that existential motivations of identity run deeper and are more highly valued than the instrumental counterparts. Yet, agents of the state got to work quickly after Spain's victory and accompanied images of celebration in national papers with political messages calling for unification and strengthening of the state. Their regional counterparts fought back with similarly instrumental political measures against the Spanish state, the most pronounced being the bullfighting ban in Catalonia because it represents Spanish culture[28] while maintaining 'correbous' as a traditional Catalan festival.[29]

The bullfighting ban in Catalonia represents a regionally bounded instrumental contestation against Spanish identity carried out by subverting the Spanish under the Catalan with political power. Regional agents successfully evoked and employed Catalonian identity against the rising Spanish identity to pass the popular legislative initiative banning bullfighting as a symbol of Spain in Catalonia. This seemingly simple contestation and rejection of Spanish national identity is highly significant, as the tide of support was also used to propel Convergència i Unió (CiU) – the Catalan nationalist party behind the popular initiative – to regain control of the regional parliament in 2010 after a seven-year hiatus following twenty-three consecutive years of being in power in Catalonia. However, merely six months later, only 3.7 percent of Catalans consider a 'crisis' of Catalonian identity a principal problem – a figure dwarfed by other topics most often cited: unemployment and job insecurity (62.7 percent), the economy (37.4 percent), immigration (23.1 percent), dissatisfaction with

28 Perez de S. Pablos, 'No a los toros, pero sin prohibirlos', *El Pais*, 1 August 2010.

29 Correbous is a Catalan tradition where bulls are let lose in the streets to be taunted after bound paper or fireworks have been attached to their horns and set on fire (L. Garrido, 'Si los toros no son tema identitario, hay que prohibir los "correbous"', *El Mundo*, 7 August 2010).

politics (16.5 percent), and relations with the Spanish state (14.4 percent).[30] CiU continued to successfully activate political action and voter support in 2011 by shifting away from instrumental motivations behind identity politics, becoming now the third-largest party in the Spanish Congress after winning a general election in Catalonia for the first time in history.[31]

The banners proclaiming the Basque Country as the oldest nation in Europe similarly represent a regionally and temporally bounded contestation motivated by the prestige of Basque identity over the Spanish. These banners were taken down in San Sebastian a week after the Spanish World Cup victory, revealing the behaviour to be a purely instrumental peak of regional self-identification for two reasons: the World Cup was over and there was no longer a need to reject the Spanish other; Jazzaldia was beginning and residents' semiotic performances against Spain were replaced by embracing European identity and the attention received during the international music festival.[32] Consequently, the relatively short duration the banners were up in the Basque Country is inversely correlated to the time Spanish flags were up throughout Spain – supporting the argument that instrumental motivations against an out-group are more punctuated but shorter lasting while existential motivations last longer and run deeper.[33]

While the more moderate PNV lost a seat in the 2011 general election (down from six in 2008), a new pro-independence nationalist party named after one of the last Basque strongholds during the Spanish conquest – Amaiur – presented itself in the election for the first time and won seven seats. This political shift is indicative of a voter base activated by identity

30 *The Economist* (Spanish version), 'Cataluna. El paro, como problema, lo que más preocupa a los catalanes frente a la relación con el estado o la identidad catalana', 25 February 2011.

31 CiU now seats sixteen deputies in the Spanish Congress – up from ten in 2008. See: À. Piñol, '¡Hemos hecho un hat-trick!', *El Pais*, 21 November 2011.

32 Jazzaldia is the longest continuous jazz festival in Europe, taking place throughout various parts of San Sebastian.

33 In this comparison, the use of the Spanish flag represents the existential shift of Spanish identity, while the Basque banners represent the instrumental peak of regional identity against the Spanish other.

politics. Discourse analysis of accounts in the Basque Country reveal that the lessening of the violence long used by Basque separatists is attributed to formal and informal regional institutions created to preserve the salience, meaningfulness and self-determination of Basque identity by protecting their cultural heritage, including the regional educational system, regional language, local celebrations and so on. It is evident that Basque separatist votes increased after Euskadi Ta Askatasuna (ETA) avowed to end violence and a more viable medium for the separatist agenda presented itself.[34]

Identity politics propelled the CiU to victory in the Catalonian parliamentary elections but their success in the 2011 Spanish general election is more ambiguous due to the political shift occurring in the midst of the European economic crisis. On the other hand, the lacklustre PNV results and success of Amaiur point to the activation of identity politics in the Basque Country and the continued, albeit peaceful, struggle for self-determination on the national stage. The identity politics in Spain continued during the 2012 Olympics and UEFA Euro 2012, as it has in the UK with the upcoming Commonwealth Games and the upcoming Scottish independence referendum.

## Conclusion

Ethnographic findings in Spain and the UK demonstrate the interaction between inclusive and exclusivist discourses of nation-building. On one hand, the states formed under the rhetoric of the nation state maintain a hegemonic discourse of exclusion and homogenization that securitizes

34 I. Sanz and A. Goyoaga, 'Basque Separatist Voters Grow after ETA Ends Violence', *Reuters*, 19 November 2011. ETA, the Basque nationalist and separatist organization proscribed as a terrorist group by Spanish and French governments, has never been directly linked to PNV. ETA announced the current ceasefire in September 2010. The ETA announcement renouncing violence was covered by *BBC News*, 'Basque Group ETA Says Armed Campaign Is Over', 20 October 2011.

the policies engaging ethnic minorities and migrants. On the other, stateless nations attempt to circumvent the state through more inclusive discourses and policies that seek to establish a heterogeneous nation, partly in response to the nation state and partly for the sake of their self-realization as nations. These are dynamic and imperfect processes that do not always overlap neatly and are at times contested by the nation state, the stateless nation and the societies of both. The overall trajectory is towards more inclusion, or what one could consider a more European identity. While both states and stateless nations are becoming more inclusive, even mutually inclusive, they are moving towards inclusiveness at different speeds at the individual, regional and national levels.

The point to take away from this chapter is that this is merely the beginning. Much attention has been given to state and EU policies as well as aggregate-level statistical analysis, but these have only presented a partial picture. Scholars need to start investigating the development of European identity through horizontal interactions as well as top-down and bottom-up approaches, but also with the ability to view the performance of European identity as 'the thing itself'. Future work should deploy more sensitive ethnographic and mixed-method approaches that do not merely rely on statistical analysis to assess a self-identification as 'European' that derives only from questionnaire responses. European identity is a dynamic and emerging phenomenon. Similar methods are required to understand the mechanism, interactions and direction of European identity as it continues to form in European society.

In the end, different political outcomes to the discourse of identity politics depend much on the appropriation of regional differences to either complement or contrast state-centred nation-building. This ongoing process has been viewed fairly negatively in the wake of the Eurocrisis without much regard to the longitudinal and cross-level implications. Nationalism took a long time to set in the modern European state. It had to be created, maintained, reified, in a political environment that thrived on the difference between the self and other. In that sense, nationalism was easier to establish in Europe than European identity. More credit should be given to the progress made in the formation of European identity over the last fifty years, which, in the grand scheme of things, is also merely the beginning.

Ultimately, more credit should be given where credit is most due – at the individual level – where billions of interactions are shaping and reshaping European identity daily.

## References


Brewer, M. B. (2001). 'The Many Faces of Social Identity: Implications for Political Psychology', *Political Psychology*, 22 (1), 115–25.

Bruter, M. (2003). 'Winning the Hearts and Minds of Europe', *Comparative Political Studies*, 36 (10), 1148–79.

Carey, S. (2002). 'Undivided Loyalties: Is National Identity an Obstacle to European Integration?', *European Union Politics*, 3 (4), 387–413.

Checkel, J. T. (2001). 'The Europeanization of Citizenship?'. In M. G. Cowles, J. Caporaso and T. Risse (eds), *Transforming Europe: Europeanization and Domestic Change*, pp. 180–97. Ithaca, NY: Cornell University Press.

—— (2005). 'International Institutions and Socialization in Europe', *International Organization*, 59 (4), 801–26.

—— (ed.) (2007). *International Institutions and Socialization in Europe*. Cambridge: Cambridge University Press.

Checkel, J. T., and Katzenstein, P. (eds) (2009). *European Identity*. Cambridge: Cambridge University Press.

Deutsch, K. (1961). 'Social Mobilization and Political Development', *American Political Science Review*, 55 (3), 493–514.

Deutsch, K. *et al.* (1957). *Political Community and the North Atlantic Area: International Organization in the Light of Historical Experience*. Princeton, NJ: Princeton University Press.

Favell, A. (2008). *Eurostars and Eurocities: Free Movement and Mobility in an Integrating Europe*. Oxford: Blackwell.

Fitjar, R. D. (2010). 'Explaining Variation in Sub-State Regional Identities in Western Europe', *European Journal of Political Research*, 49 (4), 522–44.

Fligstein, N. (2008). *The EU, European Identity, and the Future of Europe*. Oxford: Oxford University Press.

Fowler, J. H., and Kam, C. D. (2007). 'Beyond the Self: Social Identity, Altruism, and Political Participation', *Journal of Politics*, 69 (3), 813–27.

Gaertner, S. L., Dovidio, J. F., Anastasio, P. A., Bachman, B. A., and Rust, M. C. (1993). 'The Common Ingroup Identity Model: Recategorization and the Reduction of Intergroup Bias', *European Review of Social Psychology*, 4 (1), 1–26.

Garrett, G., and Tsebelis, G. (1996). 'An Institutional Critique of Intergovernmentalism', *International Organization*, 50 (2), 269–99.

Haas, E. (1958). *The Uniting of Europe: Political, Social and Economical Forces, 1950–1957*. London: Stevens & Sons.

—— (1990). *When Knowledge Is Power*. Berkeley, CA: University of California Press.

Haas, P. M. (1992). 'Introduction: Epistemic Communities and International Policy Coordination', *International Organization*, 46 (1), 1–35.

Hepburn, E. (2009). 'Introduction: Re-conceptualizing Sub-state Mobilization', *Regional & Federal Studies*, 19 (4), 477–99.

Hepburn, E., and Rosie, M. (2012). 'Immigration, Nationalism and Political Parties in Scotland'. *The New European Agenda for Integration: Regions, Multi-Level Governance and Immigrant Integration in the EU*. University of Edinburgh.

Hix, S. (1994). 'The Study of the European Community: The Challenge to Comparative Politics', *West European Politics*, 17 (1), 1–30.

—— (1998). 'The Study of the European Union II: The "New Governance" Agenda and its Rival', *Journal of European Public Policy*, 5 (1), 38–65.

Hoffmann, S. (1966). 'Obstinate or Obsolete? The Fate of the Nation-State and the Case of Western Europe', *Dædalus*, 95, 862–915.

Hogg, M. A. (2006). 'Social Identity Theory'. In P. J. Burke (ed.), *Contemporary Social Psychological Theories*, pp. 111–36. Palo Alto, CA: Stanford University Press.

Hooghe, L. (2005). 'Many Roads Lead To International Norms, but Few via International Socialization: A Case Study of the European Commission', *International Organization*, 59 (4), 861–98.

Hooghe, L., and Marks, G. (2004). 'Does Identity or Economic Reality Drive Public Opinion on European Integration?', *PS: Political Science and Politics*, 37 (3), 415–20.

—— (2008). 'A Postfunctionalist Theory of European Integration: From Permissive Consensus to Constraining Dissensus', *British Journal of Political Science*, 39 (1), 1–23.

Hussain, A., and Miller, W. (2006). *Multicultural Nationalism. Islamophobia, Anglophobia, and Devolution*. Oxford: Oxford University Press.

Inglehart, R. (1970). 'Cognitive Mobilization and European Identity', *Comparative Politics*, 3 (1), 45–70.

—— (1990). *Culture Shift in Advanced Industrial Society*. Princeton, NJ: Princeton University Press.

Jacobs, D., and Maier, R. (1998). 'European Identity: Construct, Fact and Fiction'. In M. Gastelaars and A. de Ruijter (eds), *A United Europe: The Quest for a Multifaceted Identity*, pp. 13–34, Maastircht: Shaker.

Janssen, J. I. H. (1991). 'Postmaterialism, Cognitive Mobilization and Support for European Integration', *British Journal of Political Science*, 21 (4), 443–68.

Jeram, S. (2012). 'Immigrants and the Basque Nation: Diversity as a New Marker of Identity', *Ethnic and Racial Studies*, 35 (online), 1–19.

Jupille, J., and Caporaso, J. A. (1999). 'Institutionalism and the European Union: Beyond International Relations and Comparative Politics', *Annual Review of Political Science*, 2 (1), 429–44.

Kaelberer, M. (2004). 'The Euro and European Identity: Symbols, Power and the Politics of European Monetary Union', *Review of International Studies*, 30 (2), 161–78.

Laffan, B. (1996). 'The Politics of Identity and Political Order in Europe', *Journal of Common Market Studies*, 34 (1), 81–102.

—— (2004). 'The European Union and Its Institutions as "Identity Builders"'. In R. Herrmann, T. Risse and M. Brewer (eds), *Transnational Identities: Becoming European in the EU*, pp. 75–95. Oxford: Rowman & Littlefield.

Lindberg, L. (1963). *The Political Dynamics of European Economic Integration*. Stanford, CA: Stanford University Press.

Marks, G. (1993). 'Structural Policy and Multilevel Governance in the EC'. In A. Cafruny and G. Rosenthal (eds), *The State of the European Community: The Maastricht Debates and Beyond*, pp. 491–522. Boulder, CO: Lynne Rienner.

McAllister, R. (1997). *European Union: An Historical and Political Survey*. New York: Routledge.

McDonough, P. (1995). 'Identities, Ideologies, and Interests: Democratization and the Culture of Mass Politics in Spain and Eastern Europe', *Journal of Politics*, 57 (3), 649–76.

Migdal, J. (2001). *State in Society: Studying How States and Societies Transform and Constitute One Another*. New York: Cambridge University Press.

Mitchell, J., Bennie, L., and Johns, R. (2012). *The Scottish National Party: Transition to Power*. Oxford: Oxford University Press.

Moravcsik, A. (1991). 'Negotiating the Single European Act: National Interests and Conventional Statecraft in the European Community', *International Organization*, 45 (1), 19–56.

—— (1993). 'Preferences and Power in the European Community: A Liberal Intergovernmentalist Approach', *Journal of Common Market Studies*, 31 (4), 473–524.

Mycock, A. (2012). 'SNP, Identity and Citizenship: Re-imagining State and Nation', *National Identities*, 14 (1), 53–69.

Reicher, S. (2004). 'The Context of Social Identity: Domination, Resistance, and Change', *Political Psychology*, 25 (6), 921–45.

Risse, T. (2006). 'The Euro between National and European Identity'. In R. M. Fishman and A. M. Messina (eds), *The Year of the Euro: The Cultural, Social, and Political Import of Europe's Common Currency*, pp. 65–80. Notre Dame, IN: University of Notre Dame Press.

——(2010). *A Community of Europeans?: Transnational Identities and Public Spheres*. Ithaca, NY: Cornell University Press.

Ross, G. (1995). *Jacques Delors and European Integration*. New York: Oxford University Press.

Ruggie, J. G. (1998). 'What Makes the World Hang Together? Neo-Utilitarianism and the Social Constructivist Challenge', *International Organization*, 52 (4), 855–85.

Sandholtz, W. (1992). *High-Tech Europe: The Politics of International Cooperation*. Berkeley, CA: University of California Press.

Sandholtz, W., and Sweet, A. S. (eds) (1998). *European Integration and Supranational Governance*. New York: Oxford University Press.

Sandholtz, W., and Zysman, J. (1989). '1992: Recasting the European Bargain', *World Politics*, 42 (1), 95–128.

Sassatelli, M. (2002). 'Imagined Europe', *European Journal of Social Theory*, 5 (4), 435–51.

Schaffer, F. C. (2006). 'Ordinary Language Interviewing'. In D. Yanow and P. Schwartz-Shea (eds), *Interpretation and Method: Empirical Research Methods and the Interpretive Turn*, pp. 150–60. Armonk, NY: M. E. Sharpe.

Schimmelfennig, F., and Sedelmeier, U. (eds) (2005). *The Europeanization of Central and Eastern Europe*. Ithaca, NY: Cornell University Press.

Smith, A. D. (1992). 'National Identity and the Idea of European Unity', *International Affairs*, 68 (1), 55–76.

Stets, J. E., and Burke, P. J. (2000). 'Identity Theory and Social Identity Theory', *Social Psychology Quarterly*, 63 (3), 224–37.

Tajfel, H. (1981). *Human Groups and Social Categories*. Cambridge: Cambridge University Press.

Wendt, A. (1994). 'Collective Identity Formation and the International State', *American Political Science Review*, 88 (2), 384–96.

Wiener, A. (1996). 'Practicing Citizenship beyond Modern Frontiers: The Resources of Union Citizenship'. Paper presented at the 1995–1996 EUI European Forum on Citizenship, European Citizenship: An Institutional Challenge. Florence: EUI.

MARTINA TOPIĆ

# 9 European Identity and the Far Right in Central Europe: A New Emerging Concept or a New European 'Other'?

Defining and creating concepts to explain the diversity in Europe has existed for a long time; however, nowadays these definitions present a chaotic line of classifications used to describe different regions and nations in their geographic or civilizational specificity. Therefore, there are discussions on Central Europe, Southeast Europe, the Balkans, Western Balkans, Eastern Europe, and then East-Central Europe. Following these chaotic divisions, when looking into debates on what European identity is meant to be and what the European Union (EU) claims to promote, various concepts of European identity emerge and these differ from country to country.

This chapter discusses the applicability of the terms in defining one region in a case study of the far right and its understanding of the European identity in three countries – Austria, Croatia and Hungary – supposedly belonging to the region of Central Europe and its civilizational circle.[1] Accordingly, the programmes of the following far right parties are analysed: the Freedom Party of Austria (Freiheitliche Partei Österreichs, FPÖ), the Croatian Pure Party of Rights (Hrvatska Čista Stranka Prava, HČSP) and Jobbik, the Movement for a Better Hungary (Jobbik Magyarországért Mozgalom), in the case of Hungary. The analysis has a twofold purpose. On the one hand, it analyses the programmes of the three parties in gen-

1 In Croatia's case, its territory belongs to both Central Europe (Pannonian part) and Southeast Europe (Dalmatia). However, since a concept of Central Europe exists in European studies and studies of nationalism, then Croatia, when it comes to its policy, certainly belongs to the Central European concept (its national movement from the nineteenth century, its policy of unquestionable Europeanism and so on).

eral to identify common traits amongst their political ideas, juxtaposing them with what is perceived as a general far right ideology in the West. On the other hand, the analysis concentrates on views on the meaning of 'European' in each case. The method of analysis was a critical discourse analysis, which sees the discourse as a text only (British model) and seeks to identify the so-called 'discursive topoi' (Wodak 1999). This 'discursive topoi' is then understood as a core argument that appears in the talk of the actors, which in this case are the parties' programmes. The ultimate goal is to discuss whether we are witnessing a new emerging concept of a Central European understanding of European identity in its reflection in the far right policy. In line with that, the paper will question relevance of the Central European concept for analysis.

## Defining Concepts

The notion of European identity has been an issue since 1973, when the Declaration on European Identity was introduced.[2] However, the question of belonging to the notion of Europe has never left the sphere of interest of European Union policy-makers or European public opinion and academia.

2 The Declaration on European Identity was introduced at the Copenhagen meeting in 1973 when the EU member states declared that European unification was a dynamic process open to every country that shares the same ideals. One of those ideals was the need for further unification that would go beyond mere economic collaboration. The goal was to create a European identity that would be, amongst other things, based on the diversity of cultures within Europe as a common civilization. The Declaration reads: 'The diversity of cultures within the framework of a common European civilization, the attachment to common values and principles, the increasing convergence of attitudes to life, the awareness of having specific interests in common and determination to take part in the construction of a United Europe, all give the European Identity its originality and its own dynamism'. For various discussions of the declaration, see Calhoun (2003), Kraus (2011), Mokre (2006), Topić and Sciortino (2012), Shore (2006), Vidmar Horvat (2012).

This is because the sense of belonging still largely centres on the national, while the notion of European remains contested by the EU's foreign policy, which is not always approved of by the European public. Immigration has also been in the centre of debates on the notion of European, and this issue is largely intertwined with the question of the integration of immigrants. This latter remains a contested issue, threatening the European project.[3] The issue of immigration and integration have also been a subject of interest to the far right, which calls for radical policies towards immigrants, and because of which the European far right has gained new strength. While before the Second World War the European far right largely dealt with Jews as seen as a threat to European progress, the new far right largely deals with immigrants, who are nowadays mostly Muslims, but also Hindus as well as newcomers from the new EU member states that joined the EU in the enlargement processes from 2004 onwards. Although the far right remains steadily anti-Semitic, new calls for the extermination of Jews are usually not publicly announced, and Jews are more or less safe when it comes to the European far right,[4] except in extreme cases such as Hungary.

However, the essence of the EU is economic collaboration, peace amongst member states, as well as respect towards diversity, best expressed

3 Some authors claim that 'Europe is an uncertain nation, born of confusion, with vague borders, a shifting geometry and subject to slippage, breaks and metamorphosis' (Morin 2002: 126).

4 This is quite paradoxical. Before the Second World War, the far right called for extermination of Jews while the European left remained silent. Nowadays, the far right remains silent and more or less ignores the Jews while the European left enforces the so-called new anti-Semitism expressed in strenuous criticism of Israel while ignoring the fact that, because of those critiques that equate all Jews with Israel, Jews suffer from discrimination and assaults from new immigrants from the East, mostly Muslims. However, because Muslims are victims of growing Islamophobia (and there does not seem to be the will to fully acknowledge this problem either) when they assault Jews nobody raises their voice. This is another issue in Europe and because of which the European Commission published a study on new forms of anti-Semitism and ways to combat it. This study recognized these issues, amongst others, as a new form of anti-Semitism (EUMC 2004). For further discussion, see Gerstenfeld (2004), Stern (2006), Topić (2013), Wistrich (1990, 2002, 2004).

in the EU's motto 'United in diversity'. Nonetheless, the EU has invested a lot of energy and funding in fostering intercultural collaboration and a sense of belonging to the European project founded on diversity.[5] Even though the EU invests a lot of effort in promoting integration and diversity, new concepts meant to demarcate the different still occur. While during the Cold War the division in Europe was drawn in accordance with the communist systems enforced in countries behind the so-called Iron Curtain, after the fall of communism new division lines emerged, and nowadays we are confronted with discussions on Central Europe, Southern Europe, and Eastern Europe. In the case of the last of these, everything that used to be behind the 'Iron Curtain' became Eastern Europe, and remained the 'other' constructed during the Cold War (Wolff 1999). In the case of the Central European classification, countries belonging (or supposedly belonging) to that region fostered the sense of belonging to that region to avoid the Eastern classification. Insofar as the majority of countries from the former Eastern bloc (except ex-Soviet countries) declared themselves to be Central European, that term has for a long time served as a classification for national movements in countries that claim to belong to that civilizational circle.[6] This region has also been accepted as returning to Europe after being under communist rule (Ray 2009) and this notion of the return to Europe is a concept that has a particular strength in countries claiming to belong to the Central European civilizational circle.[7]

5 The European Commission runs several programmes that foster the idea of European unity founded on diversity inside Europe, including the European Year of Intercultural Dialogue, the European City of Culture (later renamed the European Capital of Culture), Europe Day and so on. For details on these policies, see Topić and Sciortino (2012) and Vidmar Horvat (2012). These programmes were not introduced without criticism; European cultural policy has been called imperialistic (Vidmar Horvat 2012) and criticized as lacking any strategic objectives (Fisher 2012).

6 For example, in Croatia, being a part of Central Europe means not only belonging to this region geographically, but in a civilizational respect, and this is clearly visible in Croatia's tourist promotion (Topić 2012a).

7 This is one of the key factors used to describe Central Europe. The policy of unquestionable Europeanism, a 'right' to belong to Europe, and to return to Europe after

Since new concepts such as East-Central Europe and Southeast Europe have emerged, it seems that not only Europe as a whole needs its 'East' (Neumann 1999), but that countries often perceived as East by the West need their East, too, so they identify countries that claim to be a part of the Central European civilizational circle as East-Central European. The term East-Central Europe originates from Central Europe itself, where intellectuals firstly (that is, before arguing for Central Europe as a civilization and distinctive culture) argued that Hungary, Croatia, Poland and the Czech Republic belonged to the Western Church while the others under the communist rule belonged to the Eastern Church. Following this, a division emerged and, therefore, countries of the Orthodox Church became Eastern Europe while countries of the Western Church became Central Eastern Europe (Kovacs *et al.* 2009). This means that Central Europe found its East and thus its 'other', just like Europe found its East and 'other' in everything behind the so-called Iron Curtain. Today, some authors use the term East-Central Europe as a self-explanatory term for the region bordering with Austria, and this apparently applies even to countries that the above-mentioned classification considered as Central Europe (Spohn 2003).

These issues become even more complicated when it comes to the far right, because far right parties have their own countries as a starting position, and even though their people might be considered as 'other' in different countries, that does not prevent them from 'othering' the perceived others in their own countries.[8] In the past few decades, the far right has become an increasing problem in Europe, mostly because of their sudden electoral

---

being a part of the communist bloc are key objectives of the policies of the post-communist part of Central Europe (Kundera 1984; Topić *et al.* 2009).

8 The far right is often defined as an attempt to oppose the changes society undergoes and as a political ideology that implements inclusionary and exclusionary criteria (Kitschelt 1997; Minkenberg 1998, 2001, 2011). The overall emphasis of the far right is tradition, social homogeneity and a nationally defined community (Minkenberg 2011). Different authors use different terms for the far right. For example, Minkenberg uses the term radical right. However, I consider the terms radical right and far right as synonyms since there is no detailed classification that would explain in detail the variations between right-oriented parties.

successes where, in some cases, they participate in ruling the country or become parliamentary parties. Much research has been conducted on this issue and the conclusion is often that unemployment and immigration form a solid ground for the emergence and political success of the far right parties in the West (Anderson 1996; Jackman and Volpert 1996; Knigge 1998). However, as is the case with many issues, there is no agreement on this, and many studies conclude the opposite (Golder 2003).

Nonetheless, much research has shown that people who vote for far right and anti-immigrant parties mostly have a lower level of education and poor standards of living; manual workers and the unemployed particularly often vote for these political options (Anderson 1996; Knigge 1998; Lubbers *et al.* 2002). However, there are also variations, and some far right parties attract the middle classes, such as the Austrian FPÖ (Kitschelt 1997), the Belgian Vlaams Bloc (Lubbers and Scheepers 2000) and the French National Front (Mayer 1998). Some theories have also claimed that non-religious people and younger people tend to vote for far right parties, and this is explained by social disintegration; these two groups are not integrated into the society and thus find their place amongst members of the far right (Arendt 1951; Kornhauser 1960). However, what often plays a pivotal role in deciding to vote for the far right party is their anti-immigrant and favourable in-group attitude, their authoritarian stance, and political dissatisfaction (Lubbers *et al.* 2002), with the anti-immigrant attitude and political dissatisfaction proving to be the most decisive factors (Lubbers and Scheepers 2000).

## Identity Affiliation and the Far Right: Austria, Croatia and Hungary

### *Austria*

The notion of Europe has a pivotal role in Austria's national identity, and these discussions started when the Second World War (WWII) ended.

Since Austria had been annexed to Germany during WWII, it found itself in doubt about how to place itself in the future. Spohn (2003: 5) outlines that public and academic debates in Austria were centred on four crucial issues: '(1) the Anschluß to Nazi Germany as consensual or enforced or the coresponsibility or non-guilt for Nazi crimes; (2) the historical foundations of a separate Austrian national identity vis-à-vis a German identity; (3) the Austrian nation as based on ethnic-cultural or political-civic foundations of a political community; and (4) Austria as a Western oriented or a neutral nation mediating between East and West'.

The end of WWII brought debates on Austrian national identity and the extent to which this identity could be separated from its German element (Wodak 1997). The debates on how to identify Austria after Nazism ended with the conclusion that Austria had been the first victim of Nazi Germany, which had annexed it and enforced its regime, thus entirely underplaying Austria's active role in the Nazi regime (Pelinka 2001; Spohn 2003). Citizens who took leading roles in the Nazi regime were not removed from public positions, and Austrian society never faced its past as German society did. This policy influenced the appearance of the FPÖ, a far right party led by Jörg Haider, and the fact that this party managed to enter parliament and participate in governing the country as late as 1999. The FPÖ insisted on the German culture of Austria, and that this German civilizational aspect should be included in the Austrian national identity, an old debate that had dominated discussions on Austrian identity after WWII ended (Pelinka 2001; Spohn 2003). As will be explained in this chapter, the FPÖ still insists on this aspect, although not as it used to; for example, a strong emphasis on German identity has been partially replaced by Austrian patriotism. Additionally, the FPÖ's policy of underplaying Austria's role in Nazism and claiming that Austria was Hitler's first victim presented a continuation of Austria's old policy of denying responsibility for WWII and the country's active role in it. This presented populist rhetoric that found approval with a public reluctant to accept Austria's responsibility for WWII crimes.

Ever since WWII Austria has tolerated former Nazi officials in the political and the public sphere, and this brought belief that Austria was indeed the victim of Nazi Germany, and the FPÖ presents just one more denial of Austria's Nazi past (Pelinka 2001). Nonetheless, this constructionist origin of the Austrian nation has also been questioned. In this, many Austrian historians have attempted to prove that Austrian identity existed before WWII and annexation and, thus, that Austria has its own identity that is not a mere construct (Spohn 2003).

As a consequence, Austria's relations with the EU have been dominated by fear of German control. Therefore Austria as a neutral country collaborated with the neutral Scandinavian countries. Austria joined the EU only when the Scandinavian countries also applied for membership, and it became an EU member state only in 1995 (Haller 1996; Spohn 2003; Wodak 1999). However, Austria – in line with its neutral policy of being between the East and the West – remained between these two sides of Europe. But this started to change with the fall of communism, and Austria shifted its policy towards supporting the Danubian countries due to their common culture and Austro-Hungarian legacy (Spohn 2003).

European identity in Austria was significantly affected by the fall of the so-called Iron Curtain, which changed relations between Austria and Europe and also altered the sense of Austrian national identification, in that the number of those who felt very proud of Austria rose in comparison to previous decades. On the other hand, the sense of belonging to Austria has shifted from the state-oriented and civic to a more ethnocultural view, where people in Austria consider it is more relevant to feel like an Austrian and to speak German than to be a Christian, obey Austrian laws, have Austrian citizenship, be born in Austria and so on (Haller 1996). Since Austria had to redefine its neutrality after joining the EU, Austrians approved entry to the EU on the 1994 referendum; however, they remained steadily attached to their own identity and preservation of the national (Haller 1996; Spohn 2003).

This means that, as far as the far right is concerned, the most significant factor is Haider's FPÖ, a far right party that gained second place in the national elections in 1999 and established a coalition with the Austrian conservative People's Party to form the government. Because of this, Austria faced sanctions from the EU that reduced its relations with Austria to a technical level and threatened Austria with losing its right to vote in the European Parliament and with eventual expulsion from the EU (Pelinka

2001). Haider's party won 26.9 percent of votes in 1999, which was close to one-third of the total Austrian electorate and thus presented the highest entry level for any extreme party in Europe when results are compared to other European countries where the far right managed to obtain a significant proportion of votes in national elections (Marchart 2001). At the core of this success was not solely the economy, because Austria had a low unemployment rate at the time of the elections, as well as a well-managed social security system (Marchart 2001). According to various observers, 'FPÖ's electorate is typically young, male, blue-collar, relatively less educated and secular' (Pelinka 2001) – a description that is in line with the aforementioned theory of social disintegration. Additionally, while the Austrian far right historically had urban support, recent support has come from the rural area, and thus the party has lost its bourgeois label (Pelinka 2001). After the EU reduced relations with Austria because of the election of the FPÖ to a leading coalition, European identification further decreased.

### *Croatia*

In contrast, Croatia is a country that belongs to one of the Danubian neighbours mentioned above because it has a history of belonging to the Habsburg monarchy. Like Austria, Croatia also has a share of WWII history as a Nazi puppet state called the Independent State of Croatia that committed a holocaust over its Serbian and Jewish population. When Nazi Germany capitulated, Tito established the second Yugoslavia, and pushed all atrocities under the carpet instead of confronting Croatia with its past and enforcing a reconciliation process. Therefore, just like Austria, Croatia was never forced to face the past, and animosities coming from the war remained in the private sphere, spreading in an oral form.

With the dissolution of Yugoslavia, old animosities came to the surface, and Croatian Serbs rebelled against the new Croatian state, claiming that it might become Nazi-like again. Instead of guaranteeing all rights to its Serbian population and inviting them to accept the newly founded Croatian state, Franjo Tudjman, the first president since independence, declaratively guaranteed all rights, but at the same time expressed discriminatory attitudes towards Serbs and Jews (Bijelić 2006; Ramet 2005; Topić 2009, 2010; Topić *et al.* 2009). At the same time, Tudjman radically enforced historical revisionism, primarily expressed through romanticizing the notorious WWII regime. Additionally, he and his regime re-established the Catholic Church in Croatia in a significant position and in the decision-making process, leading to the revitalization of religion in Croatia. The Church took a leading role in enforcing historical revisionism and discriminatory policies, and this policy has not changed to this day, even when Tudjman no longer lives, and his party enforces less radical views on the past (although it still does not clearly distance itself from that same past) (Pavlaković 2008; Ramet 2005; Topić 2010; Topić and Vasiljević 2011a, 2011b; Topić *et al.* 2009).

When it comes to the notion of European identity, Croatia has a long history of dealing with this issue, and it presents what is often perceived to be a Central European policy of understanding Europe and Croatia's role in it. Since the nineteenth century, Croatian national movements have insisted on unquestionable Europeanism, and on the necessity to 'return to Europe'. This was one of the arguments during the nation's formation in the nineteenth century, and it continued during the twentieth century when this policy was advocated by Stjepan Radić, one of the most prominent Croatian politicians. However, policies from the nineteenth and twentieth centuries advocated by Croatian politicians, although nationally oriented (and often anti-Yugoslav), were never exclusive or extreme.

On the other hand, when Tudjman gained power in the first multi-party elections and established an independent Croatia in 1991, he also continued with the policies of Europeanism; however, back then his policies were wrapped together with discrimination and exclusion of Croatia's newly formed national minorities. Tudjman advocated 'a return to Europe' supposedly disrupted by the creation of Yugoslavia, and insisted on Croatia as the cradle of Christianity that served as an outer wall defending Europe from the Ottoman threat. The latter is a historical discourse present in argumentation of national ideologists of the nineteenth century, while the Yugoslav disruption of Croatia's return to Europe is historical revisionism at its best. On the contrary, the idea of creating the Yugoslav federation largely came from Croatian intellectuals and national ideologists because this was considered as the best way to preserve Croatia's independence and statehood, which was threatened by Hungarian nationalism and Austria's imperialism. Finally, when Tudjman's policies did not meet with approval in the EU, which at that time was in the process of strengthening its unity and collaboration, a discourse of alleged European betrayal emerged. This is again an old discourse dating from the nineteenth- and twentieth-century national ideologists, only once more Tudjman used it in a revisionist manner. However, even though Tudjman's Croatian Democratic Union has been nationalistic, ruling the country for the major part since its independence, it cannot be considered as the far right since it does not openly discriminate against Croatia's minorities, nor does it openly glorify the Nazi regime.

The only party that can be labelled as far right is the Croatian Pure Party of Rights. Unlike their Austrian colleagues, this party failed to enter parliament or participate in governing the country. Due to disappointing results before the December 2011 parliamentary elections, several other factions of the party emerged, splitting the votes. My analysis focuses on the largest of these parties, the Croatian Pure Party of Rights (HČSP), a party that openly glorifies the Nazi regime of Croatia. Additionally, this party has media coverage making an attempt to secure public support for its ideas. Although the party does not hold a significant political position in the country and thus can be considered marginal, its potential for endangering the European idea should not be neglected, due to the circumstances in the country (holocaust denial, denial of atrocities committed by Croats during the wars in the 1990s and generally denial of any wrongdoing of Croatia) and its programme that correlates in some aspects with Croatia's official policies and the sentiments amongst the citizenry.

### *Hungary*

Hungary also has a history of being a part of the Habsburg monarchy, although its role was different from Croatia's, since Hungary was the constitutive part of the monarchy, and it also had a certain control over

Croatia, which was partially subordinated to Hungary.[9] Hungary acted imperialistically in its policies, including fostering its own art and culture as a separate entity distinct from the Austrian identity, while at the same time undermining Croatian art (Szekely 2012). As in the Croatian case, Hungary also fostered an idea of being an 'Eastern bastion to Christianity', which affected the sense of the Hungarian national identity (Hunyady and Kiss 2003). Fascination with Europe can be traced throughout Hungarian history – an aspect visible not only in the official policies, but also in art and literature (Hunyady and Kiss 2003; Szekely 2012). This means that, like in the Croatian case, debates on Europe existed in the nineteenth century during the process of nation formation, and they continued throughout the twentieth century (Kovacs *et al.* 2009).

The first debates originated from the period of communism, when intellectuals (mostly historians) argued for a division between Central and Eastern Europe and Eastern Europe based on religion (Western versus Eastern Church), which was a predecessor of the argument that Central Europe should be seen as a distinctive civilization and culture (Kovacs *et al.* 2009). On the other hand, newer debates centred on the question of the place of Hungary in Europe and to what extent Hungarians are Europeans (Kovacs *et al.* 2011). After the fall of communism, however, Hungarian elites put forward enthusiastic views on European integration, though some authors claim this was not immediately met with approval from the wider public (Kovacs *et al.* 2011), until the entry to the EU became a political reality when it met with approval (Hunyady and Kiss 2003). This was because some intellectuals – mostly from the nationalistic wing – wondered whether there would be second-class members of the EU and whether there would be economic exploitation (Kovacs *et al.* 2009).

9 At the time of the Habsburg monarchy, Croatia was not united in its present form. Only Roy Croatia was Croatia, while Slavonia was a kingdom of its own that easily joined Roy Croatia in its attempt to unite several regions into a unique Croatian state. Both parts of the monarchy were subordinated to Hungarian rule while Dalmatia and Istria remained under Austrian control. During the nineteenth-century national movements there was a particular struggle to include Dalmatia and Istria in the new Croatian state.

Debates on Europe that emerged after the fall of communism were centred on divisions between the prosperous West and the barbaric East, where Central Europe was explained as more similar and attached to the West than to the East. However, all of these debates had a top-down approach, and there were no debates or research that deeply questioned the attitudes and feelings of those who did not belong to elites, and thus the whole idea of Europe and the subsequent modernization was imposed from above. Because of this, national identity remains stronger than European identity (Kovacs *et al.* 2009).

In the case of Hungary, nationalism and relations with minorities became a problem after the fall of communism (Kovacs *et al.* 2009), and this is where the far right emerged. A party considered far right in Hungary is most certainly Jobbik, a party that organizes death marches on the Hungarian Romani population and openly expresses harsh anti-Semitism, while advocating radical policies towards Hungarian minorities. Even so, the party managed to enter parliament and was elected to the European Parliament as well. Therefore, it is selected for analysis here, as it presents an important case of the far right in the EU.

## Case-Study Countries: Programme Ideologies and European Identity

### *Austria*

The Freedom Party of Austria primarily insists on freedom as the highest value. Accordingly, its programme outlines the importance of freedom of self-determination as well as freedom from 'being the plaything of international speculators and multinational firms, whether of the state, or of international semi-state institutions' (FPÖ 2012: Chapter I). In addition, the party enforces a dual understanding of the notion of Austria and Europe. Accordingly, Austria comes first, as 'Austria is more than a simple administrative unit. Its people are linked by a will for independence and belong together in regional diversity' (FPÖ 2012: Chapter III). This means that the FPÖ envisages Austria united in its regional diversity, cultivating its identity and cultural heritage. This is because the party believes that there has been a decline in the preservation of Austria's cultural heritage and low self-esteem when it comes to international politics. Article 4 (FPÖ 2012: Chapter III) states that

> Austria's social and cultural heritage justifies pride in the results, traditions and achievements. From this arose a positive self image [Patriotismus] which calls for self-assured Austrian politics and a resistance to a decline in the cultural level, and increasing efforts to revile traditions and to willfully disparage Austria:
>
> 1. As Austria played a decisive role in the all-German and all-European history and in view of the resulting cultural heritage, it is legitimate to appear on the international stage with self-confidence and pride.
>
> 2. We reject the politics that ends in – especially since Austria's entry into the EU – massive efforts to standardize and level down, to the detriment of Austria's intellectual and cultural substance.
>
> 3. The modern trend to get some public response by abusing Austria and disparaging Austrian qualities needs resolute intellectual resistance on the part of all people who believe in Austria [erfordert einen entschlossenen geistigen Widerstand aller patriotischen Kräfte].
>
> 4. Especially in the media a decline in the cultural level has been obvious for years; so we need a new intellectual and cultural move to keep Austrian traditions and regional peculiarities alive.

In its protection of Austrian cultural identity, the party recognizes indigenous groups that exist in Austria (Germans, Croats, Roma, Slovaks, Slovenians, Czechs and Hungarians) and acknowledges their own identity that caused Austrian culture to be 'moulded by them'. These groups, together with their distinctive identities, are to be protected.

What is considered problematic by many authors and advocates of a multicultural Europe is that the FPÖ recognizes as Austrian only the minorities with a historical presence in Austria, while immigrants are not mentioned. In fact, the party clearly states that Austria is 'not a country for immigration' (FPÖ 2012: Chapter III) – a statement inspired by the country's 'density of population and its limited resources', as well as by the fact that every Austrian citizen, regardless of the culture he or she belongs to, has a right to have a so-called home country (*Heimat*), which is a specific term the party uses. Immigration would, as explained, endanger 'the right to preservation and protection of cultural identity [Heimat]. We reject multi-cultural experiments that bear social conflicts with them'.

When it comes to the notion of Europe, the FPÖ has a very clear standpoint, although it is tightly intertwined with religion. In Chapter V, the party states that Christianity is the foundation of Europe (Article 1). In this it clearly ignores the policy of the EU, which removed religion from its Constitution so as to enable respect for diversity. Christianity, according to the FPÖ, has great relevance for European progress, as well as for the cultural character of Europe, and the party goes as far as to state that 'the cultural character of Christian values and traditions even embraces members of non-Christian religions and people without any confession' (FPÖ 2012: Chapter V). However, the party recognizes that Europe has been influenced by Judaism and other non-Christian religions, although it does not name them. The FPÖ believes that Christian values are to be cherished especially because they are 'endangered by different streams of thought. The increasing fundamentalism of radical Islam which is penetrating Europe, as well as hedonistic consumption, aggressive capitalism, increasing occultism, pseudo-religious sects and an omnipresent nihilism threaten the consensus of values which is in danger of getting lost' (FPÖ 2012: Chapter V).

According to the party, Europe is not to be reduced to only a geographic term. Because it is based on Christian values, its people are 'bound together by destiny and a cultural heritage which make up Europe' (FPÖ 2012: Chapter VI). The EU is not the only representative of Europe because Europe is, in this view, 'composed of a variety of peoples and ethnic groups, regions, nations and state units which have all grown up historically with shared values'. In this Europe, Austria should have a higher status because Austria has had a remarkable role in shaping its diverse ethnic character. Europe as a whole should be cherished and respected; however, it should not become a federal state, and neither does the EU represent Europe fully. The party recognizes the right of ethnic minorities throughout Europe, since minorities should have all cultural rights and a right to continuous existence and protection from assimilation tendencies. This, according to the party, also means that there should be an assumption that 'borders of settlement between peoples are not contiguous with state borders which is why many European states have ethnic minorities' (FPÖ 2012: Chapter VI). However, it is not clear how the party envisages incorporation of the cultural diversity of historical minorities while at the same time opposing the inclusion of ethics in school and insisting on the religious catechism (FPÖ 2012: Chapter V).

According to the FPÖ programme, Austria should play a special role in the protection of ethnic minorities. As outlined, Austria has to protect 'its own cultural minorities but also to act as a protector for German minorities on the territory of the former Austro-Hungarian Monarchy – minorities whose existence is threatened' (FPÖ 2012: Chapter VI) – an aspiration that is explained in even more detail in Chapter VII: A self-confident foreign policy – a common security policy, in which Article 4 states the following:

> Austria remains the protector of the German and Ladin South Tyroleans. There must remain the possibility for South Tyrol to join the Republic of Austria in a free exercise of its right to self-determination:
>
> 1. As a result of political trends South Tyrol can at any time become the plaything of internal conflicts in Italy.
>
> 2. The peoples' right to self-determination is indivisible and cannot be renounced. Until South Tyrol has realized its right to self-determination, it is Austria's historic mission to protect the population of the German and Ladin minorities in South Tyrol and the internationally protected legal status by all available peaceful means.
>
> 3. In the event of South Tyrol's secession from Italy following the exercise of its right of self-determination, the right to join the Republic of Austria must be kept open.

Going further, Article 5, on the one hand, states that Austria

> has a special historic responsibility and a duty to protect the numerous members of the German groups now living in the former territories of the Austro-Hungarian Monarchy: 1. Austria has only made a small contribution to help members of the German minorities living in difficult conditions in the former territories of the Austro-Hungarian Monarchy; 2. The preservation of these minorities with their unique culture has to be guaranteed. So it should be Austria's duty to offer these minorities a chance of economic and cultural survival.

With such policies, the party clearly expresses its imperial tendencies, even if the question of Tyrol is already a difficult issue in Austro-Italian relations. On the other hand, the party does not discuss the Austrian minority but rather considers German minorities in the territories formerly belonging to the Austro-Hungarian monarchy, which represents a continuation of the policies the party held in the past, when it considered Austrians as Germans and thus advocated preservation of German culture. However, since they replaced their open German-oriented policies with Austrian patriotism, this policy presents a combination of an old discourse and a new-found patriotic discourse because the central policy is no longer stronger unification with Germany.

The party also discusses the issue of culture and art, and it particularly implies 'culture means all forms of civilized expression' (FPÖ 2012: Chapter XV), and that culture should never be subject to any limitation. Accordingly, the party places an emphasis on language, which is something recognized as a Central European model in the theory of nationalism.[10] As Article 2 puts it, language 'is the most important medium of cultural expression. Thus it must be specially cultivated. The freedomite movement emphasizes the affiliation of Austrians to the cultural community shaped by the mother tongue which for the overwhelming majority of Austrians is German'. In this, they particularly emphasize that language is a characteristic of family, and 'is the language in which we dream, feel and think. Thus the mother tongue as the medium of cultural expression determines the cultural community we belong to. As a majority of Austrians speak the official language German … as their mother tongue, they belong to

10 This type of nationalism places a strong emphasis on the distinctive language of each nation, as language serves as one of the bases for founding nations that then have the right to exist on the European map of nation states. The other elements that form the nation vary from case to case; however, Central European nationalism is considered as an ethnic nationalism often perceived through negative lenses that are not always correct. Or, in other words, this negative prism can most certainly be applied to present national policies in that region; however, this does not always work in practice where the past is concerned. For more details on national processes in Central Europe, see Hroch (2006).

the German cultural community'. The party particularly insists that the state has to protect its culture and cultural heritage, and provinces have a distinct responsibility in this process. Because of this, the party 'decisively rejects' multicultural goals (FPÖ 2012: Chapter XV). Needless to say, when rejecting multicultural goals, the party undermines the whole idea of the EU, largely founded on respect towards each other and cherishing diversity.

*Croatia*

In Croatia, as already mentioned, the Croatian Pure Party of Rights (HČSP) is a real far right representative – a party that, in contrast to other similar parties in Europe, has not managed to meet the minimum number of votes needed to enter parliament.

When it comes to the notion of European identity, unlike in the case of Austria's Freedom Party, not much has been said; the HČSP seems to concentrate solely on Croatia, perceiving it separately from its European context. It is important to note that such an approach is not a problem that characterizes this party only, but also the general Croatian nationalist discourse.[11] However, the HČSP's opinion of the EU is largely negative, and it seems as if the party equates Yugoslavia and the EU, while in its programme strongly opposing any association of Croatia with any other state, including the union of states such as the EU. Still, like the Austrian FPÖ, in its founding principles (HČSP 2012a) the HČSP insists that advocating hatred and violence is 'against basic moral foundations of civilised mankind, and an obstacle towards achieving human rights and freedom, democracy and peaceful coexistence amongst peoples and nations. Therefore, the Croatian Pure Party of Rights opposes all political parties and views that advocate hatred and violence towards anyone'. In addition,

11 This is, for example, the case with history textbooks that take Croatia out of its regional and world contexts and present the whole history of Croatia as a constant struggle to achieve and maintain its statehood endangered by those who oppose it; see Höpken (2006), Karge (2001), Topić and Vasiljević (2011a, 2011b).

it insists that all Croatian citizens are equal before the law, regardless of race, sex, language, faith, world view, political beliefs, education or social position. The founding principles (HČSP 2012a) state that 'members of the national minorities in Croatia have the right to maintain, cherish and develop their national culture and self-esteem (use of their language, development of cultural associations, publishing newspapers, opening schools in the mother tongue, and so on) in line with international law, and they are obliged to respect the rights and interests of the Croatian people and the Croatian state'. However, at the same time, the HČSP insists that Croatian people have the right to exist as every other people, and that 'every attempt of fusion or identifying Croatian people with any other people is against the natural desire and the right of the Croatian people to its existence, so Croatian Pure Party of Rights opposes to Yugoslavism and all similar political endeavours' (HČSP 2012a).

With regard to the EU, the party states that the EU has already gained all Croatia's property and that joining the EU is wrong and should be stopped until the people come to a referendum and clearly express their negative attitude. Even though Croatian citizens voted affirmatively for joining the EU in the referendum held in January 2012, the HČSP has not yet amended this part of its programme, meaning that it still remains strongly anti-EU. Since it has proved not to have high credibility due to some of its contradictory policies,[12] this might be pure sloppiness; still,

12 In 2012 the party made an attempt to organize a so-called conference of the European nationalists to which they invited ultra-nationalistic groups and parties from several European countries. However, one of the parties invited to the conference was the Hungarian Jobbik, a party that has imperial tendencies in its programme. Those imperial tendencies include aspirations towards part of Croatian territory. For a party that claims to 'defend' apparently 'jeopardized' Croatia and its statehood this was proof of incredible ignorance. The anti-fascist scene jumped to motivate the people to organize a public protest and to pressurize the authorities to ban the conference. The authorities eventually banned it, and the HČSP then organized 'a walk in support of the Croatian generals in the Hague tribunal'. However, a few thousand people came to the streets to stop the walk while there were only a few people who came to support the party and the European nationalists. The anti-fascists also twisted roles and accused the HČSP of working against Croatian interests for inviting Jobbik, and

it might also be a sign that the party's programme will change, but that it will take a radical anti-EU stance after Croatia joins the EU, similar to the programmes of fellow far right parties inside the EU. Another reason for not joining the EU, according to the party, is the prevention of all right-oriented parties in their work because that 'supra-state', as the party calls the EU, does not allow anything but financial slavery and lack of independence and patriotism in Croatia.

The party states that it is 'strictly against all negotiations on "Balkan" and similar associations that are against the Constitution and that are ever more present in public' (HČSP 2012b). The opposition towards any association with other countries is justified by a view, according to which, only a 'free, autonomous, and independent Croatian state is the guarantee of existence, liberty and undisturbed development of the Croatian people and, therefore, Croatian Pure Party of Rights fights for liberation of all Croatian ethnic and historical space, for foundation of entirely autonomous and independent State of Croatia on that entire space, as well as for defence of that State (after the state is founded)'. The problematic term in this statement is 'State of Croatia' (Država Hrvatska), as well as the mention of Croatia's historical space. This is because Croatia's Nazi state was named the 'Independent State of Croatia' (Nezavisna Država Hrvatska) and as a Nazi puppet state had control over a large portion of the present Bosnian territory, claiming it as Croatia's historical space.

Although the HČSP declaratively guarantees all rights to national minorities, it demonstrates a problematic attitude according to which national minorities, at the same time, need to respect the 'rights and interests of the Croatian people and the Croatian state' (HČSP 2012a). This is problematic because it implies that national minorities are not loyal to Croatia – a historical discourse greatly used during the Tudjman regime in the 1990s. However, unlike Tudjman's party, which never acknowledged the participation of the Croatian Serbs in the Serbo-Croatian war in the 1990s, this radical party surprisingly acknowledges the help of 'Croatian

---

used their rhetoric of not loving Croatia, something the party often enacts against the anti-fascists (Topić and Sremac 2013).

citizens of Serbian nationality'[13] (HČSP 2012b). Furthermore, the party insists that Croatia is in crisis in all respects, and this is because it has been led by 'people from the former Yugo-Communist system', generating the present Croatian problems. The solution lies in the so-called 'de-communization' of Croatian society and purification, while the lack of these activities is justified by the 'so-called all-time reconciliation process in Croatia'. The party insists that reconciliation is impossible and that all people who had important duties during the former Yugoslavia should be removed from all public and state positions, including the education system, cultural sector, journalism and publishing, and generally from the whole of public life. This is explained as a logical historical continuation, and everything else is 'an attempt to stop the historical wheel that results in new glorification of the criminal Communist regime and justification, and even denial, of its terrible mass crimes over Croats, now skilfully wrapped in cellophane of anti-fascism' (Programme, Introduction). By saying this, the HČSP equates anti-fascism and communism, which is, in fact, a dispute between the anti-fascists and the nationalists in Croatia. In the nationalist rhetoric, anyone who is anti-fascist is automatically a communist. This is because the anti-fascists correctly insist that when ethnic Croats, who were not endangered by the notorious Nazi (Ustasha) regime, joined non-Croats in the anti-fascist people's liberation battle (*Narodnooslobodilačka borba*) this was a heroic act. While the anti-fascists subsequently insist that this is something to be remembered and cherished, the nationalists ignore it and, instead, enforce romanticized views of Croatian history, including its notorious WWII history, which is criticized and rejected by the anti-fascists.

The salute 'God and the Croats' that the HČSP uses is explained as though only God and Croats can be in power in Croatia. The justification that only God can rule Croats comes as a response to the left-oriented scene that labels this party as neo-Ustasha; however, it is noticeable that the party does not offer an explanation for its other salute 'For Home

13 I translated this literally, but it needs to be noted that the term nationality in Croatia is also colloquially used as a synonym for ethnicity.

Ready!' This is important because, whereas the first salute comes from the so-called Father of the Nation, Ante Starčević (which is indeed the case), who was not a politician with genocidal ideas,[14] the other salute is exclusively a salute from Croatia's Ustasha regime (Pavlaković 2008), and its use can be nothing else but an attempt to create sympathetic feelings towards that regime that committed a holocaust over Croatia's Serbian and Jewish population. Additionally, the party's organizational structure is also problematic because its main body, responsible for all decision-making, is called 'Glavni stan', which is a term from the Nazi Ustasha regime in which the Croatian *führer* (called *poglavnik*) observed its central governing body, called 'Glavni stan'.

The above-outlined approaches and policies are accompanied by organized commemorations for well-known Ustasha collaborators and perpetrators of the holocaust in Croatia. The party insists that the Independent State of Croatia (a Nazi state) is also a founding element of the Croatian statehood and the present Croatian state. Indeed, in its founding principles, the party openly advocates the legitimacy of the Croatia's Nazi state:

> Culture is the most important characteristic of people; it enriches men and boosts his human dignity. By desiring to disable freedom, honour and dignity, and with that also the mere existence of the Croatian people, Croatian enemies were systematically destroying the Croatian culture, and language and history in particular. In the latter, particularly wrong was the representation of the creation and actions of the Independent State of Croatia. This is why the Croatian Clear Party of Rights demands to maintain and cherish the Croatian cultural heritage, its comprehensive research, and its truthful and objective manifestation in public – and especially in the explanation of the creation and action of the Independent State of Croatia as one of the most significant periods and accomplishments in struggling for Croatian statehood and independence – and in that way to remove all consequences of anti-Croatian actions on the Croatian culture and return of honour and dignity to the

14 Ante Starčević is often attributed as a Father of the Nation, although the idea of the Croatian nation existed before him. His views were negative toward Serbs and Austrians for he considered them as the ultimate enemies of Croatian statehood; however, his views on the Croatian nation were not of ethnic orientation. Instead, he thought that being a Croat was a spiritual category in a sense that Croat can be anybody who has a Croatian spirit, regardless of ethnicity (Matić 2006; Topić 2009).

> Croatian people and then, furthermore, continuous development of all types of cultural creations as a permanent shape of enrichment of the Croatian people and raising of its human dignity into the lap of civilised manhood. (HČSP 2012a: Article 28)

This view goes against the Constitution, which strictly denies any historical continuation between the Nazi Croatian state and the present Republic of Croatia. By claiming that Croatia has its historical legacy in its Nazi past, the party is actually damaging Croatia's national interests. While from one point claiming that the so-called communists are undermining Croatia's political and economic interests, it is actually this party that is doing so, for at least two reasons: (a) if Croatia were to accept its Nazi past as a part of its legacy, its international reputation and prospects would be highly damaged, and (b) Croatia would also have to pay compensation to all victims of the holocaust in Croatia – something the authorities insist they will not do, because of the Constitutional claims that the Croatian Nazi past has no direct connection with the present Croatian state. This is also because the Croatian Nazi state is considered to have been a quisling state imposed on the Croats, who eventually stood up against it. This official discourse is very similar to the Austrian one where the Nazi collaborators also never faced any sanctions, while Austria claims to be the Hitler's first victim. Nazi perpetrators faced hardly any sanctions in Croatia. Although they are not in high politics, and neither have they ever managed to be so because Croatia became a part of Yugoslavia, some perpetrators are still living out their days in Croatia, while others are hiding in Austria or Latin America. Lastly, the Croatian Pure Party of Rights uses the coat of arms with a chessboard; however, Croatia's current coat of arms starts with a red field, while the party uses the coat of arms that starts with the white field; something the Ustashas did too.

The party expresses rage towards the so-called communists, whom they frame as 'children of the butchers from Bleiburg, where their fathers disarmed Croatian soldiers from the dignified death in battle, so today they are trying to take from the Croatian soldier every feeling of glory and the glorious victory against the Serbian aggressor' (HČSP 2012b: Section V). However, the most problematic aspect of the party's programme is Section VI on purification and so-called de-communization of Croatia, in which the party insists that all anti-fascist monuments and memorial days should be abolished because they are, as the party declares, nothing but glorifications of the communist criminals who committed atrocities over Croats. This is yet another attempt to mark all anti-fascists who advocate a ban of all pro-Ustasha policies and symbols as communists, and to equate communism with anti-fascism. In line with this, the party insists that the battle of Bleiburg was a mass crime over Croats that should be remembered, and those who committed it should be prosecuted.[15] The appropriate term for these alleged crimes is, according to the party, 'the Croatian Holocaust',[16] so that these crimes can achieve 'decent piety'. This is quite an interesting statement because nowhere in its programme does the party accept any responsibility of Croatia for the holocaust; however, it wants to use this term to describe alleged crimes against the Croats, in which they indirectly admit that the holocaust was a mass crime; however, in this argumentation and policy, Croatia apparently never took part.

Like the Austrian FPÖ, the Croatian HČSP makes reference to migrant communities. In its founding principles, the party states that the non-Croatian (in Croatian: *nehrvatski/e* means anti-Croatian) parties that ruled Croatia inflicted violence and poverty over Croats, because of which they largely left the country, while the non-Croatian population immigrated

15 The Bleiburg massacre was an alleged massacre of Croats; however, it was actually a massacre of the Ustasha army that refused to accept defeat. The HČSP, the Catholic Church and Tudjman's party have claimed it was a massacre of civilians and women and children. The latter has never been proven. There is no list of alleged atrocities or an exact number. However, officials organize commemoration in Bleiburg every year and the commemorations – led by the Catholic Church – are often accompanied by Ustasha symbols. The newly elected government in 2012 revoked official support for the commemoration; however, this event still remains an important part of the history textbooks, where the main position is given to supposed Croatian martyrdom at Bleiburg, while there is very little mention of atrocities committed by Croats, such as the holocaust over Serbs and Jews. For more details, see Höpken (2006), Topić and Vasiljević (2011a, 2011b).

16 The European Monitoring Centre on Racism and Xenophobia in 2004 offered a working definition of anti-Semitism that includes comparing the Holocaust to other crimes with which the Holocaust is made relative (EUMC 2004).

to Croatia. In this respect, the party insists that all Croats should be able to remain in the country and the diaspora should be allowed to return. With this in mind, the party clearly envisages an ethnically cleansed Croatia inhabited by a large number of ethnic Croats. However, this aspect is related to immigration, in which the party, like their Austrian colleagues, states that 'Croatia is not a country for free immigration', implying that it will not look with sympathy on potential immigration from the EU once Croatia becomes a member. This is in line with their rejection of all state unions including the EU. Nonetheless, and again like their Austrian colleagues, the party states that Croats were forced to immigrate from 'historical Croatian countries of Bosnia, Herzegovina, Boka Kotorska, Srijem, Bačka and Banat' (HČSP 2012a: Article 21). These territories today belong to other sovereign states, namely Bosnia and Herzegovina (that the party refers to as two separate entities), Montenegro (Boka Kotorska) and Serbia (Srijem, Bačka and Banat).

In terms of the economic development of Croatia, the HČSP insists that all regions should be developed equally, and that the state has the responsibility to ensure this, as well as to encourage a competitive economy. This is similar to the policy of their Austrian colleagues, who also insist on the development of all Austrian regions. In terms of the urban–rural dichotomy, the party demands that the state should ensure the development of village economies so that people do not need to leave to seek work. According to this view, living conditions in both rural and urban areas should be sufficient to enable people to live in either place instead of living in rural areas (HČSP 2012a: Article 25).

Finally, the HČSP makes reference to religion, but not to the same extent as the Austrian FPÖ. According to its founding principles, the party states that belief in God is 'the strongest reliance of noble and moral life while the lack of it causes devastation of peoples and individuals' (HČSP 2012a: Article 17). This is why the state has to help 'activities of all religious communities in fulfilling their duties, and to respect religious traditions without questioning the right of someone to believe or not to believe'. Following this, the party states that Croatian people, as other Croatian citizens in general, are religiously united so it is the duty of the HČSP to 'develop religious tolerance and love amongst members of various faiths, and with this policy to spread unity in Croatia' (HČSP 2012a: Article 17). On the other hand, in its programme, the party states that they support the founding of the Croatian society based on Christian values and morals (HČSP 2012b: Section 2). Like the Austrian party, they also state that Croatian society has been infiltrated by moral relativism, for which they accuse the West; however, the Croatian party does not mention religious catechism in schools in their programme or founding principles.

### *Hungary*

In Hungary, Jobbik, a far right political party, is the third strongest party in the country. This party does not foster an anti-immigration policy because Hungary is not a destination for immigration. Instead, they openly foster anti-Semitism and anti-Roma attitudes as well as rehabilitating Hungarian Nazi leaders, such as admiral Miklos Horthy, who compiled the list of Hungarian Jews that was later used as the basis for sending them to Auschwitz. The party deals obsessively with Israel and its alleged criminal policy as well as insisting on the creation of lists of Hungarian Jews. When this policy caused the rage of all other political parties in Hungary, it was justified as a means of finding out how many Jews possess dual Hungarian–Israeli citizenship, as dual citizenship is perceived as a security risk. However, the party has never clarified what kind of risk dual citizenship poses.

Jobbik's emphasis on anti-Semitism lies in the fact that Hungary is not a destination for immigration, while at the same time it has a history of deep anti-Semitism and a Nazi history. Therefore the party cannot promote anti-immigration policy and blame the immigrants for the situation in the country, as the other far right parties usually do. Additionally, the party also insists on persecuting the Hungarian Roma population, on whom their members (the Hungarian Guard) performed death marches several times.

Anti-Semitism in Hungary is not a new problem. It is the continuation of an old anti-Semitism that never disappeared, and nowadays exists in an open and coded manner while officials express little or no reaction to it.[17] Lately, it has become common practice to assault and intimidate Jews, while anti-Semitism is generally on the rise; however, such tendencies attract little attention from the EU. Only the United States has warned Hungary that the glorification of the Nazi past and open anti-Semitism are not going unnoticed (Heilbrunn 2012). The anti-Semitism that Jobbik fosters is a combination of an old anti-Semitism and glorification of its Nazi past, as well as a new anti-Semitism manifested in criticizing Israel above any other country in the world. In Jobbik's case, this goes to the extent that the party's programme mentions collaboration with Arab countries only, while it completely ignores Israel (Jobbik 2012). It is less important whether Jobbik – or any other party for that matter – likes Israel or not; the problem here is the radical engagement of Jobbik in demonizing Israel and the Hungarian Jews, which is why their unconditional support for Arabs in the Middle East has another dimension. In the same section, Jobbik also states that it will promote the existence of Christian communities in the Middle East, while omitting to outline that these Christian communities are particularly endangered in Arab countries (Pacini 1998). With this in mind – with prosecuting its Jewish and Roma minorities and expressing radical anti-Semitism – Jobbik represents a different case from other far right parties in Europe.

However, when analysing Jobbik's programme, it appears that the term 'far right' indeed requires some differentiation, because this party is ultra-far right in comparison to its Austrian and Croatian colleagues. While Austrian and Croatian parties at least declaratively guarantee all rights to their national minorities, whose cultures should be preserved, Jobbik also places remarkable emphasis on the minority issue and in particular on Roma[18] and Jews, but in a different sense. In its programme, Jobbik makes

17 See Markus (2007) and Todosijevic and Enyedi (2002).

18 The party calls Romani citizens 'Gypsy'; however, they do have a footnote in their manifesto stating that the term 'Gypsy' is the '[c]orrect translation into English of the endonym "Cigány," used self-referentially by the Roma of Hungary'. With this, the party explains that the term 'Gypsy' is not a term with a negative connotation, but a self-used term that they took over. For a comparison, in Croatia and Serbia (and probably elsewhere in the former Yugoslavia) the Romani population is officially

explicit reference to the Roma population and not to the Jewish one; the Jewish one is, however, extensively 'discussed' on Jobbik's official website, which is dominated by statements about Jews and Israel. When it comes to the Roma population, Jobbik states that

> The coexistence and cohesion of Magyar and Gypsy is one of the severest problems facing Hungarian society. On the occasion of 1989's regime change, great swathes of the Gypsy people lost their jobs; who subsequently found themselves unable, and in many cases unfortunately unwilling, to adapt to the new realities. Astonishing rates of unemployment were produced, which the absence or low-level of education merely exacerbated. In certain parts of the country over the last decades the situation has deteriorated to truly deplorable levels. Generations have now grown up, having never once seen their parents in work. The continuation of the Gypsy people's circumstances along their current course is nothing short of a potential time-bomb, and if it is not subject to concerted intervention, our mutual home could sink into a state of virtual civil war. At the present time a segment of the Gypsy community strive for neither integration, nor employment, nor education; and wish only that society maintain them through the unconditional provision of state benefits. (Jobbik 2012)

The reason that the party picks up on the Roma population is that they are not integrated into any country where they live so they become an easy target for discrimination – something that is not the case with Jews, who are integrated and speak the language of the country they live in. After the Holocaust, Jewish communities in Europe decreased in number and now they are not so visible. This is why Jews can no longer be the main target for discrimination or a main reason for a difficult situation in the country. On the other hand, the Roma population is visible, even if they are not numerous, due to their poor living conditions. In order to resolve this Roma issue, the party suggests reform of the social security system, as well as of the education system, and enforcement by the police. This latter

called 'Romi' (for an ethnic group), while a person who is of that origin is called *Rom* (m)/*Romkinja* (f). The term *Cigan* (m)/*Ciganka* (f) (which would be the translation of the term Gypsy) is also used, but only in a negative context. Even if the Romani do call themselves Gypsies, this would still be inappropriate when coming from the position of the majority, given its negative connotation in colloquial use.

is because of the alleged high crime rate amongst the Roma population. The party hesitates to label one whole ethnic group as criminal, but it does insist that there are certain correlations when it comes to this ethnic group and the crime rate:

> Naturally, gypsy crime does not mean that all Gypsy people are criminals, and it is an absurdity to suggest that it equates to the collective labelling of an entire community, as frequently the main victims of gypsy crime are Gypsy people themselves. What is however simply beyond dispute, is that certain specific criminological phenomena are predominantly and overwhelmingly associated with this minority, and that as a result such phenomena require the application of fitting and appropriate remedies. Law enforcement initiatives therefore, must go hand in hand with the reform of social, educational and employment policy, given that Gypsy integration [as opposed to Gypsy issues alienation] means assimilation into society-at-large, and that this process must commence at school, even in nursery school; which is why we would allocate both churches and civic and social institutions a specific role in this endeavour, given their ability to more quickly engage the Gypsy people in the necessary dialogue. (Jobbik 2012)

According to the party, instead of receiving state-funded help, everyone should get an employment offer, including public work, in order to be able to receive public assistance. This public work is envisaged as a free-of-charge community work that would qualify someone for state help. The party also proposes a revision of state subsistence for children in order to stop 'the regrettable practice of the bearing of children for the purposes of economic subsistence through the state benefits receivable'.

The party's manifesto also touches upon culture. Its creators see the current situation as an 'unhealthy, virtual autocracy, of opinion', and this is because there should be a culture and a cultural life 'which finally allows national values, Hungarian society's values, to be taken into account' (Jobbik 2012). One of the values particularly to be cherished is similar to the Austrian model, the development of rural life and culture. In the Austrian case, this is expressed in the protection of the culture of the Austrian regions, while in Hungary, rural areas are particularly mentioned. In addition, the party proposes removal of national symbols from the negative parts of history – a case similar to the situation in Croatia where the HČSP proposes the establishment of a museum of Croatia's negative history (HČSP 2012b: Purification and de-communization of Croatia). Both Croatian and Hungarian parties also propose removal of negative figures from public places, including street names.

The Jobbik party, like its Austrian and Croatian counterparts, discusses the issue of diaspora communities. The party proposes reinstallation of the Hungarian diaspora in Hungarian public life and explicitly outlines that in its view the Hungarian nation is not defined by its borders but 'by the borders of our nation' (Jobbik 2012). The party explains this by specifying that these borders of the Hungarian nation 'do not coincide with the geographical boundaries of the Hungarian Republic, given that our nation had its contiguity dismembered by the imposition of the Trianon peace diktat; to this day, the fate of those living in these fractured territories remain connected with each other by a thousand different threads' (Jobbik 2012). Because of this, the party proposes political thinking 'in terms of a nation of 15 million souls', which means they propose 'the cultural and economic reunification of the Hungarian nation, the granting of Hungarian citizenry to every Hungarian, the establishment of a Ministry of National Affairs, the promotion of efforts for self-determination, the reincorporation of beyond-the-border communities and émigrés into active Hungarian life, the promotion and development of border-transcending regional cooperation; and the coordinated development of domestic relationships between disparate nationalities' (Jobbik 2012). This would not be so different from other far right parties, and neither would it be problematic had the manifesto not continued with the following statement: 'Of course we are perfectly aware, that before all this can be achieved, the affairs of the territorially-maimed mother-country must first be put right; that the Hungarian state must be restored to the prominence its history demands; and, most crucially of all, that the plight of our disjointed nation – the Hungarian question – finally become widely known and discussed both at the EU and on the international stage' (Jobbik 2012).

This statement has been interpreted in surrounding countries as a call for the establishment of a large Hungary that would incorporate parts of those surrounding countries, and thus as a policy of imperialism. This is how the anti-fascists managed to denounce the Croatian Pure Party of Rights, a party that claims to work for protection of supposedly endangered

Croatian national interests and statehood, but then in 2012 invited Jobbik to the conference and made an attempt to establish collaboration with them, as already mentioned.[19]

Additionally, with regard to foreign affairs, the party presents an unusually radical programme. It envisages 'reincorporation into the national body of both Western and Carpathian-basin Hungarians'; however, the most problematic aspect of its foreign policy is 'the reunification of a Hungarian nation unjustly torn apart during the course of the 20th century' (Jobbik 2012). With this policy, the party clearly envisages reinvigoration of Hungarian imperialism, thus jeopardizing the sovereignty of surrounding states, which were formerly subordinated to Hungary. This is also expressed in the following statement:

> We will guarantee every Hungarian the right to Hungarian citizenship, and thus, to have their voices heard in matters concerning the national interest. We will review the treaties agreed with our neighbouring countries, and reposition them onto more sound foundations. And with every single political instrument at our disposal we shall promote and support the efforts of Hungarians beyond the border to achieve self-determination. Jobbik will diligently strive in its foreign policy, for the closer cooperation of Central-European states, on the pre-condition that the rights of the Hungarian minorities living in those states are resolved.

Jobbik is also oriented towards a Christian moral value system that should be recognized, but at the same time, there should be 'a re-examination of the regulations governing registration of new religious bodies and the operations of sects' (Manifesto: Religious affairs policy). The party

19 In this, the Croatian party clearly showed its ignorance and incompetence, which is why its gathering was a failure and had a low attendance, even though it was also intended to express support for the Croatian generals that were at that time still awaiting a second hearing at the International Criminal Tribunal for the former Yugoslavia (ICTY). They were eventually set free by the ICTY. Even though the HČSP had always claimed they would be prosecuted because of the interests of the international community, which is, in their view, clearly against Croatian statehood and sovereignty, when the generals were set free, the party did not change its rhetoric. Instead, it is now demanding liberation of less known figures that participated in leading the war between Croatia and Serbia during the 1990s.

also proposes compulsory teaching of religious or ethical education in schools. This is different from the Austrian party's manifesto that opposes the teaching of ethics and insists on catechism only (FPÖ 2012: Chapter V). The Croatian party makes no reference on this matter. Moreover, the Jobbik party particularly emphasizes the integration of Gypsy people into religious education. This policy is not quite clear because it implies that the Roma community is not religious, so Jobbik apparently envisages missionary work coming from the state in a forced form.

When it comes to the EU, the party states – similar to the Austrian party – that Europe and the EU are not 'one and the same' (Jobbik 2012: The European Union) and that Hungary 'is not a part of Europe because of its entry into the EU', but 'through the right of its history; and neither shall we in the future be rightfully termed Europeans, because we may choose to remain a member state of the Union, but rather, because we have resolved to remain true to Europe's fundamental principles'. Jobbik states that European culture is based on three 'pillars: Greek thinking, Roman law, and Christian morality', and because these three pillars are the fundamental values of Europe, it considers the Lisbon Treaty to be 'wrongheaded'. Because of this, Jobbik rejects the Treaty for it is seen as an attempt to create a United States of Europe, and instead insists on the promotion of Europe as 'a Europe of Nations'. It also objects to the EU for supposedly failing to resolve 'the concerns of national minorities living within its boundaries' (Jobbik 2012: The European Union). With this policy, the party sees Europe as founded on Christianity, which is common to all three parties, although the Croatian Pure Party of Rights insists more on faith in God than in any particular religion, and makes only one reference to Christianity, while at the same time emphasizes that it is crucial that the state fosters religious beliefs and offers financial support to all religious communities.

## Conclusion

The analysis offered here shows that there are various similarities between the far right parties discussed. For example, diaspora communities occupy a particular place in programmes of the far right and it is also common to propose imperial policies. In the case of Jobbik, this is manifested in stronger collaboration with Hungarians who live outside Hungary as well as expansion of Hungary to its 'historical' space. In the case of the FPÖ in Austria, this is represented in the right of Austrians living in South Tyrol to exercise self-determination and to become part of Austria. In the case of Croatia's HČSP, this is expressed through envisaging extension of Croatia to its 'historical' space, meaning to parts of Bosnia and Herzegovina as well as Serbia and Montenegro. These 'historical' borders are, nonetheless, borders of the Independent State of Croatia, a Nazi state established during the Second World War.

Another argument that characterizes all three parties is that diaspora should be reincorporated into the respective societies; however, it is feared that imperialistic and ethnic-oriented policies may arise from such a process. This is because the incorporation of diaspora also means incorporation of an ethnically homogeneous population and this would decrease the number of 'others'. The envisaged policies certainly present a case of a favourable in-group attitude in which members of the dominant group or the ethnic majority do not blame each other for things that go wrong, but they shift responsibility to the so-called out-group or 'other'. The only difference lies in who the 'other' is. In the case of Austria, the 'others' are immigrants who are mostly Muslims; in Hungary, they are Jews and Roma; and in Croatia, they are the anti-fascists who are also framed as descendants of the communists and who therefore do not support the idea of an independent and sovereign Croatia.

With regard to other policies, it is noticeable that all parties address the issue of religion and culture. Here, the Austrian FPÖ is the most explicit when discussing the supposedly endangered Austrian culture that should be preserved. At the same time, it insists on the German language as a language of Austrians in which they think and with which they develop their sense of belonging. Language is, thus, an important factor for identification of Austrians. The Croatian party discusses culture, but not in entirely the same way. It discusses a supposedly oppressed Croatian culture that should be preserved, but in this case, 'the enemy' is not immigration, but former communists, perceived as those who hate Croatia and continuously work towards its disappearance. In the Hungarian case, the policy is that culture should be preserved, but there is no particular mention of who is to be blamed for its lack of preservation. The tone of the manifesto of the Hungarian Jobbik party points at political elites that led Hungary towards unconditional European integration, apparently without preserving the national, which is, in this argumentation, nowadays oppressed.

This leads us to another issue, immigration. While the Hungarian party ignores the immigration issue, the other two do not. Jobbik ignores this issue because Hungary is not a destination for immigrants; however, even though Croatia is not an immigration destination either, the HČSP does discuss this issue. In Austria, which has served as an immigration destination, the FPÖ enforces populist views on immigrants, excluding them from possible integration due to the fact they believe Austrians have the right to their homeland (*Heimat*), placing it in a special position, and immigrants apparently cannot integrate or accept Austria as their *Heimat*. This is also in line with the Croatian HČSP, which also states that Croatia belongs to its citizens, while others are not welcome.

The major difference comes when we look into anti-Semitism and the position of minorities. For example, the Austrian and Croatian far right parties express no desire to intimidate Jews and place them in a position of 'other'. The FPÖ in one place even mentions the Judeo-Christian character of Europe, explicitly excluding Islam from the founding part of Europe and the European culture. Islam is also mentioned as a threat to Europe. The Croatian HČSP also ignores the Jews and guarantees all rights to Croatian minorities (thus including the Jewish one). However, it massively relativizes the Holocaust and glorifies Croatia's Nazi regime, insisting that it did not do anything wrong, and that this part of history presents a glowing episode that fostered and founded the idea of an independent Croatian state. The party also compares the Holocaust with a crime against the Ustasha army, which is regarded as a martyr, while it fails to acknowledge any wrongdoing on the part of Croatia. In the Hungarian case, there is a different situation. The Hungarian Jobbik party openly calls for discrimination of its Roma population, and expresses and advocates massive anti-Semitism. In contrast to Croatia, where the far right party is a marginal political option, in Hungary, the Jobbik party participates in governing the country, promoting policies that generate an increase in anti-Semitism in an already deeply anti-Semitic society. Discrimination against the Roma population and calls for their expulsion are also something well known from WWII, and this policy presents a logical continuation, since the Hungarian party has started to glorify the Nazi crimes and intimidate the Jews. Indeed, in all three countries, the far right parties glorify Nazi collaborators and perpetrators of the Holocaust, denying that their fellow nationals ever did anything wrong.

When it comes to the notion of Europe, the three parties differ. The Austrian and the Hungarian parties discuss Europe and the place of their respective countries within an enlarged EU. Whereas the FPÖ insists on the Europeanism of Austria and its contribution to Europe and its culture (which is, as already noted, a typical Central European discourse of Europeanism), the Jobbik party insists that Europe is more than the EU. This is because joining the EU is a voluntary decision, whereas being European and 'in Europe' means to have European views on the world and share European values. Again, this is a Central European discourse of unquestionably belonging to European civilization and culture. The Croatian HČSP, however, pays little attention to the EU and no attention at all to the notion of Europe and being a European. In fact, the party strongly opposes Croatia's EU membership, comparing the EU with the former Yugoslavia.

When looking into the elements that characterize the far right in the West – an anti-immigrant stance, a favourable in-group attitude, an authoritarian approach and political dissatisfaction – it becomes obvious that the three parties analysed here fit very well into this classification. When it comes to political dissatisfaction, they all claim that their respective countries are in crisis and that their national identity and values are not being cherished enough. Their programmes also express an anti-immigrant attitude, except in the case of Hungary, where there is no such attitude; however, there is something that can be called an 'anti-minority attitude'. This 'anti-minority attitude' is not present in the other two parties, as they accept their national minorities and offer them all rights. In the case of favourable in-group attitudes, this connotation is also present, just not at an extreme level or, at least, not to the extent that parties would cast members of the national minorities as out-groups, but there is rather a strong anti-immigration sentiment where immigrants are 'out-grouped'. Hungary is, again, a different case, as a favourable in-group attitude goes to the extreme, and works against official Hungarian minorities such as Jews and Roma. In the case of the Roma minority, this group is strenuously out-grouped and portrayed as wanting to retain their 'deviant' behaviour and not wanting to be integrated. In contrast, the Jewish group is accused of dual loyalty to Hungary and Israel and, as such, labelled as a national security threat. Additionally, a favourable in-group attitude is also expressed in the policy of enforcing the opinion that their countries should come first, which is also a characteristic of the Western far right.

Thus, it appears that far right parties in countries belonging to the so-called Central European circle follow quite a number of the policies that characterize the general far right in the West. However, common to all three parties is the glorification of the Nazi regime and, at the same time, lack of condemnation for such glorification from the respective officials or public opinion. Taking this into consideration, we can indeed talk about a Central European model; however, we cannot talk about a Central European and East-Central European model because Austria fits into this category, too, and no classification ever considered Austria as East-Central Europe. If we consider the radical exclusivity of one's nation and a strong ethnic policy as East-Central European, then only Hungary would fit, because it is only the Hungarian party that is against its national minorities. Paradoxically, it was Hungarian historians that first debated the concept of East-Central Europe, claiming not to belong there. However, when it comes to Jobbik, its programme and the fact that it presents such a strong political option in Hungary, then indeed it would be only Hungary that could be out-grouped as Eastern.

The analysis offered here focused on three countries only; however, the results would probably not be much different had it considered other countries in the region. For example, in the case of Slovakia, the available literature points out that the far right policies are very close to those found in Croatia (Chalaniova 2012; Djurašković 2008; Harris 2002). The only exception, given the available research, seems to be the Czech Republic (Vido 2012). However, if the EU and its policy-makers truly want the European project to succeed, then the region discussed and the policies promoted by its far right parties should be subject to closer inspection and deeper consideration. If, instead of dealing with the issue, the EU allows new classifications to emerge, the only outcome we can expect to see in the future is a new European 'other', rather than integration and unification based on diversity.

## References


Anderson, C. J. (1996). 'Economics, Politics and Foreigners: Populist Party Support in Denmark and Norway', *Electoral Studies*, 15 (4), 497–511.

Arendt, H. (1951). *The Origins of Totalitarianism*. New York: Harcourt, Brace & World.

Bijelić, B. (2006). 'Žene na rubu rodne jednakopravnosti'. In S. Ramet and D. Matić (eds), *Demokratska tranzicija u Hrvatskoj: Tranformacija vrijednosti, obrazovanje, mediji*, pp. 241–61. Zagreb: Alinea.

Calhoun, C. (2003). 'European Studies: Always Already There and Still in Formation', *Comparative European Politics*, 1 (1), 5–20.

Chalaniova, D. (2012). 'Cultural Diplomacy and Stereotypes in Present-Day Czech-Slovak Relations: Breaking with the Past? Hetero-stereotypes of Czechs and Slovaks Twenty Years from the Velvet Divorce'. In M. Topić and S. Rodin (eds), *Cultural Diplomacy and Cultural Imperialism: European perspective(s)*, pp. 161–89. Frankfurt am Main: Peter Lang.

Djurašković, S. (2008). 'Politike povijesti: Pregled razvoja discipline u Hrvatskoj i Slovačkoj', *Politička misao*, XLV (3–4), 201–20.

EUMC (2004). *Working Definition of Anti-Semitism* <http://fra.europa.eu/fraWebsite/material/pub/AS/AS-WorkingDefinition-draft.pdf> accessed 18 January 2012.

*Eurobarometer* 70 (2008). 'European Commission Public Opinion Survey held in Autumn 2008' <http://ec.europa.eu/public_opinion/archives/eb/eb70/eb70_hr_exec.pdf> accessed 9 December 2009.

—— 75 (2011). 'European Commission Public Opinion Survey held in May 2011' <http://ec.europa.eu/public_opinion/archives/eb/eb75/eb75_en.htm> accessed 3 November 2011.

European Communities (1973). 'The Copenhagen Summit Conference: Declaration on European Identity' <http://www.cvce.eu/viewer/-/content/02798dc9-9c69-4b7d-b2c9-f03a8db7da32/en> accessed 8 July 2012.

Fisher, R. (2012). 'Towards a Common European cultural diplomacy?', *More Europe Seminar: Culture & European Identity*, Paris, 23 May 2012.

FPÖ [Freedom Party of Austria] (2012). 'Programme' <http://www.fpoe.at/fileadmin/Contentpool/Portal/PDFs/Parteiprogramme/Parteiprogram_eng.pdf> accessed 22 November 2012.

Gerstenfeld, M. (2004). 'European Anti-Americanism and Anti-Semitism: Similarities and Differences', *Post-Holocaust and Anti-Semitism*, 16, 1 January <http://www.jcpa.org/phas/phas-16.htm> accessed 21 January 2012.

Golder, M. (2003). 'Explaining Variation in the Success of Extreme Right Parties in Western Europe', *Comparative Political Studies*, 36 (4), 432–66.

Haller, M. (1996). *Identität und Nationalstolz der Österreicher. Gesellschaftliche Ursachen und Funktionen. Herausbildung und Transformation seit 1945: Internationaler Vergleich*. Wien, Köln, Weimar: Böhlau.

Harris, E. (2002). *Nationalism and Democratisation: Politics of Slovakia and Slovenia*. Aldershot: Ashgate.

HČSP [Croatian Pure Party of Rights] (2012a). 'Founding Principles' <http://hcsp.hr/temeljna-nacela> accessed 12 November 2012.

—— (2012b). 'Programme' <http://hcsp.hr/program> accessed 12 November 2012.

Heilbrunn, J. (2012). 'Anti-Semitism Flourishes in Hungary' <http://nationalinterest.org/blog/european-union/anti-semitism-flourishes-hungary-7122> accessed 4 January 2013.

Hroch, M. (2006). *Društveni preduvjeti nacionalnih preporodoa u Europi: Komparativna analiza društvenog sastava patriotskih grupa malih europskih zemalja*. Zagreb: Srednja Europa.

Hunyady, G., and Kiss, P. (2003). 'Nation, State and National Identity in Modern Hungary'. In B. Stråth and A. Triandafyllidou (eds), *Representations of Europe and the Nation in Current and Prospective Member States: Media, Elites and Civil*

*Society*. Brussels: The European Commission <ftp://ftp.cordis.europa.eu/pub/citizens/docs/sta_media_0603.pdf> accessed 8 January 2013.

Höpken, W. (2006). 'Između građanskog identiteta i nacionalizma: udžbenici povijesti u postkomunističkoj Europi'. In S. Ramet and D. Matić (eds), *Demokratska tranzicija u Hrvatskoj: Tranformacija vrijednosti, obrazovanje, mediji*, pp. 143–69. Zagreb: Alinea.

Jackman, R. W., and Volpert, K. (1996). 'Conditions Favouring Parties of the Extreme Right in Western Europe', *British Journal of Political Science*, 26 (4), 501–21.

Jobbik (2012). 'Manifesto: Radical Change' <http://www.jobbik.com/sites/default/files/Jobbik-RADICALCHANGE2010.pdf> accessed 22 November 2012.

Karge, H. (2001). 'Istraživanja školskih udžbenika u Jugoistočnoj Europi: Problemi, projekti, perspektive'. In H. G. Fleck and I. Graovac (eds), *Dijalog povjesničara-istoričara 4*, pp. 17–31. Zagreb: Friedrich-Naumann Foundation.

Kitschelt, H. (1997). *The Radical Right in Western Europe: A Comparative Analysis*. Ann Arbor, MI: University of Michigan Press.

Knigge, P. (1998). 'The Ecological Correlates of Right-Wing Extremism in Western Europe', *European Journal of Political Research*, 34 (2), 249–79.

Kornhauser, W. (1960). *The Politics of Mass Society*. London: Routledge & Kegan Paul.

Kovacs, A., Horvath, A., and Vidra, Z. (2009). *The State of the Art: Various Paths to Modernity – Hungarian Case Report*. Report submitted to the European Commission (FP7 project: Identities and Modernities in Europe).

—— (2011). *An Overview Report: The Hungarian case*. Report submitted to the European Commission (FP7 project: Identities and Modernities in Europe).

Kraus, P. A. (2011). 'The Politics of Complex Diversity: A European Perspective', *Ethnicities*, 12 (1), 3–25.

Kundera, M. (1984). 'The Tragedy of Central Europe' <http://www.euroculture.upol.cz/dokumenty/sylaby/Kundera_Tragedy_(18).pdf> accessed 8 July 2012.

Lubbers, M., and Scheepers, P. (2000). 'Individual and Contextual Characteristics of the German Republikaner Vote: A Test of Complementary Theories', *European Journal of Political Research*, 38 (1), 63–94.

Lubbers, M., Gijsberts, M., and Scheepers, P. (2002). 'Extreme Right-Wing Voting in Western Europe', *European Journal of Political Research*, 41 (3), 345–78.

Marchart, O. (2001). 'The "Fourth Way" of the Ultra Right: Austria, Europe, and the End of Neo-Corporatism', *Capital & Class*, 25 (7), 7–14.

Markus, G. G. (2007). 'Political Cleavages and Anti-Semitism in Hungary' <http://epa.oszk.hu/02000/02051/00008/pdf/EPA02051_Tudomanyos_Kozlemenyek_18_029-041.pdf > accessed 4 January 2013.

Matić, D. (2006). 'Je li nacionalizam stvarno toliko loš: Slučaj Hrvatske'. In S. Ramet and D. Matić (eds), *Demokratska tranzicija u Hrvatskoj: tranformacija vrijednosti, obrazovanje, mediji*, pp. 261–85. Zagreb: Alinea.

Mayer, N. (1998). 'The Front National in the Plural', *Patterns of Prejudice*, 32 (1), 4–24.

Minkenberg, M. (1998). 'Context and Consequence: The Impact of the New Radical Right on the Political Process in France and Germany', *German Politics and Society*, 16 (3), 1–23.

—— (2001). 'The Radical Right in Public Office: Agenda-Setting and Policy Effects', *West European Politics*, 24 (4), 1–21.

—— (2011). *The Radical Right in Europe: An Overview*. Berlin: Verlag Bertelsmann Stiftung.

Mokre, M. (2006). 'Transnational Policy as a Prerequisite for Democracy'. In K. Robins (ed.), *The Challenge of Transcultural Diversities: Cultural Policy and Cultural Diversity*, pp. 69–80. Strasbourg: Council of Europe Publishing.

Morin, E. (2002). 'European Civilization: Properties and Challenges'. In M. Mozaffari (ed.), *Globalization and Civilizations*, pp. 125–50. London: Routledge.

Neumann, I. (1999). *Uses of the Other. 'The East' in European Identity Formation*. Minneapolis, MN: University of Minnesota Press.

Pacini, A. (ed.) (1998). *Christian Communities in the Arab Middle East: The Challenge of the Future*. Oxford: Clarendon Press.

Pavlaković, V. (2008). 'Flirting with Fascism: The Ustaša Legacy and Croatian Politics in the 1990s'. In D. Gavrilović (ed.), *The Second World War and the National Question in Ex-Yugoslavia*, pp. 115–43. Novi Sad: CHDR.

Pelinka, A. (2001). 'The Haider Phenomenon in Austria: Examining the FPÖ in European Context', *The Journal of the International Institute*, 9 (1) <http://quod.lib.umich.edu/j/jii/4750978.0009.102?rgn=main;view=fulltext> accessed 3 January 2013.

Ramet, S. P. (2005). *Thinking about Yugoslavia: Scholarly Debates about the Yugoslav Breakup and the Wars in Bosnia and Kosovo*. Cambridge: Cambridge University Press.

Ray, L. (2009). 'At the End of the Post-Communist Transformation? Normalization or Imagining Utopia?', *European Journal of Social Theory*, 12 (3), 321–36.

Shore, C. (2006). 'In Uno Plures? EU Cultural Policy and the Governance of Europe', *Cultural Analysis*, No. 5, 7–26.

Spohn, W. (2003). 'Europe and Nation in Austrian National Identity'. In B. Stråth and A. Triandafyllidou (eds), *Representations of Europe and the Nation in Current and Prospective Member States: Media, Elites and Civil Society*. Brussels: The European Commission <ftp://ftp.cordis.europa.eu/pub/citizens/docs/sta_media_0603.pdf> accessed 8 January 2013.

Stern, K. S. (2006). *Anti-Semitism Today: How It Is the Same, How It Is Different and How to Fight It.* New York: American Jewish Committee.

Szekely, M. (2012). 'Rebuilding History: The Political Meaning of the Hungarian Historical Pavilion at the 1900 Paris Universal Exhibition'. In M. Topić and S. Rodin (eds), *Cultural Diplomacy and Cultural Imperialism: European perspective(s)*, pp. 51–67. Frankfurt am Main: Peter Lang.

Todosijevic, B., and Enyedi, Z. (2002). 'Anti-Jewish Prejudice in Contemporary Hungary: A Socio-Psychological Causal Model', *Social Thought and Research*, 24 (1–2), 313–41.

Topić, M. (2009). 'Rod i nacija, očuvanje (i kreacija) nacionalnog identiteta kroz rodno diskriminacijsku nacionalističku politiku: Slučaj Hrvatske iz devedesetih', *Sociološki pregled*, XLIII (2), 185–207.

—— (2010). 'Overcoming Nationalism: "Croatian" Alan Ford as a Cross-National Bound in (Former) Yugoslavia'. In B. Stevanović, A. Kostić and Lj. Mitrović (eds), *Media and the Culture of Peace in the Balkans*, pp. 263–81. Niš: Faculty of Humanities and Social Sciences and Center for Sociological Research.

—— (2012a). 'Culture and Identity as Tools for Forging Europeanization'. In M. Topić and S. Rodin (eds), *Cultural Diplomacy and Cultural Imperialism: European Perspective(s)*, pp. 219–39. Frankfurt am Main: Peter Lang.

—— (2013, forthcoming). 'A European Intifada? On the New Form of an Old European Anti-Semitism in a New Millennium'. In M. Topić and S. Sremac (eds), *Europe as a Multiple Modernity: Multiplicity of Religious Identities and Belongings*. Newcastle upon Tyne: Cambridge Scholars Publishing.

Topić, M., and Sciortino, C. (2012). 'Cultural Diplomacy and Cultural Hegemony: A Framework for the Analysis'. In M. Topić and S. Rodin (eds), *Cultural Diplomacy and Cultural Imperialism: European Perspective(s)*, pp. 9–49. Frankfurt am Main: Peter Lang.

Topić, M., and Sremac, S. (2013, forthcoming). 'Former Nazi in United Europe? Significance, Meaning and Expressions of Radical Groups in Croatia'. In A. F. Wilson and J. Lee (eds), *Extremism, Nationalism and Transgression*. Derby: University of Derby Press.

Topić, M., and Vasiljević, S. (2011a). *WP6: Identity Construction Programs of the State and the EU – Case Study Phase II: Croatia*. Report submitted to the European Commission (FP7 project: Identities and Modernities in Europe).

—— (2011b). *WP7: Identity Construction Programs of the State and the EU – Case Study Phase III: Citizens and Modernities between National and European Paths in Croatia*. Report submitted to the European Commission (FP7 project: Identities and Modernities in Europe).

Topić, M., Vasiljević, S., and Djurašković, S. (2009). *WP4: The State of the Art: Various Paths to Modernity – Croatian Case Report*. Report submitted to the European Commission (FP7 project: Identities and Modernities in Europe).

Vidmar Horvat, K. (2012). 'The Predicament of Intercultural Dialogue: Reconsidering the Politics of Culture and Identity in the EU', *Cultural Sociology*, 6 (1), 27–44.

Vido, R. (2012). 'Czech Modernity as Secular Modernity'. Paper presented at Euroacademia International Conference *Re-Inventing Eastern Europe*, Vienna, 17–19 May <http://euroacademia.eu/wordpress/wp-content/uploads/2012/05/Roman_Vido_Czech_Modernity_as_Secular_Modernity.pdf> accessed 4 January 2013.

Wistrich, R. S. (ed.) (1990). *Anti-Zionism and Anti-Semitism in the Contemporary World*. London: Macmillan.

—— (2002). *Muslim Anti-Semitism: A Clear and Present Danger*. New York: The American Jewish Committee.

—— (2004). 'Anti-Zionism and Anti-Semitism', *Jewish Political Studies Review*, 16 (3–4), 27–31.

Wodak, R. (1997). 'Austria and its New East Central European Minorities: The Discourses of Racism'. In L. Kürti and J. Langman (eds), *Beyond Borders*, pp. 132–51. Boulder, CO: Westview Press.

—— (1999). *The Discursive Construction of National Identity*. Edinburgh: Edinburgh University Press.

Wolff, L. (1999). *Inventing Eastern Europe: The Map of Civilization on the Mind of the Enlightenment*. Stanford, CA: Stanford University Press.

# PART THREE

# Undeniable Challenges and Questionable Prospects

MIRUNA ANDREEA BALOSIN

# 10 The European Public Space: More Than Words?

The European Union (EU) appears as the first supranational system fit for the twenty-first century. The quest for a 'European consciousness' able to hold the Union together has fallen behind the process of creating a common legal and economic system (El-Tayeb 2008: 649). Despite the adoption of a common currency by the majority of EU member states, the Europeanization of identities, ways of living and orientations, and the rising of a common public space, seem to be a difficult dream to reach. In the absence of a common identity, the name of the European community is overrated; there is no true and sustainable European community. In addition, such an identity is based on the existence of a pan-European public space – a space for defining, shaping or reshaping common values, principles or practices, and in which supranational political institutions can reach the point of legitimacy.

How can we define a public space? Public space should not be mistaken for private space: while private space is dedicated to privacy, such as family life, public space is devoted to exposing and to discovering of the others. In short, everything related to social life, politics and economics is part of public space, which comprises all matters that are not private. Immanuel Kant invented the concept of public space in 1784. In his short work 'Idea for a Universal History with a Cosmopolitan Purpose' (1991), he explains that reason cannot develop entirely in a single individual; it needs variety in order to show its valuable power. A public space does not only contain people who disclose something, but it also contains the people to whom something is disclosed. Accordingly, a public space is the place where citizens can freely debate political questions.

In the twentieth century, Jürgen Habermas popularized the notion of public space/public sphere (Habermas 1989, 1997). In his opinion, public space, as a space of conciliation between individuals and the state, is fundamental to democracy. Thus, the state does not act in secrecy; it presents publicly its decisions or, even better, it takes decisions only after a public debate. With this in mind, public space is a place of political authenticity. According to Habermas (1989), the 'public sphere' consists of social spaces where individuals gather to discuss their common public affairs and to organize against arbitrary and oppressive forms of social and public power. The principles of the public sphere involve an open discussion of all issues of general concern in which discursive argumentation is employed to ascertain general interests and the public good, thus presupposing freedom of speech and assembly, a free press, and the right to participate freely in political debate and decision-making. Public space is not manipulation by the political elites, or a theatre of puppets playing on stage after the public taste. Moreover, it is not a homogeneous space for a unique public opinion; it is a space of political communication in which economic actors and civil society treat issues of common interest (Habermas 1997). In other words, public space is more than a deliberative space, where individuals exchange rational arguments respecting the ethical rules of democracy.

A European public space may be a condition for a united Europe, but unity should not be confused with standardization. The challenge is to take diversity seriously and make room for new views – whether in word or thought. Only such a rich and unrestricted exchange of ideas has the potential to form a shared identity and put it to the test. As already suggested elsewhere, 'Europe needs to find its place in the existing national, regional and local "public spheres" and the public discussion across Member States must be deepened. This is first and foremost the responsibility of the public authorities in the Member States. It is the responsibility of government, at national, regional and local level, to consult and inform citizens about public policy ... and to put in place the forums to give this debate life' (European Commission 2006: 4).

## Building a European Public Space

So far, public space has become such an all-encompassing idea that it is very difficult to understand what it stands for. That explains the multitude of adjectives surrounding this term, like 'deliberative public space', 'international public space', 'conflictive public space' and so on. It appears to be necessary to elaborate a permissive vocabulary to qualify these multiple entities contained under this umbrella term. For example, authors like Dominique Wolton (1991) and Alain Cotterau and Paul Ladrière (1992) underlined the necessity of using dissimilar names to separate similar democratic experiences of distinctive natures: while the first author proposes differentiating between common space, public space and political space, the other two want a separation between space of expression, public space and political space. The reflections of those already mentioned suggest to us not to lower politics to the rank of public space. Private space constitutes the foundation of public space. Symmetrically, the space of legitimate power or the political space (Wolton 1991) – the place where decisions are taken in the secrecy of cabinets – forms the pedestal of public space.

As acknowledged by the European Commission (2001: 7),

> European integration has delivered fifty years of stability, peace and economic prosperity. It has helped to raise standards of living, built an internal market, and strengthened the Union's voice in the world. It has achieved results, which would not have been possible by individual Member States acting on their own … Yet despite its achievements, many Europeans feel alienated from the Union's work. People do not necessarily feel less European. They still expect Europe-wide action in many domains, but they no longer trust the complex system to deliver what they want. In other words, people have disappointed expectations, but expectations nevertheless.

These phrases amplify the real political nature of the problem. In fact, for political communication to be able to build a bridge between Europe and its citizens (European Commission 2001: 3), it needs both sides to be stable. So far, this has not been the case. The European Union is in search of a new institutional system and European citizens are confused by the complexity of a global world. It was more convenient not to offer new strategies or develop new instruments to make that connection between Europe and its citizens possible, but to assign another objective to European political communication: to energize the European democracy.

As Europe becomes more concrete, the political process of unification loses support. This paradox is connected to the disputed legitimacy of the European institutions. Some authors remind us that the political construction of Europe was and is an elitist process where the citizens are more excluded than involved (Boual 1999; Wolton 1993). They mention the problems tied to the absence of real political parties, European juridical illegibility or the lack of imagination of the European elites trapped in a sterile debate between federation and confederation. Certainly, the European Parliament (1996) acknowledged the disputed legitimacy which is provoked by the low institutional power given only to the elected institution by European suffrage, or, by the fact that the member states have put off giving European citizenship a concrete content. All the explanations mentioned find their origins in an essential characteristic of the political construction of Europe: the absence of a European public space. As observed elsewhere, '[t]he European Union is not yet a polity and it lacks a public sphere. For this to emerge, actions are needed that support trans-national mobilization and political contestation, the consolidation of a European party system, as well as the emergence of a cosmopolitan identity' (Giorgi *et al.* 2001: 81). In addition, '[n]ational public authorities, civil society, and the European Union institutions need to work together to develop Europe's place in the public sphere' (European Commission 2006: 5). Giorgi *et al.* (2001) observe realistically that the needed actions are not so easy to specify, making it more challenging to measure or monitor. The authors consider that the failure to implement such actions, despite all difficulties, will only reinforce contemporary forms of nationalism and ultimately spell the end of the project of European democracy. Back in the nineteenth century, John Stuart Mill (1861) was right on one important point: a sphere for common discussion and understanding is the heartbeat of any democracy.

Jean-Marc Ferry (2000) maintains that the condition for building a European public space resides in the articulation of three principles: civility, legality and publicity. These principles constitute the patrimony of European civilization in the measure in which legality conditions the base structure and civility assures the continuity of daily practices where the results are opposable to the parties captivated by the publicity of debates, in virtue of the non-violent constraining force of public opinion. The public space, in its political dimension, is the space of democratic debate and the place of political action. Through the public space, citizens have access to political information, they can debate and form opinions, and they can choose the right persons to represent them. Thus, through the public space, citizens are not only the receivers of law but also the authors of that law (Habermas 1997).

Europeans have witnessed different attempts to reach an embryo status of a European public space. The question is how the EU institutions can breathe life into the idea of EU participatory democracy. Democracy depends on people being able to take part in public debate. To do this, they must have access to reliable information on European issues and be able to scrutinize the policy process in its various stages (European Commission 2001: 11). Major progress seemed to have been made in 2001 with the adoption of new rules giving citizens greater access to Community documents. A well-known and much debated expression of the participatory engineering approach in EU politics is the 'White Paper on European Governance'. The Commission's intention with the White Paper is to find new means 'to connect Europe with its citizens' (2001: 3). As noted,

> [t]his paper starts a process responding to the disenchantment of many of the Union's citizens. Alienation from politics is not just a European problem, it is global, national and local. But for the Union it represents a particular challenge. Given the deep level of integration already achieved, people have similar expectations for the Union as they have for domestic politics and political institutions. But the Union cannot develop and deliver policy in the same way as a national government; it must build partnerships and rely on a wide variety of actors. Expectations must be met in different ways. (European Commission 2001: 32)

The White Paper introduces five political principles – openness, participation, accountability, effectiveness and coherence. However, the concept of participation remains unclear between the notions of civil society and participation. Participation is overall perceived in instrumental ways as a means to improve the efficiency and effectiveness of European policy-making. A further critique against the White Paper is its strong focus on participation of organized interests and the neglect of non-organized citizens. According to Abels (2009: 2), '[w]hereas the Commission is highly experienced with integrating territorial as well as functional interest groups via a number of means, the challenge is to find direct channels of communication with individual citizens'.

As a direct response to the negative French and Dutch referenda on the Constitutional Treaty and at the request of the European Council, Margot Wallström, the Commission's Vice-President and Commissioner for Communication, launched a new initiative in 2005, entitled *Plan D for Democracy, Dialogue and Debate*. The purpose of Plan D is that 'any vision of the future of Europe needs to build on a clear view on citizen's needs and expectations' (European Commission 2005b: 2). Plan D calls for innovative models for citizens' communication and aims at shaping communication as a two-way street. On the launching day, 13 October 2005, Wallström stated that 'plan D is about debate, dialogue and listening. It is a means of harnessing political ideas to generate change ... Plan D aims to inject more democracy into the Union, to stimulate a wide public debate and build a new consensus on the future direction of the European Union' (European Commission 2005c).

Unfortunately, despite Wallström's promises to 'give the EU ears', the EU leaders did not listen to the citizens. Thus, Plan D did not fulfil its basic purpose and European citizens have continued to remain excluded from the decision-making process. As correctly underlined in the literature, the 'Treaty of Lisbon [was] ratified without open and public debate which is proposed by the Plan D', a fact contradictory to the 'conception of citizens as actors of political changes' (Ivic 2011: 18). Given that Plan D did not manage to bring any changes to EU policy-making, EU leaders continued to behave as they always had, oblivious to the opinions of citizens. Without either a legal base or political support, Plan D was in practice 'heavy on communications and weak on democracy' (Thomson 2011). Even if the initiative was appreciated for demonstrating that 'ordinary citizens could indeed intelligently and respectfully discuss EU issues, it was dismissed as ineffective in doing two things it was never in fact designed to do: impact EU policy and increase overall voter participation in EU elections' (Thomson 2011).

In 2010, Plan D was abandoned, its online discussion forum archived and citizens' consultations left unfunded. Instead of promising to listen to citizens, Wallström's successor, Viviane Reding, promised to give them policies to help with personal cross-border legal issues. Traditional one-way public relations returned, alongside an outdated vision of citizens. According to Ivic (2011: 19), the basic problem of this initiative can be identified in the fact that determination of European values is ignored. The concept of European values is based on the widely accepted assumptions that it is built on the homogeneous concepts of cultural and historical heritage and liberal theory. The European public sphere produced by this point of view is thin and instrumental and thus perceived only as a means to an end, and not a good in itself. However, the failure of the European Commission's Plan D can serve as a good example for other European initiatives, which should reject homogenizing assumptions and mere instrumental concepts.

The White Paper on a European Communication policy, published in February 2006, complements the previous approaches by attempting to develop further tools and initiatives for citizens' involvement. The main message was that it was time for the EU to close the gap between citizens and institutions: 'People from all walks of life should have the right to fair and full information about the European Union, and be confident that the views and concerns they express are heard by the EU institutions. The European Parliament, member states and the representation of European citizens have a special role to play, as peoples' support for the European project is a matter of common interest' (European Commission 2006: 4). The objective was therefore to contribute to the development of a European public sphere, thus a space where the debate on Europe could unfold, by following three principles: inclusiveness ('all citizens should have access ... to information of public concern'), diversity ('EU communication policy must respect the full range of views in the public debate') and participation ('Citizens should have a right to express their views, be heard and have the opportunity for dialogue with the decision-makers'). According to the White Paper, 'people feel remote from these decisions, the decision-making process and EU institutions … Despite exercising the right to elect members of the European Parliament, citizens often feel that they themselves have little opportunity to make their voices heard on European issues, and there is no obvious forum within which they can discuss these issues together. A pan-European political culture – with pan-European political groups and foundations – is still developing' (European Commission 2006: 4).

The European Union needs programmes that place citizens in the centre of its actions, that respond to their aspirations of better participating in the future of Europe, and that will allow citizens of different nationalities to meet, to interact, to confront their ideas, and develop their own reflections in a European public space that captures their diversity. Conferences, workshops and internet forums are today widely used tools for civil-society consultation, but still, they are not without limitations. It is mainly civil-society organizations that participate in consultations and less so individual citizens. The European Parliament's Agora project is a good example. The official website of the institution makes a succinct presentation, mentioning that the Citizens' Agora represents a link between the European Parliament and European civil society. It is a unique tool, in both structure and breadth, for discussing with citizens, issues on Parliament's legislative agenda. It aims not just to communicate with citizens, but genuinely to listen to them. Agora organizes a dialogue between 500 representatives from civil-society organizations and provides room for open debate with a view to building consensus or revealing diverging opinions within civil society on the analysis or the action to be undertaken to address Europe's future challenges. As the EU develops its next initiatives, European civil-society organizations are invited to express their views, bring forward their analyses and proposals and highlight the role they are willing to take in future EU actions. The Agora conclusions, as drafted by the civil-society representatives, are submitted to the European and national institutions and widely disseminated by all those involved. The first Agora forum took place in 2007 on the future of the EU; the final forum was organized in January 2011 on the economic and financial crisis and new forms of poverty.

The Commission also aims to reach out to the wider public, but still, this does not include the average citizen. In fact, the question is how to reach out to these individual citizens? What tools are suitable in the EU polity? The European Commission is as much an active as an innovative advocate of participatory engineering (Abels 2009: 3). One example is represented by the *Consultation Forum Concerning the Future Action Programme to Promote Active European Citizenship, 2007–2013*. This was the second part of an extensive two-stage consultation exercise organized by the Directorate-General for Education and Culture. Held at the beginning of February 2005, it followed closely the online public consultation, launched in December 2004, thus after a period in which over a thousand responses were received. The Forum attracted the full range of stakeholders, drawing approximately 350 actors and representatives from European civil society's non-governmental organizations (NGOs), think tanks, regional and municipal authorities, European networks, advocacy groups, trade unions, and European associations (European Commission 2005a: 2). The major objective of the occasion was to stimulate dialogue and debate and thereby advance concrete proposals, recommendations and suggestions for the preparation of the new active citizenship programme, destined to improve and strengthen the current transitional one, in time for the discussions on the financial perspectives 2007–13. Discussion points raised for reflection were aimed specifically at the possible contribution thinks tanks or civil society could bring to European policy-making, possible partnerships between such activities and those undertaken by NGOs.

Other experiments supported by the EU Commission that allow for public participation are the citizens' deliberation 'Meeting of Minds' or the 'European Citizens' Consultations' (ECCs). For example, the ECCs are more than a one-time exercise in citizen involvement. They are designed as a model for dialogue across the boundaries of geography and language and thereby aim at establishing a template for future European citizen-participation projects that: create dialogue in a multilingual and decentralized setting; empower randomly chosen citizens to set the agenda and lead information debates; and use innovative facilitation methods and modern technology to make every voice heard. The results of the ECCs were aimed to provide profound insights into the general feelings of citizens towards the EU, and into their main areas of interest. The ECCs process managed to create a truly European discussion on Europe's future, bringing citizens together and linking simultaneous national debates in all member states on a shared agenda of broad ideas and visions set by the citizens themselves.

A strong sign of the 'change' was the inclusion of the principle of participatory democracy in the 2004 Treaty establishing a constitution for Europe (Article I-47) and also in the follow-up Lisbon Treaty (Article 10 and 11) – however without explicitly mentioning the term 'participatory democracy'. Article 10 states that the functioning of the Union shall be founded on representative democracy; every citizen shall have the right to participate in the democratic life of the Union, and decisions shall be taken as openly and as closely as possible to the citizen. Article 11, for example, even introduces an instrument of direct democracy, the popular initiative, into the overall representative structure of the EU. This allows citizens some agenda-setting influence at EU level: 'Not less than one million citizens who are nationals of a significant number of member states may take the initiative of inviting the European Commission, within the framework of its powers, to submit any appropriate proposal on matters where citizens consider that a legal act of the Union is required for the purpose of implementing the Treaties' (TEU: Article 11(4)).

Since the death of Plan D, advocates of greater public involvement in the EU have pinned their hopes on the European Citizens' Initiative (ECI). The ECI represents a solution to building a space where citizenship is tied to residence and not to origin, and where the European people can enjoy complete civil rights (the right of referendum for adopting or rejecting a law and the right of initiative to propose a law). The ECI could thus create a new space inside the EU policy-making machine for ordinary EU citizens. The next section will explore how the ECI might impact future EU public engagement, including the development of a European public sphere (Thomson 2011).

The European Parliament gives a small presentation on its official website of this new tool that has allowed citizens to participate in shaping EU policy since April 2012. Put in place by the Lisbon Treaty, the citizens' initiative allows one million citizens from at least a quarter of the EU member states to ask the European Commission to propose legislation in areas that fall within its competence. The organizers of a citizens' initiative – a citizens' committee composed of at least seven EU citizens, resident in at least seven different member states – have one year to collect the necessary support. Signatures must be certified by the competent authorities in each member state. Organizers of successful initiatives will participate in a hearing at the European Parliament. The Commission will have three months to examine the initiative and decide how to act on it. One year has passed since its official introduction in April 2012, and the initiative is considered a success. There are fourteen projects registered on the Commission's official website but none reached the necessary number to be submitted to the Commission. Together with Plan D, these initiatives set out a long-term plan to reinvigorate European democracy and help the emergence of a European public sphere, where citizens are given the information and the tools to actively participate in the decision-making process and gain ownership of the European project.

## Promoting the European Public Space

For a long time, both the political and academic debates have focused on issues of territorial representation, the division of power, and guaranteeing the individual rights of citizens. More recently, it has been argued that the involvement of civil-society organizations in European policy-making may constitute a form of participatory democracy complementing representative democracy. As the principal obstacles in the EU's path to democratic reform were identified as the 'deficits of legitimacy and participation', 'representation' is one of the central topics in the current debate on EU legitimacy. According to Goehring (2002: 134), 'it is evident that different types of representation and participation have to be combined and reinforced in order to build a strong enlarged, legitimate, and political Union'. In her article, Goehring also refers to one of the EU's means to overcome its deficits, namely, the civil dialogue, and, in fact, claims that 'all types of dialogues, general, and issue-specific have the potential to bolster

EU legitimacy … As long as they are well organized, they could provide the EU with the required knowledge to improve its efficiency' (2002: 134).

There are two different kinds of legitimacy in the European Union: input and output legitimacy. The former concerns the democratic decision-making at the European level, so that a bigger involvement of citizens and interest groups can provide a higher legitimacy to the system. The output legitimacy, in contrast, concerns the EU's general efficiency and effectiveness in dealing with issues, that is to say, its ability to achieve the citizens' goals and to solve their problems. Thus, as noted by Marziali (2006: 37), '[t]he more the EU is effective, the more likely citizens accept it as an important political actor: it raises both their confidence in the institutions and the accountability of the latter vis-à-vis the citizens themselves'.

However, because of the lack of input legitimacy, the EU is an ideal venue for interest groups, which have very positive meaning: 'They bring much needed resources to policy making, implementation, and monitoring. In some accounts of how European integration develops, they help the EU to acquire more policy competencies by bringing irresistible demands to member state doorsteps, and assist in the popular identification with the European Union' (Greenwood 2004: 145). So, in this view, interest groups not only help in policy-making, but also bring the EU closer to its citizens. Put together, one can agree with authors claiming that 'interest representation brings more advantages for EU institutions – in terms of providing information, carrying issues between institutions, selling EU policies to national authorities and legitimating the policy process – than disadvantages' (McLaughlin and Greenwood 1995: 154). Still, the lack of accountability of the Council of Ministers vis-à-vis the European Parliament cannot be replaced merely by more participation of interest groups in the legislative process. On the contrary, their activity could continue to be a means to increase the trust of the citizens in EU institutions. If citizens feel the EU is a faraway institutional complex, they do not know how it works and what it does; interest groups can represent a sort of transmission belt between Brussels and the European peoples.

The absence of a European public space has not stopped certain actors from developing political actions in favour of the European construction. Numerous representatives of European civil society – syndicates, patronates,

NGOs, euro think tanks, cultural organizations and so on – express their progressive determination to participate to the European project. For these actors, the social Europe and the political Europe are complementary and inseparable. It has been stated repeatedly that think tanks' activity and the European Union are interdependent, and above all the latter needs the former to carry out its actions and policies. Nevertheless, can think tanks contribute to the emergence of a European public space?

The values, objectives and the projects of these organizations allow them to create a relationship between European institutions and citizens. First, can the European think tanks bring the ideas of the citizens to the institutions and politicians? The questions may surprise. On the one hand, European spirits are captured by the conversion to the euro; on the other hand, the think tank is often seen as a social actor capable of fighting efficiently against exclusion, and not as an engine-element of democracy. It is an element of counter-power; it becomes visible when struggling with the failures or weaknesses of the state or protesting against different administrative actions (Balosin 2010: 21). In other words, if we share the opinion of Dominique Wolton (1993), that political communication is the vector of democratic debate, think tanks, through their public critique, are the animators of this. Moreover, these associations are also actors contributing to the definition of the general interest and of the institutions that carry it.

Sometimes, the superiority given to the expertise can harm the mediation and democratization process. Stephen Boucher (2004) speaks about the ambiguous position of think tanks in their engagement in front of the general public. He underlines the existence of a dichotomy between the declarations of good intentions and reality, which shows the limited activities towards the citizens. Even if the will to promote participation and transmission of information from the citizens is incontestably present amongst the think tanks, the concretization of this principle into a declarative value remains to be proven. The European think tanks wish to handle different publics in their actions: the political decision-makers, the general public, the media, and the academic and business world. Once the research work is complete, it is necessary to present it to the public sphere. Three main activities seem to constrain the different initiatives developed by think tanks. To concretize their role as experts, campaigns must be completed close to the decision-makers. The manufacture of effective mediation needs information dissemination and a democratization of debates.

The idea of an organized civil society is very recent in the communitarian corpus: it represents one of the novelties introduced by the Treaty of Nice. This concept has to be separated from the general term of civil society, as it is limited to the active and organized part of the civil society. The idea of civil participation has been reaffirmed and expanded in the constitutional project, which introduced the concept of participative democracy as a new communitarian principle. Despite all efforts, the idea of an active role for citizens in the European process remains limited to a conceptual level. At a practical level, this civic participation has yet to develop and the idea of an effective European public space is still at a baby-step stage. Think tanks should be considered as the indispensable actors for its blooming. The establishment of think tanks encourages the creation of a space in the political and university worlds, a space that creates networks throughout Europe and contacts amongst researchers and national decision-makers of different member states. These structures have a certain impact on the problem of the democratic deficit. They play an important role in informing the general public and have an influence on the formation of a participative democracy, a potential base for a future European civic flourishing.

The Europeanization of civil society requires a twin strategy in which think tanks can perform and play a part, but to which issues of institutional reform at the EU level constitute a vital complement. First, the opportunity structures available to think tanks at EU level must be improved and a genuine attempt made to reach think tanks that hitherto have not mobilized at EU level. As a flanking measure, the role of civil society in all stages of the legislative chain must be enhanced. To that end, national governments must be obliged to openly consult relevant civil-society actors about proposed EU legislation according to a quasi-corporatist model based on a system of national committees appointed by independent commissions. Moreover, the partnership principle of EU policy must be exported to other areas of activity. This could be done particularly effectively in environmental, cohesion, consumer and social policies, involving a broad swathe of citizens and socializing them into the evolving European system. However, EU actors must not expect think tanks to tell them what they want to hear.

Instead, the Union should impose a different kind of conditionality: think tanks must address their internal democracy as the price of access to EU decision-makers. This would benefit the Union by providing opportunities for political socialization of the citizen. It would also benefit think tanks, since by adopting a more stakeholding style they would simultaneously re-emphasize their links to the public and allow supporters to identify more closely with them. In turn, this could produce a virtuous circle in terms of member/supporter commitment and involvement – a real asset for the notoriously resource-constrained NGO sector.

Second, a broader attempt to engage the public and initiate further institutional reform based on sustained public dialogue is required in order to bring the trajectories of integration and public opinion closer together. In this respect, the civil dialogue is promising, but it must be elaborated as a genuine attempt to uncover public opinion rather than as a bid to impose a particular model of reform decided a priori by either federalists or inter-governmentalists. Taken together, such measures would provide great opportunities to Europeanize civil society and thereby improve the EU's ability to manage persisting differences between its citizens.

## A Solution for the Democratic Deficit?

Democracy has become an issue in the current debates on the European Union. There are different views on the state of democracy in the EU and about the presence of a so-called democratic deficit, and whether something needs to be done to improve democracy in the EU. If citizens' participation is the 'lifeblood of democracy, then the European Union suffers from anaemia and is in desperate need for a remedy' (Abels 2009: 3). As a strategy for tackling the democratic deficit, attention is increasingly shifting towards the Europeanization of civil society, this being traditionally viewed as a means both to limit state power and to promote solidarity amongst citizens. This attempted change requires in turn actors who are both able and willing to act as agents of political socialization in the context of EU policy-making. As widely acknowledged, there is limited knowledge amongst the European public about what really goes on in Europe, specifically the division of responsibilities and competencies between the Union and the member states. If reforms of existing institutions are not enough, what else needs to be done? One possible answer to this question may be that institutional reform is inadequate in the absence of a European public space as well as of a new form of European collective identity, distinct from but not contradictory to nation-based citizenship. A European public space populated with citizens subscribing to a form of European collective identity could possibly overcome both the actual and the perceived democratic deficit.

The term democratic deficit generally signifies that the flow of influence from the people to government is disturbed in some way. In general terms, this indicates that the institutional mechanisms prescribed by a particular democratic model either are absent or fail to function correctly. In other words, the democratic deficit is closely related to an identity deficit. It is both more theoretically coherent and more practically plausible to relate the European collective identity to the democratic process itself: adequate democratic procedures would promote a sense of identification, and vice versa, leading to a 'virtuous cycle of truly European citizenship' (Giorgi *et al.* 2001: 74). Most politicians, scholars and members of the European public appear to agree that the EU suffers from a severe democratic deficit and there are various reasons why this perception seems so widespread. The 'democratic deficit' stems from both the lack of a European-wide people and of a truly European party system. Not only do people continue to think of themselves in terms of national affiliations, but political events and issues at the European level are monitored by national media from an internal perspective, and European elections are dominated by national problems (Schlesinger 1999). Still, an organization of continental scope would appear rather distant from the individual European citizen. As a multinational body, moreover, it lacks the grounding in a common history, culture, discourse, and symbolism on which most individual polities can draw (Moravcsik 2002: 604).

European Union officials seem to be aware of the issue; one of the main objectives of the Single European Act of 1986 was to 'rectify the democratic deficit in the Community's decision-making process'. In a communiqué of the EU summit, which launched the Convention, European leaders designated the EU's lack of democratic legitimacy as the 'first challenge facing Europe' (Moravcsik 2002: 610). According to Zweifel (2003), there are two sorts of deficit in the EU; a structural one and a normative one. The *structural* deficit can be found in the institutional set-up and procedures of the EU, and this can be formulated as the lack of transparency, consensus, accountability and redistribution. The *normative* deficit entails the lack of a common identity and the lack of a public sphere. Almond (1956) defines a democratic political system as one characterized by a stable and defined set of institutions and rules governing their interrelationships; a system where citizens and social groups seek to influence decisions directly or indirectly, where collective decisions have impacts on the distribution of resources, and where it is possible to establish a relation between decisions, demands and outputs. A democratic system is one in which most citizens believe that democracy is a valid normative principle. The public space is both the expression of this democratic language and the proof of its use.

The public space needed by a democratically viable European policy might take very different forms from those familiar at a national level. Its irreducible character is to offer a framework for a set of practices which are citizenship-oriented. What these practices might look like in the context of multi-governance is an open question, and 'the kinds of indicators that can be used to monitor the achievement of a European public space must be sensitive to this fundamental openness and indeterminacy. European democracy is, necessarily, a project to be defined, rather than a process to be simply observed' (Giorgi *et al.* 2000: 79). According to Micossi (2008: 1), the Union will be strong in the eyes of public opinion and member states alike if it manages to come up with solutions to the challenges of globalization, external and internal security, energy and the environment. In this respect, there is no reason why difficulties encountered over the last decade should endure, to the extent that they were a systemic consequence of poor Union functioning (Micossi 2008: 15).

The current crisis is only a symptom of a bigger problem between the EU and its citizens. Until the early 1990s, citizens seemed to accept a situation in which decisions were being taken in their name at the European level, but without their involvement in the process. Since then, however, European leaders have had to learn that the era of 'permissive consensus' was over. The French and Dutch no-votes were only the latest example in a series of lost referenda, starting with the Danish rejection of the Maastricht Treaty. Since 1992, there have been many calls for the EU to get closer to its citizens and to 'reconnect' with them. Obviously, it has not yet achieved this goal. According to the analysis of voters' motivations in the Dutch and French referenda, many seized the opportunity to express a general dissatisfaction with the EU and the way in which the European integration process has developed.

The White Paper on European Governance, published in July 2001 by the European Commission, identifies the need to reform European governance against the background of a mismatch between the concrete achievements of European integration, on the one hand, and the disappointment and alienation of Europeans, on the other. The accomplishments of European integration have predominantly been the product of the political and technocratic elite that does not have much connection with the population, and which acts without feeling the issues raised by lack of democracy and legitimacy. Even though the EU has proved to be able to deliver stability, peace and economic wealth, the people that are governed do not feel connected to and do not have influence upon the system by which they are governed. The challenge for European governance is how to close this normative gap. There is also tension in the confrontation of participation and representation in the EU. Some people claim that the participation of lobby groups in the policy process is harmful to the system of representation, while others say that participation is an important addition to representation and helps with the inclusion of more interests and public awareness of the works of the EU.

There are plenty of possibilities to engage citizens in the debate on European matters. European leaders must use this 'period of reflection' to convincingly demonstrate that they take seriously the message from the two negative referenda. Instead of 'selling' the Constitution, this present period of reflection must directly address the larger dissatisfaction that characterizes the attitude of a growing part of the population towards the EU. Public debates on European issues should be organized with the participation of politicians and civil society. New methods of participatory democracy – such as consensus conferences, deliberative polls or the formation of cross-border networks between citizens – should be considered at the national but also at the European level in order to maximize citizens' involvement in shaping policy.

As a clear signal of their determination to reach out to the citizens, European politicians need to subscribe to a hard compact that addresses the democratic and communicative deficits of the EU with concrete measures. The main aim of such a compact for citizens would be to establish an effective 'European democratic and civic space' (Kurpas *et al.* 2005).

## Conclusion

European Union institutions cannot exist in a void. They need the support of European public opinion, and if they lose it, their own future will be endangered. If more democracy at the European level is the answer – as has been claimed for decades – what can be done to foster it? Successive treaties and projects like the Constitution might be one answer. The other must be the creation of a European 'public space', 'a trans-national space where citizens from different countries can discuss the important challenges for the Union. This should help policy makers to stay in touch with European public opinion, and could guide them in identifying European projects, which mobilize public support' (European Commission 2001: 11).

There is no panacea that would bring Europe closer to its citizens and create a veritable European conscience and mentality. The solution lies in details. Journalistic and informative platforms are needed as much as think tanks to make the EU more comprehensible. It is essential to promote an active transnational participation of citizens in the European construction.

It is important to valorize mutual understanding and solidarity, in order to contribute to the intercultural dialogue inside the Union. For that, the Union must offer the necessary instruments to allow European citizens to get involved in this creation and Europeans must understand that their national universe does not end where Europe starts.

## References

Abels, G. (2009). 'Citizens' Deliberations and the EU Democratic Deficit: Is There a Model for Participatory Democracy?', *Tübinger Arbeitspapiere zur Integrationsforschung* (TAIF) <http://aei.pitt.edu/11419/1/Abels_TAIF1_2009.pdf> accessed 10 March 2013.

Almond, G. A. (1956). 'Comparing Political Systems', *Journal of Politics*, 18 (2), 391–409.

Balosin, M. A. (2010). 'Think Tanks for the Promotion of a European Public Space', *L'Europe Unie – Revue d'Etudes Europeennes*, No. 3–4, 12–16.

Boual, J. C. (1999). *Vers une société civile européenne*. La Tour d'Aigues: Editions de l'Aube.

Boucher, S. (ed.) (2004). 'L'Europe et Ses Think Tanks: Un Potentiel Inaccompli', *Etudes & Recherches*, No. 35.

Cotterau, A., and Ladrière, P. (eds) (1992). *Pouvoir et Légitimité: Figures de l'Espace Public*. Paris: Ecole des hautes études en sciences sociales.

El-Tayeb, F. (2008). 'The Birth of a European Public: Migration, Postnationality, and Race in the Uniting of Europe', *American Quarterly*, 60 (3), 649–70.

European Commission (2001). *European Governance. A White Paper*. COM(2001)428 final, Brussels <http://eur-lex.europa.eu/LexUriServ/site/en/com/2001/com2001_0428en01.pdf> accessed 12 March 2013.

—— (2005a). *Synthesis Report Consultation Forum on the Future Action Programme for Active European Citizenship 2007–2013* <http://ec.europa.eu/citizenship/pdf/doc481_en.pdf> accessed 10 February 2013.

—— (2005b). *The Commission's Contribution to the Period of Reflection and Beyond: Plan-D for Democracy, Dialogue and Debate*. COM(2005)494 final <http://eur-lex.europa.eu/LexUriServ/LexUriServ.do?uri=COM:2005:0494:FIN:EN:PDF> accessed 20 March 2013.

——(2005c). 'European Commission Launches PLAN D for Democracy, Dialogue and Debate'. *Press Release*, IP/05/1272 <http://europa.eu/rapid/press-release_IP-05-1272_en.htm> accessed 20 March 2013.

——(2006). *White Paper on a European Communication Policy*. COM(2006)0035 final <http://eur-lex.europa.eu/LexUriServ/LexUriServ.do?uri=CELEX:52006DC0035:EN:NOT> accessed 12 March 2013.

——(2011). *Guide to the European Citizens' Initiative*. Luxembourg: Publications Office of the European Union.

European Parliament (1996). 'Resolution on Participation of Citizens and Social Players in the European Union's Institutional System and the IGC', *Official Journal*, C020, 20 January1997.

Ferry, J.-M. (2000). *La question de l'État européen*. Paris: Gallimard.

Giorgi, L., Rowley, J. C., and Ney, S. (2001). 'Surveying the European Public Space: A Political and Research Agenda', *Innovation: The European Journal of Social Science Research*, 14 (1), 73–83.

Goehring, R. (2002). 'Interest Representation and Legitimacy in the European Union: The New Quest for Civil Society Formation'. In A. Warleigh and J. Fairbrass (eds), *Influence and Interests in the European Union: The New Politics of Persuasion and Advocacy*, pp. 118–38. London: Europa Publications.

Greenwood, J. (2004). 'The Search for Input Legitimacy through Organized Civil Society in the EU', *Transnational Associations*, No. 2, 145–56.

Habermas, J. (1989). *The Public Sphere*. Cambridge, MA: MIT Press.

——(1997). *Droit et démocratie*. Paris: Gallimard.

Ivic, S. (2011). 'European Commission's Plan D for Democracy, Dialogue and Debate: The Path towards Deliberation?', *Journal of Law and Conflict Resolution*, 3 (2), 14–19.

Kant, I. (1991). 'Idea for a Universal History with a Cosmopolitan Purpose'. In H. S. Reiss (ed.), *Kant: Cambridge Texts in the History of Political Thought* (2nd edn), pp. 41–53. Cambridge: Cambridge University Press.

Kurpas, S. *et al.* (2005). 'A Citizens' Compact: Reaching out to the Citizens of Europe', *EPIN Working Paper*, No. 14 <http://www.ceps.eu/files/book/1263.pdf> accessed 25 October 2012.

Marziali, V. (2006). 'Lobbying in Brussels. Interest Representation and Need for Information', *Discussion Paper: C155* <http://aei.pitt.edu/6827/1/dp_c155Marziali.pdf> accessed 10 March 2013.

McLaughlin, A. M., and Greenwood, J. (1995). 'The Management of Interest Representation in the European Union', *Journal of Common Market Studies*, 33 (1), 143–56.

Micossi, S. (2008). 'Democracy in the European Union', *CEPS Working Document*, No. 286, 1–18.

Mill, J. S. (1861 [1991]). *Considerations on Representative Government*. New York: Prometheus Books.

Moravcsik, A. (2002). 'In Defence of the "Democratic Deficit": Reassessing Legitimacy in the European Union', *Journal of Common Market Studies*, 40 (4), 603–24.

Schlesinger, P. (1999). 'Changing Spaces of Political Communication: The Case of the European Union', *Political Communication*, 16 (3), 263–79.

Thomson, J. (2011). '"A Space inside Europe for the Public" before "A European Public Space"' <http://www.involve.org.uk/wp-content/uploads/2011/03/ECI-A-Space-Inside-Europe-for-the-Public.pdf> accessed 20 March 2013.

Wolton, D. (1991). *War Game. L'information et la guerre*. Paris: Flammarion.

—— (1993). *La dernière utopie*. Paris: Flammarion.

Zweifel, T. D. (2003). 'Democratic Deficits in Comparison: Best (and Worst) Practices in European, US and Swiss Merger Regulation', *Journal of Common Market Studies*, 41 (3), 541–66.

MONICA MERUTIU

# 11 Religious Identity and Secularization in Europe

There are three constants that have left their imprints and shaped European culture and civilization, illustrated in the Athens–Rome–Jerusalem triangle: Greek thought, Roman law and the Christian faith, related to Judaism. The challenges that European civilization confronts seem more intense now in an era influenced by the process of globalization, when local problems tend to become global: terrorism and fundamentalism, violations of human rights, pathologies of reason and pathologies of faith, the crisis of democracies viewed as being reduced to procedures, incapable of sustaining themselves and lacking inspiration.

The rivalry between religion and secularization in Europe today seems deeper than anticipated by diagnoses formulated towards the end of the twentieth century. A closer analysis of the European Constitutional Treaty (2004) reveals the struggle between religion and secularization as mirrored in the controversies over mentioning Christianity or God in its Preamble. Accordingly, the question that arises is whether European unity can be stable unless it is built on durable foundations that are based on a spiritual dimension.

## Challenges at the Beginning of the Third Millennium: Identity Divides

In recent years we have witnessed a variety of surprising manifestations of religious phenomena: terrorist attacks, Christian and Muslim fundamentalisms, the increase of secularization, especially in Central and Western

Europe, the continuous decrease of numbers as far as the European traditional church members are concerned, an increased number of different sects, and the rise of Islam. In the view of Joseph Ratzinger (2005), '[w]e are living in a time of great dangers and great opportunities for man and the world; a time which is also of great responsibility for us all'. Far from being isolated, this message summarizes the situation that characterizes our world today, inviting a deeper analysis from each and every one of us. Great global problems are escalating, including 'inequality in the distribution of the goods of the earth, growing poverty, and the more threatening impoverishment and exhaustion of the earth and its resources, hunger, sicknesses that threaten the whole world and the clash of cultures' (Ratzinger 2005).

A large part of Cardinal Ratzinger's works are dedicated to the idea of Europe, its foundations, the sources conferring its identity and unity, and not least, the crises of European civilization. He characterizes the culture of Europe nowadays as radically contradicting not only Christianity, but all religious traditions. For example, in *Turning Point for Europe* (1991), Ratzinger identified three milestones in the history of the twentieth century that still have an impact today: first, the transformations after the First World War; second, the Second World War and the division of Europe between communism and capitalism; and third, the fall of communism and the disintegration of the Marxist ideology. Later, in the Preface to *Introduction to Christianity*, Ratzinger refers specifically to the two years that marked the twentieth century: 1968 and 1989. The milestone of 1968 represented 'the rebellion of a new generation, which not only considered postwar reconstruction in Europe as inadequate, full of injustice, full of selfishness and greed, but also viewed the entire course of history since the triumph of Christianity as a mistake and a failure' (2004: 11). The historic events of 1989 'brought the surprising collapse of the socialist regimes in Europe, which left behind a sorry legacy of ruined land and ruined souls' (2004: 11) and, in Ratzinger's view, they only made the atmosphere of disorientation much stronger. However, the fall of communism in 1989 was perceived as evidence that the power of faith surpassed the power of scientific socialism, and, in this context, Ratzinger connects to the personality of Karol Wojtyla, whose election in 1978 as Pope John Paul II represented a turning point for history at the end of the twentieth century. He proclaimed Christianity and communism incompatible and the Vatican together with the United States had a key role in supporting the Polish Solidarity movement, the common goal representing fighting down the 'Red danger'.

The diagnoses offered by Cardinal Ratzinger emphasize the moral problem of our times when 'morality has surrendered, and man *qua* man has surrendered' (1991: 39) and point to an argument offered by C. S. Lewis back in 1943 when Europe was experiencing the descent of morality in the time of the Second World War: 'It is the magician's bargain: give up our soul, get power in return. But once our souls, that is, our selves, have been given up, the power thus conferred will not belong to us … It is in Man's power to treat himself as a mere "natural object" … The real objection is that if man chooses to treat himself as raw material, raw material he will be' (Ratzinger 1991: 39).

The beginning of the third millennium deepened the crisis of morality and brought with it great new challenges. In an era strongly affected by globalization and scientific and technological advances, what becomes even more problematic seems to be the equation where 'the growth of our possibilities has not been matched by a comparable development of our moral energy', and, for Ratzinger, the greatest danger is to be found in this lack of balance between the progress of technology and moral energy: 'moral strength has not grown together with the development of science; rather, it has diminished, because the technical mentality relegates morality to the subjective realm, while we have need, precisely, of a public morality, a morality that is able to respond to the threats that weigh down on the existence of us all' (Ratzinger 2005).

The problem of our age is identified as a moral one: 'morality, just like religion, now belongs to the realm of the subjective; it has no place in the objective' (Ratzinger 1991: 37). That means man is the one that shapes and controls morality which confers dignity to a human being and it by no means represents something that a person should renounce: '[I]t is moral obligation that constitutes his dignity, and he does not become more free if he discards it: on the contrary, he takes a step backward, to the level of a machine, of a mere thing' (1991: 41). Ratzinger notes that 'the real untruth of the world view of which drugs and terrorism are symptoms consists in the reduction of the world to facts and in the narrowing-down of reason to the perception of what is quantitative. That which is most specific to man is shoved aside into the subjective realm and thus lacks reality' (1991: 40).

In *Europe Today and Tomorrow: Addressing the Fundamental Issues*, Ratzinger paraphrases Hans Küng's affirmation about the need for dialogue between religions in order to gain peace between them, and he claims that 'there can be no peace in the world without genuine peace between reason and faith, because without peace between reason and religion, the sources of morality and law dry up' (2004: 87). This vision mirrors the imperative of a complementarity between these two realms because of the *pathologies of reason* and *pathologies of religion* that are increasingly present in the contemporary era. Religion today needs reason in order to prevent its metamorphosis into fundamentalism and terrorism, just as reason needs religion as a complement in solving various crises, and these two dimensions are called to 'mutual healing and cleansing, each of which need the other', as transpired from the 2004 'historical encounter' between Ratzinger and Jürgen Habermas at the Catholic Academy of Bavaria in 2004. The problematic of the relationship between these two dimensions was once again analysed in the essay entitled 'In Search for Freedom: Against Reason Fallen Ill and Religion Abused'. Ratzinger (2005) condemns both pathologies as life-threatening for peace: 'But the evolution of intellect in the West, also, inclines ever more towards the destructive pathologies of reason. Was not the atom bomb already an overstepping of the frontier, where reason instead of being a constructive power, sought its potency in its capacity to destroy?' The problem of morals is once again underlined and the alarm signal points to the consequences of a reason that is detached from a moral ethos. At the same time, we live in an age that experiences the most extreme forms of what a faith without reason represents, and fundamentalism, terrorism, fanaticism are sides to this phenomenon.

The very idea of Europe is declining today and the ideal of unity appears to be an empty concept, lacking any substance, claims Ratzinger, who reminds us that, immediately after the Second World War, the goal of a united Europe represented a positive moral factor and made possible the reconciliation between the East and the West. The solution proposed for the crises of our world today is rediscovering the spiritual dimension, systematically weakened by the process of secularization.

Recent years have clearly shown that in an increasingly interdependent world, one can no longer ignore the problems humanity is confronted with. In his book *One World. The Ethics of Globalization*, Peter Singer offers an illustrative picture of such interdependence, inviting each and every one of us to

> [c]onsider two aspects of globalization: first, planes exploding as they slam into the World Trade Center, and second, the emission of carbon dioxide from the exhausts of gas-guzzling sport utility vehicles. One brought instant death and left unforgettable images that were watched on television screens all over the world; the other makes a contribution to climate change that can be detected only by scientific instruments. Yet both are indications of the way in which we are now one world, and the more subtle changes to which sport utility vehicle owners unintentionally contribute will almost certainly kill far more people than the highly visible one. (Singer 2002: 1)

Hans Küng holds that, as an indicator of modernity, economic progress can lead to inhumane consequences. Therefore he initiated the discussion of a 'global ethic', conceived in terms of an ethos of values common to global humanity, meant to 'penetrate to a deeper *ethical level*, the level of *binding values*, *irrevocable criteria*, and *inner basic attitudes*, and not remain stuck at the level of laws, codified rights and paragraphs with which issue might be taken, or at the political level of proposing concrete political solutions' (1998: 56).

In his turn, Karl-Otto Apel believes that our globalized world urgently requires a viable universal ethics. Since the late 1960s, he has been concerned with creating the basis and implementation of a global ethical concept, drawing attention to the need of our world today, in an age of science, of a planetary macro-ethics, to be distinguished from the traditional forms of ethics, micro-ethics or meso-ethics, which, in his view, were restricted to 'loyalties inside small groups or obedience to the law and order within the national state' (Apel 2000: 138). In the new reality created by globalization, the need for ethical responsibility is urgent. Pope John Paul II drew attention to the 'moral limits of the market' (Hehir 2006) and in a common declaration with the Archbishop of Athens and all Greece stated that

> we observe that man's social and scientific evolution has not been accompanied by a deeper delving into the meaning and value of life, which in every instance is a gift of God, nor by an analogous appreciation of man's unique dignity, as being created according to the Creator's image and likeness. Moreover, economic and technological development does not belong equally to all mankind but belongs only to a very small portion of it. Furthermore, the improvement of living standards has not brought about the opening of men's hearts to their neighbours who suffer hunger and are naked. (John Paul II 2007)

The accomplishments of contemporary society come to reflect the autonomy of man, who feels entitled to apply them in various modalities, moreover 'in the end, terrorism is also based on this modality of man's self-authorization, and not on the teachings of the Koran' (Ratzinger 2005).

Analysts speak today of a global resurgence of religion, an unexpected renaissance that brings the religion of the beginning of the third millennium to the front lines. Philosopher Habermas even formulated the notion of a *post-secular society*, as considered to reflect

> public recognition for the contributions that religious communities make to the reproduction of desirable motives and views. In addition, within the public consciousness of a post-secular society, a normative insight shines through, and this insight has consequences for how unbelievers should act politically towards believers. In the post-secular society, it becomes clear that the 'modernization of the public consciousness' affects both religious and worldly mentalities and changes both reflexively, albeit in different phases. If both sides comprehend the secularization of society as a complementary learning process, then they have cognitive reasons to take seriously each others' contributions to controversial topics in public life. (Habermas and Ratzinger 2005: 95)

Although the notion of a post-secular society seems debatable, one thing remains unequivocal: the phenomenon of globalization tends to strengthen identities and affirm diversity. Religions, too, are placed in competition and they tend to reveal their divergences in the new context. In a time of postmodern relativism, Catholic theologian Hans Küng claims that a global peace is conditioned by the peace between religions: 'The world is in agony. No survival without a world ethic. No world peace without peace between religions. No peace between religions without dialogue between religions' (1990: xv). The enlightened vision of Küng transcends any divergences that might characterize different religions and invites us to dialogue and to find common grounds, since we live in a time when religions ought to take a pragmatic approach towards one another and consider their convergences, beyond the doctrinal, dogmatic aspects, in order to achieve tolerance and acceptance of diversity and pluralism. Reflecting on this context, Jonathan Sacks, chief rabbi of the United Kingdom, emphasizes 'the dignity of difference' (2002: 66), claiming that, in fact, those who are confident in their faith should by no means feel threatened, but rather enlarged, by the religious world views of others:

> We must learn the art of conversation, from which truth emerges not, as in Socratic dialogues, by the refutation of falsehood but from the quite different process of letting our world be enlarged by the presence of others who think, act, and interpret reality in ways radically different of our own. We must attend to the particular, not just the universal. For when universal civilizations clash, the world shakes and lives are lost. We will make peace only when we learn that God loves difference, and so, at last, must we. God has created many cultures, civilizations and faiths but only one world in which to live together – and it is getting smaller all the time. (Sacks 2002: 23)

Recent years have been characterized by the new paradigm 'them vs. us' and they taught us in the hardest of ways the lesson that we can no longer afford isolationism when it comes to dialogue with the 'others': the 2001 attacks in the United States, the violent manifestations that followed the publication of the Danish cartoons, the murder of Theo van Gogh, the tensions and victims caused by the Regensburg speech of Benedict XVI. As Sacks sharply affirmed: 'If religion is not part of a solution, it will certainly be part of the problem' (2002: 9). In this sense, the dialogue between religions emerges as an essential step for gaining peace between religions and implicitly peace between nations. A real dialogue must arise beyond superficial encounters and polite attitudes, it must aim for a culture of dialogue through epistemic attitudes towards the *other* (Habermas 2006a).

Furthermore, Samuel Huntington's 1996 *Clash of Civilizations and the Remaking of World Order* offers an overview of the evolution of global politics after the Cold War. The thesis proposed is that the new phase of conflicts will no longer have an ideological basis, but will be one of conflicts between civilizations. The differences between them are seen as fundamental and the cleavage even more radical because of the process of globalization, when religious identities tend to differentiate civilizations most radically. Elaborating on the various aspects of the concept of civilization, Huntington argues that their central feature is religion, that great civilizations in history have been identified with the great world religions. However, the West has produced no great religion, and moreover, in the European space, political interests seem to have outperformed religious ones. Huntington analyses the revitalization of religion throughout the world, claiming that it strengthens cultural differences; as he puts it, 'cultures can change, and the nature of their impact on politics and economics can vary from one period to another. Yet the major differences in political and economic development among civilizations are clearly rooted in their different cultures' (Huntington 2003: 29).

In *The Dignity of Difference: How to Avoid the Clash of Civilizations*, Sacks emphasizes that we have entered 'the age of the politics of identity' and this is part of a larger context that integrates the global resurgence of religion, offering an explanation of 'why religion has emerged, after a long eclipse, to become so powerful a presence on the world stage, because religion is one of the great answers to the question of identity' (2002: 10). But the renaissance of religion leads also to a proliferation of fundamentalism. A paradoxical relation is manifested between secularization and fundamentalism, both being in a definite interdependence. In her book, *The Battle for God*, Karen Armstrong discusses the global role of religion and adds that these radical forms of religion are sustained by the advances of secular Western civilization: 'They may reject the scientific rationalism of the West, but they cannot escape it' (2000: 7). We may be speaking of an interdependence, especially considering that fundamentalism is largely a response to a *stimulus-motion*, and, according to Harvey Cox, is in a state of self-contradiction: on the one hand it advocates an anti-modern doctrine, which claims that the results of modernity express the evil in the world, but on the other hand it uses technology to impose itself. For Cox, fundamentalism is perceived as a subculture, extremely liberal, modern, and secular in its manifestations, therefore hypocritical.

On the other hand, Islam represents one of the major challenges faced by European society at the beginning of the twenty-first century, and the discourse that warns against the Islamization of Europe is getting stronger. Islam is the religion whose rising is the most dynamic and which is steadfast in affirming that its values are non-negotiable. Large communities of Muslims are now part of the European space, posing serious challenges when it comes to integration. Marcello Pera, Italian philosopher and former President of the Italian Senate, believes that this context mirrors an identity crisis Europe is facing: 'By embracing it and by spreading the 'anything goes' slogan underlying it, Europe shows that it no longer knows where it comes from, what it is, and where it is going. This is why Europe meets the integration of immigrants with difficulty and risks bringing about precisely that clash of identities and cultures it most wants to avoid. If Europe is not becoming a 'melting pot' like America it is because its identity is not strong enough to merge and fuse different cultures and forge them into a single entity' (Pera 2006).

Europe's responses to the Islamic challenge vary from extreme tolerance to extreme manifestations of prejudice and exclusion. Ian Buruma's overview offers a synthesis of this landscape:

> The debate over Islam in Europe is held less in a spirit of finding the truth through open disagreement than of separating friends from foes and fingering traitors, appeasers, and collaborators. This mimics the worst years of the cold war and deliberately echoes the rhetoric of World War II. Islamist radicalism is worrying enough. But we have to recognize it for what it is. To confuse Islamism (let alone Islam *per se*) with Hitler's Nazis or Stalin's Soviet Empire is not the best way to come to grips with it. (Buruma 2010: 104)

The transcendental and sacred seem to have been lost, from the perspective of religious conservatives, in a world subjugated by secularization, as is our contemporary world. Towards the end of the twentieth century, Cox identified two reasons for the unprecedented ascendance of this phenomenon: the impact of scientific technology and an impersonal urban civilization (1985). Science and its practical application, technology, seem to make life simpler for people, who no longer find reason to call on God or other supernatural beings. The urban living environment is one that concentrates modernity and imposes bureaucracy, thus making the cities spiritually disastrous (Cox 1985). This was the vision of religious fundamentalists who perceived the city as a place of bureaucracy and secular evil. Harvey Cox questions the attitude that a postmodern theology should have towards reason and science, an attitude that has remained problematic. Back in 1961, Fritjof Schuon in *Stations of Wisdom* addressed the cleavage between faith and science, and claimed that faith ignored the intellectual aspect of the human being, 'focusing especially on the sentimental, rather than on the metaphysical' (1961: 1). In this respect, it can be argued that the impact of religion in the twenty-first century is also related to the imposing of an updated vision, even a scientific one, in order to find a solution to religious fundamentalism, completely anachronistic with the global society.

The wave of secularization that followed the religious wars and increased in a world swept by globalization; the modern critique of religion (from Hegel, Feuerbach and Marx, to Nietzsche, Freud and Comte to name the peaks of this movement) with its long-term consequences that may be encountered in the radical form of secularization experienced by contemporary Europe; the current attempts to reduce any religious manifestation to silence by expelling it to the private sphere; the attacks from atheist fundamentalism, and those of religious fundamentalism; the continuous spread of relativism; these are not to be neglected as they pose serious challenges to Europe's future.

## Secular and Religious Identities

The discussions on the foundations of Europe, on the sources of its culture and civilization, are extremely passionate, and in recent years have been increased by the dynamics of globalization. The promoters of the secular discourse on Europe meet the arguments and reactions of those for whom Christianity is not a simple myth. There is no question that Europe is being confronted with an identity crisis, the causes of which are multiple; the same goes for their effects. Can we then speak of a Judeo-Christian tradition of Europe? Formulated in the United States at the end of the nineteenth century, the concept was sometimes perceived as only an instrument in the hands of politicians or religious leaders. It was intertwined with the reaction against Nazism, the attempt to avoid anti-Semitism by admitting the value Judaism had for the European space, and expressed the common values of Judaism and Christianity, which imprinted the European continent with a specific tradition, the essence of European civilization.

As has already been pointed out, three constants have continuously shaped European culture and civilization, illustrated in the Athens–Rome–Jerusalem triangle: Greek thought, Roman law and the Christian faith, related to Judaism. A complete approach of the identity sources reveals Europe through its heritages, which were best synthesised by Cardinal Ratzinger in his *Europa – verpflichtendes Erbe für die Christen* (1983), a book dedicated to European history, culture and civilization. Here, Ratzinger speaks of four heritages: Greek, Christian, Latin, and that of the modern world (the separation between faith and law). The Greeks offered a framework for the idea of Europe, in the sense that we can speak of Europe as a creation of the Greeks (as a word and as a geographic and spiritual notion). The relation between democracy and *eunomia* (the idea of the internal stability of a state and respect of an individual's personal autonomy) was one of the constituent elements of Europe. Democracy, a creation of Greece, consists in the functioning of a system of rules that guarantees the respect of the individual's personal autonomy. The Christian heritage of Europe is for Ratzinger the synthesis between the faith of Israel and the Greek spirit. The German theologian considers this complex as the foundation of European civilization. When referring to the Latin heritage, Ratzinger means the period of the Middle Ages, when Europe was synonymous with the West, Christendom and everything the Latin Church signified. Latin culture and this Latin space did not only include the Roman peoples, but also the Germanic and the Anglo-Saxon ones (Ratzinger 1983).[1]

Without awareness of these sources of identity, one cannot understand the dynamics of a civilization. The consequences of secularization

1 These arguments are addressed in more detail in Merutiu (2009).

are evident in the European space and they are manifested not only in the 'unchurching of the European population' (Casanova 2006: 65), but also in the absence of a 'feeling of belonging to one same community of values and principles' (Pera 2006). Another aspect that must be considered is that Christianity seems to be returning to its roots, and it is becoming increasingly agreed that the future of Christianity is not in Europe, but rather in regions such as Latin America, the African continent (sub-Saharan Africa), as well as the United States. From this perspective, Europe (Western and Central) is considered to be 'exceptionalist', a secular island in an increasingly religious world, as explained in works by Peter Berger, Grace Davie and Effie Fokas. For the three (2008: 10), 'most of the world today is characterized by an explosion of passionate religious movements' and only Europe is 'a geographical exception to this characterization'. Back in 1997, Berger admitted that 'what I and most other sociologists of religion wrote in the 1960s about secularization was a mistake. Our underlying argument was that secularization and modernity go hand in hand. With more modernization comes more secularization. It wasn't a crazy theory. There was some evidence for it. But I think it's basically wrong. Most of the world today is certainly not secular. It's very religious' (1997: 974). In the case of Europe, Berger added that it is characterized by a 'strong survival of religion, most of it generally Christian in nature, despite the widespread alienation from organized Churches. A shift in the institutional location of religion, then, rather than secularization, would be a more accurate description of the European situation' (1999: 10). When referring to the contemporary manifestations of secularization in the European realm, Davie (2000) speaks about the 'believing without belonging' phenomenon. This is a unique feature of the religious phenomenon at the beginning of the third millennium, its metamorphosis that transforms religion into a private and subjective faith. Casanova shows that 'an increasing majority of the European population has ceased participating in traditional religious practices, at least on a regular basis, while still maintaining relatively high levels of private individual religious beliefs' (Casanova 2006: 65).

This sentiment was mirrored in the controversies over mentioning Christianity or God in the European Constitutional Treaty (2004) Preamble. The Treaty eventually adopted a draft that makes reference to

Europe's spiritual and moral, cultural, religious and humanistic heritage. But this version of the Preamble raised further controversies as critics interpreted it as a symptom of a European identity crisis. In his 2006 lecture on *Europe, America and the Continental Drift*, Marcello Pera, one of the voices speaking of Europe's feeble religious identity, claimed that 'both statements are extremely poor and reticent, because neither of them defines exactly *what* heritage and *what* religion Europe stems from. The question then is: Can Europe unify economically, socially, and politically if it lacks the strength even to mention that Judeo-Christian religion without which it would not even exist?' Accordingly, Pera's answer was negative.

Yet Europe needs its religious foundations that give unity. In *Christian Heritage and Democracy in Europe* it was argued that 'the core of European unity cannot be stable and durable if this spiritual crisis is furthermore ignored and the spiritual dimension left aside and considered unimportant compared to the political or the economical dimensions' (Merutiu 2009). In the same context, Ratzinger, in *Europe: Today and Tomorrow* (2007), observed that the artisans of European construction were profoundly aware of the importance religion had for European civilization; as he explained it, 'history shows us that too often men act in ways contrary to all logic and reason. The fact that the politics of reconciliation (after World War II) triumphed is to the credit of a whole generation of politicians: let me recall the names of Adenauer, Schuman, De Gasperi, de Gaulle. These were objective, intelligent men who had a healthy political realism. But their realism was rooted in the firm ground of the Christian *ethos* of enlightenment, refined by reason' (Ratzinger 2007: 116).

The European construction was intimately linked to a strong spiritual dimension by its artisans, the Christian Democrats, who conceived the democratic ideal on which Europe's future depended as owing its origins exclusively to Christianity: '[D]emocracy shall be Christian or not be at all!' (Schuman 1963). Moreover, '[i]n Europe in the late 1940s Christian Democracy and Catholicism laid the foundations of the European integration movement. Europe was not merely a site for state bargains and profitable economic transactions. It was also the focus of a political movement seeking to implement a particular, religiously infused vision' (Katzenstein 2006: 32). In fact, 'almost everyone who has been really influential in the creating of the EU has been a socially minded Catholic from Schuman and Adenauer to [Jacques] Delors and [Jacques] Santer' (Hastings 1997: 122). In his turn, the president of the European Commission, Jacques Delors, many times insisted on the necessity of a 'soul for Europe' (Delors 1992).

As Habermas explained in his essay 'Why Europe Needs a Constitution', the perspectives of the personalities who initiated the project of the European Union and those responsible today for its continuation differ. In fact, the German philosopher believes that 'there is a remarkable contrast between the expectations and demands of those who pushed for European unification immediately after World War II, and those who contemplate the continuation of this project today—at the very least, a striking difference in rhetoric and ostensible aim' (Habermas cited in Rogowski and Turner 2006). As observed elsewhere, the greatest cleavage in the two discourses is that those who had the vision of unification projected it as a 'United States of Europe', while the current state of things clearly shows the renouncement of the federal ideal and even a reluctance to use the term 'federation' (Rogowski and Turner 2006: 25). When arguing for a constitution for Europe, Habermas brings to mind two puzzling aspects: first, immediate political goals and, second, dilemmas stemming from virtually irreversible decisions of the past. When addressing the first he is aware that 'while the original political aims of European integration have lost much of their relevance, they have since been replaced by an even more ambitious political agenda', while the second, 'the containment of a potentially dangerous Germany, may have lost its salience with the growing stability of democratic institutions and spread of liberal outlooks in the Federal Republic' (Rogowski and Turner 2006: 26–7). Moreover, Habermas adds that 'the "Carolingian" background of the founding fathers – Schuman, De Gasperi, Adenauer – with its explicit appeal to the Christian West, has vanished' (cited in Rogowski and Turner 2006: 154).

One of the poles that opposed the final version of the Preamble to the Constitutional Treaty and that advocated mentioning the Christian roots was the Vatican, through the voice and actions of John Paul II. In *Ecclesia in Europa* 'he renewed his impassioned call for inclusion in the new European constitution of a prominent reference to the religious foundations of European civilization, and particularly to the Christian foundations of authentic European history' (Hehir 2006: 110). Constantly preoccupied with the idea of a united Europe, John Paul II fought for a clear recognition of the Old Continent's religious roots:

> We rejoice at the success and progress of the European Union. The union of the European world in one civil entity, without her people losing their national self-awareness, traditions and identity, has been the vision of its pioneers. However, the emerging tendency to transform certain European countries into secular states without any reference to religion constitutes a retraction and a denial of their spiritual legacy. We are called to intensify our efforts so that the unification of Europe may be accomplished. We shall do everything in our power, so that the Christian roots of Europe and its Christian soul may be preserved inviolate. (John Paul II 2007)

However, as witnessed in recent years, secularization in Europe often takes the form of a 'Christophobia', and 'often it voices an almost visceral denial of any possible public dimension for Christian values' (Ratzinger and Pera 2006: 109). In the European space, the religious voices tend to be banned from the public space and exiled only to the private sphere. Advocating a balanced separation between the state and Church, Pera underlines that this separation should be implemented to set limits to the legislation of them both, in the sense that one is forbidden to pass norms over the domain of the other, but it does *not* imply that religion must be expelled from social life, or that it should be considered only a private affair. In still other words, the *secularity* of the state, which is a juridical regime, does not imply the *secularism* of the society, which is an ideological philosophy' (Pera 2006). Accordingly, he concludes that '[i]t is one thing to separate State and Church; it is quite a different thing to separate religion from the lives of the people' (Pera 2006).

Another interesting diagnosis of Europe today comes from the American intellectual George Weigel. In 'Europe's Problem – and Ours', he identifies a 'European problem' and connects his ideas with an argument referring to the European Constitutional Treaty Preamble:

> What is most disturbing, for example, about the bizarre debate over the mere mention of Christianity's contributions to European civilization in the proposed European Constitution is that the amnesiacs who wish to rewrite European history by eliminating Christianity from the historical equation are doing so in service to a thin, indeed

> anorexic, idea of procedural democracy. To deny that Christianity had anything to do with the evolution of free, law-governed, and prosperous European societies is more than a question of falsifying the past; it is also a matter of creating a future in which moral truth has no role in governance, in the determination of public policy, in understandings of justice, and in the definition of that freedom which democracy is intended to embody. (Weigel 2004: 24)

Furthermore, in his *The Cube and the Cathedral: Europe, America and the Politics without God*, Weigel encourages additional debates when claiming that 'by abandoning its spiritual roots Europe is also raising question marks about democracy itself in all parts of the Globe'; he even questions whether democracy can sustain itself 'absent the transcendent moral reference points for ordering public life that Christianity offers the political community?' (2006: 162). Weigel's arguments support the idea that there can be no politics 'fit for human beings' without an appeal to transcendence, contrary to the decision made in 2004 in Brussels, whose answer was 'yes, not only can there be a "politics" without God, there must be politics without God' (2006: 162). Accordingly, Weigel's set of questions is provocative and sharp: 'Which culture, I wondered, would better protect human rights? Which culture would more firmly secure the moral foundations of democracy? The culture that built this stunning, rational, angular, geometrically precise but essentially featureless cube? Or the culture that produced the vaulting and bosses, the gargoyles and flying buttresses, the nooks and crannies, the asymmetries and holy "unsameness" of Notre-Dame and the other great cathedrals of Europe?'

For British historian Christopher Dawson religion is the key of history and the concept of a Christian civilization is not an abstract ideal, but instead, it represents a 'real historical tradition, embodied in social institutions and manifesting itself in a many-sided cultural activity' (2011: 98). The Christian identity of Europe has represented 'the great source of European unity' and remains a historical fact, and in this sense its reality cannot be denied, 'whether we accept it or reject it as an ideal' (2011: 98). Dawson highlights his idea by connecting to historian Edward Gibbon who 'shows how religion and the authority of the Popes, "cemented the union of the Christian Republic; and gradually produced the similar manners and common jurisprudence which have distinguished from the rest of mankind the independent and even hostile nations of modern Europe"' (2011: 98). However, Dawson notes, even though 'Europe derives its form, its spiritual unity and its culture from the Christian tradition, it is no longer Christendom', but rather it has entered a 'state of disintegration and dissolution'. For him, Christianity represents the soul of Western civilization, and the real danger for Europe lies in the fact that it is giving up its religious foundation, 'and when the soul is gone the body putrefies' (2011: 98).

Weigel (2004) traces the 'European problem' back to the 'atheistic humanism' (as formulated by Henri de Lubac in 1995) of the nineteenth century, which culminated in the twentieth century: 'Why did Europe have the twentieth century it did? Why did a century that began with confident predictions about a maturing humanity reaching new heights of civilizational accomplishment produce, within four decades, two world wars, three totalitarian systems, a Cold War threatening global catastrophe, oceans of blood, mountains of corpses, Auschwitz and the Gulag? What *happened*? And why?' The answer proposed has at its centre the great figure Aleksandr Solzhenitsyn, who spoke about the 'European problem' and the 'horrors of the twentieth century', back in 1983, when delivering the Templeton Prize Lecture:

> The failings of human consciousness, deprived of its divine dimension, have been a determining factor in all the major crimes of this century. The first of these was World War I, and much of our present predicament can be traced back to it. That war ... took place when Europe, bursting with health and abundance, fell into a rage of self-mutilation that could not but sap its strength for a century or more, and perhaps forever. The only possible explanation for this is a mental eclipse among the leaders of Europe due to their lost awareness of a Supreme Power above them ... Only the loss of that higher intuition which comes from God could have allowed the West to accept calmly, after World War I, the protracted agony of Russia as she was being torn apart by a band of cannibals ... The West did not perceive that this was in fact the beginning of a lengthy process that spells disaster for the whole world. (Solzhenitsyn cited in Weigel 2004)

However, most Europeans today seem to ignore or simply overlook that most of the great accomplishments, such as the development of capitalism, the scientific revolution, the democratic ideal, appeared in a Europe shaped by Christianity and its world views. Instead, Weigel claims that

'European man has convinced himself that in order to be modern and free, he must be radically secular. That conviction has had crucial, indeed lethal, consequences for European public life and European culture; indeed, that conviction and its public consequences are at the root of Europe's contemporary crisis of civilizational morale' (Weigel 2004). And this crisis is reflected in the actions of Europeans that are no longer coherent with their history, but seem to be 'deliberately forgetting' it and therefore 'failing to create the human future of Europe' (Weigel 2004).

The clichés pointing to religion as being opposed to progress are still perpetuating. Important counter-arguments are offered, such as Rodney Stark in *The Victory of Reason: How Christianity Led to Freedom, Capitalism and Western Success* (2006), who brings compelling arguments that religion was an essential factor for the birth and development of capitalism. The author points to the fact that 'religious ideas played a vital role in the rise of capitalism in Europe', and uses a contrast with other regions such as China or even ancient Rome and Greece that had foundations that could have led to capitalism, but none of them succeeded in developing capitalism because they lacked 'ethical visions compatible with this dynamic economic system' (2006: xii). Stark argues that 'when Europeans first began to explore the globe, their greatest surprise was not the existence of Western Hemisphere but the extent of their own technological superiority over the rest of the world' and offers a complex vision that summarizes the profound relationship between Christian ethos and the making of Europe. In his turn, Habermas sustains these theses and in *Time of Transitions* emphasizes that 'in the West, Christianity not only fulfilled the initial cognitive conditions for modern structures of consciousness; it also fostered a range of motivations that formed the major theme of the economic and ethical research of Max Weber' (Habermas 2006b: 150). For Stark, the West was shaped by four primary victories of reason:

> The first was the development of faith in progress within Christian theology. The second victory was the way that faith in progress translated into technical and organizational innovations, many of them fostered by monastic estates. The third was that, thanks to Christian theology, reason informed both political philosophy and practice to the extent that responsive states, sustaining a substantial degree of personal freedom, appeared in medieval Europe. The final victory involved the application

> of reason to commerce, resulting in the development of capitalism within the safe havens provided by responsive states. These were the victories by which the West won. (Stark 2006: xiii)

The role of religion in the European identity goes beyond a significant philosophical or theological importance but it extends to comprise political, economic and social implications as well. The Judeo-Christian tradition uniquely shaped European culture and civilization. It imprinted them with concepts of liberty, human dignity and sanctity, the values of human rights and democracy, supported the birth of modern science and development of capitalism, that all mirror the presence of the *logos* in human history. As Habermas claims,

> Christianity has functioned for the normative self-understanding of modernity as more than a mere precursor or a catalyst. Egalitarian universalism, from which sprang the ideas of freedom and social solidarity, of an autonomous conduct of life and emancipation, of the individual morality of conscience, human rights and democracy, is the direct heir to the Judaic ethic of justice and Christian ethic of love. This legacy, substantially unchanged, has been the object of continual critical appropriation and reinterpretation. To this day, there is no alternative to it. And in light of the current challenges of a postnational constellation, we continue to draw on the substance of this heritage. Everything else is just postmodern talk. (Habermas 2006b: 150–1)

The constitutional crisis and the controversies it generated brought once again to light old tensions between religious and secular voices, reflecting an identity crisis that is manifested in institutional and economic weaknesses, void of meaning, and lacking cohesion and solidarity. Europe needs to rediscover its genuine identity sources, which include its religious roots, in order to escape any division and to assure a stability that is solid enough in times of secularism, but also individualized enough in a global, relative world. As the words of Weigel echo: 'These difficult first years of the twenty-first century have taught us the importance of reading world politics in new ways. Europe's crisis of civilizational morale teaches us that, while there are many lenses through which history can be read, theological lenses help us to see deeper, farther, and more truly' (Weigel 2004).

## References


Apel, K. O. (2000). 'Globalization and the Need for Universal Ethics', *European Journal of Social Theory*, 3 (2), 137–55.

Armstrong, K. (2000). *The Battle for God: A History of Fundamentalism*. New York: Random House Publishing Group.

Berger, P. L. (1997). 'Epistemological Modesty: An Interview with Peter Berger', *Christian Century*, 114, 972–8.

——(1999). 'The Desecularization of the World: A Global Overview'. In P. L. Berger (ed.), *The Desecularization of the World: Resurgent Religion and World Politics*, pp. 1–18. Washington, DC: Ethics and Public Policy Center.

Berger, P. L., Davie G., and Fokas, E. (2008). *Religious America, Secular Europe? A Theme and Variations*. Farnham: Ashgate.

Buruma, I. (2010). *Taming the Gods: Religion and Democracy on Three Continents*. Princeton, NJ: Princeton University Press.

Casanova, J. (2006). 'Religion, European Secular Identities and European Integration'. In T. Byrnes and P. J. Katzenstein (eds), *Religion in an Expanding Europe*, pp. 65–92. Cambridge: Cambridge University Press.

Cox, H. (1985). *Religion in the Secular City: Toward a Postmodern Theology*. New York: Simon & Schuster.

Davie, G. (2000). *Religion in Modern Europe: A Memory Mutates*. Oxford: Oxford University Press.

Dawson, C. (2011). *The Judgment of the Nations*. Washington, DC: The Catholic University of America Press.

Delors, J. (1992). 'Speech to the Churches'. Brussels, 4 February <http://europa.eu.int/comm/dgs/policy_advisers/activities/dialogue_religions_humanisms/issues/soul_for_Europe/index_En.htm> accessed 22 January 2013.

Habermas, J. (2006a). 'Religion in the Public Sphere', *European Journal of Philosophy*, 14 (1), 1–25.

——(2006b). *Time of Transitions*. Cambridge: Polity Press.

Habermas, J., and Ratzinger, J. (2005). *Dialectica Secularizării: Despre Rațiune si Religie*. Cluj-Napoca: Biblioteca Apostrof.

Hastings, A. (1997). *Religion and the Construction of Nationhood*. Cambridge: Cambridge University Press.

Hehir, B. (2006). 'The Old Church and the New Europe: Charting the Changes'. In T. Byrnes and P. J. Katzenstein (eds), *Religion in an Expanding Europe*, pp. 93–116. Cambridge: Cambridge University Press.

Huntington, S. (2003). *The Clash of Civilizations and the Remaking of World Order*. New York: Simon & Schuster.
John Paul II (2007). 'Common Declaration: Pope John Paul II and His Beatitude Christodoulos Archbishop of Athens and All Greece'. In J. Gros, T. F. Best and L. F. Fuchs (eds), *Growth in Agreement III: International Dialogue Texts and Agreed Statements, 1998–2005*, pp. 182–4. Geneva: World Council of Churches.
Katzenstein, P. J. (2006). 'Multiple Modernities as Limits to Secular Europeanization?' In T. Byrnes and P. J. Katzenstein (eds), *Religion in an Expanding Europe*, pp. 1–33. Cambridge: Cambridge University Press.
Küng, H. (1990). Global Responsibility: In Search for a New World Ethic. New York: Crossroad.
——(1998). *A Global Ethic and Global Responsibilities: Two Declarations*. SCM Press.
Lubac, H. de (1995). *The Drama of the Atheistic Humanism*. San Francisco, CA: Ignatius Press.
Merutiu, M. (2009). 'The Christian Heritage of Europe and Democracy', *Journal of Interdisciplinary Studies: An International Journal of Interdisciplinary and Interfaith Dialogue*, 21 (1–2), 51–66.
Pera, M. (2006). 'Europe, America and the Continental Drift', *Heritage Lectures*, No. 978, 30 November <http://www.heritage.org/research/lecture/europe-america-and-the-continental-drift> accessed 18 January 2013.
Ratzinger, J. (1983). 'Europa – Verpflichtendes Erbe Für Die Christen'. In F. König and K. Rahner (eds), *Europa: Horizonte Der Hoffnung*, pp. 61–74. Graz: Styra.
——(1991). *Turning Point for Europe?* San Francisco, CA: Ignatius Press.
——(2004). *Introduction to Christianity*. San Francisco, CA: Ignatius Press.
——(2005). 'On Europe's Crisis of Culture', *Catholic Education Resource Centre*, 1 April <http://www.catholiceducation.org/articles/politics/pg0143.htm> accessed 18 January 2013.
——(2007). *Europe: Today and Tomorrow*. San Francisco, CA: Ignatius Press.
Ratzinger, J., and Pera, M. (2006). *Without Roots: The West, Relativism, Christianity, Islam*. New York: Basic Books.
Rogowski, R., and Turner, C. (2006). *The Shape of the New Europe*. Cambridge: Cambridge University Press.
Sacks, J. (2002). *The Dignity of Difference: How to Avoid the Clash of Civilizations*. London: Continuum.
Schuman, R. (1963). *Pour l'Europe*. Paris: Nagel.
Schuon, F. (1961). *Stations of Wisdom*. London: John Murray.
Singer, P. (2002). *One World: The Ethics of Globalization*. New Haven, CT: Yale University Press.

Stark, R. (2006). *The Victory Of Reason: How Christianity Led To Freedom, Capitalism And Western Success.* New York: Random House.

Weigel, G. (2004). 'Europe's Problem – And Ours', *First Things*, No. 140 <http://www.firstthings.com/article/2007/01/europersquos-problemmdashand-ours-9> accessed 25 January 2013.

—— (2006). *The Cube and the Cathedral: Europe, America and The Politics Without God.* New York: Basic Books.

AYHAN KAYA

# 12 Europeanization or De-Europeanization: The Myth of Tolerance in Turkey

Bearing the legacy of the Ottoman Empire, modern Turkey, with more than 72 million inhabitants, is a multi-ethnic and multicultural country housing approximately fifty different Muslim and/or non-Muslim ethno-cultural groups, including Sunni Turks, Alevi Turks, Sunni Kurds, Alevi Kurds, Armenians, Georgians, Arabs, Greeks, Jews and so on (Andrews 1992). However, leaving aside the attempts made at democratization in the last decade, the Turkish state has been far from recognizing the ethnically and culturally diverse nature of Turkish society. Ethnocultural and religious minorities in Turkey have been subjected to homogenizing state policies since the establishment of the Republic in 1923.

As Turkey is a republican country, one could not find official figures about the numbers of ethnocultural and religious minorities. This chapter is designed to portray the ways in which ethnocultural and religious diversity has hitherto been managed by the modern Turkish state within the framework of the discourse of tolerance. Explicating the construction of the Turkish national identity and the modern Turkish state, this work will primarily delineate the constitutive elements of the state machinery as well as the technologies of citizenship in Turkey. Turkey's process of Europeanization will also be scrutinized in order to pave the way for a detailed analysis of the transformation of the Turkish polity from the Cold War years to the post-Cold War years with regard to the management of ethnocultural and religious diversity. The main premise of this work will be to outline the sequence of political events leading to the de-Europeanization of Turkey in the second half of the 2000s, the first half of which was mainly characterized by Europeanization of the country in several spheres of life. The hypothesis of this work is that the discourse of an 'alliance of civilizations' deployed by the Justice and Development Party (Adalet ve Kalkınma Partisi, AKP) paid off in the first half of the 2000s in a way that contributed to the Europeanization of Turkey in a time when the European Union (EU) was aspired to as a global vision; and the overwhelming use of the very same discourse has distanced Turkey from the EU due to the parochial and inward-looking polity of the EU member states.

## The Relevance of Tolerance in the Ottoman Empire and in the Turkish Republic

Ottoman multiculturalism was usually coupled with the term 'tolerance'. In fact, the concept of tolerance has a very long history in the Turkish context, tracing back to the Ottoman Empire and being used in everyday life. The equivalents of the term tolerance in the Turkish language are *tolerans*, *hoşgörü*, *tahammül*, *müsamaha*, *görmezden gelme* and *göz yumma*. The meaning of the term *hoşgörü* is depicted in the Dictionary of the Turkish Language Association (*Türk Dil Kurumu*) as 'the state of tolerating everything as much as possible'. *Hoşgörü* literally means 'seeing (the other) in a good way'. The term *tahammül* is derived from the Arabic root word *haml*, which literally means 'to pick up' or 'to bear' or 'to carry'. For example, if one picks up a book or carries a load or a burden the word *haml* would generally be used; but if one patiently bears a turmoil, or an affliction, or a humiliation, or an indignity, or an oppression, the term *tahammül* would be used. The word *müsamaha* literally means 'to forgive', and it is even claimed that the word *Masih* derives from this word in Arabic. Additionally, in Arabic, the word *tasamuh* transcends the realm of political toleration and connotes personal virtues such as patience and generosity. On the other hand, *görmezden gelme* means 'pretending not to see', and *göz yumma* literally means 'to close one's eyes' or to condone and excuse (Kaya 2013).

Most of the above-listed words used in Turkish address a kind of burden to carry on one's shoulders, so they all refer to a kind of endurance and forbearance. The very etymological meaning of the term 'tolerance' in European languages also has parallels with the use of its equivalents in the Turkish language. It does not seem to be accidental that in most languages in which tolerance has been historically debated, the words tolerance (or its synonym, sufferance) and suffering have the same source. The etymology of the term 'tolerance' is also very illustrative in understanding what it contains. It does not seem to be accidental that in most languages in which tolerance has been historically debated, the words 'tolerance' (or its synonym, sufferance) and 'suffering' have the same source. The Latin word *tolerantia* comes from *tolere*, meaning 'to bear, tolerate, suffer, endure', and the same link exists in English (through the synonym, 'sufferance'), in French (*souffrir*), Italian (*soffrire*), and even in Hebrew (*sevel-sovlanut*). This etymological fact happens to be philosophically significant. It indicates that there is no tolerance without suffering and its overcoming. Tolerating someone means recognizing an irreducible difference, a gap of alienness separating us, which nevertheless is accepted (Yovel 1998). This implies a concealed hatred or contest between the tolerating and the tolerated party. By this very otherness, the other represents a challenge to the self in the form of a potential competition over goods, power, moral values, and so on.

In French, there are many words revolving around *tolérer* such as *permettre* (permission), *souffrir* (sufferance), *endurer* (endure) and *accorder* (accord). The word *tolérer* was first used in France in 1562 by the Catholic French King to somehow let the Protestants stay in the country. The term was basically suggested by the King to set up a policy towards many types of evil and heresy, like the Protestants and Jews. The term *permettre* had even more positive connotations than the word *tolérer*, which was very negatively loaded. However, both terms revealed common assumptions about the nature of political power vis-à-vis the Church: control from above, surveillance of individual beliefs and organized pressure. Furthermore, the term *Toleranz* was used in German, and *tolerantie* in Dutch, before tolerance became common in France, the Low Countries and Switzerland (Huseman 1984).

Turkish citizens are usually proud of referring to the Millet System of the Ottoman Empire as the guarantor of tolerance, respecting the boundaries between religious communities. The official discourse celebrating the notion of tolerance is still carried out in contemporary Turkey, although it is evident that tolerance is actually nothing but a myth. For instance, research conducted by Ali Çarkoğlu and Binnaz Toprak (2006) reveals that more than half of the Turkish population is intolerant of the possibility of having gays and atheists as their neighbours. The same research also uncovers that around 42 percent of the population are intolerant to the possibility of having Greeks and Armenians as their neighbours. The ratio is 28 percent for neighbours of Kurdish origin (Çarkoğlu and Toprak 2006). The main premise of this chapter is that the myth of tolerance becomes functional in concealing the mistreatment of ethnocultural and religious minorities other than the majority of Sunni–Muslim–Turks in Turkey.

## Tolerance as a Form of Governmentality

The definition of tolerance is confined to the acceptance of Sunni Muslims and their secular counterparts under the banner of the Sunni–Muslim–Turkish nation. However, this does not mean to embrace all different kinds of ethnocultural and religious minorities. According to historian Karen Barkey (2008: 110), toleration in the Ottoman context, as well as in other imperial contexts, refers to the 'absence of persecution of people but not their acceptance into society as full and welcomed members of community'. Toleration is actually no more than a form of *governmentality*, designed to maintain peace and order in multi-ethnic and multi-nominational contexts.[1] The Ottoman imperial experience and the Turkish national experience prove that the Turkish nation tolerates those non-Muslims, non-Sunni-

1 For further information about the notion of *governmentality*, see Foucault (1979: 21). Michel Foucault describes the concept of *governmentality* as a collection of methods used by political elites to maintain their power, or as an art of acquiring power. In other words, *governmentality* refers to the practices which characterize the form of supervision a state exercises over its subjects, their wealth, misfortunes, customs, bodies, souls and habits. It is the art of governing.

Muslims and non-Turks as long as they do not disturb or go against the Sunni–Islam–Turkish order. If ethnocultural and religious minorities were to transgress, their recognition could easily turn into suppression and persecution. Against this background, this work shall claim that 'tolerance' is nothing but a myth in Turkey, like in other countries or regions, such as the Netherlands and the Balkans (Brown 2006; Hayden 2002; Walzer 1997).

In the years following the formation of the Republic, assimilationist and/or exclusionary policies of the state elite, which sought to erase social and cultural diversity, continued to accord the national identity based on Sunni Islam and Turkishness a dominant role in social and political spheres. The social forces affiliated with diverse religious, ethnic and cultural values were frequently faced with and suppressed by homogenizing policies such as the nationalist Turkish history thesis of 1932, the Sun Language Theory of 1936, the unitarian nationalist education policies (*Tevhid-i Tedrisat Kanunu*, 1924), banning the use of mother tongue and of ethnic minority names, discriminatory settlement policies put into effect on the exchange minorities and new migrants (*İskan Kanunu*, 1934), the discriminatory citizenship laws granting citizenship exclusively to Muslim-origin migrants, the imposition of wealth tax in 1942, especially on non-Muslims, and the forced migration of Kurds in the east and south-east of Turkey (Yıldız 2001).

Subsequent to the primary goal of the formation of a homogeneous nation and a unitary state, the state elite pointed at the modern and secular character of the state.[2] Without a macro socio-economic transformation, a total cultural change through the adoption of the Kemalist version of Westernization and secularism required the state elite to construct 'an imagined Turkish nation' in line with the interests of the unitary and bureaucratic state. In its configuration of secularism, the Kemalist elite did not only accommodate the Islamist identity of the individual but also dispersed the individual identity under the banner of the modern and secular Turkish nation (I. Kaya 2004). In doing so, they ensured that the individual will

2 For the Kemalist mode of secularism as a means to the project of modernist nationalism, see Cizre (1996), Göle (1997) and Keyman (1995).

was secondary to national will, and also precluded that Islam as a social power could be organized as a challenge to the unitary and bureaucratic state. Relying on the 'bureaucratic code', the state elite instrumentalized secularism, which was conceptualized as the separation of politics and religion in both public and private spheres, in order to consolidate the central state power against the potential threat of social forces affiliated with Islamic values and aims.

The regime of tolerance has become even stronger since the reign of the AKP, which came into power in 2002, following a pro-Islamist and civilizational discourse (Kaya and Tecmen 2011). The AKP's civilizational rhetoric seems to be converging with the neoliberal form of global governmentality, which is based on the celebration of cultural and religious differences. The so-called neoliberal form of governmentality mainly invests in the reification and protection of cultural, religious and civilizational boundaries, as in the Huntingtonian paradigm of the 'clash of civilizations' (Casanova 2006; Kaya 2013). However, the revitalization of the discourse of tolerance has not brought about a better treatment of ethnocultural and religious minorities, who have always been stigmatized and problematized in Turkey due to the fact that they do not fit into the definition of nation (*millet*) prescribed on the holy trinity of Sunni–Muslim–Turk. For instance, Kurds, Alevis, Circassians, Georgians, Lazis, non-Muslims and Romas disrupt the unity of the nation, as they are neither ethnically Turkish, nor religiously Muslim, nor Sunni. Similar to the modernization process of the Ottoman Empire in the nineteenth century, the recent Turkey's recent Europeanization has not yet challenged the conventional definition of the Turkish nation. What has happened so far is the restigmatization of those ethnocultural and religious minorities through their differences. As long as these groups pay their tribute to the Turkish state and accept their subaltern and secondary position, they are tolerated. Otherwise, those groups will be inclined to encounter further ontological challenges. It seems that the revitalization of the discourse of tolerance in contemporary Turkey contributes to what Wendy Brown (2006) calls the *depoliticization of the social*.

As Mircea Eliade rightly asserts, myths are inclined to be revitalized by the ruling groups when the social, political and economic conditions of a group of people become unpleasant. Eliade (1991) makes his point with the following words:

> Merely by listening to a myth, man [sic] forgets his profane conditions, his 'historical situation' as we have accustomed to call it today … [A]n Australian … a Chinese … or a Hindu, or a peasant of some European country, when he is listening to a myth, forgets, as it were, his particular situation and is projected into another world, into a Universe which is no longer his poor little universe of every day … The myth continually reactualizes the Great Time, and in so doing raises the listener to a superhuman and suprahistorical plane; which, among other things, enables him to approach a Reality that is inaccessible at the level of profane, individual existence. (Eliade 1991: 58–9)

Myths, then, become resurgent in times of crisis when the reality hits at least some members of the larger society. The myth of tolerance, for instance, is revitalized by the ruling social groups to conceal the reality of inequality, subordination and injustice experienced by those individuals or groups who fall outside the category of Sunni–Muslim–Turk. What is happening now in Turkey and elsewhere is the rise of the discourse of tolerance in a way that leads to what Brown (2006) calls the culturalization, thus depolitization, of what is social in the age of a neoliberal form of governmentality, which is primarily shaped by the process of reduction of civilization to religion. Against this background, there seems to be a discrepancy between AKP's religious-based civilizational perspective and Turkey's long-lasting European perspective of becoming a soft power in the region. One could argue that the AKP is more inclined to use the neo-Ottoman discourse of tolerance and religious-based civilization to attract the Middle Eastern populations in order to disseminate its hegemony in the region.

## Europeanization of Turkey: A Silent Revolution

The process of modernization and Europeanization of Turkey dates back to the early nineteenth century. The journey has always been full of impediments, as the process was a rather politically oriented one, leading to the emergence of social divides/faultlines within the nation. The rise of the AKP in Turkey has made some remarkable changes in the Western-oriented civilizational discourse of the Turkish political establishment. Having a pro-Islamist discourse, the AKP is now trying to generate a multi-level governance in both domestic and international platforms, and is willing to become a soft power in the region, embracing all the countries in the Middle East, Caucasus, Balkans and North Africa. It seems that such an attempt, which makes the Islamic inclinations of the AKP very apparent, is also appreciated by the European Union circles. However, it is uncertain whether such inclinations of the AKP are destined to make Turkey a member of the EU in the end.

Turkey experienced one of the most stable periods in the history of the Republic between 1999 and 2005. At the Helsinki Summit in December 1999, the European heads of state and government for the first time offered Turkey the concrete prospect of full membership of the European Union, more than four decades after its application for association with the European Economic Community (EEC) in July 1959. Subsequently, in 1963, Turkey had signed the Ankara Agreement, which foresaw the establishment of a customs union between Turkey and the EEC. Although the customs union was an economic cooperation model, Article 28 of the Agreement stipulated Turkey's membership as a long-term goal. Accordingly, this stipulation had reflections in the political realm; the economic interests of the elites had a 'conditioning effect' on democracy (Keyman and Öniş 2007: 61). In 1987, Turkey applied for full EEC membership. Although Turkey was deemed eligible for membership, in 1989 the European Commission stated that there were several economic and political difficulties that needed to be addressed before membership, 'such as the expansion of political pluralism, the state of democracy, the persistence of disputes with a member state (namely Greece), the lack of a viable solution to the Cyprus problem, relative economic backwardness, especially in macroeconomic terms, the Kurdish question, and problems related to human rights' (Müftüler-Baç 2000: 23). However, the official reason for this rejection was the internal dynamic of the EEC, namely the process of establishing a single market.

Turkey was granted the right to candidacy in the Helsinki Summit of the European Union in December 1999. Later, in 2002, the Copenhagen Summit introduced new concerns and discussions regarding the nature of European identity, the notion of Europeanization and the borders of Europe, which led to identity-based concerns regarding Turkey's place in Europe and the situation of Islamic identity in European societies. According to Keyman and Öniş, the main concern was whether the EU aspired to become a global actor or, rather, preferred inward-oriented integration. Subsequently, while the former aspiration was accommodating towards Turkish membership, the latter perceived Turkey as a liability, given the social, political and economic disparities between the EU member states and Turkey (Keyman and Öniş 2007: 48–50). For the first time, the Copenhagen Summit and the subsequent discussions linked the question of culture with European enlargement and the EU's capacity to embrace cultural differences. As some authors put it,

> [t]he discussions over Turkish accession reveal yet another dimension of 'absorption capacity', that of 'cultural' and 'social' absorption, which are directly related to the 'identity' of the Union. Jean-Louis Bourlanges, an MEP from a French centre-right party vocal on Turkish accession, has argued that the accession of Turkey will not only have a huge economic impact on the EU, but will also introduce a great deal of cultural and social heterogeneity that will endanger the formation of a solid and democratically organised political community. (Emerson *et al.* 2006: 3)

In the course of European integration, the AKP adopted a conservative democratic ideology with an emphasis on secularism, social peace, social justice, the preservation of moral values and norms, pluralism, democracy, free-market economy, civil society and good governance (Çınar and Duran 2008: 31). By using such a pragmatist discourse, the AKP aimed to mobilize socially and economically marginalized classes, in reaction to the inequalities deriving from the processes of globalization and urban life (A. Kaya

2004: 16–17). Moreover, the AKP also became attractive for the liberal and secular bourgeoisie, upper-middle and middle classes, who were disenchanted with the political system because of the political and economic instability (Özbudun and Hale 2009: 37). The AKP immediately took an initiative to raise toleration and respect for the freedom of religion and conscience, and for the protection of religious rights, such as the right to practise religion in public and private space.

Whether the AKP's discourse on conservative democracy and Islamic liberalism achieved transformation of the society into a more tolerant one with respect to the recognition of religious freedom and rights is not certain. However, it is clear that the AKP government made profound attempts to force the state and society to recognize cultural and religious differences. The protection of religious freedoms and rights became a heated debate between the Islamist and secular segments of society. One of the cases in which the AKP sought to increase tolerance vis-à-vis the social integration of Islamist forces and to foster respect for religious freedom was the government proposal of a draft-law that would enable the *Imam Hatip* (clergy high-school) graduates to study not only in the faculty of Islamic theology but also in other faculties (Özbudun and Hale 2009: 86). In doing so, it made an attempt to eradicate the constraints that had given rise to the social and economic segregation of religious and conservative segments.

Moreover, between 2002 and 2008, the AKP made several attempts to initiate amendments and decisions in the legal and institutional framework to lift the ban on the headscarf (Kaya 2009: 18). The AKP government proposed to the Constitutional Court an amendment to the articles of the Constitution concerning the ban on wearing the headscarf in universities, with the expectation that this amendment would lead to the lifting of the ban in 2008. Following the constitutional amendments, the newly elected head of the Board of the Higher Education, Yusuf Ziya Özcan, made an announcement to the universities and stated that, according to the constitutional change, the ban on wearing a headscarf in Turkish universities was lifted. However, the court ultimately repudiated the lifting of the ban.[3] As a consequence, the appearance/existence of conservative and Islamist segments in the socio-economic sphere was recognized/accepted as an everyday reality, although (in)tolerance/(dis)respect for the expression of faith and wearing religious clothing still remained a highly debated topic in the public sphere.

On the other hand, it should be thoroughly questioned whether the quest of the AKP for the recognition of religious freedom and rights through the adoption of discourses on conservative democracy was carried out equally across every social cleavage, and particularly in the case of religious minorities. Before the 2007 elections, even though the AKP took an initiative to accommodate the Alevis in the Sunni-dominant order, the party was primarily concerned with gaining more votes from the Alevis (Kaya 2009: 17). The Alevis were not equally treated in AKP's policy to transform the society to become more tolerant of the expression of faith and religious rights. The AKP failed to accommodate the Alevis in the social sphere and continued to retain the Sunni-dominant social order, since it did not recognize the *Cemevis* (Alevi communion houses) as places of worship in addition to mosques, and insisted on the inclusion of the Alevi children in the assignment of the compulsory courses of religion in secondary school education (Kaya 2009: 18). Therefore, one could contend that the AKP's policies to stimulate the social sensitivities for toleration and recognition of religious minorities and the protection of religious rights were confined to the Sunni conservative and Islamist segments.[4]

In the legal and institutional framework since February 2002, it is also possible to find various reform policies for the recognition and protection of ethnic minority rights, which manifested a great shift in the discursive position taken by the political elite. Since the Accession Partnership Programme and the National Programme (March 2001) addressed the

3 For a detailed analysis of the headscarf debate see the *Turkish Daily News* <http://www.turkishdailynews.com.tr/article.php?enewsid=95065> accessed 8 July 2012.

4 For further information on this initiative see the *Turkish Daily News* <http://www.turkishdailynews.com.tr/article.php?enewsid=80103&contact=1> accessed 10 July 2012.

recognition of ethnocultural diversity, the former coalition government and the AKP government enacted and enforced reform packages and policies to accommodate ethnocultural diversity and, in a broader sense, to secure the individual rights, liberties and human rights within the framework of the consolidation of democracy and the rule of law. With the initial reform packages put into force between 2002 and 2004, first, they reduced the role of the military in politics by removing the judges of military origin from the State Security Courts and eventually abolishing these courts, removing the military members from the High Audio Visual Board (RTÜK) and the Board of Higher Education, weakening the military impact on the judiciary, civilianizing the National Security Council and restricting its role to a consultative body, and by bringing the extra-budgetary funds of the military under the general budget of the Defence Ministry (Kaya 2009).

Secondly, they reinforced individual rights, liberties and human rights versus the authoritarian and unitary state by loosening the law on freedom of association and demonstration, abolishing the death penalty and all means and practices of torture by the security forces, revising the Penal Code, abolishing the term 'forbidden language' from the Press law, permitting limited broadcasts in Kurdish on private radio and TV channels, introducing limited broadcasts in Arabic, Circassian and various dialects of Kurdish, such as Kurmançi and Zaza, on the national radio and TV channels, and by allowing ethnic languages and dialects to be taught in private courses (Kaya 2013). Consequently, the reform packages, which were adopted to raise social awareness of tolerance and acceptance of ethnocultural minorities, encouraged ethnocultural groups to voice their claims through legitimate political channels.

Since 2001, the government has taken initiatives to remedy the civil and cultural rights of non-Muslim minorities through legal amendments. In accordance with the Copenhagen Political Criteria, the constitutional amendments expanded the individual rights and liberties to every citizen and provided the structural arrangements for democratic consolidation and enhancement of the rule of law and human rights (Oran 2004). The EU reform packages partially and gradually restored civil and cultural rights conceded to the non-Muslim minorities with the Lausanne Agreement (Oran 2004).

In the nation-state-formation process, the state elite of the Republic had inherited from the Ottomans the discourse and practices of the homogeneous nation based on Sunni Islam and the exclusion of the non-Muslim minorities. The Kemalist definition of nationalism was also discriminative against the non-Muslim minorities, since it incorporated the element of Islam into the so-called modern secular national identity. The configuration of the majority and minority elements of the Turkish nation were also inscribed in the Lausanne Agreement (1923) during the foundation of the Turkish Republic. According to Lausanne Agreement, the non-Muslim minorities were officially categorized and recognized as 'minorities' based upon their ethnic and religious differences, whereas Kurds, Alevis, Circassians and other Muslim elements belonged to the Turkish nation (*Türk Uyruklu*) constituting the majority (Oran 2000).

With the EU reform packages, the ban on establishing associations for the preservation and diffusion of languages and cultures other than Turkish and traditional to minorities was abolished; the use of the 'forbidden language' was re-legalized in the law of associations; the restrictions on learning and publishing in different languages and dialects other than Turkish were abandoned; the right of the foundations belonging to non-Muslim minorities to acquire intangible property was restored by a change in the law on foundations and was initially subjected to the decisions of the cabinet and later to the General Secretary of Foundations (*Vakıflar Genel Mudurlugu*), and the limitation on names other than Turkish was abolished by a change in the law on population. Furthermore, recently, the European Union General Secretariat in Ankara has decided to drop the use of the term 'non-Muslims' in identifying officially recognized minorities in Turkey. Seeking to update the government's terminology for the twenty-first century, Turkey's chief negotiator for European Union affairs has announced a decision to use the term 'different belief groups' instead of *gayrimüslim* ('non-Muslim') in official EU correspondence. This decision was taken after the chief negotiator, Egemen Bağış, received a letter from the Vice-Patriarch of the Ancient Syriac Orthodox Church, Yusuf Çetin, who pointed out that *Muslim* means 'believer' in Aramaic, a northwest Semitic language used in ancient times as the everyday speech of Syria. As such, the term *gayrimüslim*, which had been the preferred term for non-Muslims in Turkey, implied 'nonbelievers'.[5]

Furthermore, the discursive shift from 'majority nationalism' to 'diversity as an ideology' fostered by the governing party created an incentive for a change in everyday life in the social motivation towards toleration of ethno-religious rights of non-Muslim minorities. The political elite, the Turkish and Armenian intellectuals and civil-society organizations were induced to open public discussion on the taboo issues involving the Armenian 'genocide', Armenian ethnic minority rights, Armenian–Turkish diplomatic relations and the impact of the Armenian diaspora on the problems related to the Armenians.

Strikingly, the debates on the Armenian 'genocide' both at the state and society levels have been good examples of the rising aspiration of toleration for Armenian ethnic and cultural rights. One of these cases of the rising tolerance was the highly debated and polemical conference on 'Ottoman Armenians during the Demise of the Empire' held at Istanbul Bilgi University in 2005 (Kaya 2009). Although some ultra-nationalists brought a lawsuit against the organizers of the conference and the court partly considered their claims rightful and lawful, this conference became a good indicator of the eradication of the biased views on the Armenian issue (Kaya 2009).

On the other hand, it should also be pointed out that the EU reforms on civil and cultural rights of non-Muslim minorities could not be brought into practice in an immediate and effective way because its application was obstructed and delayed by bureaucratic obstacles and the interference of the National Security Council, the intelligence agencies and the security forces (Kaya 2009). Since 2004, none of the applications for approval of non-Muslim foundations have been approved, and only 18.66 percent of applications for the acquisition of intangible properties belonging to the

5 See, for example, <http://www.hurriyetdailynews.com/n.php?n=gayrimuslim-replaced-by-8220different-belief-groups8221-2010-06-27> accessed 10 July 2012.

existing foundations have been approved (Kaya 2009).[6] Looking at the constraints in bringing the EU reforms on non-Muslim minorities into practice, one could maintain that the dominant discourse of 'non-Turkish' and 'foreign' non-Muslim minorities is still prevalent, and therefore, the Turkish state is still reluctant to accommodate tolerance, recognition or acceptance in everyday life.

## Discourses and Practices of (In)Tolerance in the Age of Euroscepticism: Political and Social Resentment

From 17 December 2004 to 3 October 2005, when EU state and national government leaders decided to start negotiations with Turkey, tensions began to rise between nationalist, patriotic, statist, pro-status-quo groups on the one hand and pro-EU groups on the other. This was the time when the *virtuous cycle* of the period between 1999 and 2005 was replaced with the *vicious cycle*, starting from late 2005. A new nationalist and religious wave embraced the country, especially amongst middle-class and upper-middle-class groups. The actual start of the accession negotiations in 2005 was a turning point towards Euroscepticism. This was also observed in several previous cases during the accession negotiations of the 2004/2007 entrants, as political elites and the government came to realize that accession negotiations are not in fact 'negotiations' but rather a unilateral imposition from the EU. The only 'negotiable' matters that would benefit the candidate are generally some minor exceptions and hardly bargained transition periods. Furthermore, this reality of actual accession negotiations is often abused by politicians to unfoundedly blame many governmental actions on the EU. Be the 'blaming of Brussels' honest or not, the overall impact on public support is surely almost always negative.

6 For more details on the establishment of non-Muslim foundations approved by the government, see Oran (2004: 133–4).

Euroscepticism, nationalism and parochialism in Turkey were triggered by the disapproving sentiments towards the American occupation of Iraq, the limitations on national sovereignty imposed by EU integration, the high tide of the ninetieth anniversary of the Armenian 'deportation'/'genocide' amongst the Armenian diaspora (2005), the 'risk of recognition' of Southern Cyprus by Turkey for the sake of EU integration, anti-Turkey public opinion in EU countries (such as France and Austria) framed by conservative powers, and Israel's attacks on Lebanon in 2006. Against such a background, the state elite has also become very sceptical of the Europeanization process. The best way to explain the sources of such scepticism amongst the state elite is to refer to the *Sèvres Syndrome*, which is based on a fear deriving from the post-First World War era, characterized by a popular belief regarding the risk of the break-up of the Turkish state (Öniş 2004: 12).[7]

Against this background, the AKP immediately stepped back from its pro-European position, as it was perceived by the party that the EU no longer paid off. However, it was not actually the nationalist climax in the country which turned the AKP into a Euroesceptical party, but the decision of the European Court of Human Rights (ECtHR) challenging a Turkish law which bans the wearing of the Islamic headscarf at universities and other educational and state institutions. In 2005, the ECtHR heard a particularly monumental case called *Leyla Sahin v. Turkey*. It was monumental in that the Grand Chamber agreed to hear Sahin's case at all, and two previous admissions to the European Human Rights Commission concerning the Turkish headscarf issue had been ruled inadmissible. In Sahin's case, however, the outcome equalled temporary defeat for headscarf supporters. The court ruled that there had been no violation to Article 9 of the European Convention on Human Rights (freedom of thought, conscience and religion); Article 10 (freedom of expression); Article 14 (prohibition of discrimination) and Article 2, Protocol No. 1 (right to education) (ECtHR 2004). In short, the Grand Chamber concluded that the interference/

7 Sèvres Syndrome derives from the Sèvres Peace Treaty signed by the Allied Powers and the Ottoman Empire in 1920 in the aftermath of the First World War, leading to the dissolution of the Ottoman Empire.

violations of fundamental rights concerning the headscarf were acceptable and legitimate. In addition to these rulings, the Grand Chamber stated that the interference to her education triggered by her wearing a headscarf was found to be necessary to protect the rights and freedoms of others and maintain public order. While the Chamber recognized that the ban interfered with Sahin's right to publicly express her religion, it stated that the ban was acceptable if it was imposed to protect the rights of third parties, to preserve public order, and to safeguard the principles of secularism and equality in Turkey. Since the ECtHR is an institution within the framework of the Council of Europe, of which Turkey has been a member since 1949, it could be difficult to see how its judgment could have an impact on the support for EU membership. The only way, then, that Euroscepticism could be understood is as a general perception and attitude towards Europe, not just towards the EU and the prospect of membership. This is actually a remarkable phenomenon indicating that Europe and the European Union are often used interchangeably in Turkey.

The Eurosceptic attitude towards EU accession was not just found in the AKP government and amongst Turkish nationalists and pro-status quo groups. Rather, after 2005, the Kurdish people also became strongly critical of the EU reforms with a growing sentiment of Euroscepticism (Kaya 2009). In parallel with suspicion of the sufficiency and the efficiency of the AKP's attempts to recognize Kurdish identity, the revocation of the concept 'minority' in the Progress Report in 2004 provoked some Kurdish nationalists to re-emphasize their position against the Turkish majority nationalism. A considerable faction amongst the Kurds claimed that they denounced the concept 'minority' because it gave them a 'degrading', 'inferior' and 'unequal' status versus the Turkish people (Sahin 2008: 144). Rather, this faction defended their claim that the Kurdish people were one of 'the constitutive elements' of the Turkish Republic and, therefore, had a status equal to that of the Turks. Considering themselves as a 'constitutive element' rather than a minority, the Kurds fervently alleged that the characteristics that distinguish them from other minorities should be recognized, and equality to the Turkish majority in living conditions should be secured (Sahin 2008). In other words, even though this demand gives the Kurds a distinctive status in comparison to the other ethnic and religious minorities, it is sound in the sense that it remarkably denotes the right of 'equal citizenship'.

It has also been suggested that although the EU reforms on the protection of ethnic minorities culminated in an open public debate, they did not achieve a concrete and significant step towards the settlement of the Kurdish problem (Somer and Liaras 2010). The Kurdish Democratic Society Movement (DTH) declared in 2004 that the objectives of the movement involved support for EU accession, the resolution of the Kurdish problem by peaceful and democratic means and with respect to territorial integrity, and the adoption of a new democratic and universal constitution.[8] The DTH, which abandoned the secessionist and federalist claims, put forth its demands for the adoption of 'constitutional citizenship', the abolition of the 10 percent national threshold in the electoral law, the liberalization of equal participation for all political parties, and social and economic development in the Kurdish-populated regions.[9] Thus, considering the definition of 'minority' in the Turkish political context and on the Kurdish political party, one could carry on debating whether the EU reforms adopted by the AKP government aimed merely to tolerate the cultural and individual rights of the Kurdish minority or were designed as an initial stage drifting towards a national project for the resolution of the Kurdish issue and the respect/recognition/acceptance of the difference of the Kurds.

It was possible to find examples of intolerance influenced by the upsurge of radical nationalism in the practices of everyday life. In March 2005, two Kurdish children allegedly burned the Turkish flag during the

8 For more information about the declaration of the DTH see 'Eski DEP'lilerden Demokratik Toplum Hareketi' [The Democratic Society Movement from former members of the Democracy Party] <http://hurriyetim.com.tr> [22 October 2004] accessed 13 June 2012.

9 For more information on the demands of the Kurdish civil society acitivists and intellectuals, see Y. Alataş 'AB Eşiğinde Kürt Sorunu Yazı Dizisi' [The Series on the Kurdish Question on the Verge of the EU Accession], *Radikal*, 26 May 2004).

Newroz celebrations.[10] Six months after Prime Minister Erdoğan's visit to Diyarbakir in 2005, where he declared his full support for the solution of the Kurdish problem with respect to democracy, the Kurdish people in this city rioted at the funerals of four members of the Kurdistan Workers' Party (PKK) (Somer and Liaras 2010). In the following months, the casualties caused by PKK attacks increased.

It should also be underlined that Turkish majority nationalism increased as a response to the rising Kurdish nationalism as well as to Euroscepticism. In retaliation for the flag burning in Mersin (21 March 2005), some public figures started flag campaigns in the name of 'responsible statesmanship'.[11] The 'waved and unwaved flags' (Billig 1995: 10) obviously indicated cases of the rise of intolerance, where the nationalist and sceptic attitudes of both Kurdish and Turkish people were provoked in regard to the national and ethnic conflict. Hence, the intolerance, ethnic conflict and violence increased at the time when the Kurdish people were becoming increasingly critical of the suitability and the sufficiency of the AKP government's EU reforms for the recognition of ethnocultural identity and the resolution of identity-related issues, and the sceptical and nationalist attitude towards the 'other' was strengthened by both the Turks and the Kurds.

Finally, it is also possible to find striking cases where social intolerance, non-acceptance, non-recognition and even hatred towards the Armenians reached its peak and even involved violent conflict. The most conspicuous of these cases was the assassination of the prominent Armenian journalist Hrant Dink in January 2007. It was claimed by some journalists in the media that the assassination of Hrant Dink could be linked to a reaction of ultra-nationalists, who were agitated by the guilty verdict for Hrant Dink on the denigration of Turkishness in one of his articles (Kaya 2009). In 2005, Hrant Dink was sentenced to six months' conditional imprisonment on account of 'insulting Turkish national identity', according to Article 301 of

10 For more information about the incident of burning flags, see <http://webarsiv.hurriyet.com.tr/2005/03/21/616617.asp> [21 March 2005] accessed 14 July 2012.

11 Ibid.

the Penal Code; Article 301 of the Penal Code considers it criminal to publicly denigrate Turkishness, the Republic or the Grand National Assembly of Turkey, and the sentence is imprisonment for between six months and three years (Kaya 2009). Moreover, the rise of Euroscepticism and the reinvigoration of national identity as a response to the upsurge of identity politics based on ethnic and religious difference after the articulation of the concept of 'minority' in the 2005 Progress Report also aggravated intolerance and conflict between the Turkish nationalists and the Armenian minorities. For example, in March 2005 the eightieth anniversary of the Gallipoli Victory was celebrated in an exaggerated manner in retaliation for the ninetieth anniversary activities of the Armenian exodus.[12]

Hence, it is argued that the shift in the discourse from 'majority nationalism' to 'diversity as an ideology' through the EU reforms and the attempts of the AKP did not result in a substantial change in the attitude of the Sunni-Turkish majority towards the toleration and acceptance of ethno-cultural and religious diversity for non-Turks and non-Muslim minorities such as Armenians.

## The Trial for the Closure of the AKP and the Ergenekon Plot: Handing Over Power

The chief public prosecutor of the Supreme Court of Appeals filed a complaint against the AKP on 14 March 2008 and asked the Constitutional Court to close the party down, arguing that it had become a focus of anti-secular activities. Yalçınkaya requested that seventy-one politicians be banned from politics, including Prime Minister Tayyip Erdoğan and President Abdullah Gül. The Constitutional Court made its decision in

12 For more information on the celebration for the 80th anniversary of the Gallipoli Victory on 19 March 2005, see <http://webarsiv.hurriyet.com.tr/2005/03/18/615296.asp> accessed 14 June 2012.

the case on 30 July 2008, only about four-and-a-half months after the Chief Prosecutor had filed the case. Under pressure at home as well as from the international community, the Constitutional Court felt the need to take immediate action to conclude the case. The Constitutional Court rejected the Chief Prosecutor's demand: the party escaped closure and having seventy-one of its leading figures banned from politics for five years. However, the court did rule that the AKP had shown signs of being 'a focal point for anti-secular activity' and recommended the party be deprived of 50 percent of the financial aid it received from the state treasury.[13] The closure case was perceived both in Turkey and by the international community as a test case for Turkish democracy. The court's decision was a relief not only for Turkey but also for the European Union.

Following the trial, the Turkish public was engaged in a totally different discussion: the Ergenekon Plot. The Ergenekon Plot is allegedly a paramilitary organization consisting of state-centric military officers, politicians, journalists, businessmen, academics and intellectuals whose primary motivation is the survival of the strong state vis-à-vis centrifugal forces such as Kurdish and Islamist insurgents. The term Ergenekon literally refers to a mythical fertile valley in the Central Asian Altay Mountains that has a symbolic spiritual status in Turkish nationalist mythology. The legend of Ergenekon is about a she-wolf called Asena who helped Turkic tribes stranded in the Alpay Mountains by guiding them along the labyrinthine mountain passes into the flourishing Ergenekon plains, where the Turks were able to survive and reproduce as a distinct ethnic group (Ergil 2008; Ünver 2009). When the Chief Prosecutor filed the lawsuit in the Constitutional Court demanding the closure of the AKP in March 2008, Prime Minister Erdoğan immediately responded with a midnight round-up of new Ergenekon suspects. Whereas previously arrested suspects had been largely fringe figures, this time the net was widened to include some of the most prominent secular intellectuals in Turkey, such as Doğu Perinçek, leader of the Workers' Party, the editor-in-chief of

13 For further details, see <http://news.bbc.co.uk/1/hi/world/europe/7533414.stm> accessed 11 May 2012.

*Cumhuriyet*, Ilhan Selçuk, and Kemal Alemdaroğlu, a former president of Istanbul University.[14]

It appears that Erdoğan also put the offending judges under surveillance. A scandal erupted in May 2008 when the vice-president of the Constitutional Court complained that he was being followed. Uniformed police responding to his complaint found that his pursuers were undercover officers (Jenkins 2008). It was later discovered that surveillance by the National Intelligence Service was very common. This caused an uproar in Turkey, revealing further allegations with regard to new suspects within the framework of the Ergenekon case file, which was prepared on 25 July 2008, immediately prior to the Constitutional Court decision regarding the closure of the AKP. Eventually, after a long process of filing, Turkish prosecutors issued a 2,455-page indictment detailing an alleged plot to overthrow Prime Minister Recep Tayyip Erdoğan by an elaborate network of retired military officers, journalists, academics, businessmen, and other secular opponents of the ruling AKP (Rubin 2008).

Although the precise facts of the case are not yet clear, the so-called Ergenekon conspiracy appears to be a largely fictionalized construct, with an ongoing investigation geared mainly to warding off constitutional challenges to the ruling party, rather than coups. It is claimed that the moderate Islamist Gülen movement was also somehow linked to the Ergenekon Plot, but so far no allegation has been made in this regard. However, the file has very serious charges concerning the killing of Hrant Dink, several murders whose perpetrators are unknown, nationalist and jingoist agitations which pop up from time to time, attempted military coups, and cooperation between the members of the Ergenekon, the PKK and the radical Islamist Hizbollah group, leading to constant instability in the country, particularly in the southeast.

The police also uncovered documents that revealed plans for a sustained campaign of terror and intimidation against the Islamist government due to begin in early July 2008. A perfect storm of disruption was whipped up, beginning with a groundswell of popular protest, followed

14 For the details of the Ergenekon case, see Aydınlı (2011).

by a wave of assassinations and bombings, culminating in an economic crisis and army coup. Turkey's moderate Islamist government was ousted in favour of a right-wing secular dictatorship. The documents appeared to identify a thirty-member assassination squad targeting judges and other prominent figures (Tait 2008). When they made their decision regarding the closure of the AKP, the judges of the Constitutional Court were apparently influenced by the recent political events taking place within the country, as well as by the statements of major political figures coming from within European Union circles and the United States.

Against the background described above, one could claim that the AKP is likely to win the battle for power. However, this is not an absolute certainty for the AKP, since lately its culturalist, nationalist and religious discourse has been questioned by the Turkish public as well as the European Union. It has become clear that the AKP's perseverance with the headscarf issue and religious references have become disturbing to the moderate seculars and liberals as well. It is also becoming clear that the AKP is no longer able to pursue the European Union integration project with its 'alliance of civilizations' thesis. However, the AKP seems to have manufactured consent in the aftermath of the Ergenekon case and the Sledgehammer Case (*Balyoz Davasi*),[15] which has brought about the imprisonment of several high-ranking military personnel, including the former Chief of Staff. This was the moment when the AKP consolidated its political power.

15 The Sledgehammer Case ended on 21 September 2012 with the decision of the Criminal Court sentencing 330 suspects to up to two decades behind bars. This case reflects the relatively new reduction of military influence in the nation's political landscape. Former air force commander Ibrahim Fırtına, former head of the navy Özden Örnek and an ex-army commander Çetin Doğan had their initial life sentences reduced to 20 years. The trial reinforces the shift in a balance of power oriented towards more civilian authority. Fore more details on the Sledgehammer Case, see <http://edition.cnn.com/2012/09/21/world/europe/turkey-coup-trial/index.html> accessed 10 December 2012.

## Conclusion

The concept of tolerance has a very long history in the Turkish context, tracing back to the Ottoman Empire. It is also very popular in everyday life. Turks are usually proud of referring to the Millet System of the Ottoman Empire as the guarantor of tolerance, respecting the boundaries between religious communities. Such an official discourse is still carried out in contemporary Turkey, although it is evident that it is just a myth. *The myth of tolerance* has been functional in concealing the mistreatment of ethnocultural and religious minorities other than the majority of Sunni–Muslim–Turks in Turkey. The term tolerance has become more viable in the aftermath of the Helsinki Summit of the European Union in 1999. Whether a cultural diversity challenge is tackled in relation to the concept 'tolerance' or other concepts such as 'recognition'/'acceptance' or assimilation, expulsion and persecution depends on the historical form of a particular state.

The definition of tolerance is confined to the acceptance of Sunni Muslims and their secular counterparts under the banner of the Sunni–Muslim–Turkish nation. However, this does not mean it embraces all different kinds of ethnocultural and religious minorities. Turkey has been through a social, political, economic and legal transformation in the last decade, paving the way for the official recognition of the ethnocultural and religious diversity that has always been the reality of this geographical region. However, this positive mood fundamentally changed after 17 December 2004, when the EU state and national government leaders decided to start negotiations with Turkey. Following the decision of the European Commission, as well as various internal and external developments, tensions began to rise between nationalist, patriotic, statist, pro-status-quo groups on the one hand and pro-EU groups on the other. A new nationalist wave embraced the country, especially amongst middle-class and upper-middle-class groups. The electoral cycle of presidential and general elections witnessed militarist, nationalist and Eurosceptic aspirations coupled with rising violence and terror in the country. The vicious cycle still embraces Turkey in a way that de-Europeanizes the country. Several external and domestic factors were enumerated in the text to explain the ongoing process of de-Europeanization. Against this background, one could argue that the decisive move to bring Turkey back onto the European track should come from the EU member states, rather than from domestic actors. This is the only way to derail the AKP government from its ongoing civilizational and Islamist discourse, which is distancing Turkey from the EU. And this is likely to happen only if more social-democratic, liberal, post-civilizational, and post-religious forces with a global vision come into power in the member states.

## References

Andrews, P. A. (1992). *Türkiye'de Etnik Gruplar*. Istanbul: Ant Tümzamanlar Yayıncılık.

Aydınlı, E. (2011). 'Ergenekon, New Pacts, and the Decline of the Turkish "Inner State"', *Turkish Studies*, 12 (2), 227–39.

Barkey, K. (2008). *Empire of Difference: The Ottomans in Comparative Perspective*. Cambridge: Cambridge University Press.

Billig, M. (1995). *Banal Nationalism*. London: Sage.

Brown, W. (2006). *Regulating Aversion*: *Tolerance in the Age of Identity and Empire*. Princeton, NJ: Princeton University Press.

Casanova, J. (2006). 'The Long, Difficult, and Tortuous Journey of Turkey into Europe and the Dilemmas of European Civilization', *Constellations*, 13 (2), 234–47.

Çınar, M., and Duran, B. (2008). 'The Specific Evolution of Contemporay Political Islam in Turkey and its "Difference"'. In Ü. Cizre-Sakallıoğlu (ed.), *Secular and Islamic Politics in Turkey: The Making of the Justice and Development Party*, pp. 17–41. New York: Routledge.

Cizre, Ü. (1996). 'Parameters and Strategies of Islam-State Interaction in Republican Turkey', *International Journal of Middle East Studies*, 28 (2), 231–51.

Çarkoğlu, A., and Toprak, B. (2006). *Değişen Türkiye'de Din, Toplum ve Siyaset*. Istanbul: TESEV.

Eliade, M. (1991). *Images and Symbols: Studies in Religious Symbolism*. Princeton, NJ: Princeton University Press.

Emerson, M., Aydin, S., Clerck-Sachsse, De J., and Noutcheva, G. (2006). *CEPS Policy Brief*, No. 113. Brussels: Center for European Policy Studies.

Ergil, D. (2008). 'Turkey's Crisis and Future', *The Audit of Conventional Wisdom*, No. 11 <http://web.mit.edu/cis/pdf/Audit_08_08_Ergil.pdf August 2008> accessed 7 July 2012.

Foucault, M. (1979). 'Governmentality', *Ideology and Consciousness*, 6, 5–21.

Göle, N. (1997). 'Secularism and Islamism in Turkey: The Making of Elites and Counterelites', *Middle East Journal*, 51 (1), 46–58.

Hayden, R. M. (2002). 'Antagonistic Tolerance: Competitive Sharing of Religious Sites in South Asia and the Balkans', *Current Anthropology*, 43 (2), 205–31.

Huseman, W. H. (1984). 'The Expression of the Idea of Toleration in French During the Sixteenth Century', *Sixteenth Century Journal*, 15 (3), 293–310.

Jenkins, G. (2008). 'Alleged Surveillance of Senior Judges Raises Questions about Politicization of Turkish Police', *Eurasia Daily Monitor*, 20 May.

Kaya, A. (2004). 'Unity in Diversity: Ethnic and Cultural Diversity in Turkey and the European Union', *Cemoti*, 36, 15–26.

—— (2009). 'Turkey-EU Relations: The Impact of Islam on Europe'. In J. S. Nielsen *et al.* (eds), *Yearbook of Muslims in Europe*, pp. 377–402. Leiden: Brill.

—— (2013). *Europeanization and Tolerance in Turkey: The Myth of Toleration*. Basingstoke: Palgrave Macmillan.

Kaya, A., and Tecmen, A. (2011). *FP7 Project: Identities and Modernities in Europe (IME)*. SSH-CT-2009-215949. WP6 'Identity construction programmes of non-state, professional and collective actors: Case study phase II'.

Kaya, I. (2004). *Social Theory and Later Modernities: The Turkish Experience*. Liverpool: Liverpool University Press.

Keyman, E. F. (1995). 'On the Relation Between Global Modernity and Nationalism: The Crisis of Hegemony and the Rise of (Islamic) Identity in Turkey', *New Perspectives on Turkey*, No. 13, 93–120.

Keyman, E. F., and Öniş, Z. (2007). *Turkish Politics in a Changing World: Global Dynamics and Domestic Transformations*. Istanbul: Istanbul Bilgi University Press.

Müftüler-Baç, M. (2000). 'Through the Looking Glass: Turkey in Europe', *Turkish Studies*, 1 (1), 21–34.

Oran, B. (2000). 'Lingusitic Minority Rights in Turkey, the Kurds and Globalisation'. In G. Gürbey and F. Ibrahim (eds), *The Kurdish Conflict in Turkey*, pp. 151–8. New York: St. Martin's Press.

—— (2004). *Türkiye'de Azınlıklar: Kavramlar, Teori, Lausanne, İç Mevzuat, İçtihat, Uygulama*. İstanbul: İletişim Publications.

Öniş, Z. (2004). 'Turkish Modernization and Challenges for the New Europe', *Perceptions*, 9 (3), 5–28.

Özbudun, E., and Hale, W. (2009). *Islamism, Democracy and Liberalism in Turkey: the Rise of the AKP*. London: Routledge.

Rubin, M. (2008). 'Erdogan, Ergenekon, and the Struggle for Turkey', *Mideast Monitor*, 8 August <http://www.meforum.org/article/1968> accessed 11 May 2012.

Sahin, B. (2008). 'Türkiye'nin Avrupa Birligi Uyum Süreci Baglamında Kürt Sorunu: Açılımlar ve Sınırlar'. In A. Kaya and T. Tarhanlı (eds), *Türkiye'de Çogunlık ve Azınlık Politikaları: AB Sürecinde Yurttaslık Tartısmaları*, pp. 120–54. Istanbul: TESEV.

Somer, M., and Liaras, E. G. (2010). 'Turkey's New Kurdish Opening: Religious Versus Secular Values', *Middle East Policy*, XVII (2), 152–65.

Tait, R. (2008). 'Turkish Coup Plot Awakens Fear of Violent Nationalism', *The Observer*, 6 July <http://www.guardian.co.uk/world/2008/jul/06/turkey> accessed 12 June 2012.

Ünver, H. A. (2009). 'Turkey's "Deep State" and the Ergenekon Conundrum,' *The Middle East Institute Policy Brief*, No. 23 <http://www.mei.edu> accessed 12 June 2012.

Walzer, M. (1997). *On Toleration*. New Haven, CT: Yale University Press.

Yıldız, A. (2001). *Ne mutlu Türküm diyebilene: Türk ulusal kimliginin etmo-seküler sınırları (1919–1938)*. Istanbul: Iletisim Yayınları.

Yovel, Y. (1998). 'Tolerance as Grace and as Rightful Recognition', *Social Research*, 65 (4), 897–920.

BRANISLAV RADELJIĆ

# 13 Conclusion

Since the introduction of the concept of European identity in 1973, by the then nine member states of the European Community, the European continent has transformed considerably. To begin with, the integrationist project has advanced to an extent that the number of European Union (EU) member states has tripled. Understandably, such a development was largely possible due to the end of the Cold War and collapse of communism, providing the countries of Central and Eastern Europe with an opportunity to embark on their transition paths, a process that eventually resulted in accession to the EU. As Jacques Derrida suggested in the early 1990s, 'it is necessary to make ourselves the guardians of an idea of Europe, of a difference of Europe, *but* of a Europe that consists precisely of in not closing itself off in its own identity and in advancing itself in an exemplary way towards what it is not, towards the other heading or the heading of the other, indeed – and this is perhaps something else altogether – towards the other *of* the heading, which would be the beyond of this modern tradition, another border structure, another shore' (Derrida 1992: 29).

Thus, while the Western and Central Eastern European countries were proud of being in a position to talk about integration and European unity, the only non-aligned country in Europe – the Socialist Federal Republic of Yugoslavia – was faced with a crisis, wars and break-up. At this point, the Brussels administration was involved in the promotion of further integration of the European Union as well as in the disintegration of the Yugoslav federation, by recognizing Slovenia and Croatia as independent states, in January 1992, in order to protect them from the increasing Serbian aggression. Later, in 1999, the majority of EU member states supported the, in their view necessary, air strikes against the Serbian regime, to stop it from perpetrating further crimes against the Kosovo Albanians.

Once the conflicts in Yugoslavia had ended, the Europeans presented a set of initiatives providing assistance and insisting on democratization and Europeanization as prerequisites for EU candidacy and membership, at some point in the future. By expressing its interest in the Western Balkan region, the Brussels administration has tried to convince us that Europe should work towards greater unity and that the unpleasant decisions and acts carried out throughout the 1990s should not represent an obstacle to such a process. In addition, we can argue that the decision to grant EU membership to Bulgaria and Romania in 2007 confirmed the EU's commitment to the Balkan region.

The fact that those parts of Europe once considered remote can become part of the European integrationist project, and thus actively involved in the whole European identity complexity, confirms that European identity is a work in progress, largely depending on EU citizens; as one author puts it, '"identity" has acquired a twofold nature. On the one hand, it is not merely or solely contingent on convention, tradition and the past, but has assumed a future-oriented purview and experimental dynamic. On the other, citizens of the EU as they pursue these experiments are continually parsing the nature of cultural affinity and difference as they participate in the creation of a vast, multiracial and multicultural Europe' (Holmes 2009: 52).

## Deepening the Context

Generally speaking, enlargements of the European Union are often accompanied by uncertainty with regard to the willingness of the newly acceded member(s) to continue with democratization and Europeanization processes, and this has been particularly relevant in the 2004 and 2007 rounds. As might have been expected, the two rounds are also discussed in the context of European identity and the East–West divide. While relying on a historical perspective, Holly Case (2009) insists that European identity derives from national experience and, therefore, the opposition between East and West is a false concept. Moreover, it can be argued that, with further enlargements of the EU, European identity will become even more obvious, regardless of the institutions of the EU: '[A] crisis of legitimacy looms among "old" EU member states as it becomes increasingly clear that elite European institutions neither attract the interest nor share the views of the majority of the population' (Case 2009: 130). On the other hand, Neil Fligstein is more sceptical about overall progress:

> Now with enlargement of twenty-seven countries, a whole variety of people are entering the EU without a history of interacting with their counterparts across countries. The middle and upper-middle classes of what was formally Central and Eastern Europe do not necessarily feel affinity with the Western European project. There is already evidence that many of them feel ambivalent about their future in the EU, and their positions on Europe and having a European identity more closely approximate those who are sceptical than those who are optimistic (Fligstein 2009: 157)

With this in mind, the parties involved in the European identity project should be very careful when it comes to whether the final outcome is expected to be positive rather than negative.

In order to minimize the potential risks of admitting new, non-Western, states into the European Union, the Brussels authorities introduced the so-called Copenhagen criteria, in 1993, noting the following: 'Membership requires that candidate country has achieved stability of institutions guaranteeing democracy, the rule of law, human rights, respect for and protection of minorities, the existence of a functioning market economy as well as the capacity to cope with competitive pressure and market forces within the Union. Membership presupposes the candidate's ability to take on the obligations of membership including adherence to the aims of political, economic and monetary union' (EU Council 1993). More relevant for us here, the concept and relevance of European identity was mentioned in the Presidency Conclusions only once[1] – a decision that could be justi-

1 According to the Presidency Conclusions, '[t]he European Council welcomed the Commission's report on progress in the Uruguay Round to date. It underlined the need for the Community to continue to play an active part in achieving further

fied by looking at some more recent understandings and limitations. For example, according to Marion Demossier (2007: 53),

> it is necessary to distinguish European identity from Europeanisation. The concept of a European identity can be easily dismissed as an elusive and contradictory creature; it can even be regarded as utopian. However, European identity can also be defined as a political tool operationalised by various policies, decrees and programmes created by European institutions with the aim of developing a new sense of collective and political identity among the peoples of Europe (with a strict definition of belonging to a new political space, i.e. the European Union). It could also be defined as a new, hybrid form of transnational and cultural identity that is evolving progressively and might become the platform for future political allegiance. At this stage, only a minority of people – the elites, national expatriates within Europe and students educated in a European context – would belong to this category.

Thus, while taking into consideration what a European identity is expected to be – a political tool – and the spectrum of responsibilities it is supposed to be capable of addressing – various policies, decrees and programmes – we realize that the construction of such an identity can also be a top-down process in which various elites use European institutions to promote its hybrid nature amongst the peoples of Europe. However, the existing gap between the institutions and the peoples, who are highly uninformed about EU affairs and decisions, represents a serious matter of concern. In their official appearances, members of the EU elite tend to advocate a stronger European identity as well as initiatives fostering diversity at the same time, but without really questioning to what extent such an arrangement would be possible, if at all, given Europe's current social fabric.

However, at this point, we can identify some of the dominant dilemmas that can clearly question the ideal of European identity. First, the relevance of national identity is still very strong across the European Union and it is difficult to predict the extent to which the postmodernist understanding of the nation state and national identity will succeed in becoming the dominant perspective. As Fariba Salehi summarized it:

---

progress while preserving the European identity throughout the negotiations' (EU Council 1993).

> The most powerful modern institution that homogenizes and standardizes identity is the nation-state. The nation-state is a gigantic culture industry. A postmodern critique of the nation-state offers a radically different reading of the nation-state, by describing it as an apparatus of power that produces mega-narratives of identity in the name of 'people'. A postmodern theory of the nation-state deconstructs the nationalistic amount of the nation-state, and anchors the question of 'national' identity in the locus of the 'other', and in so doing erases its totalizing boundaries, challenges the political and ideological manoeuvres that assume an essentialist core in the imagined communities, and argues for the hybridity and ambivalence of national identity. (Salehi 2001: 252)

Apart from existing EU member states and their national pride, identity issues of prospective members deserve attention, as well. For example, the break-up of Yugoslavia represented an opportunity for the newly established states to foster and promote their own identity that had been suppressed before the state crisis and consequent wars. Thus, Kosovo, to name just one, might find it difficult to understand the value of replacing its own identity with a European identity, even if it could benefit from such an upgrade.

Second, so far, we have seen that many Europeans struggle with tolerance and solidarity and, in fact, their views have continued to challenge the prospect of Europe's multicultural dimension. Accordingly, without knowing whether there will be any significant progress in generating tolerance and solidarity across the European Union, discussions about European identity and European citizenship are highly speculative. Although, in 2004, EU representatives seemed confident when saying that 'Europe's identity is something that must be negotiated by its peoples and institutions ... so that European values, traditions, and conceptions of life can live on and be effective', they have not managed to bring the two sides closer together (Biedenkopf, Geremek and Michalski 2004: 8).

Future enlargements are likely to accentuate the questions of tolerance and solidarity, thus negatively affecting the construction of European identity. Adrian Favell examines the three kinds of migration that have inevitably contributed to the concept of European identity: first, the current or traditional 'ethnic' immigrations of non-Europeans into European nation states – 'immigrations [that] have visibly put black, brown, and yellow faces in white Europe' (2009: 174); second, the emergence of new intra-European 'elite' migrations supported by European free-movement laws which date back to the Treaty of Rome in 1957 (2009: 177); and third, the flows of East–West migrants – a 'generation of new Europeans [who] are ambitious, dynamic movers ready to get what's theirs from the West, while benefiting from ease of mobility back and forth from West to East' (2009: 183). All these waves of migration have contributed to the European mosaic; still, having in mind that there are some Europeans who would like to restrict (im)migration, the author correctly questions what the situation will look like one day when the EU27 (or very soon EU28) becomes EU45 or EU55.

The migration question is even more relevant when one considers that if Turkey, Bosnia and Herzegovina, Albania and Kosovo become members of the EU, then its Muslim population will amount to over 100 million. According to one analysis, '[a]fter Maastricht [1992], Catholic social doctrine was widely embraced – encompassed by the principle of subsidiarity – to guide intellectually and regulate institutionally the cognitive meanings and political exigencies of a pluralist Europe' (Holmes 2009: 63). Thus, a valid question to think about here is whether the Brussels decision-makers are ready to face a more obvious presence of Islam in the EU. For example, in one scholar's view, 'the accession of Muslim countries and the rise of far right mobilization and violence, can only be addressed effectively under a broad consensus among its members. Across Europe, however, the citizens are split regarding its cultural identity and social model' (Medrano 2009: 106). This split is accentuated even further by the fact that immigration and the Islamization of immigrants in the EU are regulated by the individual member states, not the Union. In fact, obvious differences between Germany and the Netherlands in relation to the legal status of Islam represent an additional challenge to the idea of European identity.[2]

2 In Germany, the state and religious institutions are not separated; while the Jewish community, the Catholic Church and the Protestant Church are all recognized by the state, Islam is not. In the Netherlands, the state and religious institutions are separated; the Dutch system allows all religions to establish their own institutions, including Islam.

Third, as alluded to in the previous dilemma, the fact that the European Union does not speak with a single voice is an added difficulty. Back in 1997, Soledad García understood this trend as a result of different economic and political interests that were not sufficiently explained to the citizens: 'This is due to the fact that there is considerable ambiguity in national governments' agendas attached to Economic and Monetary Union which shows them unwilling to appear responsible for the hard choices that need to be made' (García 1997: 205–6). More importantly, as García rightly predicted, the 2004 enlargement increased the 'elite ambiguity, since there seem to be many antagonistic groups in the societies of these countries with often incompatible goals, which extends to their incipient civil societies' (García 1997: 206). Given the present circumstances, the increasing national and regional differentiations are likely to continue and further question the success of a supranational European identity.

Finally, while recognizing both intergovernmental and supranational approaches to policy-making, European Union representatives recognize their own reservations with regard to future integration of the Union in general. It is this flexibility that may determine the nature of European identity: while the first approach indicates that the national governments have little interest in deepening 'integration by shifting power from their own national to the federal level as long as the status quo seems to be secure', the second approach suggests that 'as soon as the alternative to the status quo is the end of the integration and as soon as it is not about the failure of a specific policy or a specific treaty but about the EU's very existence, even decisions to abandon one more aspect of the cherished national sovereignty might be acceptable as the lesser evil' (Pelinka 2011: 27).

The above-outlined dilemmas become even more alarming if discussed in the context of the 2008 economic crisis. The crisis, although labelled as economic in its nature, has also affected the EU's political and identity achievements. As revealed by the 2011 *Eurobarometer* poll, Euroscepticism was generally on the rise, meaning that the respondents found it significantly easier to identify with their own nation state rather than with the EU. Still, when asked who they would see as capable of addressing the crisis, the majority of interviewees listed the EU first, followed by their national authorities – a feeling that could be associated with their disappointment with local leadership (*Eurobarometer* 2011). Later, the EU continued to report about growing Euroscepticism. However, as insisted by Jose Manuel Barroso, the president of the European Commission, 'we have to be clear and honest: it was not Europe that has created this crisis: this crisis was created either in the financial markets, irresponsible behaviour or some times at national level: by unsustainable debt' (*Euronews* 2013).

## A Way Forward?

The post-2008 period has been characterized by a number of valuable initiatives (Council of Europe 2013; European Commission 2012), as well as scholarly accounts, addressing questions closely related to European unity and identity, and proposing steps to be taken with regard to the overall European integrationist project (Bayley and Williams 2012; Checkel and Katzenstein 2009; Habermas 2012; Hayward and Wurzel 2012; Lucarelli, Cerutti and Schmidt 2011; Risse 2010; Sükösd and Jakubowicz 2011). For example, Jürgen Habermas's *The Crisis of the European Union: A Response* – a book that complements his 2009 title, *Europe: The Faltering Project*, in which he addressed a number of issues of crucial relevance for the future of the European Union[3] – claims that Europe is now more than ever a constitutional project. Such a claim has to do with the challenges posed by the recent EU crisis that has clearly confirmed the existence of some alarming differences amongst the EU member states that will further erode solidarity. As Habermas puts it, '[g]iven the unprecedented gravity of the problems, one would expect the politicians to lay the European cards on

3 In his 2009 work, Habermas focused on the decreasing involvement of intellectuals in debates regarding the future of Europe – a serious lack that could affect future policy-making, the presence of Islam (securitization, potential risks, greater inclusion and tolerance), the power of the Lisbon Treaty (which actually does not solve the European problems he identifies) and, lastly, the potential of the public sphere to get involved and contribute to official decisions.

the table without further delay and to take the initiative in explaining to the public the relation between the short-term costs and the true benefits, and hence the historical importance of the European project' (2012: 6). The problem is that the politicians, even though aware of the issues, do not seem ready to lay the cards because of their own fear that if they start encouraging greater supranational solidarity in the time of crisis, such an attempt could be seen as a threat to state sovereignty and thus their own careers. Moreover, EU institutions have continuously struggled to convince the public that something of a supranational character is likely to perform better than a national entity (for example, the differences in overall characteristics and performance between Germany and Greece). Accordingly, 'the expansion of communication networks and horizons of perception, the liberalization of values and attitudes, an increase in the willingness to include strangers, the strengthening of civil society initiatives and a corresponding transformation of strong identities can at best be stimulated through legal-administrative means' (Habermas 2012: 46).

Although Habermas offers some great ideas, he seems to underestimate the relevance of willingness. It can be said that back in the 1950s when the European Coal and Steel Community was launched, the six founding states made a huge step forward, followed by a number of great achievements. However, some of the later crises, including the current one, have showed that the Community's (or Union's) future can easily be questioned and it is the member states that actually question it. To put it simply, why should Germany continue to bailout Greece and, more importantly, how can the German government justify its decisions to a German public that sees the Greeks as highly problematic? Furthermore, even if EU institutions were granted greater power over the member states, this might only generate greater frustration and thus even less willingness to cooperate.

For Habermas, there is a range of possible scenarios to consider. For example, he claims that the euro is capable of deciding the fate of the EU, as the euro zone members 'will have to choose between a deepening of European cooperation and relinquishing the euro' (Habermas 2012: 122). Also, he insists on additional laws and thus a more binding nature of intergovernmental agreements as well as greater participation of European citizens in the decision-making processes (2012: 130–1). Again, here, the media play an important role: 'On the one hand, the politicians allow themselves to be enticed by the gentle pressure of the media into short-winded forms of self-promotion. On the other hand, the programming of the media lets itself become infected by this impatient occasionalism' (2012: 136). When applied to the concept of European identity, we can agree that Habermas's concerns are powerful enough to affect its progress. As we have witnessed, economic concerns are likely to penetrate political and social dimensions of the European project, putting some of them, including European identity, on standby. The problem is if their status does not change to active within a reasonable period of time; then, there is a risk that even the previously achieved progress will require revisiting. But what seems most disturbing is the disconnection between the EU elites and the peoples of Europe, thus between the rulers and the ruled, with the former often presenting themselves as the only competent ones and the latter sharing a feeling of irrelevance.

When assessing the situation surrounding the signing of the Treaty of Maastricht in 1992, Derrida noted that 'Europe takes itself to be a promontory, an advance – the avant-garde of geography and history. It advances and promotes itself as an advance, and it will have never ceased to make advances on the other: to induce, seduce, produce, and conduce, to spread out, to cultivate, to love or to violate, to love to violate, to colonize, and to colonize itself' (Derrida 1992: 49). With such multi-tasking ability in mind, it is rather difficult to imagine a Europe that is incapable of finding a solution to the growing scepticism about its own being and thus future, while sticking to its aims and objectives that have, on various occasions, resulted in right decisions.

## References

Bayley, P., and Williams, G. (eds) (2012). *European Identity: What the Media Say*. Oxford: Oxford University Press.

Biedenkopf, K., Geremek, B., and Michalski, K. (2004). *The Spiritual and Cultural Dimension of Europe: Concluding Remarks*. Brussels: Directorate-General for Research <http://cordis.europa.eu/documents/documentlibrary/104214451EN6.pdf> accessed 10 March 2013.

Case, H. (2009). 'Being European: East and West'. In J. T. Checkel and P. J. Katzenstein (eds), (2009). *European Identity*, pp. 111–31. Cambridge: Cambridge University Press.

Checkel, J. T., and Katzenstein, P. J. (eds) (2009). *European Identity*. Cambridge: Cambridge University Press.

Council of Europe (2013). 'Debates on European Identity (2013–2014)' <http://www.coe.int/t/policy-planning/Debates/Identity_Debates/default_en.asp> accessed 15 May 2013.

Demossier, M. (2007). 'The Political Structuring of Cultural Identities in the European Union'. In M. Demossier (ed.), *The European Puzzle: The Political Structuring of Cultural Identities at a Time of Transition*, pp. 49–66. Oxford: Berghahn Books.

Derrida, J. (1992). *The Other Heading: Reflections on Today's Europe*. Bloomington, IN: Indiana University Press.

EU Council (1993). 'European Council in Copenhagen, 21–22 June 1993: Conclusion of the Presidency' <http://www.consilium.europa.eu/ueDocs/cms_Data/docs/pressData/en/ec/72921.pdf> accessed 20 March 2013.

*Eurobarometer* 75 (2011). 'European Commission Public Opinion Survey held in Autumn 2011' <http://ec.europa.eu/public_opinion/archives/eb/eb75/eb75_en.htm> accessed 5 March 2013.

*Euronews* (2013). 'Euroscepticism on the Rise, Says EU Poll.' 24 April <http://www.euronews.com/2013/04/25/euroscepticism-on-the-rise-says-eu-poll/> accessed 2 May 2013.

European Commission (2012). 'The Development of European Identity/Identities: Unfinished Business' <http://ec.europa.eu/research/social-sciences/pdf/development-of-european-identity-identities_en.pdf> accessed 15 May 2013.

Favell, A. (2009). 'Immigration, Migration and Free Movement in the Making of Europe'. In J. T. Checkel and P. J. Katzenstein (eds), (2009). *European Identity*, pp. 167–89. Cambridge: Cambridge University Press.

Fligstein, N. (2009). 'Who Are the Europeans and How Does this Matter for Politics?' In J. T. Checkel and P. J. Katzenstein (eds), (2009). *European Identity*, pp. 132–66. Cambridge: Cambridge University Press.

García, S. (1997). 'European Union Identity and Citizenship'. In M. Roche and R. van Berkel (eds), *European Citizenship and Social Exclusion*, pp. 201–12. Aldershot: Ashgate.

Habermas, J. (2009). *Europe: The Faltering Project*. Cambridge: Polity Press.

—— (2012). *The Crisis of the European Union: A Response*. Cambridge: Polity Press.

Hayward, J., and Wurzel, R. K. (eds) (2012). *European Disunion: Between Sovereignty and Solidarity*. Basingstoke: Palgrave Macmillan.

Holmes, D. R. (2009). 'Experimental Identities (after Maastricht)'. In J. T. Checkel and P. J. Katzenstein (eds), (2009). *European Identity*, pp. 52–80. Cambridge: Cambridge University Press.

Lucarelli, S., Cerutti, F., and Schmidt, V. A. (eds) (2011). *Debating Political Identity and Legitimacy in the European Union*. Oxford: Routledge.

Medrano, J. D. (2009). 'The Public Sphere and the European Union's Political Identity'. In J. T. Checkel and P. J. Katzenstein (eds), *European Identity*, pp. 81–107. Cambridge: Cambridge University Press.

Pelinka, A. (2011). 'The European Union as an Alternative to the Nation-State', *International Journal of Politics, Culture and Society*, 24 (1–2), 21–30.

Risse, T. (2010). *A Community of Europeans? Transnational Identities and Public Spheres*. Ithaca, NY: Cornell University Press.

Salehi, F. (2001). 'A Postmodern Conception of the Nation State'. In A. S. Leoussi (ed), *Encyclopedia of Nationalism*, pp. 247–55. London: Transaction.

Sükösd, M., and Jakubowicz, K. (2011). *Media, Nationalism and European Identities*. Budapest: Central European University Press.

# Notes on Contributors

MIRUNA ANDREEA BALOSIN is Assistant Professor at the Faculty of European Studies, Babeş-Bolyai University in Cluj-Napoca, Romania.

FRAN CETTI is a member of the Centre for Research on Migration, Refugees and Belonging, at the University of East London, United Kingdom.

EMMA DE ANGELIS is the editor of the *RUSI Journal*, United Kingdom.

AYHAN KAYA is Professor of Politics and Director of the European Institute at Istanbul Bilgi University, Turkey.

ADAM F. KOLA is Assistant Professor and Deputy Director of the Institute of Slavonic Philology, at Nicolaus Copernicus University in Toruń, Poland.

DORA KOSTAKOPOULOU is Professor of European Union Law, European Integration and Public Policy, at the University of Warwick, United Kingdom.

MONICA MERUTIU is Assistant Professor at the Faculty of European Studies, Babeş-Bolyai University in Cluj-Napoca, Romania.

VICTOR M. OLIVIERI is a Research Fellow at the University of Edinburgh, United Kingdom, and a PhD Candidate in Comparative Politics at the University of Florida, United States.

BRANISLAV RADELJIĆ is Senior Lecturer in International Politics at the University of East London, United Kingdom.

NICK STEVENSON is Reader in Cultural Sociology at the University of Nottingham, United Kingdom.

BO STRÅTH is the Finnish Academy Distinguished Professor in Nordic, European and World History at Helsinki University, Finland.

MARTINA TOPIĆ is a Research Fellow at the Faculty of Political Science, University of Zagreb, Croatia.

# Index